THE ANGLO-SAXON POETIC RECORDS

A COLLECTIVE EDITION

I
THE JUNIUS MANUSCRIPT

Caedmon manuscript.

THE
JUNIUS MANUSCRIPT

EDITED BY

GEORGE PHILIP KRAPP

NEW YORK: COLUMBIA UNIVERSITY PRESS
LONDON: ROUTLEDGE AND KEGAN PAUL

7100 4931 5

PREFACE

This book is the first volume in a collective edition, the plan of which includes all the surviving records of Anglo-Saxon poetry. The main body of Anglo-Saxon poetry as it has come down to us is contained in four important miscellany manuscripts, the Junius Manuscript, the Vercelli Book, the Exeter Book, and the Beowulf Manuscript, each of which will constitute a separate volume in this edition. The remaining minor and more or less scattered examples of Anglo-Saxon poetry will be grouped together, in a volume or volumes of their own.

In the matter of variant readings, the task of an editor of Anglo-Saxon poetic texts is somewhat simplified by the fact that practically all Anglo-Saxon poetry is preserved in single copies. Such variant readings as an editor may attach to his text must therefore be derived from the great mass of comment which has gradually accumulated in the course of Anglo-Saxon studies. This comment is obviously of very uneven value, and to burden a modern edition with all the extant guesses at reading of the text would be a great waste of both space and effort. It becomes necessary therefore to select, and the critical judgment of the editor must be exercised to keep alive these records as illustrious examples of poetic endeavor, not as occasions for stirring the dry bones of antiquated Anglo-Saxon scholarship. With these considerations in mind, the texts of the poems in this edition are kept as free as possible of scholarly intrusions, paleographical, typographical, grammatical, or otherwise illustrative and editorial, and the necessary machinery of exposition and interpretation is placed in the introduction and in the notes, where it seems more properly to belong. The two main duties of an editor, that of preserving a faithful record of the manuscript and that of taking account of all significant contributions to the understanding of the manuscript, it is hoped will be satisfactorily met in this way. At the foot of each page of text, such departures from the manuscript as have appeared on the page are recorded, whence anyone interested may readily turn to the introduction or to the notes for the further relevant details. In order to keep the volumes within the limits of reasonable size, comment in the introduction and notes has been somewhat rigorously limited to matters pertaining to the establishment of the texts.

The text of the poems contained in this volume has been made from the collotype reproductions of the Junius Manuscript in Gollancz's *The Cædmon Manuscript* (Oxford University Press, 1927). In the very few instances in which the collotypes are not clear, readings have been recorded on the authority of Holthausen, Clubb, and Gollancz, but only when it is so stated. Modern capitalization and punctuation and, except for the use of ð and þ, Đ and Þ, modern typography have been introduced into the text, and the sectional divisions of the manuscript have been supplemented by further paragraphing for ease in reading. The abbreviations of the manuscript, all very simple, have been resolved without comment, and losses have been indicated by asterisks. Otherwise the text faithfully follows the manuscript, or if it does not, departures from the manuscript readings are always so noted.

The editor takes pleasure in acknowledging the support of the Council for Research in the Humanities of Columbia University in the preparation and publication of this work.

CONTENTS

INTRODUCTION

I

THE MANUSCRIPT

Two names must always be associated with the venerable manuscript, the contents of which are printed in this book, the name of Cædmon as possible author and the name of Franciscus Junius, the earliest of modern scholars to enter on the task of restoring to the world the knowledge of the poetry of the Anglo-Saxons. The manuscript came into the possession of Junius, a Dutch scholar long resident in England, through Archbishop Ussher, and when in 1654 Junius published at Amsterdam the poems contained in it, he described them as a poetic paraphrase of Genesis and other parts of the Scriptures by the monk Cædmon.[1] The manuscript now rests in the Bodleian Library at Oxford, where it is numbered Junius XI in token of its origin.

The connection of Cædmon with the manuscript is less direct than Junius supposed it to be, though certainly less accidental than was that of Junius. No word in the manuscript attributes any part of it to Cædmon, or, for that matter, to any other poet. The opinions of scholars differ as to the date of composition and as to the authorship of the several poems in the manuscript, and these must still be regarded as unsettled questions, but no scholar today believes that the poems were all written by Cædmon or that any part of the manuscript contains the very forms of the words which Cædmon dictated. Yet the content of the manuscript accords so closely with the description of Cædmon as poet given by Bede, especially the first poem in the manuscript, that it requires no stretching of probability to assume that the example and incentive of Cædmon's own verse accounts in large measure for the existence of these poems, and in consequence, of this manuscript.

The manuscript consists of 116 parchment folios, $12\frac{3}{4}$ inches

---

[1] For the full title of this book, see Bibliography, p. xlv.

high and varying from 7 to 7¾ inches in width. The pages have
been numbered by a modern hand from 1 to 229, the first folio,
which carries a full page illustration as frontispiece, not being
counted in the numbering. The contents of the several pages in
terms of the lines of this edition are given in Table I on p. xxxvi,
at the end of this Introduction.

Four different hands are readily observable in the handwriting
of the manuscript, the first from p. 1 to p. 212, the second from
p. 213 to p. 215, the third from p. 216 to p. 228, and the fourth
only on p. 229. Besides these scribes, account must be taken
also of other hands which appear in many corrections, additions,
and alterations in the manuscript, in the drawing of ornamental
capitals, in the drawing of numerous illustrations accompanying
the text, and in comments on these, and in a few marginal nota-
tions of a casual nature. These several groups of minor additions to the manuscript will be considered separately hereafter.

The date of the writing of the first hand in the manuscript
has been fixed at about the year 1000.[1] The three other hands
belong chronologically to one period, and between these three
and the first there was probably a difference of "less than a
generation."[2] The manuscript as a whole may be dated
therefore at about the year 1000. The first scribe wrote the
whole of the first three poems in the manuscript, GENESIS,
EXODUS, and DANIEL, and the three other scribes wrote CHRIST
AND SATAN, the concluding poem of the manuscript. The first
of the three scribes responsible for CHRIST AND SATAN wrote
pp. 213–215 of the manuscript (ll. 1–124), the second wrote
pp. 216–228 (ll. 125–709), and the third only the last page, p.
229 (ll. 710–729).

At the bottom of the illustration on p. 2 of the manuscript
appears a small medallion portrait inscribed *ælfwine*, and according to Gollancz, it seems "difficult to ignore the strong probability that the Ælfwine of our artist is to be identified with the
famous Ælfwine who became abbot of Newminster in 1035."[3]
The abbot Ælfwine appears to have been a man of varied

---

[1] See Gollancz, *The Cædmon Manuscript*, p. xviii.

[2] Clubb, *Christ and Satan*, p. xii.

[3] *The Cædmon Manuscript*, p. xxxv.

intellectual interests, though not much is known about him, and
to call him famous perhaps exaggerates his reputation.   The
bond connecting the Ælfwine of the medallion as the possible
patron of this volume with Ælfwine of Newminster at Win-
chester is therefore frail, yet the association of the names is
suggestive and plausible.

II

UNITY OF THE MANUSCRIPT

Nothing is known of the reasons for the writing of the manuscript, but it is obvious that the occasion was considered to be of
some importance, and that elaborate preparations were made
for the compiling of a large book of Anglo-Saxon poetry.   Uniform sheets of parchment were prepared, extensive illustrations
were arranged for, and a not unskillful scribe was set to work
copying the poems.   So far indeed as GENESIS, EXODUS, and
DANIEL are concerned, there can be no doubt that these are
parts of a veritable eleventh century book.   Whether these
poems were assembled at that time for copying or whether they
had already been assembled before they were copied, there
seems to be no way of determining.   With respect to CHRIST
AND SATAN, however, there may be some question whether
this poem was included in the original design of the compilation.
For one thing, it is less harmonious in subject with the other
three poems than they are with each other.   The change of
scribes and general treatment may also be significant, CHRIST
AND SATAN being much less carefully written and ornamented
than the other three poems.   There are no illustrations and no
blank spaces left for illustrations in the part of the manuscript
containing CHRIST AND SATAN, except the irrelevant design on
p. 225 (see below, p. xvi).   It looks as though interest in the
manuscript as a piece of fine book-making had fallen off after
the completion of DANIEL.   On the other hand, perhaps a fully
thought out plan was never formed for the whole manuscript.
It may have been intended to grow by accretion.   Certainly
even the plan as first made was not carried out with rigorous
oversight, since after p. 96 there are many blank spaces left for

illustrations, and some for capitals that were never inserted. The addition of CHRIST AND SATAN may have been an after-thought, perhaps even of the patron who commissioned the writing of the first three poems, and the folios on which it is written may have been added to the main body of the book after that had been completed. Yet the folios of CHRIST AND SATAN are uniform with those of the rest of the volume, except for the slight difference that they were ruled for and written with 27 lines on a page, and the first 212 pages were ruled for and written with 26 lines on a page, and the manner in which they are combined with the rest of the volume shows that if CHRIST AND SATAN was added later, "the intention, at the time of writing, was to make it an integral portion of the manuscript."[1] Perhaps it would be literally truer to modify this statement slightly and to say that if the folios on which CHRIST AND SATAN was written were added later, the intention at the time of adding them was to make them an integral part of the manu-script. But of course the folios might have been prepared before the matter to be written on them was selected. It cannot be supposed, therefore, that the folios containing CHRIST AND SATAN were once a separate manuscript which happened to be on hand and which was fortuitously attached, perhaps at a much later date, to the three preceding poems of the Junius Manuscript as we now have it. One may lament the literary judgment of the person who added CHRIST AND SATAN to GENESIS, EXODUS, and DANIEL, but there can be little doubt that in doing so, he had the manuscript as a whole before him.

It should be noted that CHRIST AND SATAN ends on p. 229 of the Junius Manuscript with the statement *Finit Liber II. Amen.* No complementing Liber I is indicated in any preced-ing part of the manuscript, but the probabilities are that Liber II comprised only CHRIST AND SATAN, and that the conclusion of DANIEL, now missing in the manuscript, ended with *Finit* or some other indication that the original design or instructions of the copyist had been carried out. GENESIS, EXODUS, and DANIEL would thus have constituted Liber I in the eyes of the person who added CHRIST AND SATAN, and who called his addition Liber II.

[1] Gollancz, *The Cædmon Manuscript*, p. xcix.

III

CORRECTIONS IN THE MANUSCRIPT

One other possible bond of connection between Liber II, containing CHRIST AND SATAN, and the three other poems of the manuscript, which for convenience we may call Liber I, may be found in the many corrections in the manuscript, perhaps by different hands, but all closely contemporary with the manuscript. These corrections are most numerous in Liber II, and in Liber II they are much more frequent in the work of the first scribe than in that of the other two. In percentages, the proportion of corrections to the number of lines is 83+ in the work of the first scribe, 19+ in the work of the second scribe, and 52+ in the few final lines written by the third scribe. In Liber I the corrections in GENESIS are of most significance, since the number of corrections in EXODUS and DANIEL is very small, and practically all of them were made by the scribe of Liber I in correction of obvious errors as he wrote. The zeal of the more general corrector, or correctors, apparently exhausted itself on CHRIST AND SATAN and GENESIS. But the number of corrections in GENESIS, including even those made by the scribe himself, is only 4+ per cent of the number of lines, and the early lines of GENESIS are much more freely corrected than the remaining much longer portion of the poem. Now if any considerable number of the corrections in GENESIS and in Liber II were made by the same person, it is highly improbable that he began with GENESIS, gradually stopped correcting until he ceased through EXODUS and DANIEL, then resumed with very much increased enthusiasm at the beginning of Liber II. It would be much more plausible to suppose that what seemed to him the untidiness of the work of the first scribe in Liber II led some reader of the manuscript to make corrections in this part, that having once begun he continued, though less extensively, through the work of the second and third scribes in Liber II, and even went back to the beginning of the whole manuscript to make a few corrections in the work of the scribe of Liber I.

Plausible though this theory may be, its credibility must rest upon positive evidence that the corrector of Liber II actually made some of the corrections of Liber I. Clubb thinks that he did, and he declares that whatever may have been the manner in which Liber II first came to be attached to Liber I, "it is clear . . . that at some later time [i.e., later than the writing of Liber I] in the eleventh century the two sections were treated as one book, because there are traces in the GENESIS of the hand of the Late West Saxon Corrector who was so active in CHRIST AND SATAN."[1] On the contrary, Gollancz is of the opinion that "there is not evidence sufficiently strong to come to any conclusion on this similarity of penmanship" between the corrections of Liber II and those of Liber I, and he declares himself unable to endorse the statement that there are traces in GENESIS of the hand that made the corrections in CHRIST AND SATAN.[2]

It is true that the evidence from handwriting is slight and inconclusive, that it neither proves nor disproves the assumption that the hand of the corrector of Liber II also appears in Liber I. The evidence of handwriting, however, permits such an assumption, and there are other things to support it. If one cannot be quite certain that the hand of the corrector of Liber II appears in Liber I, one can be more assured that his mind appears there. As has already been pointed out, the corrections in the manuscript are of different kinds. There are, first, corrections of the casual mishaps in writing which befall any scribe, as, for example, *beorte* corrected to *beorhte*, GEN. 14, *gehlilcum* corrected to *gehwilcum*, DAN. 643, *sceoden*, CHRIST AND SATAN 27, provided with an *l;* second are verbal changes and additions, as when *hebban* is corrected to *ahebban*, GEN. 259, *hof* corrected to *ahof*, EX. 253, *we* added after *nu*, DAN. 293, and *he* changed to *hig*, CHRIST AND SATAN 191; third are those corrections which may best be designated orthographic, with or without phonetic implications involved, as when *saula* is altered to *saulæ*, GEN. 185, *alda* to *ealda*, CHRIST AND SATAN 34, *æcan* to *ecan*, *id.* 46, *heleð* to *hæleð*, *id.* 47. Corrections of the first two kinds appear in about equal proportions throughout the whole manuscript, but corrections of the third kind are much more numerous in CHRIST AND SATAN than elsewhere,

[1] *Christ and Satan*, p. xv.
[2] *The Cædmon Manuscript*, p. xxix.

and in fact appear elsewhere only in the early part of GENESIS. They are fairly frequent up to l. 546 of GENESIS, but after that they appear practically not at all. But the important point is that the corrections of this third kind, which must owe their presence to the zeal of a linguistic reformer, and not merely to the logical demands of the text, are remarkably similar in character in CHRIST AND SATAN and in the first five hundred lines of GENESIS. They are concerned very largely with the spelling of words containing diphthongs, as in *liodgeard*, corrected to *leodgeard*, GEN. 229, *him* altered to *heom*, GEN. 401, *weorðan* altered to *wyrðan*, GEN. 261, *hweorfan* altered to *hwyrfan*, CHRIST AND SATAN 119, *waldend* altered to *wealdend*, GEN. 260, *forwarð* altered to *forwearð*, CHRIST AND SATAN 21; and a great many with the spelling of words in which the corrector exhibits anxiety over the proper use of *e* and *æ*, as in *tene* altered to *tyne*, GEN. 248, *alefan* altered to *alyfan*, CHRIST AND SATAN 115; *þægne* altered to *þegne*, GEN. 409, and the reverse, as in CHRIST AND SATAN 47, *heleð* corrected to *hæleð*. But striking as these agreements are, the most significant single instance of similarity between the corrections of Liber II and Liber I is to be found in the change of *heofne*, GEN. 339 and GEN. 350, by altering final *e* to *o* and adding *n* above the line, giving *heofnon*, as in CHRIST AND SATAN 10, where original *heofene* is altered to *heofenon* by altering final *e* to *o* in the same way and adding *n* above the line. It would be very remarkable if such an exceptional correction should occur independently to two different correctors. It is of course possible, but highly improbable, that a corrector in GENESIS merely followed the model of an earlier corrector in CHRIST AND SATAN, though if this was so, he must have had a combined Liber I and Liber II to work with. It by no means follows that all of the corrections in Liber I not made by the scribe were made by the corrector of Liber II, but there seems to be very good reason for supposing that some of them were, and that therefore the book as a whole, both Liber I and Liber II, lay before that first annotator of the text, whoever he was, who occupied himself with it in the eleventh century.

The value of the corrections and additions in the manuscript is greater from the orthographic and linguistic point of view than it is from that of one interested in establishing the meaning of the text of the poems. There is no indication that the eleventh century reviser or revisers had before them other copies of the texts from which they made their revisions, or that they were led to make their corrections through any desire to restore the readings of the manuscript to what they conceived to be their original forms. In the preparation of this text, the first readings of the scribes have generally been preferred to those of the correctors, but the corrections will repay study and they have all been indicated at their appropriate places at the foot of the page.

IV

ANGLO-SAXON IN THE ILLUSTRATIONS

Some of the numerous illustrations in the manuscript contain lettering in Anglo-Saxon, but only one phrase, that on p. 56, is quoted from the text which the illustrations accompany. As no illustrations are present in the manuscript after p. 96, except an unfinished design on p. 225 which has no relation to the text and is apparently there by accident, it follows that all of the illustrations relate to GENESIS. A great many blank spaces were left in Liber I of the manuscript for illustrations which were never filled in, but none in Liber II, which has neither illustrations nor spaces for them. Most of the illustrations in the manuscript are without lettering, though the intention probably was to provide inscriptions for all of them. The Anglo-Saxon and other phrases in the illustrations are as follows:

Frontispiece. A full page illustration, with the Latin phrase in a later hand *Genesis in anglico* at the top.

Page 2. God enthroned, with the marginal inscription *hælendes hehseld*. Below the illustration is the medallion portrait, with *ælfwine* inscribed on it, which has already been mentioned.

Page 3. Hu se engyl[1] ongon ofermod wesan.

---

[1] The MS. has *sengyl*. This descriptive sentence has been partly cut off by the binder of the manuscript (see Gollancz, *The Cædmon Manuscript*, p. xxxix).

Her se hælend gesceop[1] helle heom to wite.

Her se[2]

Page 6. Her he[3] gesyndrode wæter and eorðan.

Page 7. Her he todælde dæg wið nihte. The word *Salvator*, in a late hand, appears in a picture of the Deity.

Page 9. Her godes englas astigan of heouenan into paradisum. Her drihten gescop adames wif euam.

Her drihten gewearp sclep on adam and genam him an rib of þa sidan and gescop his wif of þam ribbe. The name *Eva* is written above the picture of Eve, and *michael* above a picture of Michael.

Page 13. The words *qoddā mare*, i.e., *quoddam mare*, "a certain water," are inscribed on a picture of water with fishes in it.

Page 56. Seth wæs sæli. The picture containing these words, which are in a different hand from that in the other inscriptions, is on the same page as Gen. 1138, Seth wæs gesælig.

V

MINOR ADDITIONS

Besides the corrections and additions in the manuscript already mentioned, a few minor details are to be noted: (*a*) At the top of p. 1, above the opening lines of Genesis, a late medieval hand has written *Genesis in lingua Saxania*. (*b*) Occasionally the letters *x ƀ* appear in the margin of the manuscript, as on pp. 1, 2, etc., and less frequently merely *x*, as on pp. 11, etc. The letters stand for an abbreviated prayer, *x* for *Christus*, or some form of this word, and *ƀ* for some form of *benedicere*. At the foot of p. 22 the letters *x m* (misread by various editors as *xiii*) stand in the margin, the *m* here probably representing some form of the verb *misereri*. These prayers appear only in Liber I of the manuscript. They may have been written by the scribe or the illustrator at the beginning of the day's work, but if so, the custom was not carried through sys-

---

[1] The MS. has *gesce*, the rest of *gesceop* being cut off.

[2] This is an unfinished inscription above a picture of hell. Within the picture stands the word *inferni*.

[3] *her h* has been cut off by the binder of the manuscript.

tematically even in Liber I. (c) On p. 98 at the lower left margin appear the words *healf trymt*, with a mark probably of abbreviation above *m*, and on p. 100, *healf tmt*, with the mark above the *t*. The abbreviated word stands for *tramet*, "page," and the phrase is a direction that the next half page is to be left vacant for the illustrator, as it is in both instances in the manuscript. (d) At the top of p. 164 occurs the phrase *tribus annis transactis*, the rest of the page being vacant. (e) Page 211 is also blank, except that at the bottom appears the word *innan*. This may refer to the words *innan healle*, DAN. 718, which are on p. 210 of the manuscript, facing this blank page. The word may have been an indication to the illustrator that the passage containing it should be the subject of a full page illustration, i.e., the handwriting on the wall. (f) On the margin of p. 212, opposite ll. 739–740 of DANIEL, stands the phrase *en rex uenit mansuetus tibi sion filia*.[1] (g) At the top of p. 219 stands: *omnis homo primum bonum*.

VI

SECTIONAL DIVISIONS IN THE MANUSCRIPT

The general division of the manuscript into Liber I and Liber II has already been described. Each of the four poems of the manuscript begins at the top of a page, but none has a title supplied by the scribe. A late hand has written above the opening of GENESIS the words *Genesis in lingua Saxania*, and a different hand has inserted the words *Genesis in Anglico* at the top of the full page illustration which serves as frontispiece. But the scribe himself has indicated the opening of GENESIS only by capitalizing all of the words in the first line of his text, that is, the first five words of the poem. The first word, VS, has a large, ornamental capital. The beginning of EXODUS is indicated in the same way, but the beginning of DANIEL has only the first letter of the first word capitalized, and this capital is a very plain *G*, probably made by the scribe himself, whereas the ornamental capitals at the beginning of GENESIS and EXODUS were made by a professional hand. The beginning of

---

[1] The roman letters indicate resolved abbreviations.

CHRIST AND SATAN is similar to the beginning of DANIEL. GENESIS ends on p. 142 with nothing to indicate the ending; EXODUS breaks off on p. 171, obviously incomplete, with nothing again to mark the ending. Only about one-third of p. 142 and of p. 171 was used, the rest of the pages remaining blank. DANIEL extends to the foot of p. 212, and is also incomplete, though more of the poem, including the ending, may have been contained on a folio lost between p. 212 and p. 213. CHRIST AND SATAN ends on p. 229 with *Finit Liber II. Amen.* But this poem, in spite of the ending, is also incomplete, though not because anything has been lost, since the writing on this last page occupies only about one-half of the page.

Liber I is divided into sections, in all fifty-five, which run continuously through the book. Many of these sections are numbered, and the sectional division is regularly indicated by spacing and capitalization. In general these sectional divisions correspond to natural breakings in the thought, and "it would seem that the sectional divisions, not always correctly indicated by scribes, were originally structural divisions due to the poet, influenced by general considerations as to the approximate length of a reading, say anything from about 50 to 100 lines."[1] Liber II is also divided into sections, with numberings of their own. In all there are twelve sections in Liber II; two, three, five, and six are provided with numbers, and all of them with indication of sectional division by spacing and capitalization. The sectional divisions in the manuscript are not always happily made, but this may be partly due to the accidents of transmission, though it must be acknowledged also that structure in its larger aspects was never a strong point with Anglo-Saxon poets. The origin and purpose of these structural divisions in Anglo-Saxon poetic manuscripts remains, however, more or less an open question. The Sections of the manuscript are listed in Table II, pp. xxxix–xl.

VII

CAPITALIZATION IN THE MANUSCRIPT

As in the other Anglo-Saxon manuscripts, the capitals in the Junius Manuscript are relatively infrequent and they are to a

[1] Gollancz, *The Cædmon Manuscript*, p. xxxii.

large extent sporadic.   They are of two kinds, large capitals and small capitals.   The large capitals are used at the beginnings of poems or sections in poems, and nowhere else in the manuscript. They usually run through a whole word, sometimes through several words.   The first five words of GENESIS are all written with large capitals.   Many of these large initial capitals in the manuscript are elaborately ornamental and were probably done by the same person who drew most of the illustrations and who presumably had general charge of the decoration of the book. The last of these elaborate ornamental capitals appears on p. 143, at the opening of EXODUS.   After that, spaces for large capitals are vacant or the capitals were supplied in plainer style, probably by the scribe.   Nothing further need be said about these large capitals at the beginnings of poems and sections in poems.   The practice of the manuscript in this respect is regular and obvious.   But the small capitals, though less conventionally used, are more significant.   They are not the work of the professional illustrator of the manuscript, but of the scribes themselves as they wrote.   They are not systematically used, but when they appear it is almost always possible to see a definite purpose in their use.   Proper names are sometimes but not systematically capitalized.   Most frequently the small capitals are logical and mark the beginning of a minor division in the narrative, that is, of a paragraph.   But in GEN. 198–205 the word *inc* is capitalized three times, apparently for emphasis. In GEN. 279–288 the pronoun *ic* is capitalized four times, evidently to emphasize the parallelism of phrase in this passage. In GEN. 2617–2619 the word *oðre* is capitalized twice to enforce the antithesis.   In GEN. 715 and 2750 the connective *oðþæt* is capitalized, and in l. 1248 a section begins with this word, ornamented with a large capital.   Here again the capital seems to mark a rhetorically emphatic word.[1]

In the first three poems of the manuscript, the use and the relative frequency of small capitals are about the same, though in DANIEL the scribe seems to have been more systematic than in the other two poems.   In almost every instance in which the

---

[1] Gollancz, *The Cædmon Manuscript*, p. xxx, notes that two sections in the manuscript of BEOWULF start with this same word.

scribe has used a small capital, modern custom would agree, except perhaps in the case of *Nalles*, DAN. 529, and *Wearð*, DAN. 604, and even in these two words the capitals may very well suit the taste of many modern readers. In CHRIST AND SATAN the first scribe uses small capitals freely, but the second scribe very sparingly. The few lines written by the third scribe indicate that he would have used small capitals abundantly if he had written more. These small capitals throughout the manuscript will repay study, and a full list of them will be found in Table III at the end of this Introduction.

VIII

ABBREVIATIONS IN THE MANUSCRIPT

The abbreviations in the manuscript are relatively few in number and are for the most part of familiar types. The common way of indicating abbreviations is by a stroke above the letter before the omitted latter, as in GEN. 185, *englū ḡlice*, for *englum gelice*. But abbreviations in datives like *englum*, though not uncommon in the manuscript, are by no means the regular practice, and the abbreviated form *ḡlice* is very unusual. Apparently the scribe abbreviated here in order not to start a new line, which would have run into an illustration. We may infer from this that the illustration on this page (p. 9) was drawn before the scribe wrote his text. At various other places we can see the scribe resorting to abbreviation under the momentary pressure of the necessity of gaining space. But this is not in general characteristic of the scribal habit in the manuscript. The only two words that are consistently abbreviated in the manuscript are *and* and *þæt*. The abbreviation for *and* is regularly 7. Only once or twice is this word written out as a conjunction, as *ond*, GEN. 1195, and in GEN. 1335. In this second passage it is probable that the scribe first wrote *7nd*, by mistake, and then corrected his error by changing 7 into *o* as the easiest way of disguising the miswritten symbol. This abbreviation is also frequently used in forms of *andswaru*, *andswarian*, but only three times in other *and*-compounds: in *andgiettacen*, GEN. 1539; *andsaca*, EX. 503; and *andleofan*,

CHRIST AND SATAN 520. Whether the abbreviation should be resolved as *and* or *ond* is perhaps a matter of indifference, and the practice of the manuscript in the writing of *a* or *o* before *nd* in other words is certainly far from consistent. If the conjunction had been always, or frequently, written out, no doubt the same inconsistency would have appeared in its spelling. The regular abbreviation for *þæt* is *þ̄*, and this abbreviation stands only for *þæt* in the manuscript. There are a few occurrences of the abbreviation in passages in which it might stand for something else, for example DAN. 189, *þ̄ hie*, which is a little more readily explicable as *þe hie*, "who," than as *þæt hie*, or DAN. 717, where *þa* would seem a little more appropriate than *þæt*. But when one recalls the almost unlimited opportunities the scribe had for writing the abbreviation for *þa, þe*, or other forms besides *þæt*, and did not do so, it is unreasonable to interpret the abbreviation in these few doubtful cases as meaning anything other than *þæt*. If *þæt* for the abbreviation seems at any time an inappropriate form, the difficulty must be surmounted by emendation, not by a special interpretation of the abbreviation.

IX

PUNCTUATION IN THE MANUSCRIPT

There is a good deal of punctuation of one kind and another in the manuscript. A dot under a letter is frequently used to indicate that the letter thus marked is to be deleted. Ends of sections in the manuscript sometimes have a distinctive mark, though not always, and there are a few other occurrences of sporadic punctuation in the manuscript. Attention has already been called to the use of small capitals at the beginnings of paragraphs, and this also may be considered a kind of punctuation. But the two most abundantly used marks of punctuation are accents over words, and dots marking the hemistich divisions of the lines of verse. This latter is obviously a metrical punctuation, and it is used with remarkable regularity and correctness throughout the whole manuscript. Ordinarily it consists merely of a dot between one hemistich and the following hemistich, but sometimes there is a dot and also a

check-like mark above the dot, or occasionally beneath the dot.
A few lines from p. 18 (GEN. 345 ff.) will best illustrate these
uses:

· sátan siððan ˅hét hine þǽre swéartan helle ˅ grúndes gyman ·
nalles wið god winnan ⁊ Sátán máðelode · sorgiende sprǽc · se
ðe helle forð · healdan sceolde · gi̯eman þæs grundes · wæs
ǽr godes engel · hwit on heofne[1] · oð hine his hyge forspéon ·
⁊ his ofer métto · éalra swiðost · þ he ne wolde ˅ wereda
drihtnes · word wurðian ·

The impression of a slightly unsystematic but on the whole
quite definite metrical punctuation which one derives from these
lines is confirmed by further examination of the manuscript.
Only rarely is the manuscript punctuation an unsafe guide to
the metrical reading, as on p. 39 (GEN. 839) where the manuscript reads

· uton gan on þysne weald · innan · on þisses holtes hleo ·

with *innan* set off by itself probably because the word was
emphatic or because the scribe was disturbed by the unusually
long half-line in which the word occurs. Again on p. 123 (GEN.
2600) the scribe was misled apparently by the slightly unusual
word order of the passage, thus writing

Hie dydon swa druncnum · eode seo yldre to ·

instead of

Hie dydon swa · druncnum eode · seo yldre to ·

This metrical punctuation must obviously have been of the very
greatest assistance to anyone who undertook to read the poems of
the manuscript aloud, and it is still helpful.

The accent marks of the manuscript are not so systematically
employed as the metrical marks, and indeed the purpose of them
is often far from clear. They are not used consistently to mark
long vowels, for short vowels frequently have accent marks,
nor to mark the alliterating or metrically stressed syllables of
the lines, nor to make emphatic logically or rhetorically important words in a passage. Apparently they were used for
any of these purposes, when it struck the fancy of the scribe so
to use them. But whatever may have been the purpose of

---

[1] Altered to *heofnen*.

accent marks in other Anglo-Saxon manuscripts, in the Junius Manuscript at least, the accent marks seem to be used more frequently for rhetorical emphasis than for any other purpose. A complete record of these very numerous accent marks cannot be attempted here, but for illustration all the accents on a single page (p. 14 of the manuscript, GEN. ll. 246–270) are given: téne (l. 247), hís (l. 250), gewít (l. 250), gesétt (l. 252), híe (l. 252), gesǽliglice (l. 252), swá (l. 253a), hís (l. 253), lét (l. 253), hím (l. 254), þ (l. 255), lóf (l. 256), dýran (l. 257), hís (l. 257b), lǽte (l. 258), ác (l. 259), awénde (l. 259), hít (l. 259), hím (l. 259), óngán (l. 259), hím (l. 259), úp (l. 259), síteð (l. 260), ón (l. 260), hé (l. 261), né (l. 261), hís (l. 262), ófermod (l. 262), áhóf (l. 263), hís (l. 263), héte (l. 263), ongéan (l. 264), hís (l. 265), líc (l. 265), né (l. 266), hé (l. 266), hís (l. 266), géon-gordome (l. 267), þúhte (l. 268), máran (l. 269), sé (l. 270), gód (l. 270).

Occasionally a double accent is found, as in mĕn (GEN. 451), beǎmas (GEN. 460), but these are rare, whereas the single accents are extraordinarily numerous and extraordinarily varied in their application.

Although the accents occur throughout the whole manuscript, in both Liber I and Liber II, they are very unevenly distributed. Sometimes there will be no accents throughout an extensive passage, and when the accents do occur they often come together in groups. It is quite possible that some of the accents were put in by other hands than those of the scribes, perhaps by various readers as interpretations of their reading of the manuscript.

X

UNITY OF THE POEMS IN THE MANUSCRIPT

1. GENESIS

By common consent, GENESIS has always been accepted as an appropriate title for this poem. It is, in effect, a versification of the first book of the Old Testament, though it carries the story only from the Creation to the sacrifice of Isaac, that is, through the 13th verse of the 22d chapter. But there is no telling how much more may have been contained in the poem as originally written, and how much may possibly have been lost. The sequence of events follows the Old Testament narrative without deliberate reorganization or reconstruction of the material, and the plan of the poem permitted therefore the versification of the whole of Genesis without violation of any artistic unity.

The text of the poem as it is preserved in the Junius Manuscript is a composite of the work of at least two different poets. The main body of the text, extending from l. 1 to l. 234 and from l. 852 to the end is commonly known as Genesis A, or the Older Genesis. The passage from l. 235 to l. 851 is known as Genesis B, or the Later Genesis.[1] Genesis B may certainly be regarded as an interpolation in Genesis A. The evidence that it is an interpolation was cogently presented by Sievers in *Der Heliand und die angelsächsische Genesis* (1875). Sievers pointed out the great difference in tone and in detail between Genesis A and Genesis B, and he came to the conclusion that Genesis B was not the original work of an Anglo-Saxon poet, but a translation into Anglo-Saxon from an Old Saxon poem, no longer extant, written by the author of the Old Saxon HELIAND in the early part of the ninth century. By a happy accident of discovery, this theory was placed beyond question when a fragment of the Old Saxon poem of which the Anglo-Saxon is a translation was found in 1894 in the Vatican Library.[2] The Old Saxon fragment contains twenty-five lines and one word of the twenty-sixth, corresponding to GEN. 791–817. The Anglo-Saxon translation follows the Old Saxon so closely that all thought of accidental

---

[1] Sievers, *Beiträge* L, 426, would make a threefold division of the text: ll. 1–234, Genesis A, in which he finds some slight but genuine survivals of Cædmon's work as revised by a later Genesis poet; ll. 235–851, Genesis B; and ll. 852 to the end, Genesis C, which he thinks has not the slightest connection with Cædmon. These views were more fully elaborated by Sievers in "Cædmon und Genesis," *Britannica* (Förster Festschrift), 1929, pp. 57–84. See also Klaeber, *Anglia* LIII, 225–234.

[2] See Zangemeister und Braune, *Bruchstücke der altsächsischen Bibeldichtung*, Heidelberg, 1894. In a review of this book, *ZfdPh.* XXVII (1895), 534–538, Sievers modified his earlier opinion as to the authorship of the OS. fragment and was inclined to regard it as the work of a pupil and imitator of the Heliand poet.

similarity or mere imitation is excluded. It may be taken as established, therefore, that Genesis B could not have been written before the early ninth century. Intercourse between the Saxons of the Continent and the Anglo-Saxons was not uncommon at this time, and no special knowledge of Old Saxon would be needed to enable an Anglo-Saxon to translate from that language into his own. It is quite possible, indeed, that the translation was one of the many effects of the cosmopolitan activity at Alfred's court in the second half of the ninth century.

No direct evidence is available for dating Genesis A, the Older Genesis, although the end of the seventh or the beginning of the eighth century is generally accepted as a probable time for the original composition of the poem. Sarrazin has endeavored, on the evidence of meter, to show that Genesis A is older than BEOWULF and, in fact, the oldest English literary monument.[1] Klaeber, on the evidence of apparent borrowings, also decided that Genesis A was older than BEOWULF.[2] On the other hand, Jovy was disposed to consider BEOWULF the older of the two poems,[3] while Blackburn thought Genesis A younger than BEOWULF, EXODUS, and DANIEL.[4] The same uncertainty rules concerning the other poems of the manuscript. Although Blackburn gave EXODUS as later than BEOWULF, Klaeber, working from parallel passages, considered EXODUS the older poem of the two.[5] DANIEL, except for the interpolated Prayer and Song, is, according to Thomas, older than BEOWULF,[6] and, according to Hofer, younger than Genesis A.[7] But all the arguments for relative chronology remain indecisive, through the conflicting results to be obtained by the application of different criteria. The language of Genesis A as it is preserved is, in general, West Saxon of a later period than 700, but there occur in the recorded text of the poem a number of forms which are

---

[1] *Englische Studien* XXXVIII, 170–195.
[2] *Englische Studien* XLII, 321–338.
[3] *Bonner Beiträge* V, 27.
[4] *Exodus and Daniel*, p. xxiii.
[5] *Modern Language Notes* XXXIII, 218–224.
[6] *Modern Language Review* VIII, 537–539.
[7] *Anglia* XII, 191–199.

commonly accounted for as indications of an original Anglian dialect in which the poem was composed and which were blurred over when the poem was transcribed into West Saxon.

If the poem was written in the north of England, about the year 700, time and theme fit so exactly the description of Cædmon as poet given by Bede that the ascription of the poem to Cædmon might seem to be beyond cavil. On the whole, however, modern scholars have hesitated to assign even Genesis A to Cædmon, preferring rather to characterize it as Cædmonian, or of the school of Cædmon. Nevertheless the argument is by no means all on one side. "Having weighed all the evidence," declares Gollancz, "having tested and investigated all the points at issue, I can find nothing against the authenticity of Genesis A, including even the paraphrases of the genealogies, as the work of Cædmon."[1] Against this may be placed Sievers' characterization of the notion of Cædmon as the inventor of a *Buchepos* as one of the most wrong-headed delusions that philology has ever fallen into.[2]

2. Exodus

Though long custom has established Exodus as the title for the second poem in the Junius Manuscript, the name is not well chosen. For Exodus is not in intent merely a paraphrase of the second book of the Old Testament as Genesis is of the first. On the contrary it is a carefully organized epic narrative, single in time, in place, and in action. The story moves directly to its climax in the passing of the Red Sea, and it ends swiftly after the destruction of the Egyptians. The conclusion is lacking, but if we may judge from the feeling for structure exhibited in the poem as a whole, not much can have been lost. The internal evidence of style also separates Exodus sharply from Genesis.

The main source of Exodus is the second book of the Old Testament; but of the Old Testament narrative, the poem uses only chapters xiii and xiv, with some brief allusions to earlier

[1] *The Cædmon Manuscript*, p. lxii.
[2] *Beiträge* L (1927), 426. See also his article "Cædmon und Genesis," in *Britannica* (Förster Festschrift), 1929, pp. 57–84.

and to later events in the life of Moses. A question of interpolation is raised in Exodus as in Genesis by the presence in
Exodus of ll. 362–446, which tell first, briefly, the story of
Noah's Flood, and then at greater length the story of Abraham
and Isaac. This digression is greater than many critics have
thought to be appropriate in a story of the passing of the Red
Sea, but it is not indefensible. The poet of Exodus has been
telling the story of a great flood, the flood which drowned the
evil Egyptians. What more natural than that he should pause,
having passed the highest point of interest in his narrative, to
tell about that other great flood which drowned the whole race
of wicked men, and that having spoken of Noah, he should
proceed to Abraham, with whom also, as with Noah and Moses,
God made a covenant and to whom he gave the promise of the
land of Canaan. It will be observed that this episode of Noah's
Flood and the story of Abraham, is treated in a somewhat simpler
style than the rest of the poem, and perhaps it is not too much
to suppose that the poet of Exodus, with his sensitiveness to
style, consciously reverted in this passage of falling action in
his poem to that older manner of the Cædmonian poetry as
appropriate to an episode properly belonging to the story of
Genesis. Viewed in this light, the story of Noah's Flood and
of Abraham in Exodus is not an inept interpolation, but an
evidence of the artistic skill of the poet. After this quieter
episode, the poet returns to his original theme and manner, and
except for the loss of some possibly few final lines, the poem
closes with no effect of incompleteness or disorganization.[1]

In connection with the latter part of the poem, however,
further question has been raised, not as to interpolation, but as
to possible displacement of parts. After the episode of Noah
and Abraham, the poet returns to his main theme, which he

[1] Blackburn, *Exodus and Daniel*, p. 54, thinks it possible that the scribe
was copying a defective manuscript and that in the original copy the poet
made the transitions to and from this digression more fully and explicitly.
But there is no evidence that he did so, and episodic passages like this are
frequently allusive and compact. Gollancz, *The Cædmon Manuscript*,
p. lxxii, says that though the passage may seem a digression and so have the
appearance of an interpolation, it is in his opinion "an integral part of the
poet's elaboration of his theme."

develops descriptively, ending with the account of the complete destruction of the Egyptians, corresponding to Genesis xiv. 28, and with a final statement, l. 515, "They have striven against God." The poem, as a poem, might have ended here, but as a versification of chapters xiii–xiv of Exodus it would have been incomplete, since there are three more verses in chapter xiv. As the poem stands in the manuscript, however, the poet does not proceed directly to the material of these three verses. On the contrary, the poem takes a glance into the future: "After that, Moses spake lasting counsels to the Israelites on the seashore."[1] Or *þanon*, l. 516, might be translated "at a later time," "afterwards," since there is no indication that what Moses said was said to the army at the moment of victory, nor is the matter of this passage immediately relevant or contained in chapter xiv of Exodus. It seems to be indeed a reference to Deuteronomy and to Moses as the lawgiver, an allusion therefore to matter far in advance of the theme of this poem. The allusion is very brief, however, for the poet passes quickly into a general homiletic mood, and this passage ends at l. 548 with a picture of the joys of heaven. Then follows a second passage, ll. 549–580, in which Moses actually does address the army briefly, calling their attention to the fulfillment of the Lord's promise on this day. The passage continues through l. 579 with an account of the exultation of the children of Israel—they praised the Lord, the warriors raised a song of glory, the women in turn, the greatest of folk-bands, sang a battle hymn with reverent voices. But the words of this song are not given, and apparently we have here a brief and not very exact allusion to the Song of Moses, in Exodus xv, for in the poem it is the Hebrew men and women who sing the song, not Moses. It seems quite evident that the poet avoided entering on the matter of Exodus xv, perhaps feeling—and rightly—that though the Song of Moses was excellent material for elaboration into poetry, it did not properly belong to his poem. Then comes a third passage, ll.

---

[1] This reference to the seashore should not be connected with the destruction of the Egyptians, but with Deuteronomy i. 1, where it is said that Moses spoke to all Israel "in the plain over against the Red Sea." See l. 519, note.

580–590, which concludes the poem and in which the poet returns once more to the main theme, with emphasis now on the spoiling of the Egyptians dead upon the seashore. This corresponds to Exodus xiv. 30. The remaining verse, if it was utilized, as it may well have been in the lost concluding lines, would have returned to Moses as leader of the Israelites and servant of the Lord, thus linking the end of the poem with the beginning.

But the question has been raised whether this third passage, ll. 580–590, was at the end of the poem as the poet wrote it, and whether these lines ought not to be joined directly to the preceding passage in which the final overthrow of the Egyptians has been described in detail, that is, to the passage ending at l. 515. Thus Gollancz maintains[1] that these three passages are all "integral parts of the poem, but have by some mischance been copied in the wrong order. We should expect that immediately after the overthrow of the Egyptians, the poet would describe how Israel was thus saved from the Egyptians, how they saw the Egyptians dead upon the seashore, how they 'feared the Lord, and believed the Lord, and his servant Moses,' Exodus xiv. 30, 31, the verses preceding the song of Moses." All of this Gollancz thinks is contained in ll. 580–590, and he would therefore place ll. 580–590 after l. 515; ll. 549–579, the speech of Moses to the army, he would place after l. 590; and ll. 516–548, the forward glance at Moses as the lawgiver, he would place after l. 579, as the conclusion of the poem. In other words, Gollancz would reverse the position of these passages, placing them in the order (3) ll. 580–590, (2) ll. 549–579, (1) ll. 516–548. In this interpretation the poem would be finished at the end of ll. 516–548, these lines being intended "as a fitting epilogue—Moses is the hero of the epic, and in the story of his achievements as general is added the glorification of his teaching as set forth in Deuteronomy."

That this would have been a possible arrangement of the material of the poem cannot be denied, but it is doubtful if we are doing the poet a service in thus rearranging the text. Gollancz maintains that this new arrangement makes the poem "an organic whole," but does not the placing of ll. 516–548 at

---

[1] *The Cædmon Manuscript*, p. lxxv.

the end make it less a whole than the present arrangement? To have told the exciting story of the drowning of the Egyptians and then to end with a general allusion to Moses as lawgiver, would have been an anticlimax. But the rearrangement is even worse, for the allusion to Moses as lawgiver is only a small part of ll. 516–548, and the main part of this passage is but commonplace, homiletic amplification. In its present position after l. 515 it is appropriate enough. Just as in the earlier passage about Noah and Abraham, the poet had stopped for a momentary glance backward, so now he stops for a momentary glance forward, but only a glance, for his present concern is with Moses as captain, not as lawgiver. He therefore quickly passes on to that kind of didactic sermonizing which is so frequent as episodic embellishment in Anglo-Saxon poetry, and when this is ended, he comes back to Moses in the address of Moses to the Israelites, and in conclusion to the gathering of the booty, their rightful due, from the bodies of the dead Egyptians.

The date of composition of EXODUS cannot be determined exactly, and it can be determined relatively, as has been pointed out, p. xxvi, only with some degree of probability. As to authorship, little can be said except that for stylistic reasons it seems scarcely credible that the poet or poets who wrote Genesis A, in spite of the many excellences in their kind of that poem, could have written EXODUS.

3. DANIEL

The central figure of this poem is Daniel, as it is of the Old Testament book upon which the poem is based. The poem utilizes materials from the Vulgate, Daniel i–v, ending with the Feast of Belshazzar. It opens with a conventional epic formula, followed by a short account of the Jews in Jerusalem (ll. 1–45), as introductory to the main narrative. It is incomplete at the end, probably through loss in the manuscript. The subject matter of the missing part was presumably Daniel's interpretation of the writing on the wall and the account of the slaying of Belshazzar. This would have made a fitting climax for the poem, and it seems improbable that the poem ever comprised a paraphrase of all of the Vulgate Daniel. The story moves along in regular order, except that ll. 279–439 have the appearance of being an interruption. These lines constitute a kind of lyric interlude in the general narrative course of the poem. The main content of them is the Prayer of Azariah and the Song of the Three Children, with the necessary connecting lines between these and other parts of the poem. The first of these two lyric passages, that is, ll. 279–361, Gollancz regards an an interpolation and as the work of some other poet.[1] He believes that the poet of DANIEL intentionally omitted this passage from his paraphrase, and that someone else made good the omission by inserting here a version of the Prayer already extant in an Anglo-Saxon poem. This interpolated passage was taken from a poem which has fortunately been preserved in the Exeter Book and is now commonly entitled AZARIAS. There can be no question of the practical identity of the AZARIAS and the DANIEL versions of the Prayer, but just how the one is related to the other is not quite so certain. It is clear, however, that the Prayer is awkwardly fitted into the poem DANIEL. Gollancz thinks the proper place for it was after l. 231, when the children had just been put into the fiery furnace, but that the scribe who interpolated the Prayer made a mistake and placed it after l. 278, with the result that a prayer for aid is sung after the aid had been given. The interpolater continued the interpolated passage to l. 356b, and continued it too long, since ll. 335b–356a repeat what the DANIEL poet had already paraphrased, ll. 232 ff., the account of the angel and of the pleasant summer weather in the fiery furnace. With l. 356b we apparently return to the words of the poet of DANIEL, ll. 356b–361 leading up to the introduction of the Song of the Three Children. This may be the right explanation of the presence of the Prayer in DANIEL, but it should be pointed out that even if the Prayer had been interpolated, or inserted by the poet himself, after l. 231, it would still have been awkward to have this somewhat long and irrelevant lyric thrust in just at a moment of high suspense in the action.

The Song of the Three Children, ll. 362–408, corresponds to the Benedicite in the Vulgate, Daniel iii. 52–90, the Benedicite

---

[1] *The Cædmon Manuscript*, p. lxxxvi.

proper beginning with verse 57. This Song follows the Prayer in the Exeter Book AZARIAS as in DANIEL, but the differences between the AZARIAS Song and the DANIEL Song are so great as to make of them separate versions of the same material. The DANIEL Song cannot be an interpolation, therefore, as the DANIEL Prayer may well be, though the evidence of phrasing indicates that the two versions of the Song are not independent of each other. The doubtful point is, which is the earlier of the two versions? Gollancz thinks that the poet of AZARIAS knew and in some details followed the version of the poet of DANIEL.[1] The earlier investigations of the question arrived at no convincing results, and perhaps the whole matter may be said to be still open for consideration.[2] For if it is true that DANIEL is indebted to AZARIAS for the Prayer of Azariah, i.e., DAN. 279–361, and AZARIAS is indebted to DANIEL for some of the phrasing of the Song of the Three Children, the possibilities obviously become more numerous than those of simple borrowing and interpolating. We may have to do with different poems and versions by the same author, or with collaboration, or with dependence on common sources.

The Song of the Three Children corresponds to the Benedicite in the Vulgate, Daniel iii. 57–90, but neither the poet of AZARIAS nor the poet of DANIEL used the Vulgate version of the Benedicite, but a Canticle version which differed in a number of respects from the Vulgate version.[3] A copy of this Canticle version, in Latin with an interlinear Anglo-Saxon gloss, is readily accessible in Sweet's *Oldest English Texts*, pp. 414–415, among the hymns in the Vespasian Psalter, where it is entitled *Hymnum trium puerorum*. The Vulgate passages which underlie the Prayer of Azariah and the Song of the Three Children are not present in the authorized English Bible.

4. CHRIST AND SATAN

The vexed question of unity raises its head again in connection with the fourth and last poem in the Junius Manuscript. So

---

[1] *The Cædmon Manuscript*, pp. xc-xci.

[2] See Blackburn, *Exodus and Daniel*, p. xxiv.

[3] See Steiner, *Ueber die Interpolation im angelsächsischen Gedichte Daniel* (1889), pp. 21–25.

far as the record of the manuscript goes, there is nothing to indicate that this is not a single unified poem. It begins in the usual way and it is divided into sections in the same manner as the other poems of the manuscript. The opening lines are a slight variation of the customary Anglo-Saxon epic formula for the beginning of a poem. And the poem is so uniform in content, in manner, and in language, that no separation into parts of different origin is indicated on these grounds. The chief reason for doubting the unity of the poem, for viewing it, as some have done, as a loose collection of fragments, has been found in the vague continuity of the narrative or structural interest in the poem. Grein treated the poem as a unit in the *Bibliothek* (1857), and was the first to give to it the title CHRIST AND SATAN. In his revision of Grein, Wülker (1894) divided the poem into three parts, each with a title of its own. The first part, ll. 1–364, he called Die Klagen der Gefallnen Engel, the second part, ll. 365–662, he called Christi Höllenfahrt, Auferstehung, Himmelfahrt und Kommen zum Jüngsten Gericht, and the third part, ll. 663–729, he called Versuchung Christi. These titles were well chosen, and they serve to call attention to the fact that whatever continuity the poem has, it is not that of a sustained narrative. Clubb prefers Grein's single title for the poem, but in his analysis of the structure of it, he recognizes the appropriateness of Wülker's three divisions, which he designates as Part I, The Laments of the Angels who rebelled against Christ and fell from Heaven; Part II, Events in the career of Christ from the Crucifixion to the Last Judgment; and Part III, The Temptation of Christ. Another arrangement proposes that these three parts be placed in the order I, III, II, in order to improve the logical coherence of the parts.[1] Gollancz likewise approves the three main divisions of the poem, though he thinks the second division should end with l. 596 and the third begin with l. 597.

It is obvious therefore that CHRIST AND SATAN does not contain a simple story, like GENESIS, EXODUS, and DANIEL, that in fact it is not primarily a narrative poem. It is better described as a set of lyric and dramatic amplifications of a

---

[1] R. L. Greene, *Modern Language Notes* XLIII (1928), 108–110.

number of Biblical and legendary themes of a familiar character, as a poem therefore more in the manner of Cynewulfian than in that of Cædmonian verse. In a poem of this kind one would not look for as obvious a structural form as would be expected in a narrative poem. Clubb makes a good case for the poem as "the product of a single molding spirit."[1] Gollancz also sees in the poem "a unity with three divisions," and he detects "the same type of mind at work in the various sections forming Book II of the manuscript, and the same unusual theological knowledge and outlook."[2] It is quite probable that the poet began to write without a developed plan in his mind, that his design grew as he wrote, and it is possible also that the poem was still in a growing and formative stage when the manuscript from which the extant copy was made passed out of the hands of the poet.

No single source has been found for CHRIST AND SATAN as a whole, and it is probable that it never had one. The first part, containing the laments of the fallen angels, rests upon the later legendary development of this theme, and upon the meager statements of the Old Testament. But there is little evidence that the poet in this part of his poem "was drawing from Latin documents, either Scriptural, apocryphal, or patristic."[3] A number of parallels indicate that the poet was well acquainted with the Cynewulfian poems, and certain similarities between CHRIST AND SATAN and Guthlac A seem best accounted for as the result of the use of a common source. The second part is mainly occupied with the theme of the Harrowing of Hell, the Resurrection, the Ascension (the second part ending here, at l. 596, according to Gollancz), and the Judgment Day. The general tone of this part of the poem, as well as the similarity it bears to certain extant examples of homiletic literature, suggests that this part of the poem may have had a homily for Easter Sunday as its source.[4] No homily which exactly fits the situation has been found, however, and perhaps it is not neces-

---

[1] *Christ and Satan*, p. lvi.
[2] *The Cædmon Manuscript*, p. cv.
[3] Clubb, *Christ and Satan*, p. xxxii.
[4] See Clubb, *ibid.*, pp. xxxiv ff.

sary to look for one. For manifestly an ecclesiastic as well
supplied with good pulpit material as the poet of CHRIST AND
SATAN must have been could easily write his own Easter
homily—at the same time that he was writing his poem. In
the third part of the poem, apart from passages which seem to be
due to his own imagination, the poet "would seem to have
depended upon his well-stocked, but not especially accurate,
memory of Gospel story."[1]

With respect to authorship, the most definite thing that can
be said is that CHRIST AND SATAN was not written by Cædmon
and is not a Cædmonian poem. Its closest literary relations
are with Cynewulfian poetry, and this connection is important
also in determining the date of composition of the poem. It
seems most probable that the poem was written in the eighth
century, but according to Clubb, what we know does not "war-
rant assigning a more precise period for the composition of
CHRIST AND SATAN than 790–830."[2]

XI

TABLE I

CONTENTS OF THE PAGES OF THE MANUSCRIPT

GENESIS

Page	Line	to	Line	Page	Line	to	Line
1	1 Us		32 norðdæle	15	271 folcge-		
2	33 ham		48 meahtan		stælna		296 habban
4	49 Him		81 dream-	16	297 ealra		309 deoflum
			hæbben-	17	309 Forþon		324 tomiddes
			dra	18	325 brand		358 hean
5	82 Wæron		114 arærde	19	358 on		388 geweald
6	114 and		134 grund	21	389 Ac		408 þencean
8	135 Þa		168 gefetero	22	409 Gif		441 lare
9	169 Ne		185 gelice	23	442 Angan		476 hean
10	186 þa		205 eall	24	476 heofon		490 wann
11	206 Þa		209 gefylled	25	491 Wearp		521 hearra
12	210 fremum		234 nemnað	26	521 þas		552 wyrð
13	235 ac		245 woldon	27	552 swa		585 ic
14	246 Hæfde		270 mihte	28	585 geornlice		598 com

[1] Clubb, *Christ and Satan*, p. xli.
[2] *Christ and Satan*, p. lx.

¹ Written twice in MS., at the end and at the beginning of a page.

XII

TABLE II

SECTIONS OF THE MANUSCRIPT

The sectional divisions as they are contained in the manuscript are given according to the lines of this edition in the following table, the numbers in square brackets not being present in the manuscript.

[Liber I]
    [I] GEN. 1–81
    [II] GEN. 82–134
    [III] GEN. 135–168[1]

    [IV] GEN. 169–234[2]
    [V] GEN. 235–245[3]
    [VI] GEN. 246–324
    VII GEN. 325–388[4]

---

[1] Incomplete at the end owing to the loss of probably three folios between pages 8 and 9, which contained the end of [III] and the opening of [IV].

[2] Incomplete at the beginning owing to the loss of folios in the manuscript.

[3] Incomplete at the beginning owing to the loss of probably two folios between pages 12 and 13.

[4] Section VII begins with *brand*, in the middle of a sentence, and Section [VI] ends with *tomiddes*, probably through a mistake of the illustrator. The original ending of [VI] was probably l. 320 and the beginning of VII was l. 321 (Gollancz, *The Cædmon Manuscript*, p. cix).

|---|---|---|---|---|
VII[I]	Gen. 389–441[1]		XXXVIIII	Gen. 2691–2771
[IX–X]	Missing[2]		XL	Gen. 2772–2833
[XI]	Gen. 442–546		XLI	Gen. 2834–2936
[XII]	Gen. 547–683		XLII	Ex. 1–62
[XIII]	Gen. 684–820		[XLIII]	Ex. 63–106
[XIV]	Gen. 821–871		[XLIIII]	Ex. 107–141[7]
[XV]	Gen. 872–917		[XLV]	Ex. 142–251
XVI	Gen. 918–1001		XLVI	Ex. 252–318
XVII	Gen. 1002–1081		XLVII	Ex. 319–446
XVIII	Gen. 1082–1166		[XLVIII]	Missing
[X][3]VIIII	Gen. 1167–1247		XLVIIII	Ex. 447–590
XX	Gen. 1248–1326		L	Dan. 1–103
XXI	Gen. 1327–1406		LI	Dan. 104–223
XXII	Gen. 1407–1482		[LII]	Dan. 224–361
XXIII	Gen. 1483–1554		LIII	Dan. 362–494
XXIIII	Gen. 1555–1636		[LIV]	Dan. 495–674
XXV	Gen. 1637–1718		LV	Dan. 675–764
[XXVI]	Gen. 1719–1804		[Liber II]	
[XXVII]	Gen. 1805–1889		[I]	Chr. and Sat. 1–74
[ ]	Gen. 1890–1959[4]		II	Chr. and Sat. 75–124
XXVIII	Gen. 1960–2017		III	Chr. and Sat. 125–188
XXVIIII	Gen. 2018–2095		[IV]	Chr. and Sat. 189–223
[XXX]	Gen. 2096–2172		V	Chr. and Sat. 224–253
[XXXI]	Gen. 2173–2260		VI	Chr. and Sat. 254–314
[XXXII]	Gen. 2261–2337		[VII]	Chr. and Sat. 315–364
[XXXIII]	Gen. 2338–2398		[VIII]	Chr. and Sat. 365–440
XXXIIII	Gen. 2399–2418[5]		[IX]	Chr. and Sat. 441–511
XXXV	Gen. 2419–2512		[X]	Chr. and Sat. 512–556
[XXXVI]	Gen. 2513–2575[6]		[XI]	Chr. and Sat. 557–596
XXXVII	Gen. 2576–2620		[XII]	Chr. and Sat. 597–729
XXXVIII	Gen. 2621–2690			

[1] Incomplete at the end through the loss of a number of folios. Marked VII at the bottom of p. 19, probably a mistake for VIII.

[2] Sections IX and X must be assumed to be missing because counting back from XVI, the next numbered section in the manuscript, all the sections from XV to XI appear regularly in the manuscript, though without numbering, and VIII follows regularly after numbered VII.

[3] The X for the nineteenth number was apparently omitted inadvertently.

[4] The section following this is numbered XXVIII and the one before it is without number, but follows in order after XXV and [XXVI]. Apparently the scribe omitted to count this section.

[5] A leaf has been cut out of the manuscript between pages 110 and 111.

[6] The beginning of [XXXVI] is lacking, a leaf having been cut out between pages 116 and 117.

[7] This section begins at the middle of a sentence. It is incomplete at the end through the loss of two folios.

XIII

Table III

SMALL CAPITALS IN THE MANUSCRIPT

Since the small capitals are sometimes merely the ordinary small letters made larger, it is not always possible to tell whether a letter was intended to be a capital or not.   If the capitals had rhetorical value, as it seems they must have had, the scribe may have felt that there were degrees of capitalization, a feeling that would be reflected in the size of his letters.   In the following lists, only those words are listed in which the capital letter is distinctly different from the ordinary small latter, and in all instances only the first letter of the word is capitalized. Occasionally the conventions of Modern English have required the substitution in the text of a small letter for the capitals of the manuscript.

GENESIS

65 Sceof [*MS.*	666 Ic	1296 Ic	1661 Ða
Sceop]	673 Gehyran	1314 Noe	1710 Abraham
79 Frea	715 Oðþæt	1325 Symle	1744 Ða
103 Ne	760 Nu	1335 Ond	1754 Gif
198 Inc	790 Adam	1339 Swilce	1767 Him
201 Inc	816 Nu	1345 Gewit	1779 Him
205 Inc	842 Sæton	1346 Ic	1793 Him
233 Swilce	867 Ic	1356 Him	1820 Abraham
236*b* Inc [*but*	897 Me	1363 Him	1854 Ac
not inc *in*	925 Abead	1367 Noe	1873 Ða
*236*a]	939 Hwæt	1390 Þa	1880 Ongunnon
279 Ic	952 No	1392 Siððan	1904 Ac
280 Ic	961 Gesæton	1411 Gelædde	1927 Him
283 Ic [*but not*	965 Ongunnon	1443 Noe	1945 Abraham
ic *in 282*b]	1022 Him	1449 He	1973 Him
288 Ic	1023 Ne	1460 Gewat	2003 Hæfde
347 Satan	1036 Him	1464 Ða	2045 Him
401 Ne	1055 Se	1476 Þa	2049 Rincas
438 Sittan	1063 Se	1493 He	2136 Him
484 Sceolde	1069 Siððan	1512 Tymað	2180 Ne
599 Heo	1138 Seth	1543 Ða	2187 Him
617 Sæge	1172 Se	1555 Noe	2188 Næfre
636*a* Sum	1240 Sem	1562 Ða	2201 Ic
655 Adam	1285 Noe	1588 Ða	2221 Me

2228 Her	2484 Þa	2626 Þy	2750 Oðþæt
2234 Þa	2500 Gif	2628 Þa	2791 Þa
2256 Hire	2513 Him	2630 Þa	2804 Þa
2274 Ic	2519 Ic	2636 Ongan	2807 Sweotol
2280 Hire	2526 Him	2641 Him	2824 Gyld
2286 Ic	2528 Þu	2643 Hwæt	2846 Þa
2296 Heo	2535 Þa	2653 Him	2860 Ne
2326 Ic	2540 Þa	2655 Agif	2880 Ða
2353 Him	2542 Þa	2666 Þa	2885 Gewat
2358 Ic	2571 Nu	2672 Heht	2890 Wit
2363 Hwæðre	2591 Ne	2674 Þa	2893 Abraham
2370 Abraham	2593 Ac	2694 Ac	2902 Ongan
2408 Ic	2600 Hie	2698 Ic	2908 Þa
2426 Þa	2607 Idesa	2708 Ic	2912 Him
2428 Hie	2615 Of	2719 Sealde	2914 Abraham
2466 Her	2617 Oðre	2721 Spræc	2926 Ða¹
2473 Onfoð	2619 Oðre	2736 Abraham	2932 Abrægd
2476 Him			

EXODUS

19 Heah	120 Hæfde	259 Ne	419 Ne
22 Ða	124 Nymðe	266 Ne	426 Hu
30 Hæfde	135 Ðær	276 Hof	526 Run
33 Þa	164 Wonn	278 Hwæt	549 Swa
54 Fyrd	183 Hæfde	326 Þracu	554 Micel
From	197 Hæfdon	377 Swa	563 Gesittað
93 Him	208 Hæfde	415 Ne	

DANIEL

4 Siððan	145a Ne	268 Geseah	486 Swa
33 Þa	154 Him	288 Swa	508 Ðuhte
52 Gesamnode	158 Ða	309 Ne	523 Þa
65 Gehlodon	163 Ða	409 Ða	529 Nalles
79 Het	168 No	414 Nu	546 He
96 Þa	170 Ac	416 Ða	562 Swa
106 No	178 Þa	427 Aban	585 Gehyge
116 Þa	200 Oft	430 Het	589 Oft
119 No	209 Ða	440 Ða	593 No
127 Þa	241 Hreohmod	444 Hyssas	598 Ongan
136 Næron	250 Ða	448 Gebead	604 Wearð
141 Ne	254 Ðær	452 Agæf	608 Ðu
143 Ge	263 Næs	458 Þa	

---

¹ The capital in this word and in Ða, l. 2880, is a large small ð, though usually even the small capital of this letter is Ð.

BIBLIOGRAPHY

I. MANUSCRIPT AND REPRODUCTIONS

1705 WANLEY, HUMPHREY. Antiquæ literaturæ Septentrionalis Liber Alter. Seu Humphredi Wanleii Librorum Vett. Septentrionalium, qui in Angliæ Bibliothecis extant, nec non multorum Vett. Codd. Septentrionalium alibi extantium Catalogus Historico-Criticus, cum totius Thesauri linguarum Septentrionalium sex Indicibus. Oxoniae . . . MDCCV. Description of the MS., p. 77.

1833 ELLIS, HENRY. Account of Cædmon's Metrical Paraphrase of Scripture History, an illuminated manuscript of the Tenth Century, preserved in the Bodleian Library at Oxford. London, 1833. Originally published in *Archaeologia* XXIV, 329–343. Contains reproductions of the MS. illustrations.

1872 SIEVERS, EDUARD. Collationen angelsächsischer Gedichte. *Zeitschrift für deutsches Altertum* XV, 456–467. The poems of the Junius MS., pp. 457–461.

1887 STODDARD, FRANCIS H. Accent Collation of Cædmon's Genesis B. *Modern Language Notes* II, 165–174. Collation with Thorpe's report of the accents.

1888 STODDARD, FRANCIS H. The Cædmon Poems in MS. Junius XI. *Anglia* X, 157–167. Description of the MS., especially the gatherings and chapter numbering.

1895 PIPER, PAUL. Die Heliandhandschriften. *Jahrbuch des Vereins für niederdeutsche Sprachforschung* XXI, 17–59. Collation of Genesis B, pp. 58–59.

1927 GOLLANCZ, ISRAEL. The Cædmon Manuscript of Anglo-Saxon Biblical Poetry, Junius XI in the Bodleian Library. Oxford, 1927. Complete, full-sized facsimile of the MS.

II. COMPLETE TEXTS

1655 JUNIUS, FRANCIS. Cædmonis Monachi Paraphrasis Poetica Genesios ac præcipuarum Sacræ paginæ Historiarum, abhinc annos M.LXX. Anglo-Saxonicè conscripta, & nunc primùm edita . . . Amstelodami . . . MDCLV.

1832 THORPE, BENJAMIN. Cædmon's Metrical Paraphrase of Parts of the Holy Scriptures, in Anglo-Saxon. London, 1832. With a literal rendering in Modern English.

1851, BOUTERWEK, KARL W. Cædmon's des Angelsachsen biblische
1854 Dichtungen. 1. Theil, Gütersloh, 1854; 2. Theil, Elberfeld, 1851. The Text appeared as 1. Abth., Elberfeld, 1849, paged 1–192. 1. Theil was completed by 3. Abth., Gütersloh, 1854, paged i-ccxxxviii and 193–353, containing Kirchen- und literarhistorische Einleitung, Übersetzung, and Erläuterungen.

1857 GREIN, CHRISTIAN W. M. Bibliothek der angelsächsischen Poesie. 1. Band, Göttingen, 1857. The Junius XI poems, pp. 1–114, 129–148.

1894 WÜLKER, RICHARD P. Bibliothek der angelsächsischen Poesie. 2. Band, Leipzig, 1894. The Junius XI poems, pp. 318–562.

III. EDITIONS OF SEPARATE TEXTS

1. Genesis A

1914 HOLTHAUSEN, FERDINAND. Die ältere Genesis mit Einleitung, Anmerkungen, Glossar und der lateinischen Quelle. Heidelberg, 1914. Addenda and errata in *Anglia* XLVI (1922), 60–62.

2. Genesis B

1875 SIEVERS, EDUARD. Der Heliand und die angelsächsische Genesis. Halle, 1875.

1894 ZANGEMEISTER, KARL, and WILHELM BRAUNE. Bruchstücke der altsächsischen Bibeldichtung aus der Bibliotheca Palatina. Heidelberg, 1894. Old Saxon Genesis, pp. 42–55.

1897 PIPER, PAUL. Die altsächsische Bibeldichtung (Heliand und Genesis). Stuttgart, 1897. Genesis B, pp. 460–486.

1903 BEHAGHEL, OTTO. Heliand und Genesis. Halle, 1903 (3d ed., 1922). Genesis B, pp. 211–235.

1913 KLAEBER, FR. The Later Genesis and Other Old English and Old Saxon Texts Relating to the Fall of Man. Heidelberg, 1913. Contains also Genesis A 852–964, Christ and Satan 408–419, 468–492, and the Old Saxon text of Genesis 791–817.

3. Exodus

1883 HUNT, THEODORE W. Cædmon's Exodus and Daniel. Edited from Grein. Boston, 1883 (2d ed., 1885; 3d ed., 1888).

1907 BLACKBURN, FRANCIS A. Exodus and Daniel, Two Old English Poems Preserved in MS. Junius 11 in the Bodleian Library of the University of Oxford, England. Boston and London, 1907.

4. Daniel

1883 HUNT, THEODORE W. See under 3.

1907 BLACKBURN, FRANCIS A. See under 3.

1907 SCHMIDT, WILHELM. Die altenglische Dichtung 'Daniel' (Bearbeiteter Text). Halle, 1907.

1907 SCHMIDT, WILHELM. Die altenglischen Dichtungen Daniel und Azarias. Bearbeiteter Text mit metrischen, sprachlichen und textkritischen Bemerkungen, sowie einem Wörterbuche. *Bonner Beiträge* XXIII, 1–84.

5. Christ and Satan

1925 CLUBB, MERREL D. Christ and Satan, an Old English Poem. New Haven, 1925.

IV. PARTIAL TEXTS

1826 CONYBEARE, JOHN J. Illustrations of Anglo-Saxon Poetry. London, 1826. Genesis 356–378, Exodus 447–463a, 489–494a, with translations in Latin.

1838 LEO, HEINRICH. Altsächsische und angelsächsische Sprachproben. Halle, 1838. Genesis 547–820.

1849 KLIPSTEIN, LOUIS F. Analecta Anglo-Saxonica. Vol. II. New York, 1849. Genesis 1–820, 1371–1482, 1964–2017, 2542–2575, Exodus 68–85, 107–129, 447–513.

1850 ETTMÜLLER, LUDWIG. Engla and Seaxna Scôpas and Bôceras. Quedlinburg and Leipzig, 1850. Genesis 246–964, Christ and Satan 1–223, 365–511.

1852 GREVERUS, J. P. E. Cædmon's Schöpfung und Abfall der bösen Engel aus dem Angelsächsischen übersetzt nebst Anmerkungen. Oldenburg, 1852. Genesis 1–441, with a German translation.

1854 GREVERUS, J. P. E. Cædmon's Sündenfall aus dem Angel-
     sächsischen übersetzt nebst Anmerkungen. Oldenburg,
     1854. Genesis 442–964, with a German translation.

1861 RIEGER, MAX. Alt- und angelsächsisches Lesebuch. Gies-
     sen, 1861. Genesis 246–321, 347–452, Christ and Satan
     159–188.

1870 MARCH, FRANCIS A. Introduction to Anglo-Saxon. An
     Anglo-Saxon Reader, with Philological Notes, a Brief
     Grammar, and a Vocabulary. New York, 1870. Genesis
     103–134, 347–388, Exodus 68–85, 106–134, 154–182.

1875 CARPENTER, STEPHEN H. An Introduction to the Study
     of the Anglo-Saxon Language. Boston, 1875. Genesis
     103–134, 143–163, 169–191, 206–215, 239–245, 261–397a,
     432–437, 1285–1482, Exodus 54–62, 68–85, 87b–97, 107b–
     140a, 154–306, 447–515.

1876 SWEET, HENRY. An Anglo-Saxon Reader. Oxford, 1876
     (9th ed., revised by C. T. Onions, 1922). Genesis 246–441.

1880 KÖRNER, KARL. Einleitung in das Studium des Angel-
     sächsischen. 2. Teil. Heilbronn, 1880. Genesis 246–441,
     2846–2936, Exodus 1–67, 252–306, Daniel 1–103, with
     German translations.

1888 KLUGE, FRIEDRICH. Angelsächsisches Lesebuch. Halle,
     1888. Genesis 1–441, Exodus 1–361, 447–590.

1891 BRIGHT, JAMES W. An Anglo-Saxon Reader. New York,
     1891 (4th ed., 1917). Genesis 2846–2936.

1893 MACLEAN, G. E. An Old and Middle English Reader. New
     York, 1893. Genesis 2846–2936, based on Zupitza.

1909 WILLIAMS, O. T. Short Extracts from Old English Poetry.
     Bangor, 1909. Genesis 969b–1021, 1356–1399, 1407–1476a,
     1960–2013a, 2018–2089a, 2406b–2418, 2535–2562a, 2576–
     2586, Exodus 252–298, 397–442, 447–487, Daniel 224–267,
     495–522, 546–582, 695–740, Christ and Satan 19–64, 75–124,
     383–434, 679–722.

1911 NAPIER, ARTHUR S. See under VI.

1913 KLAEBER, FR. The Later Genesis. See under III, 2.

1913 FÖRSTER, MAX. Altenglisches Lesebuch für Anfänger.
     Heidelberg, 1913 (3d ed., 1928). Genesis 2885–2936.

1915 ZUPITZA, J., and J. SCHIPPER. Alt- und Mittelenglisches
     Übungsbuch. 11th edition, Wien and Leipzig, 1915.
     Genesis 2846–2936. This first appeared as J. Zupitza,
     Altenglisches Übungsbuch, Wien, 1874.

1919 WYATT, ALFRED J. An Anglo-Saxon Reader. Cambridge, 1919. Genesis 304–437.
1922 SEDGEFIELD, W. J. An Anglo-Saxon Verse Book. Manchester, 1922. Exodus 1–361, 447–590.
1923 CRAIGIE, W. A. Specimens of Anglo-Saxon Poetry. I. Biblical and Classical Themes. Edinburgh, 1923. Genesis 12–46, 65–77, 103–166, 187–205, 246–598, 1002–1054, 1285–1482, 1644–1701, 1960–2045, 2049–2095, 2261–2298, 2399–2458, 2492–2512, 2535–2575, 2846–2936, Exodus 54–134, 154–188, 252–304, 397–515, 549–579, Daniel 104–162, 188–278, 335–354, 430–453, 495–588, 612–644, 671–746, Christ and Satan 1–74.
1926 CRAIGIE, W. A. Specimens of Anglo-Saxon Poetry. II. Early Christian Lore and Legend. Edinburgh, 1926. Christ and Satan 665–709.
1926 WYATT, ALFRED J. The Threshold of Anglo-Saxon. New York, 1926. Genesis 533b–546, 812b–826.
1927 TURK, MILTON H. An Anglo-Saxon Reader. New York, 1927. Genesis 2846–2936.
1929 KRAPP, GEORGE P., and ARTHUR G. KENNEDY. An Anglo-Saxon Reader. New York, 1929. Genesis 1356–1482.

V. TRANSLATIONS[1]

1826 CONYBEARE, JOHN J. See under IV.
1832 THORPE, BENJAMIN. See under II.
1852 GREVERUS, J. P. E. See under IV.
1854 GREVERUS, J. P. E. See under IV.
1854 BOUTERWEK, KARL W. See under II.
1857 GREIN, C. W. M. Dichtungen der Angelsachsen stabreimend übersetzt. Vol. I, pp. 1–118, 128–148. Göttingen, 1857.
1860 BOSANQUET, W. H. F. The Fall of Man or Paradise Lost of Cædmon. London, 1860. Genesis 1–956.
1880 KÖRNER, KARL. See under IV.
1896 GURTEEN, S. HUMPHREYS. See under VI.
1902 COOK, ALBERT S., and CHAUNCEY B. TINKER. Select Translations from Old English Poetry. Boston, 1902. Genesis 1–131a, 246–457a, Exodus 98–128, 154–165, 477–506a.

[1] The interleaved copy of the edition of the manuscript by Junius in the Harvard University Library, the same copy which was used by Thorpe in the preparation of his edition, contains an autograph translation by W. D. Conybeare of Genesis 1–2265 and Exodus 1–482.

1   BIBLIOGRAPHY

1903 JOHNSON, WILLIAM S.   Translation of the Old English Exodus. *Journal of English and Germanic Philology* V, 44–57.
1915 MASON, LAWRENCE.   Genesis A, translated from the Old English.   New York, 1915.
1916 KENNEDY, CHARLES W.   The Cædmon Poems, translated into English Prose.   London, 1916.   Contains reproductions of the illustrations.
1921 SPAETH, J. DUNCAN.   Old English Poetry.   Translations into Alliterative Verse, with Introductions and Notes.   Princeton, 1921.   Genesis 246–764 (with slight omissions), Exodus 447–515.
1927 GORDON, ROBERT K.   Anglo-Saxon Poetry.   London and Toronto, 1927.   Genesis 1–111, 235–851, 1960–2095, Exodus 1–306, 447–590, Daniel 1–45, 224–488a, Christ and Satan 1–223, 365–467.

VI. CRITICAL DISCUSSIONS

1845 BOUTERWEK, KARL W.   Über Cædmon den ältesten angelsächsischen Dichter, und desselben metrische Paraphrase der heiligen Schrift.   Beilage zum Jahresbericht über das Gymnasium zu Elberfeld, September, 1845.
1845 BOUTERWEK, KARL W.   De Cedmone poeta Anglo-Saxonum vetustissimo brevis dissertatio.   Elberfeld, 1845.
1856 DIETRICH, FRANZ.   Zu Cädmon.   *Zeitschrift für deutsches Altertum* X, 310–367.   Textual and interpretative notes.
1859 SANDRAS, S. G.   De Carminibus Anglo-Saxonicis Cædmoni adjudicatis disquisitio.   Paris, 1859.
1860 GÖTZINGER, ERNST.   Über die Dichtungen des Angelsachsen Cædmon und deren Verfasser.   Göttingen, 1860.
1865 GREIN, CHRISTIAN W. M.   Zur Textkritik der angelsächsischen Dichter.   *Germania* X, 416–429.   Errata and textual notes on the Bibliothek; the Junius XI poems, pp. 417–420.
1875 WATSON, ROBERT SPENCE.   Cædmon, the First English Poet.   London, 1875.
1875 STROBL, JOSEPH.   Angelsächsische Studien.   *Germania* XX, 292–305.   Textual notes on Exodus.
1882 BALG, HUGO.   Der Dichter Cædmon und seine Werke.   Bonn, 1882.
1882 EBERT, ADOLF.   Zur angelsächsischen Genesis.   *Anglia* V, 124–133.   Genesis 852–2936 not by Cædmon; comparison with Vulgate text.

1882 EBERT, ADOLF. Zum Exodus. *Anglia* V, 409–410. Exodus 362–446 an integral part of the poem.

1883 KÜHN, ALBIN. Über die angelsächsischen Gedichte von Christ und Satan. Halle, 1883.

1883 ZIEGLER, HEINRICH. Der poetische Sprachgebrauch in den sogenannten Cædmonschen Dichtungen. Münster, 1883.

1883 GROSCHOPP, FRIEDRICH. Das angelsächsische Gedicht Christ und Satan. *Anglia* VI, 248–276. Also separately, Halle, 1883.

1883 GROTH, ERNST J. Composition und Alter der altenglischen (angelsächsischen) Exodus. Göttingen, 1883.

1884 HÖNNCHER, ERWIN. Studien zur angelsächsischen Genesis. Zur Interpolation der angelsächsischen Genesis. Vers 235–851. *Anglia* VII, 469–496. Also separately, Halle, 1884. Genesis B an interpolation on linguistic, not literary grounds.

1884 HOFER, OSCAR. Der syntaktische Gebrauch des Dativs und Instrumentals in den Cædmon beigelegten Dichtungen. *Anglia* VII, 355–404. Also separately, Halle, 1884.

1885 HÖNNCHER, ERWIN. Über die Quellen der angelsächsischen Genesis. *Anglia* VIII, 41–84.

1885 SIEVERS, EDUARD. Zu Codex Junius XI. *Beiträge* X, 195–199. Metrical and dialectal notes.

1885 SIEVERS, EDUARD. Zur Rhythmik des germanischen Alliterationsverses. II. *Beiträge* X, 451–545. Textual and metrical notes to the Junius XI poems, pp. 512–515.

1886 MULLER, J. M. Ags. Genesis 431. *Beiträge* XI, 363–364. Meaning of *onwendan*.

1887 SIEVERS, EDUARD. Zur Rhythmik des germanischen Alliterationsverses. III. *Beiträge* XII, 454–482. Textual and metrical notes to the Junius XI poems, pp. 475–477.

1888 KEMPF, ERNST. Darstellung der Syntax in der sogenannten Cædmon'schen Exodus. Halle, 1888.

1889 RAU, MAX. Germanische Altertümer in der angelsächsischen Exodus. Leipzig, 1889.

1889 HOFER, OSCAR. Über die Entstehung des angelsächsischen Gedichtes Daniel. *Anglia* XII, 158–204. Textual notes, pp. 199–204.

1889 KONRATH, M. Zu Exodus 351*b*–353*a*. *Englische Studien* XII, 138–139.

1889 LAWRENCE, JOHN. On Codex Junius XI. *Anglia* XII, 598–605. Comments on Stoddard and Hofer; MS. variants unrecorded by Grein and Kluge.

1889 STEINER, GEORG. Über die Interpolation im angelsächsischen Gedichte Daniel. Leipzig, 1889. Daniel 279–408 an interpolation.

1889 HEINZE, ALFRED. Zur altenglischen Genesis. Berlin, 1889. Disagrees with A. Ebert, *Anglia* V, 124; examines use of Vulgate as a source.

1890 MERRILL, K., and C. F. McCLUMPHA. The Parallelisms of the Anglo-Saxon Genesis. *Modern Language Notes* V, 328–349.

1891 SEYFARTH, HERMANN. Der syntaktische Gebrauch des Verbums in dem Cædmon beigelegten angelsächsischen Gedicht von der Genesis. Leipzig, 1891.

1893 LAWRENCE, JOHN. Chapters on Alliterative Verse. London, 1893. "Metrical Pointing in Codex Junius XI: its relation to theories of O. E. Verse-Structure: collation with Thorpe," pp. 1–37.

1893 SPAETH, J. D. Die Syntax des Verbums in dem angelsächsischen Gedicht Daniel. Leipzig, 1893.

1893 FERRELL, C. C. Teutonic Antiquities in the Anglosaxon Genesis. Halle, 1893.

1894 BRIGHT, JAMES W. The Anglo-Saxon Poem Genesis, ll. 2906–7. *Modern Language Notes* IX, 350–351.

1894 HEMPL, GEORGE. Cædmon's Genesis, 2906–7. *Academy* XLV, 331.

1894 BRADLEY, HENRY. Cædmon's Genesis, 2906–7. *Academy* XLV, 350.

1894 HOLTHAUSEN, FERDINAND. Beiträge zur Erklärung und Textkritik altenglischer Dichter. *Indogermanische Forschungen* IV, 379–388.

1894 COSIJN, PETER J. Anglosaxonica. *Beiträge* XIX, 441–461. Textual notes on Genesis and Exodus, pp. 444–461.

1894 COSIJN, PETER J. Zu Genesis 204. *Beiträge* XIX, 526.

1894 GRAZ, FRIEDRICH. Die Metrik der sog. Cædmonschen Dichtungen mit Berücksichtigung der Verfasserfrage. Weimar, 1894. (Stud. zum germanischen Alliterationsvers, 3. Heft.) From the point of view of the "Vierhebungstheorie"; see M. Kaluza in Nos. 1 and 2 of the same series.

1895 STECHE, GEORG. Der syntaktische Gebrauch der Conjunctionen in dem angelsächsischen Gedichte von der Genesis. Leipzig, 1895.

1895 COSIJN, PETER J. Anglosaxonica. II. *Beiträge* XX, 98–116. Textual notes on Genesis, Exodus, and Daniel.

1895 GRAZ, FRIEDRICH. Beiträge zur Textkritik der sogenannten
Cædmon'schen Dichtungen. *Englische Studien* XXI, 1–27.

1895 SIEVERS, EDUARD. Wie man Conjecturen macht. *Beiträge*
XX, 553. Note on Graz, *Englische Studien* XXI, 2.

1895 HOLTHAUSEN, FERDINAND. [Review of Grein-Wülker, Vol.
II, Part II.] *Anglia*, Beiblatt V, 193–198, 225–234. Textual notes on the Junius XI poems, pp. 227–233.

1896 GRAZ, FRIEDRICH. Beiträge zur Textkritik der sogenannten
Cædmonschen Genesis. *In* Festschrift zum 70. Geburts-
tage Oskar Schade, Königsberg, 1896, pp. 67–77.

1896 GURTEEN, S. HUMPHREYS. The Epic of the Fall of Man: a
Comparative Study of Cædmon, Dante and Milton. New
York and London, 1896. Contains a verse translation of
Genesis 1–964.

1896 COSIJN, PETER J. Anglosaxonica. III. *Beiträge* XXI, 8–26.
Textual notes on Christ and Satan, pp. 21–25.

1897 NAPIER, A. Zu Daniel 266–7. *Archiv* XCVIII, 397.

1897 BRADLEY, HENRY. Daniel 266–7. *Archiv* XCIX, 127.

1898 LAWRENCE, JOHN. A Mutilated Word in Codex Junius XI.
Modern Quarterly of Language I (*Mod. Lang. Quarterly* II),
50. *Wreccum*, Exodus 533.

1899 MÜRKENS, GERHARD. Untersuchungen über das altenglische
Exoduslied. *Bonner Beiträge* II, 62–117. Textual notes,
pp. 113–117.

1900 HOLTHAUSEN, FERDINAND. [Review of *Bonner Beiträge* II;
see Mürkens, above.] *Literaturblatt* XXI, 62–64.

1900 JOVY, HANS. Untersuchungen zur altenglischen Genesis-
dichtung. *Bonner Beiträge* V, 1–32. Textual notes,
pp. 27–32.

1901 FULTON, EDWARD. The Anglo-Saxon Daniel 320–325.
Modern Language Notes XVI, 122–123.

1902 BRIGHT, JAMES W. Notes on the Cædmonian Exodus.
Modern Language Notes XVII, 424–426.

1902 GASKIN, ROBERT T. Cædmon the First English Poet.
3d ed., London, 1902.

1902 HOLTHAUSEN, FERDINAND. Zur altsächsischen und jüngeren
altenglischen Genesis. *Anglia*, Beiblatt XIII, 266. Genesis 813–814.

1903 BINZ, GUSTAV. [Review of *Bonner Beiträge* II; see Mürkens,
above.] *Anglia*, Beiblatt XIV, 353–360.

1903 BRIGHT, JAMES W. Jottings on the Cædmonian Christ and
Satan. *Modern Language Notes* XVIII, 129–131.

1903 BECHTEL, FRITZ. Ein Einwand gegen den äolischen Homer. *In* Γέρας, Abhandlungen zur indogermanischen Sprachgeschichte, Göttingen, 1903, pp. 17–32. Examination of the Old Saxon elements in Genesis B in relation to the analogous problem of an Aeolic Homer.

1903 KOCK, ERNST A. Interpretations and Emendations of Early English Texts. III. *Anglia* XXVII 218–237.

1904 KLAEBER, FR. Zu altenglischen Dichtungen. *Archiv* CXIII, 146–149.

1905 HOLTHAUSEN, FERDINAND. Zur Quellenkunde und Textkritik der altengl. Exodus. *Archiv* CXV, 162–163.

1905 GRÜTERS, OTTO. Über einige Beziehungen zwischen altsächsischer und altenglischer Dichtung. *Bonner Beiträge* XVlI, 1–50. Comparison of Genesis B, considered as a translation from Old Saxon, with the Christ, pp. 5–34.

1905 ROUTH, JAMES E., JR. Two Studies on the Ballad Theory of the Beowulf. Baltimore, 1905. Note on Exodus 580, p. 54.

1906 ROBINSON, F. N. A Note on the Sources of the Old Saxon Genesis. *Modern Philology* IV, 389–396.

1907 HOLTHAUSEN, FERDINAND. Zur Textkritik altenglischer Dichtungen. *Englische Studien* XXXVII, 198–211.

1907 HOLTHAUSEN, FERDINAND. Zur altenglischen Literatur. IV. *Anglia*, Beiblatt XVIII, 201–208. Textual notes; note on sources of Exodus.

1907 DETHLOFF, ROBERT. Darstellung der Syntax im angelsächsischen Gedicht Daniel. Rostock,1907.

1907 MEYER, ERNST. Darstellung der syntaktischen Erscheinungen in dem angelsächsischen Gedicht Christ und Satan. Rostock, 1907.

1907 WALTER, LUDWIG. Der syntaktische Gebrauch des Verbums in dem angelsächsischen Gedichte Christ und Satan. Rostock, 1907.

1907 SARRAZIN, GREGOR. Zur Chronologie und Verfasserfrage angelsächsischer Dichtungen. *Englische Studien* XXXVIII, 145–195. "Das Beowulflied und die ältere Genesis," pp. 170–195.

1909 WILLIAMS, O. T. A Note on Exodus, ll. 56 ff. *Modern Language Review* IV, 507–508. Explanation of guðmyrce.

1909 KLAEBER, FR. [Review of Blackburn's Exodus and Daniel.] *Englische Studien* XLI, 105–113.

1910 HOLTHAUSEN, FERDINAND. Zur altenglischen Literatur. IX. *Anglia*, Beiblatt XXI, 12–14.

1910 RICHTER, CARL. Chronologische Studien zur angelsächsischen Literatur auf Grund sprachlich-metrischer Kriterien. Halle, 1910. The Junius XI poems, pp. 16–18, 23–35.

1910 SCHMITZ, THEODOR. Die Sechstakter in der altenglischen Dichtung. *Anglia* XXXIII, 1–76, 172–218. Contains discussions of long lines in the Junius XI poems, with textual notes.

1910 KLAEBER, FR. Die ältere Genesis und der Beowulf. *Englische Studien* XLII, 321–338.

1911 GAJŠEK, STEPHANIE VON. Milton und Cædmon. Wien, 1911.

1911 GEROULD, GORDON H. The Transmission and Date of Genesis B. *Modern Language Notes* XXVI, 129–133.

1911 FRINGS, THEODOR, and WOLF VON UNWERTH. Miscellen zur ags. Grammatik. *Beiträge* XXXVI, 559–562. Note on *wergum*, Christ and Satan 42.

1911 NAPIER, ARTHUR S. The Old English Exodus, ll. 63–134. *Modern Language Review* VI, 165–168. Assumes misplacement of leaves; gives critical text of passage in question.

1911 MOORE, SAMUEL. The Old English Genesis, ll. 1145 and 1446–8. *Modern Language Review* VI, 199–202.

1911 MOORE, SAMUEL. On the Sources of the Old-English Exodus. *Modern Philology* IX, 83–108.

1912 BRIGHT, JAMES W. On the Anglo-Saxon Poem Exodus. *Modern Language Notes* XXVII, 13–19. Textual notes.

1912 HOLTHAUSEN, FERDINAND. Zur altenglischen Literatur. XIII. *Anglia*, Beiblatt XXIII, 83–89.

1912 SPERBER, H. Exegetische Miszellen. *Beiträge* XXXVII, 148–156. Note on Christ and Satan 42.

1912 SIEVERS, EDUARD. Zu Satan 42. *Beiträge* XXXVII, 339–340.

1912 BRIGHT, JAMES W. The Relation of the Cædmonian Exodus to the Liturgy. *Modern Language Notes* XXVII, 97–103.

1913 FRINGS, THEODOR. Christ und Satan. *Zeitschrift für deutsche Philologie* XLV, 216–236. Grammar and MS. corrections as tests of age and authorship.

1913 SEIFFERT, FRIEDRICH. Die Behandlung der Wörter mit auslautenden ursprünglich silbischen Liquiden oder Nasalen und mit Kontraktionsvokalen in der Genesis A und im Beowulf. Halle, 1913.

1913 KLAEBER, FR. Notes on Old English Poems. *Journal of English and Germanic Philology* XII, 252–261.

1913 SARRAZIN, GREGOR. Von Kädmon bis Kynewulf. Eine
litterarhistorische Studie. Berlin, 1913. "I. Kädmon," p.
13–37; "II. Kädmons Nachfolger," pp. 38–51.

1913 THOMAS, P. G Beowulf and Daniel A. *Modern Language
Review* VIII, 537–539. Criteria of date; Daniel A older than
Beowulf.

1913 WIENERS, REINHOLD. Zur Metrik des Codex Junius XI.
Köln, 1913. Textual notes, pp. 54–69.

1913 KAMP, ANTON. Die Sprache der altenglischen Genesis;
eine Lautuntersuchung. Weimar, 1913.

1913 KLAEBER, FR. Notizen zur jüngeren Genesis. *Anglia*
XXXVII, 539–542.

1915 HALFTER, OTTO. Die Satzverknüpfung in der älteren Genesis.
Berlin, 1915.

1915 BRADLEY, HENRY. The Numbered Sections in Old English
Poetical MSS. *Proceedings of the British Academy* VII
(1915–1916), 165–187. Exposition of his theory that the
numbered sections in the MSS. represent the contents of the
loose leaves of earlier (archetypal) MSS.

1916 BRADLEY, HENRY. Some Emendations in Old English Texts.
Modern Language Review XI, 212–215.

1917 HOLTHAUSEN, FERDINAND. Zu altenglischen Denkmälern.
Englische Studien LI, 180–188. Textual notes.

1917 SISAM, KENNETH. The Cædmonian Exodus 492. *Modern
Language Notes* XXXII, 48.

1917 THOMAS, P. G. The O.E. Exodus. *Modern Language Review*
XII, 343–345. Textual notes.

1918 KOCK, ERNST A. Interpretations and Emendations of Early
English Poetry. IV *Anglia* XLII, 99–124.

1918 KOCK, ERNST A. Jubilee Jaunts and Jottings. 250 Contri-
butions to the Interpretation and Prosody of Old West
Teutonic Alliterative Poetry. *Lunds Universitets Årsskrift*,
N.F., Avd. 1, Bd. 14, Nr. 26.

1918 HOLTHAUSEN, FERDINAND. Zu alt- und mittelenglischen
Denkmälern. *Anglia*, Beiblatt XXIX, 283–285. Note on
Exodus 79.

1918 KLAEBER, FR. Concerning the Relation between Exodus
and Beowulf. *Modern Language Notes* XXXIII, 218–224.
Criteria of date; Exodus older than Beowulf.

1919 HOLTHAUSEN, FERDINAND. [Review of Kock, Jubilee Jaunts
and Jottings.] *Anglia*, Beiblatt XXX, 1–5.

1919 KOCK, ERNST A. Kontinentalgermanische Streifzüge. *Lunds Universitets Årsskrift*, N.F., Avd. 1, Bd. 15, Nr. 3.

1919 KOCK, ERNST A. Interpretations and Emendations of Early English Texts. V. *Anglia* XLIII, 298–312.

1920 KLAEBER, FR. [Review of Kock, Jubilee Jaunts and Jottings.] *Journal of English and Germanic Philology* XIX, 409–413.

1920 BRADLEY, HENRY. The 'Cædmonian' Genesis. *Essays and Studies* VI, 7–29. Oxford, 1920. Appreciation of Genesis B.

1920 HOLTHAUSEN, FERDINAND. Zu altenglischen Dichtungen. *Anglia* XLIV, 346–356.

1920 KOCK, ERNST A. Interpretations and Emendations of Early English Texts. VI. *Anglia* XLIV, 97–114; VII. *Anglia* XLIV, 245–260.

1921 HOLTHAUSEN, FERDINAND. Zu altenglischen Gedichten. *Anglia*, Beiblatt XXXII, 136–138. Notes on Kock, *Anglia* XLIV, 106 f.

1921 SEDGEFIELD, W. J. Suggested Emendations in Old English Poetical Texts. *Modern Language Review* XVI, 59–61.

1921 KOCK, ERNST A. Interpretations and Emendations of Early English Texts. VIII. *Anglia* XLV, 105–131.

1921 MCKILLOP, ALAN D. Illustrative Notes on Genesis B. *Journal of English and Germanic Philology* XX, 28–38. Originality of Genesis B.

1922 KOCK, ERNST A. Plain Points and Puzzles. 60 Notes on Old English Poetry. *Lunds Universitets Årsskrift*, N.F., Avd. 1, Bd. 17, Nr. 7.

1922 KOCK, ERNST A. Interpretations and Emendations of Early English Texts. IX. *Anglia* XLVI, 63–96; X. *Anglia* XLVI, 173–190.

1922 HOLTHAUSEN, FERDINAND. Studien zur altenglischen Dichtung. *Anglia* XLVI, 52–62. Addenda and Errata to his edition of Genesis A, pp. 60–62.

1924 CRAWFORD, S. J. A Latin Parallel for Part of the Later Genesis? *Anglia* XLVIII, 99–100.

1925 KLAEBER, FR. Zur jüngeren Genesis. *Anglia* XLIX, 361–375. Addenda to his edition of Genesis B.

1925 CRAWFORD, S. J. The Cædmon Poems. *Anglia* XLIX, 279–284. Influence upon Cædmon of the Confession of Faith.

1925 STRAUSS, OTTO. Beiträge zur Syntax der im Codex Junius enthaltenen altenglischen Dichtungen. *Die neueren Sprachen*, 6. Beiheft, 172–182.

1925 BERTHOLD, LUISE. Die Quellen für die Grundgedanken von
      V. 235–851 der altsächsisch-angelsächsischen Genesis.
      In Germanica, Eduard Sievers zum 75. Geburtstage, Halle,
      1925, pp. 380–401.

1927 KLAEBER, FR. Weitere Randglossen zu Texterklärungen.
      Anglia, Beiblatt XXXVIII, 354–360.

1928 GREENE, RICHARD L. A Rearrangement of Christ and Satan.
      Modern Language Notes XLIII, 108–110.

1928 CLUBB, MERREL D. The Second Book of the 'Cædmonian'
      Manuscript. *Modern Language Notes* XLIII, 304–306.

1929 KLAEBER, FR. Jottings on Old English Poems. *Anglia*
      LIII, 225–234.

1929 SIEVERS, EDUARD. Cædmon und Genesis. *In* Britannica,
      Max Förster zum 60. Geburtstage, Leipzig, 1929, pp.
      57–84.

GENESIS

GENESIS

Us is riht micel   ðæt we rodera weard,
wereda wuldorcining,   wordum herigen,
modum lufien!   He is mægna sped,
heafod ealra   heahgesceafta,
5 frea ælmihtig.   Næs him fruma æfre,
or geworden,   ne nu ende cymþ
ecean drihtnes,   ac he bið a rice
ofer heofenstolas.   Heagum þrymmum
soðfæst and swiðfeorm   sweglbosmas heold,
10 þa wæron gesette   wide and side
þurh geweald godes   wuldres bearnum,
gasta weardum.   Hæfdon gleam and dream,
and heora ordfruman,   engla þreatas,
beorhte blisse.   Wæs heora blæd micel!
15 þegnas þrymfæste   þeoden heredon,
sægdon lustum lof,   heora liffrean
demdon, drihtenes   dugeþum wæron
swiðe gesælige.   Synna ne cuþon,
firena fremman,   ac hie on friðe lifdon,
20 ece mid heora aldor.   Elles ne ongunnon
ræran on roderum   nymþe riht and soþ,
ærðon engla weard   for oferhygde
dwæl on gedwilde.   Noldan dreogan leng
heora selfra ræd,   ac hie of siblufan
25 godes ahwurfon.   Hæfdon gielp micel
þæt hie wið drihtne   dælan meahton
wuldorfæstan wic   werodes þrymme,
sid and swegltorht.   Him þær sar gelamp,
æfst and oferhygd,   and þæs engles mod
30 þe þone unræd ongan   ærest fremman,
wefan and weccean,   þa he worde cwæð,

9 swiðfeorm] swið ferom   14 beorhte] beorte *with* h *added above the line*
23 dwæl] dæl

niþes ofþyrsted, þæt he on norðdæle
ham and heahsetl heofena rices
agan wolde. Þa wearð yrre god
35 and þam werode wrað þe he ær wurðode
wlite and wuldre. Sceop þam werlogan
wræclicne ham weorce to leane,
helleheafas, hearde niðas.
Heht þæt witehus wræcna bidan,
40 deop, dreama leas, drihten ure,
gasta weardas, þa he hit geare wiste,
synnihte beseald, susle geinnod,
geondfolen fyre and færcyle,
rece and reade lege. Heht þa geond þæt rædlease hof
45 weaxan witebrogan. Hæfdon hie wrohtgeteme
grimme wið god gesomnod; him þæs grim lean becom!
  Cwædon þæt heo rice, reðemode,
agan woldan, and swa eaðe meahtan.
Him seo wen geleah, siððan waldend his,
50 heofona heahcining, honda arærde,
hehste wið þam herge. Ne mihton hygelease.
mæne wið metode, mægyn bryttigan,
ac him se mæra mod getwæfde,
bælc forbigde. Þa he gebolgen wearð,
55 besloh synsceaþan sigore and gewealde,
dome and dugeðe, and dreame benam
his feond, friðo and gefean ealle,
torhte tire, and his torn gewræc
on gesacum swiðe selfes mihtum
60 strengum stiepe. Hæfde styrne mod,
gegremed grymme, grap on wraðe
faum folmum, and him on fæðm gebræc
yrre on mode; æðele bescyrede
his wiðerbrecan wuldorgestealdum.
65   Sceof þa and scyrede scyppend ure
oferhidig cyn engla of heofnum,
wærleas werod. Waldend sende

52 bryttigan] bryttigin   63 yrre] yr *at the end of a line*   65 Sceof] Sceop

laðwendne here   on langne sið,
geomre gastas;   wæs him gylp forod,
70 beot forborsten,   and forbiged þrym,
wlite gewemmed.   Heo on wrace syððan
seomodon swearte,   siðe ne þorfton
hlude hlihhan,   ac heo helltregum
werige wunodon   and wean cuðon,
75 sar and sorge,   susl þrowedon
þystrum beþeahte,   þearl æfterlean
þæs þe heo ongunnon   wið gode winnan.
Þa wæs soð swa ær   sibb on heofnum,
fægre freoþoþeawas,   frea eallum leof,
80 þeoden his þegnum;   þrymmas weoxon
duguða mid drihtne,   dreamhæbbendra.
   Wæron þa gesome,   þa þe swegl buað,
wuldres eðel.   Wroht wæs asprungen,
oht mid englum   and orlegnið,
85 siððan herewosan   heofon ofgæfon,
leohte belorene.   Him on laste setl,
wuldorspedum welig,   wide stodan
gifum growende   on godes rice,
beorht and geblædfæst,   buendra leas,
90 siððan wræcstowe   werige gastas
under hearmlocan   heane geforan.
   Þa þeahtode   þeoden ure
modgeþonce,   hu he þa mæran gesceaft,
eðelstaðolas   eft gesette,
95 swegltorhtan seld,   selran werode,
þa hie gielpsceaþan   ofgifen hæfdon,
heah on heofenum.   Forþam halig god
under roderas feng,   ricum mihtum,
wolde þæt him eorðe   and uproder
100 and sid wæter   geseted wurde
woruldgesceafte   on wraðra gield,
þara þe forhealdene   of hleo sende.
   Ne wæs her þa giet   nymþe heolstersceado
wiht geworden,   ac þes wida grund

82 buað] buan   100 geseted] gesetet *the final* t *perhaps altered from* d

105 stod deop and dim,   drihtne fremde,
     idel and unnyt.   On þone eagum wlat
     stiðfrihþ cining,   and þa stowe beheold,
     dreama lease,   geseah deorc gesweorc
     semian sinnihte   sweart under roderum,
110 wonn and weste,   oðþæt þeos woruldgesceaft
     þurh word gewearð   wuldorcyninges.
        Her ærest gesceop   ece drihten,
     helm eallwihta,   heofon and eorðan,
     rodor arærde,   and þis rume land
115 gestaþelode   strangum mihtum,
     frea ælmihtig.   Folde wæs þa gyta
     græs ungrene;   garsecg þeahte
     sweart synnihte,   side and wide,
     wonne wægas.   Þa wæs wuldortorht
120 heofonweardes gast   ofer holm boren
     miclum spedum.   Metod engla heht,
     lifes brytta,   leoht forð cuman
     ofer rumne grund.   Raþe wæs gefylled
     heahcininges hæs;   him wæs halig leoht
125 ofer westenne,   swa se wyrhta bebead.
        Þa gesundrode   sigora waldend
     ofer laguflode   leoht wið þeostrum,
     sceade wið sciman.   Sceop þa bam naman,
     lifes brytta.   Leoht wæs ærest
130 þurh drihtnes word   dæg genemned,
     wlitebeorhte gesceaft.   Wel licode
     frean æt frymðe   forþbæro tid,
     dæg æresta;   geseah deorc sceado
     sweart swiðrian   geond sidne grund.
135   Þa seo tid gewat   ofer timber sceacan
     middangeardes,   metod æfter sceaf
     scirum sciman,   scippend ure,
     æfen ærest.   Him arn on last,
     þrang þystre genip,   þam þe se þeoden self
140 sceop nihte naman.   Nergend ure

116 gyta] gyt *with a following letter erased*   119 wægas] wẹgas   131 ge-
sceaft] gescaft   135 timber] tiber

hie gesundrode;   siðða æfre
drugon and dydon   drihtnes willan,
ece ofer eorðan.   Ða com oðer dæg,
leoht æfter þeostrum.   Heht þa lifes weard
145 on mereflode   middum weorðan
hyhtlic heofontimber.   Holmas dælde
waldend ure   and geworhte þa
roderas fæsten;   þæt se rica ahof
up from eorðan   þurh his agen word,
150 frea ælmihtig.   Flod wæs adæled
under heahrodore   halgum mihtum,
wæter of wætrum,   þam þe wuniað gyt
under fæstenne   folca hrofes.
     þa com ofer foldan   fus siðian
155 mære mergen þridda.   Næron metode ða gyta
widlond ne wegas nytte,   ac stod bewrigen fæste
folde mid flode.   Frea engla heht
þurh his word wesan   wæter gemæne,
þa nu under roderum   heora ryne healdað,
160 stowe gestefnde.   Ða stod hraðe
holm under heofonum,   swa se halga bebead,
sid ætsomne,   ða gesundrod wæs
lago wið lande.   Geseah þa lifes weard
drige stowe,   dugoða hyrde,
165 wide æteowde,   þa se wuldorcyning
eorðan nemde.   Gesette yðum heora
onrihtne ryne,   rumum flode,
and gefetero
                    *   *   *
     Ne þuhte þa gerysne   rodora wearde,
170 þæt Adam leng   ana wære
neorxnawonges,   niwre gesceafte,
hyrde and healdend.   Forþon him heahcyning,
frea ælmihtig   fultum tiode;
wif aweahte   and þa wraðe sealde,
175 lifes leohtfruma,   leofum rince.

150 Flod] fold   155 metode] *Final* e *above the line*   gyta] gyt *with a*
following letter erased   170 Adam] *Followed by* e *erased*

He þæt andweorc   of Adames
lice aleoðode,   and him listum ateah
rib of sidan.   He wæs reste fæst,
and softe swæf,   sar ne wiste,
180 earfoða dæl,   ne þær ænig com
blod of benne,   ac him brego engla
of lice ateah   liodende ban,
wer unwundod,   of þam worhte god
freolice fæmnan.   Feorh in gedyde,
185 ece saula.   Heo wæron englum gelice,
þa wæs Eve,   Adames bryd,
gaste gegearwod.   Hie on geogoðe bu
wlitebeorht wæron   on woruld cenned
meotodes mihtum.   Man ne cuðon
190 don ne dreogan,   ac him drihtnes wæs
bam on breostum   byrnende lufu.
þa gebletsode   bliðheort cyning,
metod alwihta,   monna cynnes
ða forman twa,   fæder and moder,
195 wif and wæpned.   He þa worde cwæð:
"Temað nu and wexað,   tudre fyllað
eorðan ælgrene,   incre cynne,
sunum and dohtrum.   Inc sceal sealt wæter
wunian on gewealde   and eall worulde gesceaft.
200 Brucað blæddaga   and brimhlæste
and heofonfugla.   Inc is halig feoh
and wilde deor   on geweald geseald,
and lifigende,   ða ðe land tredað,
feorheaceno cynn,   ða ðe flod wecceð
205 geond hronrade.   Inc hyrað eall."
þa sceawode   scyppend ure
his weorca wlite   and his wæstma blæd,
niwra gesceafta.   Neorxnawong stod
god and gastlic,   gifena gefylled

---

184 freolice] freo licu   gedyde] ge *added above the line*   185 saula]
Final a *altered to* æ   gelice] ḡlice *the final* e *in a different ink*   186 Eve]
Not in MS.   190 ne] *Abbreviation for* and, *with a dot beneath and* ne *added
above*

210 fremum forðweardum.   Fægere leohte
þæt liðe land   lago yrnende,
wylleburne.   Nalles wolcnu ða giet
ofer rumne grund   regnas bæron,
wann mid winde,   hwæðre wæstmum stod
215 folde gefrætwod.   Heoldon forðryne
eastreamas heora   æðele feower
of þam niwan   neorxnawonge.
þa wæron adælede   drihtnes mihtum
ealle of anum,   þa he þas eorðan gesceop,
220 wætre wlitebeorhtum,   and on woruld sende.
þæra anne hatað ylde,   eorðbuende,
Fison folcweras;   se foldan dæl
brade bebugeð   beorhtum streamum
Hebeleac utan.   On þære eðyltyrf
225 niððas findað   nean and feorran
gold and gymcynn,   gumþeoda bearn,
ða selestan,   þæs þe us secgað bec.
þonne seo æftre   Ethiopia
land and liodgeard   beligeð uton,
230 ginne rice,   þære is Geon noma.
þridda is Tigris,   seo wið þeodscipe,
ea inflede,   Assirie belið.
Swilce is seo feorðe,   þa nu geond folc monig
weras Eufraten   wide nemnað.
                    *   *   *
235 "ac niotað inc þæs oðres ealles,   forlætað þone ænne beam,
wariað inc wið þone wæstm.   Ne wyrð inc wilna gæd."
        Hnigon þa mid heafdum   heofoncyninge
georne togenes   and sædon ealles þanc,
lista and þara lara.   He let heo þæt land buan,
240 hwærf him þa to heofenum   halig drihten,
stiðferhð cyning.   Stod his handgeweorc
somod on sande,   nyston sorga wiht

218 adælede] *A letter erased and* d *written above the line before the final* e
221 þæra] þære   anne] *Not in MS.*   222 se] sæ   223 bebugeð] *With*
u *altered to* i   229 liodgeard] liod geard *with* i *altered to* e   232 Assirie]
assirię   238 togenes] *First* e *altered from* a *by the scribe*

to begrornianne,   butan heo godes willan
lengest læsten.   Heo wæron leof gode
245 ðenden heo his halige word   healdan woldon.
    Hæfde se alwalda   engelcynna
þurh handmægen,   halig drihten,
tene getrimede,   þæm he getruwode wel
þæt hie his giongorscipe   fyligan wolden,
250 wyrcean his willan,   forþon he him gewit forgeaf
and mid his handum gesceop,   halig drihten.
Gesett hæfde he hie swa gesæliglice,   ænne hæfde he swa
                                      swiðne geworhtne,
swa mihtigne on his modgeþohte,   he let hine swa
                                      micles wealdan,
hehstne to him on heofona rice,   hæfde he hine swa
                                      hwitne geworhtne,
255 swa wynlic wæs his wæstm on heofonum   þæt him com from
                                      weroda drihtne,
gelic wæs he þam leohtum steorrum.   Lof sceolde he
                                      drihtnes wyrcean,
dyran sceolde he his dreamas on heofonum,   and sceolde
                                      his drihtne þancian
þæs leanes þe he him on þam leohte gescerede—   þonne
                                      læte he his hine lange wealdan.
Ac he awende hit him to wyrsan þinge,   ongan him winn
                                      up ahebban
260 wið þone hehstan heofnes waldend,   þe siteð on þam
                                      halgan stole.
Deore wæs he drihtne urum;   ne mihte him bedyrned
                                      weorðan
þæt his engyl ongan   ofermod wesan,
ahof hine wið his hearran,   sohte hetespræce,

---

245 ðenden] *Glossed in the margin* þa hwile   246 alwalda] *With* e *added
above the line before the first* a   248 tene] tęne *with* y *above the first* e
getrimede] *With* i *altered to* y   250 him] hịm *with* eo *written above* i   255
wæstm] wæwtm   258 læte] *With* æ *altered to* e   259 awende, ahebban]
wende *and* hebban, *initial* a *added above the line in both words by the scribe*
260 waldend] *With* e *added above the line before* a   261 urum] urę *with* v̄
above e   weorðan] węorðan, *with* y *above* eo   263 hearran] herran *with*
a *above the line after* e

gylpword ongean,   nolde gode þeowian,
265 cwæð þæt his lic wære   leoht and scene,
hwit and hiowbeorht.   Ne meahte he æt his hige findan
þæt he gode wolde   geongerdome,
þeodne þeowian.   Þuhte him sylfum
þæt he mægyn and cræft   maran hæfde
270 þonne se halga god   habban mihte
folcgestælna.   Feala worda gespæc
se engel ofermodes.   Þohte þurh his anes cræft
hu he him strenglicran   stol geworhte,
heahran on heofonum;   cwæð þæt hine his hige speone
275 þæt he west and norð   wyrcean ongunne,
trymede getimbro;   cwæð him tweo þuhte
þæt he gode wolde   geongra weorðan.
"Hwæt sceal ic winnan?" cwæð he.   "Nis me wihtæ
þearf
hearran to habbanne.   Ic mæg mid handum swa fela
280 wundra gewyrcean.   Ic hæbbe geweald micel
to gyrwanne   godlecran stol,
hearran on heofne.   Hwy sceal ic æfter his hyldo ðeowian,
bugan him swilces geongordomes?   Ic mæg wesan god
swa he.
Bigstandað me strange geneatas,   þa ne willað me æt
þam striðe geswican,
285 hæleþas heardmode.   Hie habbað me to hearran gecorene,
rofe rincas;   mid swilcum mæg man ræd geþencean,
fon mid swilcum folcgesteallan.   Frynd synd hie mine
georne,
holde on hyra hygesceaftum.   Ic mæg hyra hearra wesan,
rædan on þis rice.   Swa me þæt riht ne þinceð,
290 þæt ic oleccan   awiht þurfe
gode æfter gode ænegum.   Ne wille ic leng his geongra
wurþan."

---

267 he] *Added above the line*   274 heahran] *A letter erased before* r, *probably* o, *and the second* h *altered from* n   cwæð] *Followed by a large caret-shaped mark, with space before and after for one letter; the space between* cwæð *and* þæt *probably left inadvertently*   speone] speoṅne   277 weorðan] weorð *with* an *added above the line*

þa hit se allwalda eall gehyrde,
þæt his engyl ongan ofermede micel
ahebban wið his hearran and spræc healic word
295 dollice wið drihten sinne, sceolde he þa dæd ongyldan,
worc þæs gewinnes gedælan, and sceolde his wite habban,
ealra morðra mæst. Swa deð monna gehwilc
þe wið his waldend winnan ongynneð
mid mane wið þone mæran drihten. þa wearð se mihtiga gebolgen,
300 hehsta heofones waldend, wearp hine of þan hean stole.
Hete hæfde he æt his hearran gewunnen, hyldo hæfde
his ferlorene,
gram wearð him se goda on his mode. Forþon he sceolde
grund gesecean
heardes hellewites, þæs þe he wann wið heofnes waldend.
Acwæð hine þa fram his hyldo and hine on helle wearp,
305 on þa deopan dala, þær he to deofle wearð,
se feond mid his geferum eallum. Feollon þa ufon of
heofnum
þurhlonge swa þreo niht and dagas,
þa englas of heofnum on helle, and heo ealle forsceop
drihten to deoflum. Forþon heo his dæd and word
310 noldon weorðian, forþon he heo on wyrse leoht
under eorðan neoðan, ællmihtig god,
sette sigelease on þa sweartan helle.
þær hæbbað heo on æfyn ungemet lange,
ealra feonda gehwilc, fyr edneowe,
315 þonne cymð on uhtan easterne wind,
forst fyrnum cald. Symble fyr oððe gar,
sum heard geswinc habban sceoldon.
Worhte man hit him to wite, (hyra woruld wæs ge-
hwyrfed),
forman siðe, fylde helle
320 mid þam andsacum. Heoldon englas forð
heofonrices hehðe, þe ær godes hyldo gelæston.

---

317 geswinc] gewrinc   319 siðe] sið *with* e *added in a different hand, and a curved stroke of the pen below* e

Lagon þa oðre fynd on þam fyre,   þe ær swa feala
                                             hæfdon
gewinnes wið heora waldend.   Wite þoliað,
hatne heaðowelm   helle tomiddes,
325 brand and brade ligas,   swilce eac þa biteran recas,
þrosm and þystro,   forþon hie þegnscipe
godes forgymdon.   Hie hyra gal beswac,
engles oferhygd,   noldon alwaldan
word weorþian,   hæfdon wite micel,
330 wæron þa befeallene   fyre to botme
on þa hatan hell   þurh hygeleaste
and þurh ofermetto,   sohton oþer land,
þæt wæs leohtes leas   and wæs liges full,
fyres fær micel.   Fynd ongeaton
335 þæt hie hæfdon gewrixled   wita unrim
þurh heora miclan mod   and þurh miht godes
and þurh ofermetto   ealra swiðost.
   Þa spræc se ofermoda cyning,   þe ær wæs engla scynost,
hwitost on heofne   and his hearran leof,
340 drihtne dyre,   oð hie to dole wurdon,
þæt him for galscipe   god sylfa wearð
mihtig on mode yrre.   Wearp hine on þæt morðer innan,
niðer on þæt niobedd,   and sceop him naman siððan,
cwæð se hehsta   hatan sceolde
345 Satan siððan,   het hine þære sweartan helle
grundes gyman,   nalles wið god winnan.
Satan maðelode,   sorgiende spræc,
se ðe helle forð   healdan sceolde,
gieman þæs grundes.   Wæs ær godes engel,
350 hwit on heofne,   oð hine his hyge forspeon
and his ofermetto   ealra swiðost,
þæt he ne wolde   wereda drihtnes

---

328 alwaldan] *With* e *above the line after* w   330 wæron] wæro *with* n
added above the line   336 heora] herra, *the first* r *changed to* o   339
hwitost] *A second* t *added above the line after* i   339 heofne] *The final* e
altered to o *and* n *added above the line*   344 cwæð se] *With the abbreviation
for* þæt *inserted between*   346 winnan] widnan   349 gieman] giẹman
with y *added above* ie   350 heofne] *Final* e *altered to* o *and* n *added above
the line*

word wurðian. Weoll him on innan
hyge ymb his heortan,   hat wæs him utan
355 wraðlic wite. He þa worde cwæð:
"Is þæs ænga styde   ungelic swiðe
þam oðrum ham   þe we ær cuðon,
hean on heofonrice,   þe me min hearra onlag,
þeah we hine for þam alwaldan   agan ne moston,
360 romigan ures rices. Næfð he þeah riht gedon
þæt he us hæfð befælled   fyre to botme,
helle þære hatan,   heofonrice benumen;
hafað hit gemearcod   mid moncynne
to gesettanne. Þæt me is sorga mæst,
365 þæt Adam sceal,   þe wæs of eorðan geworht,
minne stronglican   stol behealdan,
wesan him on wynne,   and we þis wite þolien,
hearm on þisse helle. Wa la, ahte ic minra handa
geweald
and moste ane tid   ute weorðan,
370 wesan ane winterstunde,   þonne ic mid þys werode—
Ac licgað me ymbe   irenbenda,
rideð racentan sal. Ic eom rices leas;
habbað me swa hearde   helle clommas
fæste befangen. Her is fyr micel,
375 ufan and neoðone. Ic a ne geseah
laðran landscipe. Lig ne aswamað,
hat ofer helle. Me habbað hringa gespong,
sliðhearda sal   siðes amyrred,
afyrred me min feðe;   fet synt gebundene,
380 handa gehæfte. Synt þissa heldora
wegas forworhte,   swa ic mid wihte ne mæg
of þissum lioðobendum. Licgað me ymbe
heardes irenes   hate geslægene

---

356 þæs] *With* æ *altered to* e   ænga] *With* i *added above the line after* n
styde] *With* y *canceled and* e *written above it*   357 ham] *Not in MS.*   358a
on] *Added in the margin; the first word on p. 19*   359 alwaldan] *With* e
added above the line after w   361 befælled] *With* y *written above* æ   371
irenbenda] *With a long* s *added at end*   382 ymbe] ymb *with a following*
e *erased, and* utan *added above the line*

grindlas greate.   Mid þy me god hafað
385 gehæfted be þam healse,   swa ic wat he minne hige cuðe;
and þæt wiste eac   weroda drihten,
þæt sceolde unc Adame   yfele gewurðan
ymb þæt heofonrice,   þær ic ahte minra handa geweald.
Ac ðoliaþ we nu þrea on helle,   (þæt syndon þystro
                                    and hæto),
390 grimme, grundlease.   Hafað us god sylfa
forswapen on þas sweartan mistas;   swa he us ne mæg
                                    ænige synne gestælan,
þæt we him on þam lande lað gefremedon,   he hæfð us
                        þeah þæs leohtes bescyrede,
beworpen on ealra wita mæste.   Ne magon we þæs wrace
                                    gefremman,
geleanian him mid laðes wihte   þæt he us hafað þæs
                        leohtes bescyrede.
395 He hæfð nu gemearcod anne middangeard,   þær he hæfð
                                    mon geworhtne
æfter his onlicnesse.   Mid þam he wile eft gesettan
heofona rice mid hluttrum saulum.   We þæs sculon
                                    hycgan georne,
þæt we on Adame,   gif we æfre mægen,
and on his eafrum swa some,   andan gebetan,
400 onwendan him þær willan sines,   gif we hit mægen
                                    wihte aþencan.
Ne gelyfe ic me nu þæs leohtes furðor   þæs þe he him
                        þenceð lange niotan,
þæs eades mid his engla cræfte.   Ne magon we þæt on
                                    aldre gewinnan,
þæt we mihtiges godes mod onwæcen.   Uton oðwendan
                                    hit nu monna bearnum,
þæt heofonrice, nu we hit habban ne moton,   gedon þæt
                                    hie his hyldo forlæten,
405 þæt hie þæt onwendon þæt he mid his worde bebead.
                Þonne weorð he him wrað on mode,
ahwet hie from his hyldo.   Þonne sculon hie þas helle
                                    secan

401 him] hjm *with* eo *written above*   niotan] i *altered to* e

and þas grimman grundas.   Þonne moton we hie us to
                             giongrum habban,
fira bearn on þissum fæstum clomme.   Onginnað nu ymb
                             þa fyrde þencean!
Gif ic ænegum þægne   þeodenmadmas
410 geara forgeafe,   þenden we on þan godan rice
gesælige sæton   and hæfdon ure setla geweald,
þonne he me na on leofran tid   leanum ne meahte
mine gife gyldan,   gif his gien wolde
minra þegna hwilc   geþafa wurðan,
415 þæt he up heonon   ute mihte
cuman þurh þas clustro,   and hæfde cræft mid him
þæt he mid feðerhoman   fleogan meahte,
windan on wolcne,   þær geworht stondað
Adam and Eue   on eorðrice
420 mid welan bewunden,   and we synd aworpene hider
on þas deopan dalo.   Nu hie drihtne synt
wurðran micle,   and moton him þone welan agan
þe we on heofonrice   habban sceoldon,
rice mid rihte;   is se ræd gescyred
425 monna cynne.   Þæt me is on minum mode swa sar,
on minum hyge hreoweð,   þæt hie heofonrice
agan to aldre.   Gif hit eower ænig mæge
gewendan mid wihte   þæt hie word godes
lare forlæten,   sona hie him þe laðran beoð.
430 Gif hie brecað his gebodscipe,   þonne he him abolgen
                             wurðeþ;
siððan bið him se wela onwended   and wyrð him wite
                             gegarwod,
sum heard hearmscearu.   Hycgað his ealle,
hu ge hi beswicen!   Siððan ic me sefte mæg
restan on þyssum racentum,   gif him þæt rice losað.
435 Se þe þæt gelæsteð,   him bið lean gearo
æfter to aldre,   þæs we her inne magon
on þyssum fyre forð   fremena gewinnan.

409 þægne] æ *altered to* e   417 feðerhoman] *The first* e *altered from* æ *and* ð
altered from d   425 minum mode] mode minum *with marks for transposing*
431 gegarwod] *With* e *above the line before* a

Sittan læte ic hine wið me sylfne,   swa hwa swa þæt sec-
                                             gan cymeð
on þas hatan helle,   þæt hie heofoncyninges
440 unwurðlice   wordum and dædum
lare"

*   *   *

Angan hine þa gyrwan   godes andsaca,
fus on frætwum,   (hæfde fæcne hyge),
hæleðhelm on heafod asette and þone full hearde geband,
445 spenn mid spangum;   wiste him spræca fela,
wora worda.   Wand him up þanon,
hwearf him þurh þa helldora,   (hæfde hyge strangne),
leolc on lyfte   laþwendemod,
swang þæt fyr on twa   feondes cræfte;
450 wolde dearnunga   drihtnes geongran,
mid mandædum   men beswican,
forlædan and forlæran,   þæt hie wurdon lað gode.
He þa geferde   þurh feondes cræft
oððæt he Adam   on eorðrice,
455 godes handgesceaft,   gearone funde,
wislice geworht,   and his wif somed,
freo fægroste,   swa hie fela cuðon
godes gegearwigean,   þa him to gingran self
metod mancynnes   mearcode selfa.
460 And him bi twegin   beamas stodon
þa wæron utan   ofætes gehlædene,
gewered mid wæstme,   swa hie waldend god,
heah heofoncyning   handum gesette,
þæt þær yldo bearn   moste on ceosan
465 godes and yfeles,   gumena æghwilc,
welan and wawan.   Næs se wæstm gelic!
Oðer wæs swa wynlic,   wlitig and scene,
liðe and lofsum,   þæt wæs lifes beam;

445 spenn] *With* o *added after* e   446 wora worda] *Glossed in the margin*
wraþra worda   451 men] *With a second* n *added above the line*   453
geferde] geferede *with* e *after* t *erased*   459 metod] metot   460 twegin] i
altered to e   466 and wawan] *Repeated in the margin because blurred in*
the text   467 and scene] *Repeated in the margin because blurred in the text*

moste on ecnisse   æfter lybban,
470 wesan on worulde,   se þæs wæstmes onbat,
swa him æfter þy   yldo ne derede,
ne suht sware,   ac moste symle wesan
lungre on lustum   and his lif agan,
hyldo heofoncyninges   her on worulde,
475 habban him to wæron   witode geþingþo
on þone hean heofon,   þonne he heonon wende.
Þonne wæs se oðer   eallenga sweart,
dim and þystre;   þæt wæs deaðes beam,
se bær bitres fela.   Sceolde bu witan
480 ylda æghwilc   yfles and godes
gewand on þisse worulde.   Sceolde on wite a
mid swate and mid sorgum   siððan libban,
swa hwa swa gebyrgde   þæs on þam beame geweox.
Sceolde hine yldo beniman   ellendæda,
485 dreamas and drihtscipes,   and him beon deað scyred.
Lytle hwile   sceolde he his lifes niotan,
secan þonne landa   sweartost on fyre.
Sceolde feondum þeowian,   þær is ealra frecna mæste
leodum to langre hwile.   Þæt wiste se laða georne,
490 dyrne deofles boda   þe wið drihten wann.
      Wearp hine þa on wyrmes lic   and wand him þa
                                             ymbutan
þone deaðes beam   þurh deofles cræft,
genam þær þæs ofætes   and wende hine eft þanon
þær he wiste handgeweorc   heofoncyninges.
495 Ongon hine þa frinan   forman worde
se laða mid ligenum: "Langað þe awuht,
Adam, up to gode?   Ic eom on his ærende hider
feorran gefered,   ne þæt nu fyrn ne wæs
þæt ic wið hine sylfne sæt.   Þa het he me on þysne sið
                                             faran,
500 het þæt þu þisses ofætes æte,   cwæð þæt þin abal and
                                             cræft

---

473 agan] *Second* a *altered from* o   475 witode] witod *with final* e *above the*
line   geþingþo] geþing, *then* þ *added on an erasure and* o *above the line*
476 he] heo   481 gewand] *With* o *added above the line after* n

and þin modsefa   mara wurde,
and þin lichoma   leohtra micle,
þin gesceapu   scenran,   cwæð þæt þe æniges sceattes
                                              ðearf
ne wurde on worulde.   Nu þu willan hæfst,
505 hyldo geworhte   heofoncyninges,
to þance geþenod   þinum hearran,
hæfst þe wið drihten dyrne geworhtne.   Ic gehyrde hine
                                        þine dæd and word
lofian on his leohte   and ymb þin lif sprecan.
Swa þu læstan scealt   þæt on þis land hider
510 his bodan bringað.   Brade synd on worulde
grene geardas,   and god siteð
on þam hehstan   heofna rice,
ufan alwalda.   Nele þa earfeðu
sylfa habban   þæt he on þysne sið fare,
515 gumena drihten,   ac he his gingran sent
to þinre spræce.   Nu he þe mid spellum het
listas læran.   Læste þu georne
his ambyhto,   nim þe þis ofæt on hand,
bit his and byrige.   þe weorð on þinum breostum rum,
520 wæstm þy wlitegra.   þe sende waldend god,
þin hearra þas helpe   of heofonrice."
    Adam maðelode   þær he on eorðan stod,
selfsceafte guma: "þonne ic sigedrihten,
mihtigne god,   mæðlan gehyrde
525 strangre stemne,   and me her stondan het,
his bebodu healdan,   and me þas bryd forgeaf,
wlitesciene wif,   and me warnian het
þæt ic on þone deaðes beam   bedroren ne wurde,
beswicen to swiðe,   he cwæð þæt þa sweartan helle
530 healdan sceolde   se ðe bi his heortan wuht
laðes gelæde.   Nat þeah þu mid ligenum fare
þurh dyrne geþanc   þe þu drihtnes eart
boda of heofnum.   Hwæt, ic þinra bysna ne mæg,

503 sceattes] sceates   506 hearran] hearan   509 þis] þs *with* i *inserted*
above the line   519 byrige] byrige   521 helpe] *Final* e *altered to* a
of] f *blurred, the result of changing* n *to* f?

worda ne wisna wuht oncnawan,
535 siðes ne sagona. Ic wat hwæt he me self bebead,
nergend user, þa ic hine nehst geseah;
he het me his word weorðian and wel healdan,
læstan his lare. Þu gelic ne bist
ænegum his engla þe ic ær geseah,
540 ne þu me oðiewdest ænig tacen
þe he me þurh treowe to onsende,
min hearra þurh hyldo. Þy ic þe hyran ne cann,
ac þu meaht þe forð faran. Ic hæbbe me fæstne geleafan
up to þam ælmihtegan gode þe me mid his earmum
worhte,
545 her mid handum sinum. He mæg me of his hean rice
geofian mid goda gehwilcum, þeah he his gingran ne
sende."
Wende hine wraðmod þær he þæt wif geseah
on eorðrice Euan stondan,
sceone gesceapene, cwæð þæt sceaðena mæst
550 eallum heora eaforum æfter siððan
wurde on worulde: "Ic wat, inc waldend god
abolgen wyrð, swa ic him þisne bodscipe
selfa secge, þonne ic of þys siðe cume
ofer langne weg, þæt git ne læstan wel
555 hwilc ærende swa he easten hider
on þysne sið sendeð. Nu sceal he sylf faran
to incre andsware; ne mæg his ærende
his boda beodan; þy ic wat þæt he inc abolgen wyrð,
mihtig on mode. Gif þu þeah minum wilt,
560 wif willende, wordum hyran,
þu meaht his þonne rume ræd geþencan.
Gehyge on þinum breostum þæt þu inc bam twam
meaht
wite bewarigan, swa ic þe wisie.
Æt þisses ofetes! Þonne wurðað þin eagan swa leoht
565 þæt þu meaht swa wide ofer woruld ealle
geseon siððan, and selfes stol

540 ne] *Repeated after* me *but with cancel marks beneath*   546 geofian]
With y *above* e

herran þines, and habban his hyldo forð.
Meaht þu Adame eft gestyran,
gif þu his willan hæfst and he þinum wordum getrywð.
570 Gif þu him to soðe sægst hwylce þu selfa hæfst
bisne on breostum, þæs þu gebod godes
lare læstes, he þone laðan strið,
yfel andwyrde an forlæteð
on breostcofan, swa wit him bu tu
575 an sped sprecað. Span þu hine georne
þæt he þine lare læste, þy læs gyt lað gode,
incrum waldende, weorðan þyrfen.
Gif þu þæt angin fremest, idesa seo betste,
forhele ic incrum herran þæt me hearmes swa fela
580 Adam gespræc, eargra worda.
Tyhð me untryowða, cwyð þæt ic seo teonum georn,
gramum ambyhtsecg, nales godes engel.
Ac ic cann ealle swa geare engla gebyrdo,
heah heofona gehlidu; wæs seo hwil þæs lang
585 þæt ic geornlice gode þegnode
þurh holdne hyge, herran minum,
drihtne selfum; ne eom ic deofle gelic."
Lædde hie swa mid ligenum and mid listum speon
idese on þæt unriht, oðþæt hire on innan ongan
590 weallan wyrmes geþeaht, (hæfde hire wacran hige
metod gemearcod), þæt heo hire mod ongan
lætan æfter þam larum; forþon heo æt þam laðan onfeng
ofer drihtnes word deaðes beames
weorcsumne wæstm. Ne wearð wyrse dæd
595 monnum gemearcod! Þæt is micel wundor
þæt hit ece god æfre wolde
þeoden þolian, þæt wurde þegn swa monig
forlædd be þam lygenum þe for þam larum com.
Heo þa þæs ofætes æt, alwaldan bræc
600 word and willan. Þa meahte heo wide geseon
þurh þæs laðan læn þe hie mid ligenum beswac,
dearnenga bedrog, þe hire for his dædum com,
þæt hire þuhte hwitre heofon and eorðe,

603 þuhte] þuht e *with a letter erased between* t *and* e

and eall þeos woruld wlitigre,   and geweorc godes
605 micel and mihtig,   þeah heo hit þurh monnes geþeaht
ne sceawode;   ac se sceaða georne
swicode ymb þa sawle   þe hire ær þa siene onlah,
þæt heo swa wide   wlitan meahte
ofer heofonrice.   Þa se forhatena spræc
610 þurh feondscipe   (nalles he hie freme lærde):
"Þu meaht nu þe self geseon,   swa ic hit þe secgan ne
                                                   þearf,
Eue seo gode,   þæt þe is ungelic
wlite and wæstmas,   siððan þu minum wordum getruw-
                                                   odest,
læstes mine lare.   Nu scineð þe leoht fore
615 glædlic ongean   þæt ic from gode brohte
hwit of heofonum;   nu þu his hrinan meaht.
Sæge Adame   hwilce þu gesihðe hæfst
þurh minne cime cræfta.   Gif giet þurh cuscne siodo
læst mina lara,   þonne gife ic him þæs leohtes genog
620 þæs ic þe swa godes   gegired hæbbe.
Ne wite ic him þa womcwidas,   þeah he his wyrðe ne sie
to alætanne;   þæs fela he me laðes spræc."
   Swa hire eaforan sculon   æfter lybban:
þonne hie lað gedoð,   hie sculon lufe wyrcean,
625 betan heora hearran hearmcwyde   and habban his hyldo
                                                   forð.

   Þa gieng to Adame   idesa scenost,
wifa wlitegost   þe on woruld come,
forþon heo wæs handgeweorc   heofoncyninges,
þeah heo þa dearnenga   fordon wurde,
630 forlæd mid ligenum,   þæt hie lað gode
þurh þæs wraðan geþanc   weorðan sceolden,
þurh þæs deofles searo   dom forlætan,
hierran hyldo,   hefonrices þolian
monige hwile.   Bið þam men full wa
635 þe hine ne warnað   þonne he his geweald hafað!
   Sum heo hire on handum bær,   sum hire æt heortan læg,

610 feondscipe] feonscipe *with* d *above the line after* n   625 and] ond
written out   626 gieng] gien   631 sceolden] *The second* e *altered to* o

æppel unsælga, þone hire ær forbead
drihtna drihten, deaðbeames ofet,
and þæt word acwæð wuldres aldor,
640 þæt þæt micle morð menn ne þorfton
þegnas þolian, ac he þeoda gehwam
hefonrice forgeaf, halig drihten,
widbradne welan, gif hie þone wæstm an
lætan wolden þe þæt laðe treow
645 on his bogum bær, bitre gefylled;
þæt wæs deaðes beam þe him drihten forbead.
Forlec hie þa mid ligenum se wæs lað gode,
on hete heofoncyninges, and hyge Euan,
wifes wac geþoht, þæt heo ongan his wordum truwian,
650 læstan his lare, and geleafan nom
þæt he þa bysene from gode brungen hæfde
þe he hire swa wærlice wordum sægde,
iewde hire tacen and treowa gehet,
his holdne hyge. Þa heo to hire hearran spræc:
655 "Adam, frea min, þis ofet is swa swete,
bliðe on breostum, and þes boda sciene,
godes engel god, ic on his gearwan geseo
þæt he is ærendsecg uncres hearran,
hefoncyninges. His hyldo is unc betere
660 to gewinnanne þonne his wiðermedo.
Gif þu him heodæg wuht hearmes gespræce,
he forgifð hit þeah, gif wit him geongordom
læstan willað. Hwæt scal þe swa laðlic strið
wið þines hearran bodan? Unc is his hyldo þearf;
665 he mæg unc ærendian to þam alwaldan,
heofoncyninge. Ic mæg heonon geseon
hwær he sylf siteð, (þæt is suð and east),
welan bewunden, se ðas woruld gesceop;
geseo ic him his englas ymbe hweorfan
670 mid feðerhaman, ealra folca mæst,
wereda wynsumast. Hwa meahte me swelc gewit gifan,
gif hit gegnunga god ne onsende,

---

644 laðe] lað   656 bliðe] blið   661 gespræce] gespręce   667 hwær]
hær *with* w *added above the line after* h

　　　heofones waldend?　Gehyran mæg ic rume
　　　and swa wide geseon　on woruld ealle
675　ofer þas sidan gesceaft, ic mæg swegles gamen
　　　gehyran on heofnum.　Wearð me on hige leohte
　　　utan and innan,　siðþan ic þæs ofætes onbat.
　　　Nu hæbbe ic his her on handa,　herra se goda;
　　　gife ic hit þe georne.　Ic gelyfe þæt hit from gode come,
680　broht from his bysene,　þæs me þes boda sægde
　　　wærum wordum.　Hit nis wuhte gelic
　　　elles on eorðan,　buton swa þes ar sægeð,
　　　þæt hit gegnunga　from gode come."
　　　　Hio spræc him þicce to　and speon hine ealne dæg
685　on þa dimman dæd　þæt hie drihtnes heora
　　　willan bræcon.　Stod se wraða boda,
　　　legde him lustas on　and mid listum speon,
　　　fylgde him frecne;　wæs se feond full neah
　　　þe on þa frecnan fyrd　gefaren hæfde
690　ofer langne weg;　leode hogode
　　　on þæt micle morð　men forweorpan,
　　　forlæran and forlædan,　þæt hie læn godes,
　　　ælmihtiges gife　an forleten,
　　　heofenrices geweald.　Hwæt, se hellsceaða
695　gearwe wiste　þæt hie godes yrre
　　　habban sceoldon　and hellgeþwing,
　　　þone nearwan nið　niede onfon,
　　　siððan hie gebod godes　forbrocen hæfdon,
　　　þa he forlærde　mid ligenwordum
700　to þam unræde　idese sciene,
　　　wifa wlitegost,　þæt heo on his willan spræc.
　　　wæs him on helpe　handweorc godes
　　　to forlæranne.
　　　　Heo spræc ða to Adame　idesa sceonost
705　ful þiclice,　oð þam þegne ongan
　　　his hige hweorfan,　þæt he þam gehate getruwode
　　　þe him þæt wif　wordum sægde.
　　　　Heo　dyde　hit　þeah　þurh　holdne　hyge,　nyste　þæt　þær
　　　　　　　　　　　　　　　　　　　　　　　　　hearma　swa　fela,

696 hellgeþwing] hell geþwin *with a letter following erased*　　702 him] hire

fyrenearfeða, fylgean sceolde
710 monna cynne, þæs heo on mod genam
þæt heo þæs laðan bodan   larum hyrde,
ac wende þæt heo hyldo   heofoncyninges
worhte mid þam wordum   þe heo þam were swelce
tacen oðiewde   and treowe gehet,
715 oðþæt Adame   innan breostum
his hyge hwyrfde   and his heorte ongann
wendan to hire willan.   He æt þam wife onfeng
helle and hinnsið,   þeah hit nære haten swa,
ac hit ofetes noman   agan sceolde;
720 hit wæs þeah deaðes swefn   and deofles gespon,
hell and hinnsið   and hæleða forlor,
menniscra morð,   þæt hie to mete dædon,
ofet unfæle.   Swa hit him on innan com,
hran æt heortan,   hloh þa and plegode
725 boda bitre gehugod,   sægde begra þanc
hearran sinum: "Nu hæbbe ic þine hyldo me
witode geworhte,   and þinne willan gelæst
to ful monegum dæge.   Men synt forlædde,
Adam and Eue.   Him is unhyldo
730 waldendes witod,   nu hie wordcwyde his,
lare forleton.   Forþon hie leng ne magon
healdan heofonrice,   ac hie to helle sculon
on þone sweartan sið.   Swa þu his sorge ne þearft
beran on þinum breostum,   þær þu gebunden ligst,
735 murnan on mode,   þæt her men bun
þone hean heofon,   þeah wit hearmas nu,
þreaweorc þoliað,   and þystre land,
and þurh þin micle mod   monig forleton
on heofonrice   heahgetimbro,
740 godlice geardas.   Unc wearð god yrre
forþon wit him noldon   on heofonrice
hnigan mid heafdum   halgum drihtne
þurh geongordom;   ac unc gegenge ne wæs
þæt wit him on þegnscipe   þeowian wolden.
745 Forþon unc waldend wearð   wrað on mode,
on hyge hearde,   and us on helle bedraf,

GENESIS

on þæt fyr fylde   folca mæste,
and mid handum his   eft on heofonrice
rihte rodorstolas   and þæt rice forgeaf
750 monna cynne.   Mæg þin mod wesan
bliðe on breostum,   forþon her synt bu tu gedon:
ge þæt hæleða bearn   heofonrice sculon
leode forlætan   and on þæt lig to þe
hate hweorfan,   eac is hearm gode,
755 modsorg gemacod.   Swa hwæt swa wit her morðres þoliað,
hit is nu Adame   eall forgolden
mid hearran hete   and mid hæleða forlore,
monnum mid morðes cwealme.   Forþon is min mod gehæled,
hyge ymb heortan gerume,   ealle synt uncre hearmas gewrecene
760 laðes þæt wit lange þoledon.   Nu wille ic eft þam lige near,
Satan ic þær secan wille;   he is on þære sweartan helle
hæft mid hringa gesponne."   Hwearf him eft niðer
boda bitresta;   sceolde he þa bradan ligas
secan helle gehliðo,   þær his hearra læg
765 simon gesæled.   Sorgedon ba twa,
Adam and Eue,   and him oft betuh
gnornword gengdon;   godes him ondredon,
heora herran hete,   heofoncyninges nið
swiðe onsæton;   selfe forstodon
770 his word onwended.   Þæt wif gnornode,
hof hreowigmod,   (hæfde hyldo godes,
lare forlæten),   þa heo þæt leoht geseah
ellor scriðan   þæt hire þurh untreowa
tacen iewde   se him þone teonan geræd,
775 þæt hie helle nið   habban sceoldon,
hynða unrim;   forþam him higesorga
burnon on breostum.   Hwilum to gebede feollon
sinhiwan somed,   and sigedrihten
godne gretton   and god nemdon,
780 heofones waldend,   and hine bædon

752 heofonrice] heofon rices

þæt hie his hearmsceare   habban mosten,
georne fulgangan,   þa hie godes hæfdon
bodscipe abrocen.   Bare hie gesawon
heora lichaman;   næfdon on þam lande þa giet
785 sælða gesetena,   ne hie sorge wiht
weorces wiston,   ac hie wel meahton
libban on þam lande,   gif hie wolden lare godes
forweard fremman.   Þa hie fela spræcon
sorhworda somed,   sinhiwan twa.
790   Adam gemælde   and to Euan spræc:
"Hwæt, þu Eue, hæfst   yfele gemearcod
uncer sylfra sið.   Gesyhst þu nu þa sweartan helle
grædige and gifre.   Nu þu hie grimman meaht
heonane gehyran.   Nis heofonrice
795 gelic þam lige,   ac þis is landa betst,
þæt wit þurh uncres hearran þanc   habban moston,
þær þu þam ne hierde   þe unc þisne hearm geræd,
þæt wit waldendes   word forbræcon,
heofoncyninges.   Nu wit hreowige magon
800 sorgian for þis siðe.   Forþon he unc self bebead
þæt wit unc wite   warian sceolden,
hearma mæstne.   Nu slit me hunger and þurst
bitre on breostum,   þæs wit begra ær
wæron orsorge   on ealle tid.
805 Hu sculon wit nu libban   oððe on þys lande wesan,
gif her wind cymð,   westan oððe eastan,
suðan oððe norðan?   Gesweorc up færeð,
cymeð hægles scur   hefone getenge,
færeð forst on gemang,   se byð fyrnum ceald.
810 Hwilum of heofnum   hate scineð,
blicð þeos beorhte sunne,   and wit her baru standað,
unwered wædo.   Nys unc wuht beforan
to scursceade,   ne sceattes wiht
to mete gemearcod,   ac unc is mihtig god,
815 waldend wraðmod.   To hwon sculon wit weorðan nu?
Nu me mæg hreowan   þæt ic bæd heofnes god,
waldend þone godan,   þæt he þe her worhte to me

781 his] *Written in above the line*

of liðum minum,   nu þu me forlæred hæfst
on mines herran hete.   Swa me nu hreowan mæg
820 æfre to aldre   þæt ic þe minum eagum geseah."
        Ða spræc Eue eft,   idesa scienost,
wifa wlitegost;   hie wæs geweorc godes,
þeah heo þa on deofles cræft   bedroren wurde:
"Þu meaht hit me witan,   wine min Adam,
825 wordum þinum;   hit þe þeah wyrs ne mæg
on þinum hyge hreowan   þonne hit me æt heortan deð."
        Hire þa Adam   andswarode:
"Gif ic waldendes   willan cuðe,
hwæt ic his to hearmsceare   habban sceolde,
830 ne gesawe þu no sniomor,   þeah me on sæ wadan
hete heofones god   heonone nu þa,
on flod faran,   nære he firnum þæs deop,
merestream þæs micel,   þæt his o min mod getweode,
ac ic to þam grunde genge,   gif ic godes meahte
835 willan gewyrcean.   Nis me on worulde niod
æniges þegnscipes,   nu ic mines þeodnes hafa
hyldo forworhte,   þæt ic hie habban ne mæg.
Ac wit þus baru ne magon   bu tu ætsomne
wesan to wuhte.   Uton gan on þysne weald innan,
840 on þisses holtes hleo."   Hwurfon hie ba twa,
togengdon gnorngende   on þone grenan weald,
sæton onsundran,   bidan selfes gesceapu
heofoncyninges,   þa hie þa habban ne moston
þe him ær forgeaf   ælmihtig god.
845 Þa hie heora lichoman   leafum beþeahton,
weredon mid ðy wealde,   wæda ne hæfdon;
ac hie on gebed feollon   bu tu ætsomne
morgena gehwilce,   bædon mihtigne
þæt hie ne forgeate   god ælmihtig,
850 and him gewisade   waldend se goda,
hu hie on þam leohte forð   libban sceolden.
        Þa com feran   frea ælmihtig
ofer midne dæg,   mære þeoden,
on neorxnawang   neode sine;

826 þinum] þinu   828 ic] *Added above the line after* gif

855 wolde neosian   nergend usser,
    bilwit fæder,   hwæt his bearn dyde;
    wiste forworhte   þam he ær wlite sealde.
    Gewitan him þa gangan   geomermode
    under beamsceade   blæde bereafod,
860 hyddon hie on heolstre,   þa hie halig word
    drihtnes gehyrdon,   and ondredon him.
    Þa sona ongann   swegles aldor
    weard ahsian   woruldgesceafta,
    het him recene to   rice þeoden
865 his sunu gangan.   Him þa sylfa oncwæð,
    hean hleoðrade   hrægles þearfa:
    "Ic wreo me her   wæda leasne,
    liffrea min,   leafum þecce.
    Scyldfull mine   sceaðen is me sare,
870 frecne on ferhðe;   ne dear nu forð gan
    for ðe andweardne.   Ic eom eall eall nacod."
        Him ða ædre god   andswarede:
    "Saga me þæt, sunu min,   for hwon secest ðu
    sceade sceomiende?   Þu sceonde æt me
875 furðum ne anfenge,   ac gefean eallum.
    For hwon wast þu wean   and wrihst sceome,
    gesyhst sorge,   and þin sylf þecest
    lic mid leafum,   sagast lifceare
    hean hygegeomor,   þæt þe sie hrægles þearf,
880 nymþe ðu æppel   ænne byrgde
    of ðam wudubeame   þe ic þe wordum forbead?"
        Him þa Adam eft   andswarode:
    "Me ða blæda on hand   bryd gesealde,
    freolucu fæmne,   freadrihten min,
885 ðe ic þe on teonan geþah.   Nu ic þæs tacen wege
    sweotol on me selfum.   Wat ic sorga ðy ma."
        Ða ðæs Euan frægn   ælmihtig god:
    "Hwæt druge þu, dohtor,   dugeþa genohra,
    niwra gesceafta   neorxnawanges,

857 þam] þa   875 ne] *Not in MS.*   876 þu] *The* þ *of* þu *perhaps crowded*
in by a corrector   880 byrgde] st *added above the line*   883 ða] ðe *with*
e *canceled and* a *written above*   885 nu ic] ic *added above the line after* nu

890 growendra gifa,   þa þu gitsiende
    on beam gripe,   blæda name
    on treowes telgum,   and me on teonan
    æte þa unfreme,   Adame sealdest
    wæstme þa inc wæron   wordum minum
895 fæste forbodene?"   Him þa freolecu mæg,
    ides æwiscmod   andswarode:
    "Me nædre beswac   and me neodlice
    to forsceape scyhte   and to scyldfrece,
    fah wyrm þurh fægir word,   oðþæt ic fracoðlice
900 feondræs gefremede,   fæhðe geworhte,
    and þa reafode,   swa hit riht ne wæs,
    beam on bearwe   and þa blæda æt."
        Þa nædran sceop   nergend usser,
    frea ælmihtig   fagum wyrme
905 wide siðas   and þa worde cwæð:
    "Þu scealt wideferhð   werig þinum
    breostum bearm tredan   bradre eorðan,
    faran feðeleas,   þenden þe feorh wunað,
    gast on innan.   Þu scealt greot etan
910 þine lifdagas.   Swa þu laðlice
    wrohte onstealdest,   þe þæt wif feoð,
    hatað under heofnum   and þin heafod tredeð
    fah mid fotum sinum.   Þu scealt fiersna sætan
    tohtan niwre;   tuddor bið gemæne
915 incrum orlegnið   a þenden standeð
    woruld under wolcnum.   Nu þu wast and canst,
    lað leodsceaða,   hu þu lifian scealt."
        Ða to Euan god   yrringa spræc:
    "Wend þe from wynne!   Þu scealt wæpnedmen
920 wesan on gewealde,   mid weres egsan
    hearde genearwad,   hean þrowian
    þinra dæda gedwild,   deaðes bidan,
    and þurh wop and heaf   on woruld cennan
    þurh sar micel   sunu and dohtor."
925   Abead eac Adame   ece drihten,

906 werig] werg   907 bradre] brade   908 feorh] feoh *with* r *added above*
the line after o   917 hu] nu

lifes leohtfruma,   laðæ ærende:
"Þu scealt oðerne   eðel secean,
wynleasran wic,   and on wræc hweorfan
nacod niedwædla,   neorxnawanges
930 dugeðum bedæled;   þe is gedal witod
lices and sawle.   Hwæt, þu laðlice
wrohte onstealdest;   forþon þu winnan scealt
and on eorðan þe   þine andlifne
selfa geræcan,   wegan swatig hleor,
935 þinne hlaf etan,   þenden þu her leofast,
oðþæt þe to heortan   hearde gripeð
adl unliðe   þe þu on æple ær
selfa forswulge;   forþon þu sweltan scealt."
        Hwæt, we nu gehyrað   hwær us hearmstafas
940 wraðe onwocan   and woruldyrmðo.
Hie þa wuldres weard   wædum gyrede,
scyppend usser;   het heora sceome þeccan
frea frumhrægle;   het hie from hweorfan
neorxnawange   on nearore lif.
945 Him on laste beleac   liðsa and wynna
hihtfulne ham   halig engel
be frean hæse   fyrene sweorde;
ne mæg þær inwitfull   ænig geferan
womscyldig mon,   ac se weard hafað
950 miht and strengðo,   se þæt mære lif
dugeðum deore   drihtne healdeð.
No hwæðre ælmihtig   ealra wolde
Adame and Euan   arna ofteon,
fæder æt frymðe,   þeah þe hie him from swice,
955 ac he him to frofre let   hwæðere forð wesan
hyrstedne hrof   halgum tunglum
and him grundwelan   ginne sealde;
het þam sinhiwum   sæs and eorðan
tuddorteondra   teohha gehwilcre
960 to woruldnytte   wæstmas fedan.
        Gesæton þa æfter synne   sorgfulre land,
eard and eðyl   unspedigran

954 hie] he   959 gehwilcre] gehilcre

fremena gehwilcre   þonne se frumstol wæs
þe hie æfter dæde of   adrifen wurdon.
965   Ongunnon hie þa   be godes hæse
bearn astrienan,   swa him metod bebead.
Adames and Euan   aforan wæron
freolicu twa   frumbearn cenned,
Cain and Abel.   Us cyðað bec,
970   hu þa dædfruman   dugeþa stryndon,
welan and wiste,   willgebroðor.
Oðer his to eorðan   elnes tilode,
se wæs ærboren;   oðer æhte heold
fæder on fultum,   oðþæt forð gewat
975   dægrimes worn.   Hie þa drihtne lac
begen brohton.   Brego engla beseah
on Abeles gield   eagum sinum,
cyning eallwihta,   Caines ne wolde
tiber sceawian.   Þæt wæs torn were
980   hefig æt heortan.   Hygewælm asteah
beorne on breostum,   blatende nið,
yrre for æfstum.   He þa unræden
folmum gefremede,   freomæg ofsloh,
broðor sinne,   and his blod ageat,
985   Cain Abeles.   Cwealmdreore swealh
þæs middangeard,   monnes swate.
    Æfter wælswenge   wea wæs aræred,
tregena tuddor.   Of ðam twige siððan
ludon laðwende   leng swa swiðor
990   reðe wæstme.   Ræhton wide
geond werþeoda   wrohtes telgan,
hrinon hearmtanas   hearde and sare
drihta bearnum,   (doð gieta swa),
of þam brad blado   bealwa gehwilces
995   sprytan ongunnon.   We þæt spell magon,
wælgrimme wyrd,   wope cwiðan,
nales holunge;   ac us hearde sceod
freolecu fæmne   þurh forman gylt

---

980 Hygewælm asteah] hyge wælmos teah   987 aræred] *The second* r
written over an erased letter

þe wið metod æfre   men gefremeden,
1000 eorðbuende,   siððan Adam wearð
of godes muðe   gaste eacen.
Ða worde frægn   wuldres aldor
Cain, hwær Abel   eorðan wære.
Him ða se cystleasa   cwealmes wyrhta
1005 ædre æfter þon   andswarode:
"Ne can ic Abeles   or ne fore,
hleomæges sið,   ne ic hyrde wæs
broðer mines."   Him þa brego engla,
godspedig gast   gean þingade:
1010   "Hwæt, befealdest þu   folmum þinum
wraðum on wælbedd   wærfæstne rinc,
broðor þinne,   and his blod to me
cleopað and cigeð.   þu þæs cwealmes scealt
wite winnan   and on wræc hweorfan,
1015 awyrged to widan aldre.   Ne seleð þe wæstmas eorðe
wlitige to woruldnytte,   ac heo wældreore swealh
halge of handum þinum;   forþon heo þe hroðra oftihð,
glæmes grene folde.   þu scealt geomor hweorfan,
arleas of earde þinum,   swa þu Abele wurde
1020 to feorhbanan;   forþon þu flema scealt
widlast wrecan,   winemagum lað."
Him þa ædre Cain   andswarode:
"Ne þearf ic ænigre   are wenan
on woruldrice,   ac ic forworht hæbbe,
1025 heofona heahcyning,   hyldo þine,
lufan and freode;   forþon ic lastas sceal
wean on wenum   wide lecgan,
hwonne me gemitte   manscyldigne,
se me feor oððe neah   fæhðe gemonige,
1030 broðorcwealmes.   Ic his blod ageat,
dreor on eorðan.   þu to dæge þissum
ademest me fram duguðe   and adrifest from
earde minum.   Me to aldorbanan
weorðeð wraðra sum.   Ic awyrged sceal,
1035 þeoden, of gesyhðe   þinre hweorfan."

1011 wærfæstne] wær fæsne   1022 ædre] *Not in MS.*

    Him þa selfa oncwæð   sigora drihten:
"Ne þearft ðu þe ondrædan   deaðes brogan,
feorhcwealm nu giet,   þeah þu from scyle
freomagum feor   fah gewitan.
1040 Gif þe monna hwelc   mundum sinum
aldre beneoteð,   hine on cymeð
æfter þære synne   seofonfeald wracu,
wite æfter weorce."   Hine waldend on,
tirfæst metod,   tacen sette,
1045 freoðobeacen frea,   þy læs hine feonda hwilc
mid guðþræce   gretan dorste
feorran oððe nean.   Heht þa from hweorfan
meder and magum   manscyldigne,
cnosle sinum.   Him þa Cain gewat
1050 gongan geomormod   gode of gesyhðe,
wineleas wrecca,   and him þa wic geceas
eastlandum on,   eðelstowe
fædergeardum feor,   þær him freolecu mæg,
ides æfter æðelum   eaforan fedde.
1055 Se æresta wæs   Enos haten,
frumbearn Caines.   Siððan fæsten ongon
mid þam cneomagum   ceastre timbran;
þæt wæs under wolcnum   weallfæstenna
ærest ealra   þara þe æðelingas,
1060 sweordberende,   settan heton.
Þanon his eaforan   ærest wocan,
bearn from bryde,   on þam burhstede.
Se yldesta wæs   Iared haten,
sunu Enoses.   Siððan wocan,
1065 þa þæs cynnes   cneowrim icton,
mægburg Caines.   Malalehel wæs
æfter Iarede   yrfes hyrde
fæder on laste,   oðþæt he forð gewat.
    Siððan Mathusal   magum dælde,
1070 bearn æfter bearne   broðrum sinum
æðelinga gestreon,   oðþæt aldorgedal

1040 þe] *Not in MS.*   1056 fæsten] *Not in MS.*   1069 Mathusal]
matusal *with* h *above the line after* t

frod fyrndagum   fremman sceolde,
lif oflætan.   Lameh onfeng
æfter fæder dæge   fletgestealdum,
1075 botlgestreonum.   Him bryda twa,
idesa on eðle   eaforan feddon,
Ada and Sella;   þara anum wæs
Iabal noma,   se þurh gleawne geþanc
herbuendra   hearpan ærest
1080 handum sinum   hlyn awehte,
swinsigende sweg,   sunu Lamehes.
    Swylce on ðære mægðe   maga wæs haten
on þa ilcan tid   Tubal Cain,
se þurh snytro sped   smiðcræftega wæs,
1085 and þurh modes gemynd   monna ærest,
sunu Lamehes,   sulhgeweorces
fruma wæs ofer foldan,   siððan folca bearn
æres cuðon   and isernes,
burhsittende,   brucan wide.
1090   Þa his wifum twæm   wordum sægde
Lameh seolfa,   leofum gebeddum,
Adan and Sellan   unarlic spel:
    "Ic on morðor ofsloh   minra sumne
hyldemaga;   honda gewemde
1095 on Caines   cwealme mine,
fylde mid folmum   fæder Enoses,
ordbanan Abeles,   eorðan sealde
wældreor weres.   Wat ic gearwe
þæt þam lichryre   on last cymeð
1100 soðcyninges   seofonfeald wracu,
micel æfter mane.   Min sceal swiðor
mid grimme gryre   golden wurðan
fyll and feorhcwealm,   þonne ic forð scio."
    Þa wearð Adame   on Abeles gyld
1105 eafora on eðle   oþer feded,
soðfæst sunu,   þam wæs Seth noma.
Se wæs eadig   and his yldrum ðah
freolic to frofre,   fæder and meder,

1088 æres] ærest   1093 sumne] sune   1098 ic] *Not in MS.*

Adames and Euan,   wæs Abeles gield
1110 on woruldrice.   þa word acwæð
ord moncynnes: "Me ece sunu
sealde selfa   sigora waldend,
lifes aldor   on leofes stæl,
þæs þe Cain ofsloh,   and me cearsorge
1115 mid þys magotimbre   of mode asceaf
þeoden usser.   Him þæs þanc sie!"
Adam hæfde,   þa he eft ongan
him to eðelstæfe   oðres strienan
bearnes be bryde,   beorn ellenrof,
1120 XXX and C   þisses lifes,
wintra on worulde.   Us gewritu secgað
þæt her eahtahund   iecte siððan
mægðum and mæcgum   mægburg sine
Adam on eorðan;   ealra hæfde
1125 nigenhund wintra
and XXX eac,   þa he þas woruld
þurh gastgedal   ofgyfan sceolde.
Him on laste Seth   leod weardode,
eafora æfter yldrum;   eþelstol heold
1130 and wif begeat.   Wintra hæfde
fif and hundteontig   þa he furðum ongan
his mægburge   men geicean
sunum and dohtrum.   Sethes eafora
se yldesta wæs   Enos haten;
1135 se nemde god   niðþa bearna
ærest ealra,   siððan Adam stop
on grene græs   gaste geweorðad.
Seth wæs gesælig;   siððan strynde
seofon winter her   suna and dohtra
1140 and eahtahund.   Ealra hæfde
XII and nigonhund,   þa seo tid gewearð
þæt he friðgedal   fremman sceolde.
Him æfter heold,   þa he of worulde gewat,

1111–1112 sunu sealde] sealde sunu   1118 eðelstæfe] edulf stæfe   1120
and] *The runic symbol for* w *instead of the usual abbreviation for* and
1128 leod] leof   1131 he] heo   1133 Sethes] sedes   1140 and] ond

Enos yrfe,   siððan eorðe swealh
1145 sædberendes   Sethes lice.
He wæs leof gode   and lifde her
wintra hundnigontig   ær he be wife her
þurh gebedscipe   bearn astrynde;
him þa cenned wearð   Cainan ærest
1150 eafora on eðle.   Siððan eahtahund
and fiftyno   on friðo drihtnes
gleawferhð hæleð   geogoðe strynde,
suna and dohtra;   swealt, þa he hæfde,
frod fyrnwita,   V and nigonhund.
1155   Þære cneorisse wæs   Cainan siððan
æfter Enose   aldordema,
weard and wisa.   Wintra hæfde
efne hundseofontig   ær him sunu woce.
þa wearð on eðle   eafora feded,
1160 mago Cainanes,   Malalehel wæs haten.
Siððan eahtahund   æðelinga rim
and feowertig eac   feorum geicte
Enoses sunu.   Ealra nigonhund
wintra hæfde   þa he woruld ofgeaf
1165 and tyne eac,   þa his tiddæge
under rodera rum   rim wæs gefylled.
Him on laste heold   land and yrfe
Malalehel siððan   missera worn.
Se frumgara   fif and sixtig
1170 wintra hæfde   þa he be wife ongann
bearna strynan.   Him bryd sunu
meowle to monnum brohte.   Se maga wæs
on his mægðe,   mine gefræge,
guma on geogoðe,   Iared haten.
1175 Lifde siððan   and lissa breac
Malalehel lange,   mondreama her,
woruldgestreona.   Wintra hæfde
fif and hundnigontig,   þa he forð gewat,

1148 þurh] þur   1154 -wita] a *altered from* e   1155 Cainan] cain *with two letters following erased*   1160 Cainanes] caines   1162 feowertig] feowertigum

and eahtahund;   eaforan læfde
1180 land and leodweard.   Longe siððan
Geared gumum   gold brittade.
Se eorl wæs æðele,   æfæst hæleð,
and se frumgar his   freomagum leof.
Fif and hundteontig   on fyore lifde
1185 wintra gebidenra   on woruldrice
and syxtig eac   þa seo sæl gewearð
þæt his wif sunu   on woruld brohte;
se eafora wæs   Enoc haten,
freolic frumbearn.   Fæder her þa gyt
1190 his cynnes forð   cneorim icte,
eaforan eahtahund;   ealra hæfde
V and syxtig,   þa he forð gewat,
and nigonhund eac   nihtgerimes,
wine frod wintres,   þa he þas woruld ofgeaf
1195 and Geared þa   gleawum læfde
land and leodweard,   leofum rince.
Enoch siððan   ealdordom ahof,
freoðosped folces wisa,   nalles feallan let
dom and drihtscipe,
1200 þenden he hyrde wæs   heafodmaga.
Breac blæddaga,   bearna strynde
þreohund wintra.   Him wæs þeoden hold,
rodera waldend.   Se rinc heonon
on lichoman   lisse sohte,
1205 drihtnes duguðe,   nales deaðe swealt
middangeardes,   swa her men doþ,
geonge and ealde,   þonne him god heora
æhta and ætwist   eorðan gestreona
on genimeð   and heora aldor somed,
1210 ac he cwic gewat   mid cyning engla
of þyssum lænan   life feran
on þam gearwum   þe his gast onfeng
ær hine to monnum   modor brohte.
He þam yldestan   eaforan læfde
1215 folc, frumbearne;   V and syxtig

1191 eaforan] eafora   1195 and] ond *written out*   1211 feran] frean

wintra hæfde þa he woruld ofgeaf,
and eac III hund. Þrage siððan
Mathusal heold maga yrfe,
se on lichoman lengest þissa
1220 worulddreama breac. Worn gestrynde
ær his swyltdæge suna and dohtra;
hæfde frod hæle, þa he from sceolde
niþþum hweorfan, nigonhund wintra
and hundseofontig to. Sunu æfter heold,
1225 Lamech leodgeard, lange siððan
woruld bryttade. Wintra hæfde
twa and hundteontig þa seo tid gewearð
þæt se eorl ongan æðele cennan,
sunu and dohtor. Siððan lifde
1230 fif and hundnigontig, frea moniges breac
wintra under wolcnum, werodes aldor,
and V hund eac; heold þæt folc teala,
bearna strynde, him byras wocan,
eaforan and idesa. He þone yldestan
1235 Noe nemde, se niððum ær
land bryttade siððan Lamech gewat.
Hæfde æðelinga aldorwisa
V hund wintra þa he furðum ongan
bearna strynan, þæs þe bec cweðaþ.
1240 Sem wæs haten sunu Noes,
se yldesta, oðer Cham,
þridda Iafeth. Þeoda tymdon
rume under roderum, rim miclade
monna mægðe geond middangeard
1245 sunum and dohtrum. Ða giet wæs Sethes cynn,
leofes leodfruman on lufan swiðe
drihtne dyre and domeadig,
oðþæt bearn godes bryda ongunnon
on Caines cynne secan,
1250 wergum folce, and him þær wif curon
ofer metodes est monna eaforan,

1219 þissa] þisse   1232 and] *Not in MS.*   1234 eaforan] eafora
1235 Noe] noę

scyldfulra mægð   scyne and fægere.

   Þa reordade   rodora waldend
wrað moncynne   and þa worde cwæð:
1255 "Ne syndon me on ferhðe freo   from gewitene
cneorisn Caines,   ac me þæt cynn hafað
sare abolgen.   Nu me Sethes bearn
torn niwiað   and him to nimað
mæged to gemæccum   minra feonda;
1260 þær wifa wlite   onwod grome,
idesa ansien,   and ece feond
folcdriht wera,   þa ær on friðe wæron."
   Siððan hundtwelftig   geteled rime
wintra on worulde   wræce bisgodon
1265 fæge þeoda,   hwonne frea wolde
on wærlogan   wite settan
and on deað slean   dædum scyldige
gigantmæcgas,   gode unleofe,
micle mansceaðan,   metode laðe.
1270   Þa geseah selfa   sigoro waldend
hwæt wæs monna   manes on eorðan
and þæt hie wæron   womma ðriste,
inwitfulle.   He þæt unfægere
wera cneorissum   gewrecan þohte,
1275 forgripan gumcynne   grimme and sare,
heardum mihtum.   Hreaw hine swiðe
þæt he folcmægþa   fruman aweahte,
æðelinga ord,   þa he Adam sceop,
cwæð þæt he wolde   for wera synnum
1280 eall aæðan   þæt on eorðan wæs,
forleosan lica gehwilc   þara þe lifes gast
fæðmum þeahte.   Eall þæt frea wolde
on ðære toweardan   tide acwellan
þe þa nealæhte   niðða bearnum.
1285   Noe wæs god,   nergende leof,
swiðe gesælig,   sunu Lameches,
domfæst and gedefe.   Drihten wiste

1264 bisgodon] bisgodon *with* e *added above the line after* s   1283 toweardan]
The second a *made by altering* e

þæt þæs æðelinges   ellen dohte
breostgehygdum;   forðon him brego sægde,
1290 halig æt hleoðre,   helm allwihta,
hwæt he fah werum   fremman wolde;
geseah unrihte   eorðan fulle,
side sælwongas   synnum gehladene,
widlum gewemde.   Þa waldend spræc,
1295 nergend usser,   and to Noe cwæð:
"Ic wille mid flode   folc acwellan
and cynna gehwilc   cucra wuhta,
þara þe lyft and flod   lædað and fedað,
feoh and fuglas.   Þu scealt frið habban
1300 mid sunum þinum,   ðonne sweart wæter,
wonne wælstreamas   werodum swelgað,
sceaðum scyldfullum.   Ongyn þe scip wyrcan,
merehus micel.   On þam þu monegum scealt
reste geryman,   and rihte setl
1305 ælcum æfter agenum   eorðan tudre.
Gescype scylfan   on scipes bosme.
Þu þæt fær gewyrc   fiftiges wid,
ðrittiges heah   and þreohund lang
elngemeta,   and wið yða gewyrc
1310 gefeg fæste.   Þær sceal fæsl wesan
cwiclifigendra   cynna gehwilces
on þæt wudufæsten   wocor gelæded
eorðan tudres;   earc sceal þy mare."
Noe fremede   swa hine nergend heht,
1315 hyrde þam halgan   heofoncyninge,
ongan ofostlice   þæt hof wyrcan,
micle merecieste.   Magum sægde
þæt wæs þrealic þing   þeodum toweard,
reðe wite.   Hie ne rohton þæs!
1320   Geseah þa ymb wintra worn   wærfæst metod
geofonhusa mæst   gearo hlifigean,
innan and utan   eorðan lime

1306 gescype] y *made by altering* i (*or* u, *Holthausen*)   1307 þæt] þær
1308 and] *Not in MS.*   1314 fremede] freme   1319 ne] *A letter, apparently* g, *erased before* n

gefæstnod wið flode, fær Noes,
þy selestan.   Þæt is syndrig cynn;
1325 symle bið þy heardra   þe hit hreoh wæter,
swearte sæstreamas   swiðor beatað.
   Ða to Noe cwæð   nergend usser:
"Ic þe þæs mine,   monna leofost,
wære gesylle,   þæt þu weg nimest
1330 and feora fæsl   þe þu ferian scealt
geond deop wæter   dægrimes worn
on lides bosme.   Læd, swa ic þe hate,
under earce bord   eaforan þine,
frumgaran þry,   and eower feower wif.
1335 Ond þu seofone genim   on þæt sundreced
tudra gehwilces   geteled rimes,
þara þe to mete   mannum lifige,
and þara oðerra   ælces twa.
Swilce þu of eallum   eorðan wæstmum
1340 wiste under wægbord   werodum gelæde,
þam þe mid sceolon   mereflod nesan.
Fed freolice   feora wocre
oð ic þære lafe   lagosiða eft
reorde under roderum   ryman wille.
1345 Gewit þu nu mid hiwum   on þæt hof gangan,
gasta werode.   Ic þe godne wat,
fæsthydigne;   þu eart freoðo wyrðe,
ara mid eaforum.   Ic on andwlitan
nu ofor seofon niht   sigan læte
1350 wællregn ufan   widre eorðan.
Feowertig daga   fæhðe ic wille
on weras stælan   and mid wægþreate
æhta and agend   eall acwellan
þa beutan beoð   earce bordum
1355 þonne sweart racu   stigan onginneð."
   Him þa Noe gewat,   swa hine nergend het,
under earce bord   eaforan lædan,

1335 Ond] *Written out in MS., a large* O *over the abbreviation?*   1338
oðerra] oðe ra *with an erasure after* e

weras on wægþæl and heora wif somed;
and eall þæt to fæsle frea ælmihtig
1360 habban wolde under hrof gefor
to heora ætgifan, swa him ælmihtig
weroda drihten þurh his word abead.
Him on hoh beleac heofonrices weard
merehuses muð mundum sinum,
1365 sigora waldend, and segnade
earce innan agenum spedum
nergend usser. Noe hæfde,
sunu Lameches, syxhund wintra
þa he mid bearnum under bord gestah,
1370 gleaw mid geogoðe, be godes hæse,
dugeðum dyrum. Drihten sende
regn from roderum and eac rume let
willeburnan on woruld þringan
of ædra gehwære, egorstreamas
1375 swearte swogan. Sæs up stigon
ofer stæðweallas. Strang wæs and reðe
se ðe wætrum weold; wreah and þeahte
manfæhðu bearn middangeardes
wonnan wæge, wera eðelland;
1380 hof hergode, hygeteonan wræc
metod on monnum. Mere swiðe grap
on fæge folc feowertig daga,
nihta oðer swilc. Nið wæs reðe,
wællgrim werum; wuldorcyninges
1385 yða wræcon arleasra feorh
of flæschoman. Flod ealle wreah,
hreoh under heofonum hea beorgas
geond sidne grund and on sund ahof
earce from eorðan and þa æðelo mid,
1390 þa segnade selfa drihten,
scyppend usser, þa he þæt scip beleac.
Siððan wide rad wolcnum under
ofer holmes hrincg hof seleste,
for mid fearme. Fære ne moston

1358 wægþæl] *The second* æ *altered to* e   1388 sidne] d *written over* n *erased*

1395 wægliðendum   wætres brogan
hæste hrinon,   ac hie halig god
ferede and nerede.   Fiftena stod
deop ofer dunum   se drenceflod
monnes elna;   þæt is mæro wyrd!
1400 Þam æt niehstan   wæs nan to gedale,
nymþe heof wæs ahafen   on þa hean lyft,
þa se egorhere   eorðan tuddor
eall acwealde,   buton þæt earce bord
heold heofona frea,   þa hine halig god
1405 ece upp forlet   edmodne flod
streamum stigan,   stiðferhð cyning.
      Þa gemunde god   mereliðende,
sigora waldend   sunu Lameches
and ealle þa wocre   þe he wið wætre beleac,
1410 lifes leohtfruma,   on lides bosme.
Gelædde þa wigend   weroda drihten
worde ofer widland.   Willflod ongan
lytligan eft.   Lago ebbade,
sweart under swegle.   Hæfde soð metod
1415 eaforum egstream   eft gecyrred,
torhtne ryne,   regn gestilled.
      For famig scip   L and C
nihta under roderum,   siððan nægledbord,
fær seleste,   flod up ahof,
1420 oðþæt rimgetæl   reðre þrage
daga forð gewat.   Ða on dunum gesæt
heah mid hlæste   holmærna mæst,
earc Noes,   þe Armenia
hatene syndon.   Þær se halga bad,
1425 sunu Lameches,   soðra gehata
lange þrage,   hwonne him lifes weard
frea ælmihtig   frecenra siða
reste ageafe,   þæra he rume dreah
þa hine on sunde   geond sidne grund

1398 se] sæ *blurred and imperfectly altered to* se   1401 heof] heo   1405
edmodne] ed monne   flod] *Not in MS.*   1416 torhtne] torht   1428
þæra] þære

1430 wonne yða   wide bæron.

    Holm wæs heononweard;   hæleð langode,
wægliðende,   swilce wif heora,
hwonne hie of nearwe   ofer nægledbord
ofer streamstaðe   stæppan mosten
1435 and of enge ut   æhta lædan.
    Þa fandode   forðweard scipes,
hwæðer sincende   sæflod þa gyt
wære under wolcnum.   Let þa ymb worn daga
þæs þe heah hlioðo   horde onfengon
1440 and æðelum eac   eorðan tudres
sunu Lameches   sweartne fleogan
hrefn ofer heahflod   of huse ut.
    Noe tealde   þæt he on neod hine,
gif he on þære lade   land ne funde,
1445 ofer sid wæter   secan wolde
on wægþele.   Eft him seo wen geleah,
ac se feonde gespearn   fleotende hreaw;
salwigfeðera   secan nolde.
    He þa ymb seofon niht   sweartum hrefne
1450 of earce forlet   æfter fleogan
ofer heah wæter   haswe culufran
on fandunga   hwæðer famig sæ
deop þa gyta   dæl ænigne
grenre eorðan   ofgifen hæfde.
1455 Heo wide hire   willan sohte
and rume fleah.   Nohweðere reste fand,
þæt heo for flode   fotum ne meahte
land gespornan   ne on leaf treowes
steppan for streamum,   ac wæron steap hleoðo
1460 bewrigen mid wætrum.   Gewat se wilda fugel
on æfenne   earce secan
ofer wonne wæg,   werig sigan,
hungri to handa   halgum rince.
    Ða wæs culufre eft   of cofan sended
1465 ymb wucan wilde.   Seo wide fleah
oðþæt heo rumgal   restestowe

1447 feonde] feond   1451 heah] hea *with final* h *added above the line*

 fægere funde and þa fotum stop
on beam hyre; gefeah bliðemod
þæs þe heo gesittan swiðe werig
1470 on treowes telgum torhtum moste.
 Heo feðera onsceoc, gewat fleogan eft
mid lacum hire, liðend brohte
elebeames twig an to handa,
grene blædæ. þa ongeat hraðe
1475 flotmonna frea þæt wæs frofor cumen,
earfoðsiða bot. þa gyt se eadega wer
ymb wucan þriddan wilde culufran
ane sende. Seo eft ne com
to lide fleogan, ac heo land begeat,
1480 grene bearwas; nolde gladu æfre
under salwed bord syððan ætywan
on þellfæstenne, þa hire þearf ne wæs.
 þa to Noe spræc nergend usser,
heofonrices weard, halgan reorde:
1485 "þe is eðelstol eft gerymed,
lisse on lande, lagosiða rest
fæger on foldan. Gewit on freðo gangan
ut of earce, and on eorðan bearm
of þam hean hofe hiwan læd þu
1490 and ealle þa wocre þe ic wægþrea on
liðe nerede þenden lago hæfde
þrymme geþeahtne þriddan eðyl."
 He fremede swa and frean hyrde,
stah ofer streamweall, swa him seo stefn bebead,
1495 lustum miclum, and alædde þa
of wægþele wraðra lafe.
 þa Noe ongan nergende lac
rædfæst reðran, and recene genam
on eallum dæl æhtum sinum,
1500 ðam ðe him to dugeðum drihten sealde,
gleaw to þam gielde, and þa gode selfum
torhtmod hæle tiber onsægde,

1469 gesittan] gesette 1491 liðe] hliðe 1492 geþeahtne] geþeahte
þriddan] þridda

cyninge engla.   Huru cuð dyde
nergend usser,   þa he Noe
1505 gebletsade   and his bearn somed,
þæt he þæt gyld on þanc   agifen hæfde
and on geogoðhade   godum dædum
ær geearnod   þæt him ealra wæs
ara este   ælmihtig god,
1510 domfæst dugeþa.   þa gyt drihten cwæð,
wuldris aldor   word to Noe:
    "Tymað nu and tiedrað,   tires brucað,
mid gefean fryðo;   fyllað eorðan,
eall geiceað.   Eow is eðelstol
1515 and holmes hlæst   and heofonfuglas
and wildu deor   on geweald geseald,
eorðe ælgrene   and eacen feoh.
Næfre ge mid blode   beodgereordu
unarlice   eowre þicgeað,
1520 besmiten mid synne   sawldreore.
Ælc hine selfa   ærest begrindeð
gastes dugeðum   þæra þe mid gares orde
oðrum aldor oðþringeð.   Ne ðearf he þy edleane gefeon
modgeþance,   ac ic monnes feorh
1525 to slagan sece   swiðor micle,
and to broðor banan,   þæs þe blodgyte,
wællfyll weres   wæpnum gespedeð,
morð mid mundum.   Monn wæs to godes
anlicnesse   ærest gesceapen.
1530 Ælc hafað magwlite   metodes and engla
þara þe healdan wile   halige þeawas.
Weaxað and wridað,   wilna brucað,
ara on eorðan;   æðelum fyllað
eowre fromcynne   foldan sceatas,
1535 teamum and tudre.   Ic eow treowa þæs
mine selle,   þæt ic on middangeard
næfre egorhere   eft gelæde,
wæter ofer widland.   Ge on wolcnum þæs

1508 þæt] þa   1515a and] *Not in MS.*   heofonfuglas] heofon fugla
1517 feoh] *With* r *written above* h   1522 þæra] þære   1525 sece] seðe

oft and gelome andgiettacen
1540 magon sceawigan, þonne ic scurbogan
minne iewe, þæt ic monnum þas
wære gelæste, þenden woruld standeð.''
  Ða wæs se snotra sunu Lamehes
of fere acumen flode on laste
1545 mid his eaforum þrim, yrfes hyrde
(and heora feower wif;
nemde wæron Percoba, Olla,
Olliua, Olliuani),
wærfæst metode, wætra lafe.
1550 Hæleð hygerofe hatene wæron,
suna Noes Sem and Cham,
Iafeð þridda. From þam gumrincum
folc geludon and gefylled wearð
eall þes middangeard monna bearnum.
1555   Ða Noe ongan niwan stefne
mid hleomagum ham staðelian
and to eorðan him ætes tilian;
won and worhte, wingeard sette,
seow sæda fela, sohte georne
1560 þa him wlitebeorhte wæstmas brohte,
geartorhte gife, grene folde.
  Ða þæt geeode, þæt se eadega wer
on his wicum wearð wine druncen,
swæf symbelwerig, and him selfa sceaf
1565 reaf of lice. Swa gerysne ne wæs,
læg þa limnacod. He lyt ongeat
þæt him on his inne swa earme gelamp,
þa him on hreðre heafodswima
on þæs halgan hofe heortan clypte.
1570 Swiðe on slæpe sefa nearwode
þæt he ne mihte on gemynd drepen
hine handum self mid hrægle wryon
and sceome þeccan, swa gesceapu wæron
werum and wifum, siððan wuldres þegn
1575 ussum fæder and meder fyrene sweorde

1539 and] *Not in MS.*   1549 metode] metod   1567 inne] innne

on laste beleac   lifes eðel.
Þa com ærest   Cam in siðian,
eafora Noes,   þær his aldor læg,
ferhðe forstolen.   Þær he freondlice
1580 on his agenum fæder   are ne wolde
gesceawian,   ne þa sceonde huru
hleomagum helan,   ac he hlihende
broðrum sægde,   hu se beorn hine
reste on recede.   Hie þa raðe stopon,
1585 heora andwlitan   in bewrigenum
under loðum listum,   þæt hie leofum men
geoce gefremede;   gode wæron begen,
Sem and Iafeð.   Ða of slæpe onbrægd
sunu Lamehes,   and þa sona ongeat
1590 þæt him cynegodum   Cham ne wolde,
þa him wæs are þearf,   ænige cyðan
hyldo and treowa.   Þæt þam halgan wæs
sar on mode,   ongan þa his selfes bearn
wordum wyrgean,   cwæð, he wesan sceolde
1595 hean under heofnum,   hleomaga þeow,
Cham on eorþan;   him þa cwyde syððan
and his fromcynne   frecne scodon.
    Þa nyttade   Noe siððan
mid sunum sinum   sidan rices
1600 ðreohund wintra   þisses lifes,
freomen æfter flode,   and fiftig eac, þa he forð gewat.
    Siððan his eaforan   ead bryttedon,
bearna stryndon;   him wæs beorht wela.
Þa wearð Iafeðe   geogoð afeded,
1605 hyhtlic heorðwerod   heafodmaga,
sunu and dohtra.   He wæs selfa til,
heold a rice,   eðeldreamas,
blæd mid bearnum,   oðþæt breosta hord,
gast ellorfus   gangan sceolde
1610 to godes dome.   Geomor siððan
fæder flettgesteald   freondum dælde,

1579 ferhðe] ferðe *with* h *above the line after* r

swæsum and gesibbum,   sunu Iafeðes;
þæs teames wæs   tuddor gefylled
unlytel dæl   eorðan gesceafta.
1615   Swilce Chames suno   cende wurdon,
eaforan on eðle;   þa yldestan
Chus and Chanan   hatene wæron,
ful freolice feorh,   frumbearn Chames.
Chus wæs æðelum   heafodwisa,
1620   wilna brytta   and worulddugeða
broðrum sinum,   botlgestreona,
fæder on laste,   siððan forð gewat
Cham of lice,   þa him cwealm gesceod.
Se magoræswa   mægðe sinre
1625   domas sægde,   oðþæt his dogora wæs
rim aurnen.   Þa se rinc ageaf
eorðcunde ead,   sohte oðer lif,
fæder Nebroðes.   Frumbearn siððan
eafora Chuses   yrfestole weold,
1630   widmære wer,   swa us gewritu secgeað,
þæt he moncynnes   mæste hæfde
on þam mældagum   mægen and strengo.
Se wæs Babylones   bregorices fruma,
ærest æðelinga;   eðelðrym onhof,
1635   rymde and rærde.   Reord wæs þa gieta
eorðbuendum   an gemæne.
Swilce of Cames   cneorisse woc
wermægða fela;   of þam widfolce
cneorim micel   cenned wæron.
1640   Þa wearð Seme   suna and dohtra
on woruldrice   worn afeded,
freora bearna,   ær ðon frod cure
wintrum wælreste   werodes aldor.
On þære mægðe   wæron men tile,
1645   þara an wæs   Eber haten,
eafora Semes;   of þam eorle woc
unrim þeoda,   þa nu æðelingas,

1617 Chanan] cham   1628 Nebroðes] nebreðer   1630 swa] wwa
1637 Swilce] Svilce   1638 widfolce] wid folc   1642 frod] forð

ealle eorðbuend, Ebrei hata.

Gewiton him þa eastan æhta lædan,
1650 feoh and feorme. Folc wæs anmod;
rofe rincas sohton rumre land,
oðþæt hie becomon corðrum miclum,
folc ferende, þær hie fæstlice
æðelinga bearn, eard genamon.
1655 Gesetton þa Sennar sidne and widne
leoda ræswan; leofum mannum
heora geardagum grene wongas,
fægre foldan, him forðwearde
on ðære dægtide duguðe wæron,
1660 wilna gehwilces weaxende sped.
Ða þær mon mænig be his mægwine,
æðeling anmod, oðerne bæd
þæs hie him to mærðe, ær seo mengeo eft
geond foldan bearm tofaran sceolde,
1665 leoda mægðe on landsocne
burh geworhte and to beacne torr
up aræde to rodortunglum.
þæs þe hie gesohton Sennera feld,
swa þa foremeahtige folces ræswan,
1670 þa yldestan oft and gelome
liðsum gewunedon; larum sohton
weras to weorce and to wrohtscipe,
oðþæt for wlence and for wonhygdum
cyðdon cræft heora, ceastre worhton
1675 and to heofnum up hlædræ rærdon,
strengum stepton stænenne weall
ofer monna gemet, mærða georne,
hæleð mid honda. Þa com halig god
wera cneorissa weorc sceawigan,
1680 beorna burhfæsten, and þæt beacen somed,
þe to roderum up ræran ongunnon
Adames eaforan, and þæs unrædes
stiðferhð cyning steore gefremede,

1664 bearm] bearn   1674 ceastre] ea *altered from some other letter, probably* m   1676 stænenne] stænnene

þa he reðemod   reorde gesette
1685 eorðbuendum   ungelice,
þæt hie þære spæce   sped ne ahton.

   þa hie gemitton   mihtum spedge,
teoche æt torre,   getalum myclum,
weorces wisan,   ne þær wermægða
1690 ænig wiste   hwæt oðer cwæð.
Ne meahte hie gewurðan   weall stænenne
up forð timbran,   ac hie earmlice
heapum tohlocon,   hleoðrum gedælde;
wæs oðerre   æghwilc worden
1695 mægburh fremde,   siððan metod tobræd
þurh his mihta sped   monna spræce.
Toforan þa   on feower wegas
æðelinga bearn   ungeþeode
on landsocne.   Him on laste bu
1700 stiðlic stantorr   and seo steape burh
samod samworht   on Sennar stod.

   Weox þa under wolcnum   and wriðade
mægburh Semes,   oðþæt mon awoc
on þære cneorisse,   cynebearna rim,
1705 þancolmod wer,   þeawum hydig.
Wurdon þam æðelinge   eaforan acende,
in Babilone   bearn afeded
freolicu tu,   and þa frumgaran,
hæleð higerofe,   hatene wæron
1710 Abraham and Aaron;   þam eorlum wæs
frea engla bam   freond and aldor.
   Ða wearð Aarone   eafora feded,
leoflic on life,   ðam wæs Loth noma.
   Ða magorincas   metode geþungon,
1715 Abraham and Loth,   unforcuðlice,
swa him from yldrum   æðelu wæron
on woruldrice;   forðon hie wide nu
dugeðum demað   drihtfolca bearn.

1693 tohlocon] tohlodon   1694 oðerre] oðere   1710 wæs] wees *with the first* e *altered to* a   1711 freond] freod   1718 drihtfolca bearn] drihta bearnum

þa þæs mæles wæs   mearc agongen
1720 þæt him Abraham   idese brohte,
wif to hame,   þær he wic ahte,
fæger and freolic.   Seo fæmne wæs
Sarra haten,   þæs þe us secgeað bec.
Hie þa wintra fela   woruld bryttedon,
1725 sinc ætsomne,   sibbe heoldon
geara mengeo.   Nohwæðre gifeðe wearð
Abrahame þa gyt   þæt him yrfeweard
wlitebeorht ides   on woruld brohte,
Sarra Abrahame,   suna and dohtra.
1730 Gewat him þa mid cnosle   ofer Caldea folc
feran mid feorme   fæder Abrahames;
snotor mid gesibbum   secean wolde
Cananea land.   Hine cneowmægas,
metode gecorene   mid siðedon
1735 of þære eðeltyrf,   Abraham and Loth.
Him þa cynegode   on Carran
æðelinga bearn   eard genamon,
weras mid wifum.   On þam wicum his
fæder Abrahames   feorh gesealde,
1740 wærfæst hæle;   wintra hæfde
twa hundteontig,   geteled rime,
and fife eac,   þa he forð gewat
misserum frod   metodsceaft seon.
Ða se halga spræc,   heofonrices weard,
1745 to Abrahame,   ece drihten:
"Gewit þu nu feran   and þine fare lædan,
ceapas to cnosle.   Carran ofgif,
fæder eðelstol.   Far, swa ic þe hate,
monna leofost,   and þu minum wel
1750 larum hyre,   and þæt land gesec
þe ic þe ælgrene   ywan wille,
brade foldan.   Þu gebletsad scealt
on mundbyrde   minre lifigan.
Gif ðe ænig   eorðbuendra
1755 mid wean greteð,   ic hine wergðo on

1722 wæs] *Added above the line*   1747 Carran] carram

mine sette   and modhete,
longsumne niŏ;   lisse selle,
wilna wæstme   þam þe wurŏiaŏ.
þurh þe eorŏbuende   ealle onfoŏ,
1760 folcbearn freoŏo   and freondscipe,
blisse minre   and bletsunge
on woruldrice.   Wriŏende sceal
mægŏe þinre   monrim wesan
swiŏe under swegle   sunum and dohtrum,
1765 oŏþæt fromcyme   folde weorŏeŏ,
þeodlond monig   þine gefylled."
    Him þa Abraham gewat   æhte lædan
of Egipta   eŏelmearce,
gumcystum god,   golde and seolfre
1770 swiŏfeorm and gesælig,   swa him sigora weard,
waldend usser   þurh his word abead,
ceapas from Carran;   sohton Cananea
lond and leodgeard.   þa com leof gode
on þa eŏelturf   idesa lædan,
1775 swæse gebeddan   and his suhtrian
wif on willan.   Wintra hæfde
fif and hundseofontig   ŏa he faran sceolde,
Carran ofgifan   and cneowmagas.
    Him þa feran gewat   fæder ælmihtiges
1780 lare gemyndig   land sceawian
geond þa folcsceare   be frean hæse
Abraham wide,   oŏþæt ellenrof
to Sicem com   siŏe spedig,
cynne Cananeis.   þa hine cyning engla
1785 Abrahame   iewde selfa,
domfæst wereda   and drihten cwæŏ:
    "þis is seo eorŏe   þe ic ælgrene
tudre þinum   torhte wille
wæstmum gewlo   on geweald don,
1790 rume rice."   þa se rinc gode
wibed worhte   and þa waldende

1758 wilna] n *over* l *erased?*   1764 swegle] segle *with* w *added above the*
line after s   1783 Sicem] siem

lifes leohtfruman   lac onsægde
gasta helme.   Him þa gyt gewat
Abraham eastan   eagum wlitan
1795 on landa cyst,   (lisse gemunde
heofonweardes gehat,   þa him þurh halig word
sigora selfcyning   soð gecyðde),
oðþæt drihtweras   duguþum geforan
þær is botlwela   Bethlem haten.
1800 Beorn bliðemod   and his broðor sunu
forð oferforan   folcmæro land
eastan mid æhtum,   æfæste men
weallsteapan hleoðu,   and him þa wic curon
þær him wlitebeorhte   wongas geþuhton.
1805   Abraham þa   oðere siðe
wibed worhte.   He þær wordum god
torhtum cigde,   tiber onsægde
his liffrean,   (him þæs lean ageaf
nalles hneawlice   þurh his hand metend),
1810 on þam gledstyde   gumcystum til.
Ðær ræsbora   þrage siððan
wicum wunode   and wilna breac,
beorn mid bryde,   oðþæt brohþrea
Cananea wearð   cynne getenge,
1815 hunger se hearda,   hamsittendum,
wælgrim werum.   Him þa wishydig
Abraham gewat   on Egypte,
drihtne gecoren,   drohtað secan,
fleah wærfæst wean;   wæs þæt wite to strang.
1820   Abraham maðelode,   geseah Egypta
hornsele hwite   and hea byrig
beorhte blican;   ongan þa his bryd frea,
wishydig wer,   wordum læran:
"Siððan Egypte   eagum moton
1825 on þinne wlite wlitan   wlance monige,
þonne æðelinga   eorlas wenað,
mæg ælfscieno,   þæt þu min sie

1795 landa] lande   1809 hneawlice] hnea lice *with space for one letter between*

   beorht gebedda, þe wile beorna sum
   him geagnian. Ic me onegan mæg
1830 þæt me wraðra sum wæpnes ecge
   for freondmynde feore beneote.
   Saga þu, Sarra, þæt þu sie sweostor min,
   lices mæge, þonne þe leodweras
   fremde fricgen hwæt sie freondlufu
1835 ellðeodigra uncer twega,
   feorren cumenra. Þu him fæste hel
   soðan spræce; swa þu minum scealt
   feore gebeorgan, gif me freoðo drihten
   on woruldrice, waldend usser,
1840 an ælmihtig, swa he ær dyde,
   lengran lifes. Se us þas lade sceop,
   þæt we on Egiptum are sceolde
   fremena friclan and us fremu secan."
   Þa com ellenrof eorl siðian,
1845 Abraham mid æhtum on Egypte,
   þær him folcweras fremde wæron,
   wine uncuðe. Wordum spræcon
   ymb þæs wifes wlite wlonce monige,
   dugeðum dealle; him drihtlicu mæg,
1850 on wlite modgum mænegum ðuhte,
   cyninges þegnum. Hie þæt cuð dydon
   heora folcfrean þæt fægerro lyt
   for æðelinge idesa sunnon,
   ac hie Sarran swiðor micle,
1855 wynsumne wlite wordum heredon,
   oðþæt he lædan heht leoflic wif to
   his selfes sele. Sinces brytta,
   æðelinga helm heht Abrahame
   duguðum stepan. Hwæðere drihten wearð,
1860 frea Faraone fah and yrre
   for wifmyne; þæs wraðe ongeald
   hearde mid hiwum hægstealdra wyn.
   Ongæt hwæðere gumena aldor

1829 onegan] on agen 1836 feorren] n *altered from* m 1852 þæt] *Abbreviation for* and 1853 idesa] idese

hwæt him waldend wræc   witeswingum;
1865 heht him Abraham to   egesum geðreadne
brego Egipto,   and his bryd ageaf,
wif to gewealde;   heht him wine ceosan,
ellor æðelingas,   oðre dugeðe.
Abead þa þeodcyning   þegnum sinum,
1870 ombihtscealcum,   þæt hie hine arlice
ealles onsundne   eft gebrohten
of þære folcsceare,   þæt he on friðe wære.
    Ða Abraham   æhte lædde
of Egypta   eðelmearce;
1875 hie ellenrofe   idese feredon,
bryd and begas,   þæt hie to Bethlem
on cuðe wic   ceapas læddon,
eadge eorðwelan   oðre siðe,
wif on willan   and heora woruldgestreon.
1880 Ongunnon him þa bytlian   and heora burh ræran,
and sele settan,   salo niwian.
Weras on wonge   wibed setton
neah þam þe Abraham   æror rærde
his waldende   þa westan com.
1885 Þær se eadga eft   ecan drihtnes
niwan stefne   noman weorðade;
tilmodig eorl   tiber onsægde
þeodne engla,   þancode swiðe
lifes leohtfruman   lisse and ara.
1890   Wunedon on þam wicum,   hæfdon wilna geniht
Abraham and Loth.   Ead bryttedon,
oðþæt hie on þam lande   ne meahton leng somed
blædes brucan   and heora begra þær
æhte habban,   ac sceoldon arfæste,
1895 þa rincas þy   rumor secan
ellor eðelseld.   Oft wæron teonan
wærfæstra wera   weredum gemæne,
heardum hearmplega.   Þa se halga ongan
ara gemyndig   Abraham sprecan
1900 fægre to Lothe: "Ic eom fædera þin

1879 on] *Abbreviation for* and

sibgebyrdum,   þu min suhterga.
Ne sceolon unc betweonan   teonan weaxan,
wroht wriðian—   ne þæt wille god!
Ac wit synt gemagas;   unc gemæne ne sceal
1905 elles awiht,   nymþe eall tela
lufu langsumu.   Nu þu, Loth, geþenc,
þæt unc modige   ymb mearce sittað,
þeoda þrymfæste   þegnum and gesiððum,
folc Cananea   and Feretia,
1910 rofum rincum.   Ne willað rumor unc
landriht heora;   forðon wit lædan sculon,
teon of þisse stowe,   and unc staðolwangas
rumor secan.   Ic ræd sprece,
bearn Arones,   begra uncer,
1915 soðne secge.   Ic þe selfes dom
life, leofa.   Leorna þe seolfa
and geþancmeta   þine mode
on hwilce healfe   þu wille hwyrft don,
cyrran mid ceape,   nu ic þe cyst abead."
1920   Him þa Loth gewat   land sceawigan
be Iordane,   grene eorðan.
Seo wæs wætrum weaht   and wæstmum þeaht,
lagostreamum leoht,   and gelic godes
neorxnawange,   oðþæt nergend god
1925 for wera synnum   wylme gesealde
Sodoman and Gomorran,   sweartan lige.
Him þa eard geceas   and eðelsetl
sunu Arones   on Sodoma byrig;
æhte sine   ealle lædde,
1930 beagas from Bethlem   and botlgestreon,
welan, wunden gold.   Wunode siððan
be Iordane   geara mænego.
Þær folcstede   fægre wæron,
men arlease,   metode laðe.
1935 Wæron Sodomisc cynn   synnum þriste,
dædum gedwolene;   drugon heora selfra

1912 teon of] teon wit of   1924 neorxna-] neoxna   oðþæt] on þæt
1929 ealle lædde] *Not in MS.*

ecne unræd. Æfre ne wolde
þam leodþeawum   Loth onfon,
ac he þære mægðe   monwisan fleah,
1940 þeah þe he on þam lande   lifian sceolde,
facen and fyrene,   and hine fægre heold,
þeawfæst and geþyldig   on þam þeodscipe,
emne þon gelicost,   lara gemyndig,
þe he ne cuðe   hwæt þa cynn dydon.
1945   Abraham wunode   eðeleardum
Cananea forð. Hine cyning engla,
metod moncynnes   mundbyrde heold,
wilna wæstmum   and worulddugeðum,
lufum and lissum;   forþon his lof secgað
1950 wide under wolcnum   wera cneorisse,
foldwonga bearn. He frean hyrde
estum on eðle,   ðenden he eardes breac,
halig and higefrod;   næfre hleowlora
æt edwihtan   æfre weorðeð
1955 feorhberendra   forht and acol,
mon for metode,   þe him æfter a
þurh gemynda sped   mode and dædum,
worde and gewitte,   wise þance,
oð his ealdorgedal   oleccan wile.
1960   Ða ic aldor gefrægn   Elamitarna
fromne folctogan,   fyrd gebeodan,
Orlahomar;   him Ambrafel
of Sennar   side worulde
for on fultum. Gewiton hie feower þa
1965 þeodcyningas   þrymme micle
secan suð ðanon   Sodoman and Gomorran.
  Ða wæs guðhergum   be Iordane
wera eðelland   wide geondsended,
folde feondum. Sceolde forht monig
1970 blachleor ides   bifiende gan
on fremdes fæðm;   feollon wergend
bryda and beaga,   bennum seoce.

1938 Loth] leoht   1951 foldwonga] full wona   1953 hleowlora] hleor lora
1957 mode] mod

Him þa togeanes   mid guðþræce
fife foran   folccyningas
1975 sweotum suðon,   woldon Sodome burh
wraðum werian;   þa wintra XII
norðmonnum ær   niede sceoldon
gombon gieldan   and gafol sellan,
oðþæt þa leode   leng ne woldon
1980 Elamitarna   aldor swiðan
folcgestreonum,   ac him from swicon.
   Foron þa tosomne   (francan wæron hlude),
wraðe wælherigas.   Sang se wanna fugel
under deoreðsceaftum,   deawigfeðera,
1985 hræs on wenan.   Hæleð onetton
on mægencorðrum,   modum þryðge,
oðþæt folcgetrume   gefaren hæfdon
sid tosomne   suðan and norðan,
helmum þeahte.   Þær wæs heard plega,
1990 wælgara wrixl,   wigcyrm micel,
hlud hildesweg.   Handum brugdon
hæleð of scæðum   hringmæled sweord,
ecgum dihtig.   Þær wæs eaðfynde
eorle orlegceap,   se ðe ær ne wæs
1995 niðes genihtsum.   Norðmen wæron
suðfolcum swice;   wurdon Sodomware
and Gomorre,   goldes bryttan,
æt þæm lindcrodan   leofum bedrorene,
fyrdgesteallum.   Gewiton feorh heora
2000 fram þam folcstyde   fleame nergan,
secgum ofslegene;   him on swaðe feollon
æðelinga bearn,   ecgum ofþegde,
willgesiððas.   Hæfde wigsigor
Elamitarna   ordes wisa,
2005 weold wælstowe.   Gewat seo wæpna laf
fæsten secan.   Fynd gold strudon,
ahyðdan þa mid herge   hordburh wera,
Sodoman and Gomorran,   þa sæl ageald,
mære ceastra.   Mægð siðedon,

1986 þryðge] þrydge   2007 ahyðdan] ahudan

2010 fæmnan and wuduwan, freondum beslægene,
from hleowstole. Hettend læddon
ut mid æhtum Abrahames mæg
of Sodoma byrig. We þæt soð magon
secgan furður, hwelc siððan wearð
2015 æfter þæm gehnæste herewulfa sið,
þara þe læddon Loth and leoda god,
suðmonna sinc, sigore gulpon.
Him þa secg hraðe gewat siðian,
an gara laf, se ða guðe genæs,
2020 Abraham secan. Se þæt orlegweorc
þam Ebriscan eorle gecyðde,
forslegen swiðe Sodoma folc,
leoda duguðe and Lothes sið.
Þa þæt inwitspell Abraham sægde
2025 freondum sinum; bæd him fultumes
wærfæst hæleð willgeðoftan,
Aner and Manre, Escol þriddan,
cwæð þæt him wære weorce on mode,
sorga sarost, þæt his suhtriga
2030 þeownyd þolode; bæd him þræcrofe
þa rincas þæs ræd ahicgan,
þæt his hyldemæg ahreded wurde,
beorn mid bryde. Him þa broðor þry
æt spræce þære spedum miclum
2035 hældon hygesorge heardum wordum,
ellenrofe, and Abrahame
treowa sealdon, þæt hie his torn mid him
gewræcon on wraðum, oððe on wæl feollan.
Þa se halga heht his heorðwerod
2040 wæpna onfon. He þær wigena fand,
æscberendra, XVIII
and CCC eac þeodenholdra,
þara þe he wiste þæt meahte wel æghwylc
on fyrd wegan fealwe linde.
2045 Him þa Abraham gewat and þa eorlas þry

2032 ahreded] ahred   2038 feollan] feallan   2040 onfon] ofon *with* n
added above the line before f   2042 þeodenholdra] þeonden holdra

þe him ær treowe sealdon   mid heora folcgetrume;
wolde his mæg huru,
Loth alynnan   of laðscipe.
Rincas wæron rofe,   randas wægon
2050 forð fromlice   on foldwege.
Hildewulfas   herewicum neh
gefaren hæfdon.   Þa he his frumgaran,
wishydig wer,   wordum sægde,
Þares afera,   him wæs þearf micel
2055 þæt hie on twa healfe
grimme guðgemot   gystum eowdon
heardne handplegan;   cwæð þæt him se halga,
ece drihten,   eaðe mihte
æt þam spereniðe   spede lænan.
2060   Þa ic neðan gefrægn   under nihtscuwan
hæleð to hilde.   Hlyn wearð on wicum
scylda and sceafta,   sceotendra fyll,
guðflana gegrind;   gripon unfægre
under sceat werum   scearpe garas,
2065 and feonda feorh   feollon ðicce,
þær hlihende   huðe feredon
secgas and gesiððas.   Sigor eft ahwearf
of norðmonna   niðgeteone,
æsctir wera.   Abraham sealde
2070 wig to wedde,   nalles wunden gold,
for his suhtrigan,   sloh and fylde
feond on fitte.   Him on fultum grap
heofonrices weard.   Hergas wurdon
feower on fleame,   folccyningas,
2075 leode ræswan.   Him on laste stod
hihtlic heorðwerod,   and hæleð lagon,
on swaðe sæton,   þa þe Sodoma
and Gomorra   golde berofan,
bestrudon stigwitum.   Him þæt stiðe geald
2080 fædera Lothes.   Fleonde wæron

2046 folcgetrume] folce getrume   2049 wæron] waron   rofe] f *altered
from* r   wægon] g *altered from* r?   2055 hie] he   2058 eaðe] eað
2080 wæron] *Not in MS.*

Elamitarna   aldorguðe
dome bedrorene,   oðþæt hie Domasco
unfeor wæron.   Gewat him Abraham ða
on þa wigrode   wiðertrod seon
2085 laðra monna.   Loth wæs ahreded,
eorl mid æhtum,   idesa hwurfon,
wif on willan.   Wide gesawon
freora feorhbanan   fuglas slitan
on ecgwale.   Abraham ferede
2090 suðmonna eft   sinc and bryda,
æðelinga bearn,   oðle nior,
mægeð heora magum.   Næfre mon ealra
lifigendra her   lytle werede
þon wurðlicor   wigsið ateah,
2095 þara þe wið swa miclum   mægne geræsde.
    Þa wæs suð þanon   Sodoma folce
guðspell wegen,   hwelc gromra wearð
feonda fromlad.   Gewat him frea leoda,
eorlum bedroren,   Abraham secan,
2100 freonda feasceaft.   Him ferede mid
Solomia   sinces hyrde;
þæt wæs se mæra   Melchisedec,
leoda bisceop.   Se mid lacum com
fyrdrinca fruman   fægre gretan,
2105 Abraham arlice,   and him on sette
godes bletsunge,   and swa gyddode:
    "Wæs ðu gewurðod   on wera rime
for þæs eagum   þe ðe æsca tir
æt guðe forgeaf!   Þæt is god selfa,
2110 se ðe hettendra   herga þrymmas
on geweald gebræc,   and þe wæpnum læt
rancstræte forð   rume wyrcan,
huðe ahreddan   and hæleð fyllan.
On swaðe sæton;   ne meahton siðwerod
2115 guðe spowan,   ac hie god flymde,
se ðe æt feohtan   mid frumgarum
wið ofermægnes   egsan sceolde

2096 folce] folc   2097 wegen] wegan   2107 Wæs] wær

handum sinum,   and halegu treow,
seo þu wið rodora weard   rihte healdest."

2120   Him þa se beorn   bletsunga lean
þurh hand ageaf,   and þæs hereteames
ealles teoðan sceat   Abraham sealde
godes bisceope.   Þa spræc guðcyning,
Sodoma aldor,   secgum befylled,

2125 to Abrahame   (him wæs ara þearf):
"Forgif me mennen   minra leoda,
þe þu ahreddest   herges cræftum
wera wælclommum!   Hafa þe wunden gold
þæt ær agen wæs   ussum folce,

2130 feoh and frætwa!   Læt me freo lædan
eft on eðel   æðelinga bearn,
on weste wic   wif and cnihtas,
earme wydewan!   Eaforan syndon deade,
folcgesiðas,   nymðe fea ane,

2135 þe me mid sceoldon   mearce healdan."
Him þa Abraham   andswarode
ædre for eorlum,   elne gewurðod,
dome and sigore,   drihtlice spræc:
"Ic þe gehate,   hæleða waldend,

2140 for þam halgan,   þe heofona is
and þisse eorðan   agendfrea,
wordum minum,   nis woruldfeoh,
þe ic me agan wille,
sceat ne scilling,   þæs ic on sceotendum,

2145 þeoden mæra,   þines ahredde,
æðelinga helm,   þy læs þu eft cweðe
þæt ic wurde,   willgesteallum,
eadig on eorðan   ærgestreonum
Sodoma rices;   ac þu selfa most heonon

2150 huðe lædan,   þe ic þe æt hilde gesloh,
ealle buton dæle   þissa drihtwera,
Aneres and Mamres   and Escoles.

2135–2136 mid . . . Abraham] *Written in above the line*   2137 gewurðod]
ge *written over an erasure*   2141 and] *Not in MS.*   2149 rices] rice
selfa] *Not in MS.*

Nelle ic þa rincas   rihte benæman,
ac hie me fulleodon   æt æscþræce,
2155 fuhton þe æfter frofre.   Gewit þu ferian nu
ham hyrsted gold   and healsmægeð,
leoda idesa.   Þu þe laðra ne þearft
hæleða hildþræce   hwile onsittan,
norðmanna wig;   ac nefuglas
2160 under beorhhleoþum   blodige sittað,
þeodherga wæle   þicce gefylled."
    Gewat him þa se healdend   ham siðian
mid þy hereteame   þe him se halga forgeaf,
Ebrea leod   arna gemyndig.
2165 Þa gen Abrahame   eowde selfa
heofona heahcyning   halige spræce,
trymede tilmodigne   and him to reordode:
"Meda syndon micla þina!   Ne læt þu þe þin mod
                                       asealcan,
wærfæst willan mines!   Ne þearft þu þe wiht ondrædan,
2170 þenden þu mine lare læstest,   ac ic þe lifigende her
wið weana gehwam   wreo and scylde
folmum minum;   ne þearft þu forht wesan."
    Abraham þa   andswarode,
dædrof drihtne sinum,   frægn hine dægrime frod:
2175   "Hwæt gifest þu me,   gasta waldend,
freomanna to frofre,   nu ic þus feasceaft eom?
Ne þearf ic yrfestol   eaforan bytlian
ænegum minra,   ac me æfter sculon
mine woruldmagas   welan bryttian.
2180 Ne sealdest þu me sunu;   forðon mec sorg dreceð
on sefan swiðe.   Ic sylf ne mæg
ræd ahycgan.   Gæð gerefa min
fægen freobearnum;   fæste mynteð
ingeþancum   þæt me æfter sie
2185 eaforan sine   yrfeweardas.

2159 ac nefuglas] eacne fuglas   2160 blodige] blodig   2161 wæle]
wæl   2164 gemyndig] gem *at end of a line with* m *partly erased, and*
myndig *at beginning of the next line*   2171 gehwam] wa *written over an
erasure*   2174 frægn] æg *written over an erasure*

Geseoð þæt me of bryde   bearn ne wocon."
    Him þa ædre god   andswarode:
"Næfre gerefan   rædað þine
eafora yrfe,   ac þin agen bearn
2190 frætwa healdeð,   þonne þin flæsc ligeð.
Sceawa heofon,   and hyrste gerim,
rodores tungel,   þa nu rume heora
wuldorfæstne wlite   wide dælað
ofer brad brymu   beorhte scinan.
2195 Swilc bið mægburge   menigo þinre
folcbearnum frome.   Ne læt þu þin ferhð wesan
sorgum asæled.   Gien þe sunu weorðeð,
bearn of bryde   þurh gebyrd cumen,
se ðe æfter bið   yrfes hyrde,
2200 gode mære.   Ne geomra þu!
Ic eom se waldend   se þe for wintra fela
of Caldea   ceastre alædde,
feowera sumne,   gehet þe folcstede
wide to gewealde.   Ic þe wære nu,
2205 mago Ebrea,   mine selle,
þæt sceal fromcynne   folde þine,
sidland manig,   geseted wurðan,
eorðan sceatas   oð Eufraten,
and from Egypta   eðelmearce
2210 swa mid niðas   swa Nilus sceadeð
and eft Wendelsæ   wide rice.
Eall þæt sculon agan   eaforan þine,
þeodlanda gehwilc,   swa þa þreo wæter
steape stanbyrig   streamum bewindað,
2215 famige flodas   folcmægða byht."
    Þa wæs Sarran   sar on mode,
þæt him Abrahame   ænig ne wearð
þurh gebedscipe   bearn gemæne,
freolic to frofre.   Ongann þa ferhðcearig

2191 and] *Not in MS*.   2195 mægburge] mæg burh   2197 asæled]
æsæled   2203 feowera] o *altered from* w   2210b swa] twa   2211
Wendelsæ] wendeð sæ   2216 Sarran] sar *at end of a line, followed by a
letter erased, possibly* a, *with* ran *at beginning of next line*

2220 to were sinum wordum mæðlan:
   "Me þæs forwyrnde waldend heofona,
   þæt ic mægburge moste þinre
   rim miclian roderum under
   eaforum þinum. Nu ic eom orwena
2225 þæt unc se eðylstæf æfre weorðe
   gifeðe ætgædere. Ic eom geomorfrod!
   Drihten min, do swa ic þe bidde!
   Her is fæmne, freolecu mæg,
   ides Egyptisc, an on gewealde.
2230 Hat þe þa recene reste gestigan,
   and afanda hwæðer frea wille
   ænigne þe yrfewearda
   on woruld lætan þurh þæt wif cuman."
   Þa se eadega wer idese larum
2235 geðafode, heht him þeowmennen
   on bedd gan bryde larum.
   Hire mod astah þa heo wæs magotimbre
   be Abrahame eacen worden.
   Ongan æfþancum agendfrean
2240 halsfæst herian, higeþryðe wæg,
   wæs laðwendo, lustum ne wolde
   þeowdom þolian, ac heo þriste ongan
   wið Sarran swiðe winnan.
   Þa ic þæt wif gefrægn wordum cyðan
2245 hire mandrihtne modes sorge,
   sarferhð sægde and swiðe cwæð:
   "Ne fremest þu gerysnu and riht wið me.
   Þafodest þu gena þæt me þeowmennen,
   siððan Agar ðe, idese laste,
2250 beddreste gestah, swa ic bena wæs,
   drehte dogora gehwam dædum and wordum
   unarlice. Þæt Agar sceal ongieldan,
   gif ic mot for þe mine wealdan,
   Abraham leofa. Þæs sie ælmihtig,

2225 se] seo   eðylstæf] *Followed by a letter erased; a second* f?   2251
drehte] drehta   gewham] geham   2252 Agar] agan   ongieldan] *Not
in MS.*

2255 drihtna drihten, dema mid unc twih."
    Hire þa ædre andswarode
wishidig wer wordum sinum:
    "Ne forlæte ic þe, þenden wit lifiað bu,
arna lease, ac þu þin agen most
2260 mennen ateon, swa þin mod freoð."
    Ða wearð unbliðe Abrahames cwen,
hire worcþeowe wrað on mode,
heard and hreðe, higeteonan spræc
fræcne on fæmnan. Heo þa fleon gewat
2265 þrea and þeowdom; þolian ne wolde
yfel and ondlean, þæs ðe ær dyde
to Sarran, ac heo on sið gewat
westen secan. Þær hie wuldres þegn,
engel drihtnes an gemitte
2270 geomormode, se hie georne frægn:
    "Hwider fundast þu, feasceaft ides,
siðas dreogan? Þec Sarre ah."
    Heo him ædre andswarode:
"Ic fleah wean, wana wilna gehwilces,
2275 hlæfdigan hete, hean of wicum,
tregan and teonan. Nu sceal tearighleor
on westenne witodes bidan,
hwonne of heortan hunger oððe wulf
sawle and sorge somed abregde."
2280   Hire þa se engel andswarode:
"Ne ceara þu feor heonon fleame dælan
somwist incre, ac þu sece eft,
earna þe ara, eaðmod ongin
dreogan æfter dugeðum, wes drihtenhold.
2285 Þu scealt, Agar, Abrahame sunu
on woruld bringan. Ic þe wordum nu
minum secge, þæt se magorinc sceal
mid yldum wesan Ismahel haten.
    Se bið unhyre, orlæggifre,
2290 and wiðerbreca wera cneorissum,

2255 drihtna] *Not in MS.* twih] twig *with* h *above* g   2290 and] *Not in MS.*

magum sinum;   hine monige on
wraðe winnað   mid wæpenþræce.
Of þam frumgaran   folc awæcniað,
þeod unmæte.   Gewit þu þinne eft
2295 waldend secan;   wuna þæm þe agon!"
       Heo þa ædre gewat   engles larum
hire hlafordum,   swa se halga bebead,
godes ærendgast,   gleawan spræce.
Þa wearð Abrahame   Ismael geboren,
2300 efne þa he on worulde   wintra hæfde
VI and LXXX.   Sunu weox and ðah,
swa se engel ær   þurh his agen word,
fæle freoðoscealc,   fæmnan sægde.
       Þa se ðeoden   ymb XIII gear,
2305 ece drihten,   wið Abrahame spræc:
       "Leofa, swa ic þe lære,   læst uncre wel
treowrædenne!   Ic þe on tida gehwone
duguðum stepe.   Wes þu dædum from
willan mines!   Ic þa wære forð
2310 soðe gelæste,   þe ic þe sealde geo
frofre to wedde,   þæs þin ferhð bemearn.
Þu scealt halgian   hired þinne.
Sete sigores tacn   soð on gehwilcne
wæpnedcynnes,   gif þu wille on me
2315 hlaford habban   oððe holdne freond
þinum fromcynne.   Ic þæs folces beo
hyrde and healdend,   gif ge hyrað me
breostgehygdum   and bebodu willað
min fullian.   Sceal monna gehwilc
2320 þære cneorisse   cildisc wesan
wæpnedcynnes,   þæs þe on woruld cymð,
ymb seofon niht   sigores tacne
geagnod me,   oððe of eorðan
þurh feondscipe   feor adæled,
2325 adrifen from duguðum.   Doð swa ic hate!
Ic eow treowige,   gif ge þæt tacen gegaþ

2293 frumgaran] frum garum   awæcniað] apæcniað   2306 Leofa] *In the margin,* lyfa

soðgeleafan. Þu scealt sunu agan,
bearn be bryde þinre, þone sculon burhsittende
ealle Isaac hatan. Ne þearf þe þæs eaforan sceomigan,
2330 ac ic þam magorince mine sylle
godcunde gife gastes mihtum,
freondsped fremum. He onfon sceal
blisse minre and bletsunge,
lufan and lisse. Of þam leodfruman
2335 brad folc cumað, bregowearda fela
rofe arisað, rices hyrdas,
woruldcyningas wide mære."
    Abraham ða ofestum legde
hleor on eorðan, and mid hucse bewand
2340 þa hleoðorcwydas on hige sinum,
modgeðance. He þæs mældæges
self ne wende þæt him Sarra,
bryd blondenfeax bringan meahte
on woruld sunu; wiste gearwe
2345 þæt þæt wif huru wintra hæfde
efne C, geteled rimes.
He þa metode oncwæð missarum frod:
    "Lifge Ismael larum swilce,
þeoden, þinum, and þe þanc wege,
2350 heardrædne hyge, heortan strange,
to dreoganne dæges and nihtes
wordum and dædum willan þinne."
    Him þa fægere frea ælmihtig,
ece drihten, andswarode:
2355   "Þe sceal wintrum frod on woruld bringan
Sarra sunu, soð forð gan
wyrd æfter þissum wordgemearcum.
Ic Ismael estum wille
bletsian nu, swa þu bena eart
2360 þinum frumbearne, þæt feorhdaga
on woruldrice worn gebide,
tanum tudre. Þu þæs tiða beo!
Hwæðre ic Isace, eaforan þinum,
geongum bearne, þam þe gen nis

2365 on woruld cumen, willa spedum
 dugeða gehwilcre on dagum wille
 swiðor stepan and him soðe to
 modes wære mine gelæstan,
 halige higetreowa, and him hold wesan."
2370 Abraham fremede swa him se eca bebead,
 sette friðotacen be frean hæse
 on his selfes sunu, heht þæt segn wegan
 heah gehwilcne, þe his hina wæs
 wæpnedcynnes, wære gemyndig,
2375 gleaw on mode, ða him god sealde
 soðe treowa, and þa seolf onfeng
 torhtum tacne. A his tir metod,
 domfæst cyning, dugeðum iecte
 on woruldrice; he him þæs worhte to,
2380 siððan he on fære furðum meahte
 his waldendes willan fremman.

 * * *

 Þa þæt wif ahloh wereda drihtnes
 nalles glædlice, ac heo gearum frod
 þone hleoðorcwyde husce belegde
2385 on sefan swiðe. Soð ne gelyfde,
 þæt þære spræce sped folgode.
 Þa þæt gehyrde heofona waldend,
 þæt on bure ahof bryd Abrahames
 hihtleasne hleahtor, þa cwæð halig god:
2390 "Ne wile Sarran soð gelyfan
 wordum minum. Sceal seo wyrd swa þeah
 forð steallian swa ic þe æt frymðe gehet.
 Soð ic þe secge, on þas sylfan tid
 of idese bið eafora wæcned.
2395 Þonne ic þas ilcan oðre siðe
 wic gesece, þe beoð wordgehat
 min gelæsted. Þu on magan wlitest,
 þin agen bearn, Abraham leofa!"
 Gewiton him þa ædre ellorfuse

2368 gelæstan] gelætan 2369 higetreowa] hige treawa 2372 wegan]
wesan 2396 wordgehat] worn gehat

2400 æfter þære spræce   spedum feran
of þam hleoðorstede,   halige gastas,
lastas legdon,   (him wæs Lothes mæg
sylfa on gesiððe),   oðþæt hie on Sodoman,
weallsteape burg,   wlitan meahton.
2405 Gesawon ofer since   salo hlifian,
reced ofer readum golde.   Ongan þa rodera waldend,
arfæst wið Abraham sprecan,   sægde him unlytel spell:
"Ic on þisse byrig   bearhtm gehyre,
synnigra cyrm   swiðe hludne,
2410 ealogalra gylp,   yfele spræce
werod under weallum habban;   forþon wærlogona sint,
folces firena hefige.   Ic wille fandigan nu,
mago Ebrea,   hwæt þa men don,
gif hie swa swiðe   synna fremmað
2415 þeawum and geþancum,   swa hie on þweorh sprecað
facen and inwit;   þæt sceal fyr wrecan,
swefyl and sweart lig   sare and grimme,
hat and hæste   hæðnum folce."

                *   *   *

Weras basnedon   witelaces,
2420 wean under weallum,   and heora wif somed.
Duguðum wlance   drihtne guldon
god mid gnyrne,   oðþæt gasta helm,
lifes leohtfruma   leng ne wolde
torn þrowigean,   ac him to sende
2425 stiðmod cyning   strange twegen
aras sine,   þa on æfentid
siðe gesohton   Sodoma ceastre.
Hie þa æt burhgeate   beorn gemitton
sylfne sittan   sunu Arones,
2430 þæt þam gleawan were   geonge þuhton
men for his eagum.   Aras þa metodes þeow
gastum togeanes,   gretan eode

2402 Lothes] leohtes   2409 synnigra] g *altered from some other letter,
perhaps* f   2412 folces] folce   2416 fyr] *Not in MS.*   2418 hat]
Followed by a letter erased, probably e   2419 witelaces] wite loccas

cuman cuðlice, cynna gemunde
riht and gerisno, and þam rincum bead
2435 nihtfeormunge. Him þa nergendes
æðele ærendracan andswarodon:
"Hafa arna þanc, þara þe þu unc bude!
Wit be þisse stræte stille þencað
sæles bidan, siððan sunnan eft
2440 forð to morgen metod up forlæt."
Þa to fotum Loth
þam giestum hnah, and him georne bead
reste and gereorda and his recedes hleow
and þegnunge. Hie on þanc curon
2445 æðelinges est, eodon sona,
swa him se Ebrisca eorl wisade,
in undor edoras. Þær him se æðela geaf,
gleawferhð hæle, giestliðnysse
fægre on flette, oðþæt forð gewat
2450 æfenscima. Þa com æfter niht
on last dæge. Lagustreamas wreah,
þrym mid þystro þisses lifes,
sæs and sidland. Comon Sodomware,
geonge and ealde, gode unleofe
2455 corðrum miclum cuman acsian,
þæt hie behæfdon herges mægne
Loth mid giestum. Heton lædan ut
of þam hean hofe halige aras,
weras to gewealde, wordum cwædon
2460 þæt mid þam hæleðum hæman wolden
unscomlice, arna ne gymden.
Þa aras hraðe, se ðe oft ræd ongeat,
Loth on recede, eode lungre ut,
spræc þa ofer ealle æðelinga gedriht
2465 sunu Arones, snytra gemyndig:
"Her syndon inne unwemme twa
dohtor mine. Doð, swa ic eow bidde
(ne can þara idesa owðer gieta

2433 cuman] cum *with* an *added above the line*   2436 ærendracan] ærendran
2439 sunnan] sunne

þurh gebedscipe   beorna neawest)
2470 and geswicað þære synne.   Ic eow sylle þa,
ær ge sceonde   wið gesceapu fremmen,
ungifre yfel   ylda bearnum.
Onfoð þæm fæmnum,   lætað frið agon
gistas mine,   þa ic for gode wille
2475 gemundbyrdan,   gif ic mot, for eow."
    Him þa seo mænigeo   þurh gemæne word,
arlease cyn,   andswarode:
    "Þis þinceð gerisne   and riht micel,
þæt þu ðe aferige   of þisse folcsceare.
2480 Þu þas werðeode   wræccan laste
freonda feasceaft   feorran gesohtest,
wineþearfende.   Wilt ðu, gif þu most,
wesan usser her   aldordema,
leodum lareow?"   Þa ic on Lothe gefrægn
2485 hæðne heremæcgas   handum gripan,
faum folmum.   Him fylston wel
gystas sine,   and hine of gromra þa,
cuman arfæste,   clommum abrugdon
in under edoras,   and þa ofstlice
2490 anra gehwilcum   ymbstandendra
folces Sodoma   fæste forsæton
heafodsiena.   Wearð eal here sona
burhwarena blind.   Abrecan ne meahton
reðemode   reced æfter gistum,
2495 swa hie fundedon,   ac þær frome wæron
godes spellbodan.   Hæfde gistmægen
stiðe strengeo,   styrnde swiðe
werode mid wite.   Spræcon wordum þa
fæle freoðoscealcas   fægre to Lothe:
2500   "Gif þu sunu age   oððe swæsne mæg,
oððe on þissum folcum   freond ænigne
eac þissum idesum   þe we her on wlitað,
alæde of þysse leodbyrig,   þa ðe leofe sien,
ofestum miclum,   and þin ealdor nere,
2505 þy læs þu forweorðe   mid þyssum wærlogan.

2482 wineþearfende] þine þearfende

Unc hit waldend heht   for wera synnum
Sodoma and Gomorra   sweartan lige,
fyre gesyllan   and þas folc slean,
cynn on ceastrum   mid cwealmþrea
2510 and his torn wrecan.   Þære tide is
neah geþrungen.   Gewit þu nergean þin
feorh foldwege.   Þe is frea milde."
         *   *   *
Him þa ædre Loth   andswarode:
"Ne mæg ic mid idesum   aldornere mine
2515 swa feor heonon   feðegange
siðe gesecan.   Git me sibblufan
and freondscipe   fægre cyðað,
treowe and hyldo   tiðiað me.
Ic wat hea burh   her ane neah,
2520 lytle ceastre.   Lyfað me þær
are and reste,   þæt we aldornere
on Sigor up   secan moten.
Gif git þæt fæsten   fyre willað
steape forstandan,   on þære stowe we
2525 gesunde magon   sæles bidan,
feorh generigan."   Him þa freondlice
englas arfæste   andswaredon:
"Þu scealt þære bene,   nu þu ymb þa burh sprycest,
tiða weorðan.   Teng recene to
2530 þam fæstenne;   wit þe friðe healdað
and mundbyrde.   Ne moton wyt
on wærlogum   wrecan torn godes,
swebban synnig cynn,   ær ðon þu on Sægor þin
bearn gelæde   and bryd somed."
2535   Þa onette   Abrahames mæg
to þam fæstenne.   Feðe ne sparode
eorl mid idesum,   ac he ofstum forð
lastas legde,   oðþæt he gelædde
bryd mid bearnum   under burhlocan
2540 in Sægor his.   Þa sunne up,
folca friðcandel,   furðum eode,

2528 sprycest] spryst

þa ic sendan gefrægn swegles aldor
swefl of heofnum and sweartne lig
werum to wite, weallende fyr,
2545 þæs hie on ærdagum drihten tyndon
lange þrage. Him þæs lean forgeald
gasta waldend! Grap heahþrea
on hæðencynn. Hlynn wearð on ceastrum,
cirm arleasra cwealmes on ore,
2550 laðan cynnes. Lig eall fornam
þæt he grenes fond goldburgum in,
swylce þær ymbutan unlytel dæl
sidre foldan geondsended wæs
bryne and brogan. Bearwas wurdon
2555 to axan and to yslan, eorðan wæstma,
efne swa wide swa ða witelac
reðe geræhton rum land wera.
Strudende fyr steapes and geapes,
swogende leg, forswealh eall geador
2560 þæt on Sodoma byrig secgas ahton
and on Gomorra. Eall þæt god spilde,
frea mid þy folce. Þa þæt fyrgebræc,
leoda lifgedal, Lothes gehyrde
bryd on burgum, under bæc beseah
2565 wið þæs wælfylles. Us gewritu secgað
þæt heo on sealtstanes sona wurde
anlicnesse. Æfre siððan
se monlica (þæt is mære spell)
stille wunode, þær hie strang begeat
2570 wite, þæs heo wordum wuldres þegna
hyran ne wolde. Nu sceal heard and steap
on þam wicum wyrde bidan,
drihtnes domes, hwonne dogora rim,
woruld gewite. Þæt is wundra sum,
2575 þara ðe geworhte wuldres aldor.
    Him þa Abraham gewat ana gangan
mid ærdæge þæt he eft gestod

2559 leg] *Not in MS.*   geador] eador   2573 hwonne] hwone *with a*
second n *above the line after* o   2577 he eft] heft

þær wordum ær   wið his waldend spræc
frod frumgara.   He geseah from foldan up
2580 wide fleogan   wælgrimne rec.
Hie þæs wlenco onwod   and wingedrync
þæt hie firendæda   to frece wurdon,
synna þriste,   soð ofergeaton,
drihtnes domas,   and hwa him dugeða forgeaf,
2585 blæd on burgum.   Forþon him brego engla
wylmhatne lig   to wræce sende.
Waldend usser   gemunde wærfæst þa
Abraham arlice,   swa he oft dyde
leofne mannan.   Loth generede,
2590 mæg þæs oðres,   þa seo mænegeo forwearð.
Ne dorste þa   dædrof hæle
for frean egesan   on þam fæstenne
leng eardigean,   ac him Loth gewat
of byrig gangan   and his bearn somed
2595 wælstowe fyrr   wic sceawian,
oðþæt hie be hliðe   heare dune
eorðscræf fundon.   Þær se eadega Loth
wærfæst wunode,   waldende leof,
dægrimes worn   and his dohtor twa.

                    *   *   *

2600 Hie dydon swa;   druncnum eode
seo yldre to   ær on reste
heora bega fæder.   Ne wiste blondenfeax
hwonne him fæmnan to bryde   him bu wæron,
on ferhðcofan   fæste genearwod
2605 mode and gemynde,   þæt he mægða sið
wine druncen   gewitan ne meahte.
Idesa wurdon eacne,   eaforan brohtan
willgesweostor   on woruld sunu
heora ealdan fæder.   Þara æðelinga
2610 modor oðerne   Moab nemde,
Lothes dohter,   seo on life wæs
wintrum yldre.   Us gewritu secgeað,

2587 wærfæst] wær fæst *with* ær *written over an erasure*   2604 genearwod]
genearwot

godcunde bec,   þæt seo gingre
hire agen bearn   Ammon hete.
2615 Of þam frumgarum   folces unrim,
þrymfæste twa   þeoda awocon.
Oðre þara mægða   Moabitare
eorðbuende   ealle hatað,
widmære cynn,   oðre weras nemnað,
2620 æðelinga bearn,   Ammonitare.
Gewat him þa mid bryde   broðor Arones
under Abimelech   æhte lædan
mid his hiwum.   Hæleðum sægde
þæt Sarra his   sweostor wære,
2625 Abraham wordum   (bearh his aldre),
þy he wiste gearwe   þæt he winemaga,
on folce lyt   freonda hæfde.
Þa se þeoden his   þegnas sende,
heht hie bringan   to him selfum.
2630 Þa wæs ellþeodig   oðre siðe
wif Abrahames   from were læded
on fremdes fæðm.   Him þær fylste þa
ece drihten,   swa he oft dyde,
nergend usser.   Com nihtes self,
2635 þær se waldend læg   wine druncen.
Ongan þa soðcyning   þurh swefn sprecan
to þam æðelinge   and him yrre hweop:
"Þu Abrahames   idese gename,
bryde æt beorne.   Þe abregdan sceal
2640 for þære dæde   deað of breostum
sawle þine."   Him symbelwerig
sinces brytta   þurh slæp oncwæð:
"Hwæt, þu æfre,   engla þeoden,
þurh þin yrre wilt   aldre lætan,
2645 heah beheowan,   þæne þe her leofað
rihtum þeawum,   bið on ræde fæst,

2615 folces] folc   2620 Ammonitare] ammontare *with* i *above the line*
after n   2624 his] hi *with* s *added above the line*   2629 hie] *Not in MS.*
2631 Abrahames] abrames   2642 sinces] synna   2645 beheowan]
beheopan   þæne] þære

modgeþance, and him miltse
to þe seceð? Me sægde ær
þæt wif hire wordum selfa
2650 unfricgendum, þæt heo Abrahames
sweostor wære. Næbbe ic synne wið hie,
facna ænig gefremed gena."
   Him þa ædre eft ece drihten,
soðfæst metod, þurh þæt swefn oncwæð:
2655   "Agif Abrahame idese sine,
wif to gewealde, gif þu on worulde leng,
æðelinga helm, aldres recce.
He is god and gleaw, mæg self wið god sprecan,
geseon sweglcyning. Þu sweltan scealt
2660 mid feo and mid feorme, gif ðu þam frumgaran
bryde wyrnest. He abiddan mæg,
gif he ofstum me ærendu wile
þeawfæst and geþyldig þin abeodan,
þæt ic þe lissa lifigendum giet
2665 on dagum læte duguþa brucan
sinces gesundne." Þa slæpe tobrægd
forht folces weard. Heht him fetigean to
gesprecan sine, spedum sægde
eorlum Abimeleh, egesan geðread,
2670 waldendes word. Weras him ondredon
for þære dæde drihtnes handa
sweng æfter swefne. Heht sylf cyning
him þa Abraham to ofstum miclum.
   Þa reordode rice þeoden:
2675 "Mago Ebrea, þæs þu me wylle
wordum secgean, hu geworhte ic þæt,
siððan þu usic under, Abraham, þine
on þas eðelturf æhta læddest,
þæt þu me þus swiðe searo renodest?
2680 Þu ellþeodig usic woldest
on þisse folcsceare facne besyrwan,

2658 wið god] *Not in MS.* 2662 ærendu] ærenda 2667 Heht] heht
with e *altered from* a 2668 gesprecan] sprecan 2676 geworhte] orht *on
an erasure* (Holthausen)

synnum besmitan,   sægdest wordum
þæt Sarra þin   sweostor wære,
lices mæge,   woldest laðlice
2685 þurh þæt wif on me   wrohte alecgean,
ormæte yfel.   We þe arlice
gefeormedon,   and þe freondlice
on þisse werþeode   wic getæhton,
land to lissum.   Þu us leanast nu,
2690 unfreondlice   fremena þancast!"
      Abraham þa   andswarode:
"Ne dyde ic for facne   ne for feondscipe
ne for wihte þæs   ic þe wean uðe.
Ac ic me, gumena baldor,   guðbordes sweng
2695 leodmagum feor   lare gebearh,
siððan me se halga   of hyrde frean,
mines fæder   fyrn alædde.
Ic fela siððan   folca gesohte,
wina uncuðra,   and þis wif mid me,
2700 freonda feasceaft.   Ic þæs færes a
on wenum sæt   hwonne me wraðra sum
ellþeodigne   aldre beheowe,
se ðe him þas idese eft   agan wolde.
Forðon ic wigsmiðum   wordum sægde
2705 þæt Sarra min   sweostor wære,
æghwær eorðan   þær wit earda leas
mid wealandum   winnan sceoldon.
Ic þæt ilce dreah   on þisse eðyltyrf,
siððan ic þina,   þeoden mæra,
2710 mundbyrde geceas.   Ne wæs me on mode cuð,
hwæðer on þyssum folce   frean ælmihtiges
egesa wære,   þa ic her ærest com.
Forþon ic þegnum   þinum dyrnde
and sylfum þe   swiðost micle
2715 soðan spræce,   þæt me Sarra
bryde laste   beddreste gestah."

2685 þurh] þur *with* h *added above the line*   2697 alædde] alæded   2702
ellþeodigne] elþeodigne *with a second* l *above the line before* þ   2715
Sarra] sarran

þa ongan Abimæleh   Abraham swiðan
woruldgestreonum   and him his wif ageaf.
Sealde him to bote,   þæs þe he his bryd genam,
2720 gangende feoh   and glæd seolfor
and weorcþeos.   Spræc þa wordum eac
to Abrahame   æðelinga helm:
"Wuna mid usic   and þe wic geceos
on þissum lande   þær þe leofost sie,
2725 eðelstowe,   þe ic agan sceal.
Wes us fæle freond,   we ðe feoh syllað!"
Cwæð þa eft raðe   oðre worde
to Sarran   sinces brytta:
"Ne þearf ðe on edwit   Abraham settan,
2730 ðin freadrihten,   þæt þu flettpaðas,
mæg ælfscieno,   mine træde,
ac him hygeteonan   hwitan seolfre
deope bete.   Ne ceara incit duguða
of ðisse eðyltyrf   ellor secan,
2735 winas uncuðe,   ac wuniað her."
Abraham fremede   swa hine his aldor heht,
onfeng freondscipe   be frean hæse,
lufum and lissum.   He wæs leof gode.
Forðon he sibbe   gesælig dreah
2740 and his scippende   under sceade gefor,
hleowfeðrum þeaht,   her þenden lifde.
Þa gien wæs yrre   god Abimelehe
for þære synne   þe he wið Sarrai
and wið Abrahame   ær gefremede,
2745 þa he gedælde   him deore twa,
wif and wæpned.   He þæs weorc gehleat,
frecne wite.   Ne meahton freo ne þeowe
heora bregoweardas   bearnum ecan
monrim mægeð,   ac him þæt metod forstod,
2750 oðþæt se halga   his hlaforde

2721 weorcþeos] weorc feos *with* s *altered from* h (*Holthausen*)   spræc]
Written twice in MS.   2727 eft] *Followed by erasure of two letters;* þa eft
written over an erasure (*Holthausen*)   2730 flettpaðas] flett waðas   2748
ecan] agan

Abraham ongan   arna biddan
ecne drihten.   Him engla helm
getigðode,   tuddorsped onleac
folccyninge   freora and þeowra,
2755 wera and wifa;   let weaxan eft
heora rimgetel   rodora waldend,
ead and æhta.   Ælmihtig wearð
milde on mode,   moncynnes weard,
Abimeleche,   swa hine Abraham bæd.
2760   Þa com feran   frea ælmihtig
to Sarrai,   swa he self gecwæð,
waldend usser,   hæfde wordbeot
leofum gelæsted,   lifes aldor
eaforan and idese.   Abrahame woc
2765 bearn of bryde,   þone brego engla,
ær ðy magotudre   modor wære
eacen be eorle,   Isaac nemde.
Hine Abraham on   mid his agenc hand
beacen sette,   swa him bebead metod,
2770 wuldortorht ymb wucan,   þæs þe hine on woruld
to moncynne   modor brohte.
     Cniht weox and þag,   swa him cynde wæron
æðele from yldrum.   Abraham hæfde
wintra hundteontig   þa him wif sunu
2775 on þanc gebær.   He þæs ðrage bad,
siððan him ærest   þurh his agen word
þone dægwillan   drihten bodode.
     Þa seo wyrd gewearð   þæt þæt wif geseah
for Abrahame   Ismael plegan,
2780 ðær hie æt swæsendum   sæton bu tu,
halig on hige,   and heora hiwan eall,
druncon and drymdon.   Þa cwæð drihtlecu mæg,
bryd to beorne: "Forgif me, beaga weard,
min swæs frea,   hat siðian
2785 Agar ellor   and Ismael
lædan mid hie!   Ne beoð we leng somed

2751 arna] arra   2758 weard] wearð   2768 mid] *Not in MS.*   2774
hundteontig] hunteontig   2784 siðian] siððan

willum minum, gif ic wealdan mot.
Næfre Ismael wið Isace,
wið min agen bearn yrfe dæleð
2790 on laste þe, þonne þu of lice
aldor asendest." Þa wæs Abrahame
weorce on mode þæt he on wræc drife
his selfes sunu, þa com soð metod
freom on fultum, wiste ferhð guman
2795 cearum on clommum. Cyning engla spræc
to Abrahame, ece drihten:
"Læt þe aslupan sorge of breostum,
modgewinnan, and mægeð hire,
bryde þinre! Hat bu tu aweg
2800 Agar feran and Ismael,
cniht of cyððe! Ic his cynn gedo
brad and bresne bearna tudre,
wæstmum spedig, swa ic þe wordum gehet."
Þa se wer hyrde his waldende,
2805 draf of wicum dreorigmod tu,
idese of earde and his agen bearn.
*   *   *
"Sweotol is and gesene þæt þe soð metod
on gesiððe is, swegles aldor,
se ðe sigor seleð snytru mihtum
2810 and þin mod trymeð,
godcundum gifum. Forðon ðe giena speow,
þæs þu wið freond oððe feond fremman ongunne
wordum oððe dædum. Waldend scufeð,
frea on forðwegas folmum sinum
2815 willan þinne. Þæt is wide cuð
burhsittendum. Ic þe bidde nu,
wine Ebrea, wordum minum,
þæt þu tilmodig treowa selle,
wæra þina, þæt þu wille me
2820 wesan fæle freond fremena to leane,
þara þe ic to duguðum ðe gedon hæbbe,
siððan ðu feasceaft feorran come

2809 snytru] snytrum   2814 on] *Not in MS.*

on þas werþeode   wræccan laste.
Gyld me mid hyldo,   þæt ic þe hneaw ne wæs
2825 landes and lissa.   Wes þissum leodum nu
and mægburge   minre arfæst,
gif þe alwalda,   ure drihten,
scirian wille,   se ðe gesceapu healdeð,
þæt þu randwigum   rumor mote
2830 on ðisse folcsceare   frætwa dælan,
modigra gestreon,   mearce settan."
Ða Abraham   Abimelehe
wære sealde   þæt he wolde swa.
    Siððan wæs se eadega   eafora þares
2835 in Filistea   folce eardfæst,
leod Ebrea   lange þrage,
feasceaft mid fremdum.   Him frea engla
wic getæhte   þæt weras hata ð
burhsittende   Bersabea lond.
2840 Ðær se halga   heahsteap reced,
burh timbrede   and bearo sette,
weobedd worhte,   and his waldende
on þam glædstede   gild onsægde,
lac geneahe,   þam þe lif forgeaf,
2845 gesæliglic   swegle under.
    Þa þæs rinces   se rica ongan
cyning costigan,   cunnode georne
hwilc þæs æðelinges   ellen wære,
stiðum wordum   spræc him stefne to:
2850   "Gewit þu ofestlice,   Abraham, feran,
lastas lecgan   and þe læde mid
þin agen bearn.   Þu scealt Isaac me
onsecgan, sunu ðinne,   sylf to tibre.
Siððan þu gestigest   steape dune,
2855 hrincg þæs hean landes,   þe ic þe heonon getæce,
up þinum agnum fotum,   þær þu scealt ad gegærwan,
bælfyr bearne þinum,   and blotan sylf
sunu mid sweordes ecge,   and þonne sweartan lige
leofes lic forbærnan   and me lac bebeodan."

2838 þæt] þær   2839 lond] lono

2860   Ne forsæt he þy siðe,   ac sona ongann
       fysan to fore.   Him wæs frean engla
       word ondrysne   and his waldend leof.
       Þa se eadga   Abraham sine
       nihtreste ofgeaf.   Nalles nergendes
2865 hæse wiðhogode,   ac hine se halga wer
       gyrde grægan sweorde,   cyðde þæt him gasta weardes
       egesa on breostum wunode.   Ongan þa his esolas bætan
       gamolferhð goldes brytta,   heht hine geonge twegen
       men mid siðian.   Mæg wæs his agen þridda
2870 and he feorða sylf.   Þa he fus gewat
       from his agenum hofe   Isaac lædan,
       bearn unweaxen,   swa him bebead metod.
       Efste þa swiðe   and onette
       forð foldwege,   swa him frea tæhte
2875 wegas ofer westen,   oðþæt wuldortorht,
       dæges þriddan up   ofer deop wæter
       ord aræmde.   Þa se eadega wer
       geseah hlifigan   hea dune
       swa him sægde ær   swegles aldor.
2880   Ða Abraham spræc   to his ombihtum:
       "Rincas mine,   restað incit
       her on þissum wicum.   Wit eft cumað,
       siððan wit ærende   uncer twega
       gastcyninge   agifen habbað."
2885   Gewat him þa se æðeling   and his agen sunu
       to þæs gemearces   þe him metod tæhte,
       wadan ofer wealdas.   Wudu bær sunu,
       fæder fyr and sweord.   Ða þæs fricgean ongann
       wer wintrum geong   wordum Abraham:
2890   "Wit her fyr and sweord,   frea min, habbað;
       hwær is þæt tiber,   þæt þu torht gode
       to þam brynegielde   bringan þencest?"
           Abraham maðelode   (hæfde on an gehogod
       þæt he gedæde   swa hine drihten het):
2895 "Him þæt soðcyning   sylfa findeð,

2861 frean] frea   2862 waldend] waldende   2894 gedæde] *The final* e
erased or rubbed   swa] s *altered from small capital* h

moncynnes weard,   swa him gemet þinceð."
   Gestah þa stiðhydig   steape dune
up mid his eaforan,   swa him se eca bebead,
þæt he on hrofe gestod   hean landes
2900 on þære stowe   þe him se stranga to,
wærfæst metod   wordum tæhte.
Ongan þa ad hladan,   æled weccan,
and gefeterode   fet and honda
bearne sinum   and þa on bæl ahof
2905 Isaac geongne,   and þa ædre gegrap
sweord be gehiltum,   wolde his sunu cwellan
folmum sinum,   fyre scencan
mæges dreore.   Þa metodes ðegn,
ufan engla sum,   Abraham hlude
2910 stefne cygde.   He stille gebad
ares spræce   and þam engle oncwæð.
Him þa ofstum to   ufan of roderum
wuldorgast godes   wordum mælde:
   "Abraham leofa,   ne sleah þin agen bearn,
2915 ac þu cwicne abregd   cniht of ade,
eaforan þinne!   Him an wuldres god!
Mago Ebrea,   þu medum scealt
þurh þæs halgan hand,   heofoncyninges,
soðum sigorleanum   selfa onfon,
2920 ginfæstum gifum.   Þe wile gasta weard
lissum gyldan   þæt þe wæs leofre his
sibb and hyldo   þonne þin sylfes bearn."
   Ad stod onæled.   Hæfde Abrahame
metod moncynnes,   mæge Lothes,
2925 breost geblissad,   þa he him his bearn forgeaf,
Isaac cwicne.   Ða se eadega bewlat,
rinc ofer exle,   and him þær rom geseah
unfeor þanon   ænne standan,
broðor Arones,   brembrum fæstne.
2930 Þone Abraham genam   and hine on ad ahof
ofestum miclum   for his agen bearn.
Abrægd þa mid þy bille,   brynegield onhread,

2900 stowe] *Not in MS.*   2907 scencan] sencan   2921 leofre] leofra

reccendne weg   rommes blode,
onbleot þæt lac gode,   sægde leana þanc
2935 and ealra þara sælða   þe he him sið and ær,
gifena drihten,   forgifen hæfde.

2935 sælða] *Not in MS.*

EXODUS

EXODUS

Hwæt! We feor and neah   gefrigen habaðˇ
ofer middangeard   Moyses domas,
wræclico wordriht,   wera cneorissum,—
in uprodor   eadigra gehwam
5 æfter bealusiðe   bote lifes,
lifigendra gehwam   langsumne ræd,—
hæleðum secgan.   Gehyre se ðe wille!
  Þone on westenne   weroda drihten,
soðfæst cyning,   mid his sylfes miht
10 gewyrðode,   and him wundra fela,
ece alwalda,   in æht forgeaf.
He wæs leof gode,   leoda aldor,
horsc and hreðergleaw,   herges wisa,
freom folctoga.   Faraones cyn,
15 godes andsacan,   gyrdwite band,
þær him gesealde   sigora waldend,
modgum magoræswan,   his maga feorh,
onwist eðles,   Abrahames sunum.
Heah wæs þæt handlean   and him hold frea,
20 gesealde wæpna geweald   wið wraðra gryre,
ofercom mid þy campe   cneomaga fela,
feonda folcriht.   Ða wæs forma sið
þæt hine weroda god   wordum nægde,
þær he him gesægde   soðwundra fela,
25 hu þas woruld worhte   witig drihten,
eorðan ymbhwyrft   and uprodor,
gesette sigerice,   and his sylfes naman,
ðone yldo bearn   ær ne cuðon,
frod fædera cyn,   þeah hie fela wiston.
30   Hæfde he þa geswiðed   soðum cræftum

8 weroda] werode   11 forgeaf] for geǎf, *i.e.*, a *deleted and then restored*
15 andsacan] andsaca   17 magoræswan] mago ræs wum   22 feonda]
Written twice

and gewurðodne   werodes aldor,
Faraones feond,   on forðwegas.
þa wæs ingere   ealdum witum
deaðe gedrenced   drihtfolca mæst;
35 hordwearda hryre   heaf wæs geniwad,
swæfon seledreamas,   since berofene.
Hæfde mansceaðan   æt middere niht
frecne gefylled,   frumbearna fela,
abrocene burhweardas.   Bana wide scra ð,
40 la ð leodhata,   land drysmyde
deadra hræwum,   dugo ð for ð gewat,
wop wæs wide,   worulddreama lyt.
Wæron hleahtorsmi ðum   handa belocene,
alyfed la ðsi ð   leode gretan;
45 folc ferende,   feond wæs bereafod,
hergas on helle.   Heofung þider becom,
druron deofolgyld.   Dæg wæs mære
ofer middangeard   þa seo mengeo for.
Swa þæs fæsten dreah   fela missera,
50 ealdwerige,   Egypta folc,
þæs þe hie widefer ð   wyrnan þohton
Moyses magum,   gif hie metod lete,
on langne lust   leofes si ðes.
   Fyrd wæs gefysed,   from se ðe lædde,
55 modig magoræswa,   mægburh heora.
Oferfor he mid þy folce   fæstena worn,
land and leodweard   la ðra manna,
enge anpa ðas,   uncu ð gelad,
o ðþæt hie on Gu ðmyrce   gearwe bæron,
60 (wæron land heora   lyfthelme beþeaht),
mearchofu morheald.   Moyses ofer þa,
fela meoringa,   fyrde gelædde.
   Heht þa ymb twa niht   tirfæste hæle ð,
si ððan hie feondum   o ðfaren hæfdon,

34 gedrenced] renced *written over an erasure in a large and different hand*
40 drysmyde] dryrmyde   45 feond] freond   46 Heofung] heofon
55 magoræswa] mago ræwa   63 Heht] EHT *with space for a capital*
tirfæste] tir fæstne

65 ymbwicigean   werodes bearhtme
   mid ælfere   Æthanes byrig,
   mægnes mæste   mearclandum on.
   Nearwe genyddon   on norðwegas,
   wiston him be suðan   Sigelwara land,
70 forbærned burhhleoðu,   brune leode,
   hatum heofoncolum.   þær halig god
   wið færbryne   folc gescylde,
   bælce oferbrædde   byrnendne heofon,
   halgan nette   hatwendne lyft.
75 Hæfde wederwolcen   widum fæðmum
   eorðan and uprodor   efne gedæled,
   lædde leodwerod,   ligfyr adranc,
   hate heofontorht.   Hæleð wafedon,
   drihta gedrymost.   Dægsceades hleo
80 wand ofer wolcnum;   hæfde witig god
   sunnan siðfæt   segle ofertolden,
   swa þa mæstrapas   men ne cuðon,
   ne ða seglrode   geseon meahton,
   eorðbuende   ealle cræfte,
85 hu afæstnod wæs   feldhusa mæst,
   siððan he mid wuldre   geweorðode
   þeodenholde.   þa wæs þridda wic
   folce to frofre.   Fyrd eall geseah
   hu þær hlifedon   halige seglas,
90 lyftwundor leoht;   leode ongeton,
   dugoð Israhela,   þæt þær drihten cwom
   weroda drihten,   wicsteal metan.
   Him beforan foran   fyr and wolcen
   in beorhtrodor,   beamas twegen,
95 þara æghwæðer   efngedælde
   heahþegnunga   haliges gastes,
   deormodra sið   dagum and nihtum.
       þa ic on morgen gefrægn   modes rofan
   hebban herebyman   hludan stefnum,
100 wuldres woman.   Werod eall aras,

66 Æthanes] ætanes *with* h *added above the line after* t   79 Dægsceades]
dæg scealdes   81 segle] swegle

modigra mægen,   swa him Moyses bebead,
mære magoræswa,   metodes folce,
fus fyrdgetrum.   Forð gesawon
lifes latþeow   lifweg metan;
105 swegl siðe weold,   sæmen æfter
foron flodwege.   Folc wæs on salum,
hlud herges cyrm.   Heofonbeacen astah
æfena gehwam,   oðer wundor,
syllic æfter sunne   setlrade beheold,
110 ofer leodwerum   lige scinan,
byrnende beam.   Blace stodon
ofer sceotendum   scire leoman;
scinon scyldhreoðan,   sceado swiðredon,
neowle nihtscuwan   neah ne mihton
115 heolstor ahydan;   heofoncandel barn.
Niwe nihtweard   nyde sceolde
wician ofer weredum,   þy læs him westengryre,
har hæðbroga,   holmegum wederum
on ferclamme   ferhð getwæfde.
120 Hæfde foregenga   fyrene loccas,
blace beamas;   bellegsan hweop
in þam hereþreate,   hatan lige,
þæt he on westenne   werod forbærnde,
nymðe hie modhwate   Moyses hyrde.
125   Scean scir werod,   scyldas lixton,
gesawon randwigan   rihte stræte,
segn ofer sweoton,   oðþæt sæfæsten
landes æt ende   leodmægne forstod,
fus on forðweg.   Fyrdwic aras;
130 wyrpton hie werige,   wiste genægdon
modige meteþegnas,   hyra mægen beton.
Bræddon æfter beorgum,   siððan byme sang,
flotan feldhusum.   Þa wæs feorðe wic,
randwigena ræst,   be þan readan sæ.

---

107 hlud] LUD *with space before for a large capital, and a small* h *in the*
margin   herges] heriges   109 sunne] sunnan   113 sceado] sceaðo
118 hæðbroga] broga *not in MS.*   119 on ferclamme] ofer clamme   ge-
twæfde] getwæf   128 leodmægne] leo mægne

135   Ðær on fyrd hyra   færspell becwom,
       oht inlende. Egsan stodan,
       wælgryre weroda; wræcmon gebad
       laðne lastweard, se ðe him lange ær
       eðelleasum onnied gescraf,
140   wean witum fæst. Wære ne gymdon,
       ðeah þe se yldra cyning ær ge
                   *   *   *

       þa wearð yrfeweard ingefolca,
       manna æfter maðmum, þæt he swa miceles geðah.
       Ealles þæs forgeton siððan grame wurdon
145   Egypta cyn ymbe antwig;
       ða heo his mægwinum morðor fremedon,
       wroht berenedon, wære fræton.
       Wæron heaðowylmas heortan getenge,
       mihtmod wera; manum treowum
150   woldon hie þæt feorhlean facne gyldan,
       þætte hie þæt dægweorc dreore gebohte,
       Moyses leode, þær him mihtig god
       on ðam spildsiðe spede forgefe.
       þa him eorla mod ortrywe wearð
155   siððan hie gesawon of suðwegum
       fyrd Faraonis forð ongangan,
       oferholt wegan, eored lixan,
       (garas trymedon, guð hwearfode,
       blicon bordhreoðan, byman sungon),
160   þufas þunian, þeod mearc tredan,
       on hwæl
                   *   *   *

       Hreopon herefugolas, hilde grædige,
       deawigfeðere ofer drihtneum,
       wonn wælceasega. Wulfas sungon
165   atol æfenleoð ætes on wenan,
       carleasan deor, cwyldrof beodan
       on laðra last leodmægnes fyl.
       Hreopon mearcweardas middum nihtum,

---

142 þa] A *with space before for a large capital*   145 ymbe] ymb   146 heo]
Written twice in MS.   151 hie] he   162 Hreopon] hwreopån   167 fyl]
ful   168 middum] midum *with a second* d *added above the line before* u

fleah fæge gast,   folc wæs gehæged.
170   Hwilum of þam werode   wlance þegnas
mæton milpaðas   meara bogum.
Him þær segncyning   wið þone segn foran,
manna þengel,   mearcþreate rad;
guðweard gumena   grimhelm gespeon,
175 cyning cinberge,   (cumbol lixton),
wiges on wenum,   wælhlencan sceoc,
het his hereciste   healdan georne
fæst fyrdgetrum.   Freond onsegon
laðum eagan   landmanna cyme.
180 Ymb hine wægon   wigend unforhte,
hare heorowulfas   hilde gretton,
þurstige þræcwiges,   þeodenholde.
Hæfde him alesen   leoda dugeðe
tireadigra   twa þusendo,
185 þæt wæron cyningas   and cneowmagas,
on þæt eade riht,   æðelum deore.
Forðon anra gehwilc   ut alædde
wæpnedcynnes,   wigan æghwilcne
þara þe he on ðam fyrste   findan mihte.
190 Wæron ingemen   ealle ætgædere,
cyningas on corðre.   Cuð oft gebad
horn on heape   to hwæs hægstealdmen,
guðþreat gumena,   gearwe bæron.
Swa þær eorp werod,   ecan læddon,
195 lað æfter laðum,   leodmægnes worn,
þusendmælum;   þider wæron fuse.
Hæfdon hie gemynted   to þam mægenheapum
to þam ærdæge   Israhela cynn
billum abreotan   on hyra broðorgyld.
200 Forþon wæs in wicum   wop up ahafen,
atol æfenleoð,   egesan stodon,
weredon wælnet,   þa se woma cwom.
Flugon frecne spel,   feond wæs anmod,
werud wæs wigblac,   oððæt wlance forsceaf

176 wælhlencan] hwæl hlencan   178 fyrdgetrum] syrd getrum   on-
segon] onsigon   181 heorowulfas] heora wulfas

205 mihtig engel,   se ða menigeo beheold,
þæt þær gelaðe mid him   leng ne mihton
geseon tosomne;   sið wæs gedæled.
Hæfde nydfara   nihtlangne fyrst,
þeah ðe him on healfa gehwam   hettend seomedon,
210 mægen oððe merestream;   nahton maran hwyrft.
Wæron orwenan   eðelrihtes,
sæton æfter beorgum   in blacum reafum,
wean on wenum;   wæccende bad
eall seo sibgedriht   somod ætgædere
215 maran mægenes,   oð Moyses bebead
eorlas on uhttid   ærnum bemum
folc somnigean,   frecan arisan,
habban heora hlencan,   hycgan on ellen,
beran beorht searo,   beacnum cigean
220 sweot sande near.   Snelle gemundon
weardas wigleoð,   werod wæs gefysed,
brudon ofer burgum,   (byman gehyrdon),
flotan feldhusum,   fyrd wæs on ofste.
Siððan hie getealdon   wið þam teonhete
225 on þam forðherge   feðan twelfe
moderofra;   mægen wæs onhrered.
Wæs on anra gehwam   æðelan cynnes
alesen under lindum   leoda duguðe
on folcgetæl   fiftig cista;
230 hæfde cista gehwilc   cuðes werodes
garberendra,   guðfremmendra,
X hund geteled,   tireadigra.
Þæt wæs wiglic werod;   wace ne gretton
in þæt rincgetæl   ræswan herges,
235 þa þe for geoguðe   gyt ne mihton
under bordhreoðan   breostnet wera
wið flane feond   folmum werigean,
ne him bealubenne   gebiden hæfdon
ofer linde lærig,   licwunde swor,
240 gylpplegan gares.   Gamele ne moston,
hare heaðorincas,   hilde onþeon,

216 bemum] benum   226 moderofra] mode rofa   233 wace] wac

gif him modheapum   mægen swiðrade,
ac hie be wæstmum   on wig curon,
hu in leodscipe   læstan wolde
245 mod mid aran,   eac þan mægnes cræft,
garbeames feng.
   Þa wæs handrofra   here ætgædere,
fus forðwegas.   Fana up gerad,
beama beorhtost;   bidon ealle þa gen
250 hwonne siðboda   sæstreamum neah
leoht ofer lindum   lyftedoras bræc.
   Ahleop þa for hæleðum   hildecalla,
bald beohata,   bord up ahof,
heht þa folctogan   fyrde gestillan,
255 þenden modiges meðel   monige gehyrdon.
   Wolde reordigean   rices hyrde
ofer hereciste   halgan stefne,
werodes wisa   wurðmyndum spræc:
   "Ne beoð ge þy forhtran,   þeah þe Faraon brohte
260 sweordwigendra   side hergas,
eorla unrim!   Him eallum wile
mihtig drihten   þurh mine hand
to dæge þissum   dædlean gyfan,
þæt hie lifigende   leng ne moton
265 ægnian mid yrmðum   Israhela cyn.
Ne willað eow andrædan   deade feðan,
fæge ferhðlocan,   fyrst is æt ende
lænes lifes.   Eow is lar godes
abroden of breostum.   Ic on beteran ræd,
270 þæt ge gewurðien   wuldres aldor,
and eow liffrean   lissa bidde,
sigora gesynto,   þær ge siðien.
Þis is se ecea   Abrahames god,
frumsceafta frea,   se ðas fyrd wereð,
275 modig and mægenrof,   mid þære miclan hand."
   Hof ða for hergum   hlude stefne
lifigendra leod,   þa he to leodum spræc:

---

243 on] *Not in MS.*   248 gerad] rad   249 bidon] buton   253 ahof]
hof *with a prefixed above the line*   277 leod] þeod

"Hwæt, ge nu eagum to   on lociað,
folca leofost,   færwundra sum,
280 hu ic sylfa sloh   and þeos swiðre hand
grene tacne   garsecges deop.
Yð up færeð,   ofstum wyrceð
wæter wealfæsten.   Wegas syndon dryge,
haswe herestræta,   holm gerymed,
285 ealde staðolas,   þa ic ær ne gefrægn
ofer middangeard   men geferan,
fage feldas,   þa forð heonon
in ece tid   yðe þeahton,
sælde sægrundas.   Suðwind fornam
290 bæðweges blæst,   brim is areafod,
sand sæcir spaw.   Ic wat soð gere
þæt eow mihtig god   miltse gecyðde,
eorlas ærglade.   Ofest is selost
þæt ge of feonda   fæðme weorðen,
295 nu se agend   up arærde
reade streamas   in randgebeorh.
Syndon þa foreweallas   fægre gestepte,
wrætlicu wægfaru,   oð wolcna hrof."
      Æfter þam wordum   werod eall aras,
300 modigra mægen.   Mere stille bad.
Hofon herecyste   hwite linde,
segnas on sande.   Sæweall astah,
uplang gestod   wið Israhelum
andægne fyrst.   Wæs seo eorla gedriht
305 anes modes,
fæstum fæðmum   freoðowære heold.
Nalles hige gehyrdon   haliges lare,
siððan leofes leoþ   læste near
sweg swiðrode   and sances bland.
310   þa þæt feorðe cyn   fyrmest eode,
wod on wægstream,   wigan on heape,
ofer grenne grund,   Iudisc feða

283 wæter wealfæsten] wæter 7 wealfæsten   288 tid] *Not in MS.*   290
brim] bring   291 spaw] span

on orette   on uncuð gelad
for his mægwinum. Swa him mihtig god
315 þæs dægweorces deop lean forgeald,
siððan him gesælde sigorworca hreð,
þæt he ealdordom agan sceolde
ofer cynericu, cneowmaga blæd.
    Hæfdon him to segne, þa hie on sund stigon,
320 ofer bordhreoðan beacen aræred
in þam garheape, gyldenne leon,
drihtfolca mæst, deora cenost.
Be þam herewisan hynðo ne woldon
be him lifigendum lange þolian,
325 þonne hie to guðe garwudu rærdon
ðeoda ænigre. Þracu wæs on ore,
heard handplega, hægsteald modige
wæpna wælslihtes, wigend unforhte,
bilswaðu blodige, beadumægnes ræs,
330 grimhelma gegrind, þær Iudas for.
    Æfter þære fyrde flota modgade,
Rubenes sunu. Randas bæron
sæwicingas ofer sealtne mersc,
manna menio; micel angetrum
335 eode unforht. He his ealdordom
synnum aswefede, þæt he siðor for
on leofes last. Him on leodsceare
frumbearnes riht freobroðor oðþah,
ead and æðelo; he wæs gearu swa þeah.
340   Þær forð æfter him folca þryðum
sunu Simeones sweotum comon;
þridde þeodmægen (þufas wundon
ofer garfare) guðcyste onþrang
deawig sceaftum. Dægwoma becwom
345 ofer garsecge, godes beacna sum,
morgen mæretorht; mægen forð gewat.
    Þa þær folcmægen for æfter oðrum,

313 on orette on uncuð gelad] an on orette un cuð gelad   321 leon] leor
326 þracu] þraca   327 handplega] hand plega *with* hand *imperfectly
altered from* heard   334 manna] man   340 forð] *Not in MS.* 345 gar-
secge] gar secges

isernhergum. An wisode
mægenþrymmum mæst, þy he mære wearð,
350 on forðwegas folc æfter wolcnum,
cynn æfter cynne. Cuðe æghwilc
mægburga riht, swa him Moises bead,
eorla æðelo. Him wæs an fæder,
leof leodfruma, landriht geþah,
355 frod on ferhðe, freomagum leof.
Cende cneowsibbe cenra manna
heahfædera sum, halige þeode,
Israela cyn, onriht godes,
swa þæt orþancum ealde reccað
360 þa þe mægburge mæst gefrunon,
frumcyn feora, fæderæðelo gehwæs.
Niwe flodas Noe oferlað,
þrymfæst þeoden, mid his þrim sunum,
þone deopestan drencefloda
365 þara ðe gewurde on woruldrice.
Hæfde him on hreðre halige treowa;
forþon he gelædde ofer lagustreamas
maðmhorda mæst, mine gefræge.
On feorhgebeorh foldan hæfde
370 eallum eorðcynne ece lafe,
frumcneow gehwæs, fæder and moder
tuddorteondra, geteled rime
mismicelra þonne men cunnon,
snottor sæleoda. Eac þon sæda gehwilc
375 on bearm scipes beornas feredon,
þara þe under heofonum hæleð bryttigað.
Swa þæt wise men wordum secgað
þæt from Noe nigoða wære
fæder Abrahames on folctale.
380 Þæt is se Abraham se him engla god
naman niwan asceop; eac þon neah and feor
halige heapas in gehyld bebead,
werþeoda geweald; he on wræce lifde.

Siððan he gelædde   leofost feora
385 haliges hæsum;   heahlond stigon
sibgemagas,   on Seone beorh.
Wære hie þær fundon,   wuldor gesawon,
halige heahtreowe,   swa hæleð gefrunon.
Þær eft se snottra   sunu Dauides,
390 wuldorfæst cyning,   witgan larum
getimbrede   tempel gode,
alh haligne,   eorðcyninga
se wisesta   on woruldrice,
heahst and haligost,   hæleðum gefrægost,
395 mæst and mærost,   þara þe manna bearn,
fira æfter foldan,   folmum geworhte.
To þam meðelstede   magan gelædde
Abraham Isaac.   Adfyr onbran;
fyrst ferhðbana   no þy fægenra wæs.
400 Wolde þone lastweard   lige gesyllan,
in bælblyse   beorna selost,
his swæsne sunu   to sigetibre,
angan ofer eorðan   yrfelafe,
feores frofre,   ða he swa forð gebad,
405 leodum to lafe,   langsumne hiht.
He þæt gecyðde,   þa he þone cniht genam
fæste mid folmum,   folccuð geteag
ealde lafe,   (ecg grymetode),
þæt he him lifdagas   leofran ne wisse
410 þonne he hyrde   heofoncyninge.
Up aræmde   Abraham þa;
se eorl wolde slean   eaferan sinne
unweaxenne,   ecgum reodan
magan mid mece,   gif hine metod lete.
415 Ne wolde him beorht fæder   bearn ætniman,
halig tiber,   ac mid handa befeng.
Þa him styran cwom   stefn of heofonum,

<hr>

384 gelædde] gelifde *with* i *altered to* æ *and* d *added above the line after* d
392 alh] alhn   399 fægenra] fæg ra *with space between* g *and* r *for one letter*
405 langsumne] *Final* e *obscured by a defect in the MS.*   411 Abraham
þa] *Not in MS.*   413 ecgum] eagum   414 metod] god

wuldres hleoðor,   word æfter spræc:
"Ne sleh þu, Abraham,   þin agen bearn,
420 sunu mid sweorde!   Soð is gecyðed,
nu þin cunnode   cyning alwihta,
þæt þu wið waldend   wære heolde,
fæste treowe,   seo þe freoðo sceal
in lifdagum   lengest weorðan,
425 awa to aldre   unswiciendo.
Hu þearf mannes sunu   maran treowe?
Ne behwylfan mæg   heofon and eorðe
his wuldres word,   widdra and siddra
þonne befæðman mæge   foldan sceattas,
430 eorðan ymbhwyrft   and uprodor,
garsecges gin   and þeos geomre lyft.
He að swereð,   engla þeoden,
wyrda waldend   and wereda god,
soðfæst sigora,   þurh his sylfes lif,
435 þæt þines cynnes   and cneowmaga,
randwiggendra,   rim ne cunnon,
yldo ofer eorðan,   ealle cræfte
to gesecgenne   soðum wordum,
nymðe hwylc þæs snottor   in sefan weorðe
440 þæt he ana mæge   ealle geriman
stanas on eorðan,   steorran on heofonum,
sæbeorga sand,   sealte yða;
ac hie gesittað   be sæm tweonum
oð Egipte   incaðeode
445 land Cananea,   leode þine,
freobearn fæder,   folca selost."
              *   *   *
Folc wæs afæred,   flodegsa becwom
gastas geomre,   geofon deaðe hweop.
Wæron beorhhliðu   blode bestemed,
450 holm heolfre spaw,   hream wæs on yðum,
wæter wæpna ful,   wælmist astah.
Wæron Egypte   eft oncyrde,
flugon forhtigende,   fær ongeton,

428 widdra] id *on an erasure*   432 He] ne   442 sand] sund

woldon herebleaðe   hamas findan,
455 gylp wearð gnornra.   Him ongen genap
atol yða gewealc,   ne ðær ænig becwom
herges to hame,   ac behindan beleac
wyrd mid wæge.   Þær ær wegas lagon,
mere modgode,   mægen wæs adrenced.
460 Streamas stodon,   storm up gewat
heah to heofonum,   herewopa mæst.
Laðe cyrmdon,   (lyft up geswearc),
fægum stæfnum,   flod blod gewod.
Randbyrig wæron rofene,   rodor swipode
465 meredeaða mæst,   modige swulton,
cyningas on corðre,   cyre swiðrode
sæs æt ende.   Wigbord scinon
heah ofer hæleðum,   holmweall astah,
merestream modig.   Mægen wæs on cwealme
470 fæste gefeterod,   forðganges weg
searwum æsæled,   sand basnodon,
witodre fyrde,   hwonne waðema stream,
sincalda sæ,   sealtum yðum
æflastum gewuna   ece staðulas,
475 nacud nydboda,   neosan come,
fah feðegast,   se ðe feondum geneop.
Wæs seo hæwene lyft   heolfre geblanden,
brim berstende   blodegesan hweop,
sæmanna sið,   oðþæt soð metod
480 þurh Moyses hand   modge rymde,
wide wæðde,   wælfæðmum sweop.
Flod famgode,   fæge crungon,
lagu land gefeol,   lyft wæs onhrered,
wicon weallfæsten,   wægas burston,
485 multon meretorras,   þa se mihtiga sloh
mid halige hand,   heofonrices weard,
on werbeamas.   Wlance ðeode
ne mihton forhabban   helpendra pað,
merestreames mod,   ac he manegum gesceod
490 gyllende gryre.   Garsecg wedde,

470 weg] nep   471 basnodon] barenodon   487 on] *Not in MS.*

up ateah, on sleap. Egesan stodon,
weollon wælbenna. Witrod gefeol
heah of heofonum   handweorc godes,
famigbosma   flodwearde sloh,
495 unhleowan wæg,   alde mece,
þæt ðy deaðdrepe   drihte swæfon,
synfullra sweot. Sawlum lunnon
fæste befarene,   flodblac here,
siððan hie on bugon   brun yppinge,
500 modewæga mæst. Mægen eall gedreas
ða gedrencte wæron   dugoð Egypta,
Faraon mid his folcum. He onfond hraðe,
siððan grund gestah   godes andsaca,
þæt wæs mihtigra   mereflodes weard;
505 wolde heorufæðmum   hilde gesceadan,
yrre and egesfull. Egyptum wearð
þæs dægweorces   deop lean gesceod,
forðam þæs heriges   ham eft ne com
ealles ungrundes   ænig to lafe,
510 þætte sið heora   secgan moste,
bodigean æfter burgum   bealospella mæst,
hordwearda hryre,   hæleða cwenum,
ac þa mægenþreatas   meredeað geswealh,
spelbodan eac. Se ðe sped ahte,
515 ageat gylp wera. Hie wið god wunnon!
    þanon Israhelum   ece rædas
on merehwearfe   Moyses sægde,
heahþungen wer,   halige spræce,
deop ærende. Dægword nemnað
520 swa gyt werðeode,   on gewritum findað
doma gehwilcne,   þara ðe him drihten bebead
on þam siðfate   soðum wordum,
gif onlucan wile   lifes wealhstod,
beorht in breostum,   banhuses weard,

492 witrod] wit rod   499 on bugon] on bogum   501 gedrencte] þegedrecte   wæron] Not in MS.   502 onfond] on feond   503 grund] Not
in MS.   505 heorufæðmum] huru fæðmum   510 heora] heoro   514
eac] Not in MS.   517 Moyses] moyse   519 Dægword] dæg weorc

525 ginfæsten god   gastes cægon.
    Run bið gerecenod,   ræd forð gæð,
    hafað wislicu   word on fæðme,
    wile meagollice   modum tæcan
    þæt we gesne ne syn   godes þeodscipes,
530 metodes miltsa.   He us ma onlyhð,
    nu us boceras   beteran secgað
    lengran lifwynna.   þis is læne dream,
    wommum awyrged,   wreccum alyfed,
    earmra anbid.   Eðellease
535 þysne gystsele   gihðum healdað,
    murnað on mode,   manhus witon
    fæst under foldan,   þær bið fyr and wyrm,
    open ece scræf.   Yfela gehwylces
    swa nu regnþeofas   rice dælað,
540 yldo oððe ærdeað.   Eftwyrd cymð,
    mægenþrymma mæst   ofer middangeard,
    dæg dædum fah.   Drihten sylfa
    on þam meðelstede   manegum demeð,
    þonne he soðfæstra   sawla lædeð,
545 eadige gastas,   on uprodor,
    þær is leoht and lif,   eac þon lissa blæd;
    dugoð on dreame   drihten herigað,
    weroda wuldorcyning,   to widan feore.
      Swa reordode   ræda gemyndig
550 manna mildost,   mihtum swiðed,
    hludan stefne;   here stille bad
    witodes willan,   wundor ongeton,
    modiges muðhæl;   he to mænegum spræc:
      "Micel is þeos menigeo,   mægenwisa trum,
555 fullesta mæst,   se ðas fare lædeð;
    hafað us on Cananea   cyn gelyfed
    burh and beagas,   brade rice;
    wile nu gelæstan   þæt he lange gehet
    mid aðsware,   engla drihten,
560 in fyrndagum   fæderyncynne,

532 lifwynna] lyft wynna   535 healdað] healdeð   538 gehwylces]
gehylces   546 is] *Not in MS.*   556 us on] ufon

gif ge gehealdað   halige lare,
þæt ge feonda gehwone   forð ofergangað,
gesittað sigerice   be sæm tweonum,
beorselas beorna.   Bið eower blæd micel!"
565   Æfter þam wordum   werod wæs on salum,
sungon sigebyman,   (segnas stodon),
on fægerne sweg;   folc wæs on lande,
hæfde wuldres beam   werud gelæded,
halige heapas,   on hild godes.
570 Life gefegon   þa hie oðlæded hæfdon
feorh of feonda dome,   þeah ðe hie hit frecne geneðdon,
weras under wætera hrofas.   Gesawon hie þær weallas
standan,
ealle him brimu blodige þuhton,   þurh þa heora beado-
searo wægon.
Hreðdon hildespelle,   siððan hie þam herge wiðforon;
575 hofon hereþreatas   hlude stefne,
for þam dædweorce   drihten heredon,
weras wuldres sang;   wif on oðrum,
folcsweota mæst,   fyrdleoð golan
aclum stefnum,   eallwundra fela.
580   Þa wæs eðfynde   Afrisc neowle
on geofones staðe   golde geweorðod.
Handa hofon   halswurðunge,
bliðe wæron,   bote gesawon,
heddon herereafes,   hæft wæs onsæled.
585 Ongunnon sælafe   segnum dælan
on yðlafe,   ealde madmas,
reaf and randas.   Heo on riht sceodon
gold and godweb,   Iosepes gestreon,
wera wuldorgesteald.   Werigend lagon
590 on deaðstede,   drihtfolca mæst.

590 gefegon] gefeon   574 herge] *Not in MS.*   578 golan] galan   580
neowle] meowle   587 sceodon] sceo   590 mæst] mæ

DANIEL

DANIEL

Gefrægn ic Hebreos   eadge lifgean
in Hierusalem,   goldhord dælan,
cyningdom habban,   swa him gecynde wæs,
siððan þurh metodes mægen   on Moyses hand
5 wearð wig gifen,   wigena mænieo,
and hie of Egyptum   ut aforon,
mægene micle.   Þæt wæs modig cyn!
  Þenden hie þy rice   rædan moston,
burgum wealdan,   wæs him beorht wela.
10 Þenden þæt folc mid him   hiera fæder wære
healdan woldon,   wæs him hyrde god,
heofonrices weard,   halig drihten,
wuldres waldend.   Se ðam werude geaf
mod and mihte,   metod alwihta,
15 þæt hie oft fela folca   feore gesceodon,
heriges helmum,   þara þe him hold ne wæs,
oðþæt hie wlenco anwod   æt winþege
deofoldædum,   druncne geðohtas.
  Þa hie æcræftas   ane forleton,
20 metodes mægenscipe,   swa no man scyle
his gastes lufan   wið gode dælan.
  Þa geseah ic þa gedriht   in gedwolan hweorfan,
Israhela cyn   unriht don,
wommas wyrcean.   Þæt wæs weorc gode!
25 Oft he þam leodum   to lare sende,
heofonrices weard,   halige gastas,
þa þam werude   wisdom budon.
Hie þære snytro   soð gelyfdon
lytle hwile,   oðþæt hie langung beswac
30 eorðan dreamas   eces rædes,
þæt hie æt siðestan   sylfe forleton
drihtnes domas,   curon deofles cræft.

9 wealdan] weoldon   22 þa] þe   25 to] *Not in MS.*   29 hie] me

þa wearð reðemod   rices ðeoden,
unhold þeodum   þam þe æhte geaf.
35 Wisde him æt frymðe,   ða ðe on fruman ær ðon
wæron mancynnes   metode dyrust,
dugoða dyrust,   drihtne leofost;
herepað tæhte   to þære hean byrig,
eorlum elðeodigum,   on eðelland
40 þær Salem stod   searwum afæstnod,
weallum geweorðod.   To þæs witgan foron,
Caldea cyn,   to ceastre forð,
þær Israela   æhta wæron,
bewrigene mid weorcum;   to þam þæt werod gefor,
45 mægenþreat mære,   manbealwes georn.
Awehte þone wælnið   wera aldorfrea,
Babilones brego,   on his burhstede,
Nabochodonossor,   þurh niðhete,
þæt he secan ongan   sefan gehygdum
50 hu he Israelum   eaðost meahte
þurh gromra gang   guman oðþringan.
Gesamnode þa   suðan and norðan
wælhreow werod,   and west foran
herige hæðencyninga   to þære hean byrig.
55 Israela   eðelweardas
hæfdon lufan, lifwelan,   þenden hie let metod.
þa ic eðan gefrægn   ealdfeonda cyn
winburh wera.   þa wigan ne gelyfdon,
bereafodon þa receda wuldor   readan golde,
60 since and seolfre,   Salomones templ.
Gestrudan gestreona   under stanhliðum,
swilc eall swa þa eorlas   agan sceoldon,
oðþæt hie burga gehwone   abrocen hæfdon,
þara þe þam folce   to friðe stodon.
65 Gehlodon him to huðe   hordwearda gestreon,
feoh and frætwa,   swilc þær funden wæs,
and þa mid þam æhtum   eft siðedon,

---

34 þeodum] þeoden   35 Wisde] wisðe   38 herepað] herepoð   tæhte]
Not in MS.   53 foran] faran   56 hæfdon] *Not in MS.*   57 ic] eac
66 feoh] fea   frætwa] freos

and gelæddon eac   on langne sið
Israela cyn,   on eastwegas
70 to Babilonia,   beorna unrim,
under hand hæleð   hæðenum deman.
Nabochodonossor   him on nyd dyde
Israela bearn   ofer ealle lufen,
wæpna lafe   to weorcþeowum.
75 Onsende þa   sinra þegna
worn þæs werudes   west toferan,
þæt him þara leoda   land geheolde,
eðne eðel,   æfter Ebreum.
   Het þa secan   sine gerefan
80 geond Israela   earme lafe,
hwilc þære geogoðe   gleawost wære
boca bebodes,   þe þær brungen wæs.
Wolde þæt þa cnihtas   cræft leornedon,
þæt him snytro on sefan   secgan mihte,
85 nales ðy þe he þæt moste   oððe gemunan wolde
þæt he þara gifena   gode þancode
þe him þær to duguðe   drihten scyrede.
Þa hie þær fundon   þry freagleawe
æðele cnihtas   and æfæste,
90 ginge and gode   in godsæde;
an wæs Annanias,   oðer Azarias,
þridda Misael,   metode gecorene.
Þa þry comon   to þeodne foran,
hearde and higeþancle,   þær se hæðena sæt,
95 cyning corðres georn,   in Caldea byrig.
Þa hie þam wlancan   wisdom sceoldon,
weras Ebrea,   wordum cyðan,
higecræft heane,   þurh halig mod,
þa se beorn bebead,   Babilone weard,
100 swiðmod cyning,   sinum þegnum,
þæt þa frumgaras   be feore dæde,
þæt þam gengum þrym   gad ne wære
wiste ne wæde   in woruldlife.

73 ofer] otor   76 west] wes   77 leoda] leode   88 þry] to   97 cyðan]
cyðdon

þa wæs breme   Babilone weard,
105 mære and modig   ofer middangeard,
egesful ylda bearnum.   No he æ fremede,
ac in oferhygde   æghwæs lifde.
þa þam folctogan   on frumslæpe,
siððan to reste gehwearf   rice þeoden,
110 com on sefan hwurfan   swefnes woma,
hu woruld wære   wundrum geteod,
ungelic yldum   oð edsceafte.
Wearð him on slæpe   soð gecyðed,
þætte rices gehwæs   reðe sceolde gelimpan,
115 eorðan dreamas,   ende wurðan.
þa onwoc wulfheort,   se ær wingal swæf,
Babilone weard.   Næs him bliðe hige,
ac him sorh astah,   swefnes woma.
No he gemunde   þæt him meted wæs.
120   Het þa tosomne   sinra leoda
þa wiccungdom   widost bæron,
frægn þa ða mænigeo   hwæt hine gemætte,
þenden reordberend   reste wunode.
Wearð he on þam egesan   acol worden,
125 þa he ne wisse   word ne angin
swefnes sines;   het him secgan þeah.
þa him unbliðe   andswaredon
deofolwitgan   (næs him dom gearu
to asecganne   swefen cyninge):
130   "Hu magon we swa dygle,   drihten, ahicgan
on sefan þinne,   hu ðe swefnede,
oððe wyrda gesceaft   wisdom bude,
gif þu his ærest ne meaht   or areccan?"
þa him unbliðe   andswarode
135 wulfheort cyning,   witgum sinum:
    "Næron ge swa eacne   ofer ealle men
modgeþances   swa ge me sægdon,
and þæt gecwædon,   þæt ge cuðon
mine aldorlege,   swa me æfter wearð,

107 æghwæs] æghæs *with* w *added above the line after* h   119 meted] metod
138 gecwædon] gcwædon

140 oððe ic furðor   findan sceolde.
    Nu ge mætinge   mine ne cunnon,
    þa þe me for werode   wisdom berað.
    Ge sweltað deaðe,   nymþe ic dom wite
    soðan swefnes,   þæs min sefa myndgað.''
145   Ne meahte þa seo mænigeo   on þam meðelstede
    þurh witigdom   wihte aþencean
    ne ahicgan,   þa hit forhæfed gewearð
    þætte hie sædon   swefn cyninge,
    wyrda gerynu,   oðþæt witga cwom,
150 Daniel to dome,   se wæs drihtne gecoren,
    snotor and soðfæst,   in þæt seld gangan.
    Se wæs ordfruma   earmre lafe
    þære þe þam hæðenan   hyran sceolde.
    Him god sealde   gife of heofnum
155 þurh hleoðorcwyde   haliges gastes,
    þæt him engel godes   eall asægde
    swa his mandrihten   gemæted wearð.
     Ða eode Daniel,   þa dæg lyhte,
    swefen reccan   sinum frean,
160 sægde him wislice   wereda gesceafte,
    þætte sona ongeat   swiðmod cyning
    ord and ende   þæs þe him ywed wæs.
    Ða hæfde Daniel   dom micelne,
    blæd in Babilonia   mid bocerum,
165 siððan he gesæde   swefen cyninge,
    þæt he ær for fyrenum   onfon ne meahte,
    Babilonie weard,   in his breostlocan.
    No hwæðere þæt Daniel   gedon mihte
    þæt he wolde metodes   mihte gelyfan,
170 ac he wyrcan ongan   weoh on felda
    þam þe deormode   Diran heton,
    se wæs on ðære ðeode   ðe swa hatte,
    bresne Babilonige.   Þære burge weard
    anne manlican   ofer metodes est,
175 gyld of golde,   gumum arærde,

141 Nu] Ne   142 berað] bereð   152 wæs] þæs   170 weoh] woh

for þam þe gleaw ne wæs,   gumrices weard,
reðe and rædleas,   riht

    * * *

 Þa wearð hæleða hlyst   þa hleoðor cwom
byman stefne   ofer burhware.
180 Þa hie for þam cumble   on cneowum sæton,
onhnigon to þam herige   hæðne þeode,
wurðedon wihgyld,   ne wiston wræstran ræd,
efndon unrihtdom,   swa hyra aldor dyde,
mane gemenged,   mode gefrecnod.
185 Fremde folcmægen,   swa hyra frea ærest,
unræd efnde,   (him þæs æfter becwom
yfel endelean),   unriht dyde.
 Þær þry wæron   on þæs þeodnes byrig,
eorlas Israela,   þæt hie a noldon
190 hyra þeodnes dom   þafigan onginnan,
þæt hie to þam beacne   gebedu rærde,
ðeah ðe ðær on herige   byman sungon.
Ða wæron æðelum god   Abrahames bearn,
wæron wærfæste,   wiston drihten
195 ecne uppe,   ælmihtigne.
 Cnihtas cynegode   cuð gedydon,
þæt hie him þæt gold   to gode noldon
habban ne healdan,   ac þone hean cyning,
gasta hyrde,   ðe him gife sealde.
200 Oft hie to bote   balde gecwædon
þæt hie þæs wiges   wihte ne rohton,
ne hie to þam gebede   mihte gebædon
hæðen heriges wisa,   þæt hie þider hweorfan wolden,
guman to þam gyldnan gylde,   þe he him to gode ge-
             teode.
205 Þegnas þeodne sægdon   þæt hie þære geþeahte wæron,
hæftas hearan,   in þisse hean byrig,
þa þis hegan ne willað,   ne þysne wig wurðigean,
þe ðu þe to wuldre   wundrum teodest.
 Ða him bolgenmod   Babilone weard

---

193 god] *Not in MS.*   195 ælmihtigne] ælmihtne   208 wuldre] *Not
in MS.*

210 yrre andswarode, eorlum onmælde
    grimme þam gingum, and geocre oncwæð,
    þæt hie gegnunga gyldan sceolde
    oððe þrowigean þreanied micel,
    frecne fyres wylm, nymðe hie friðes wolde
215 wilnian to þam wyrrestan, weras Ebrea,
    guman to þam golde, þe he him to gode teode.
    Noldon þeah þa hyssas hyran larum
    in hige hæðnum. Hogedon georne
    þæt æ godes ealle gelæste,
220 and ne awacodon wereda drihtne,
    ne þan mæ gehwurfe in hæðendom,
    ne hie to facne freoðo wilnedan,
    þeah þe him se bitera deað geboden wære.
    Þa wearð yrre anmod cyning, het he ofn onhætan
225 to cwale cnihta feorum forðam þe hie his cræftas
                                            onsocon.
    Þa he wæs gegleded, swa he grimmost mihte,
    frecne fyres lige, þa he þyder folc samnode,
    and gebindan het, Babilone weard,
    grim and gealhmod, godes spelbodan.
230 Het þa his scealcas scufan þa hyssas
    in bælblyse, beornas geonge.
    Gearo wæs se him geoce gefremede; þeah þe hie swa
                                            grome nydde
    in fæðm fyres lige, hwæðere heora feorh generede
    mihtig metodes weard. Swa þæt mænige gefrunon,
235 halige him þær help geteode, sende him of hean rodore
    god, gumena weard, gast þone halgan.
    Engel in þone ofn innan becwom þær hie þæt aglac
                                            drugon,
    freobearn fæðmum beþeahte under þam fyrenan hrofe.
    Ne mihte þeah heora wlite gewemman owiht
240 wylm þæs wæfran liges, þa hie se waldend nerede.
    Hreohmod wæs se hæðena þeoden, het hie hraðe
                                            bærnan.

221 gehwurfe] gen hwyrfe   226 gegleded] gelæded   227 he] þe *with* þ
altered to h   239 owiht] *Not in MS.*

Æled wæs ungescead micel.   Þa wæs se ofen onhæted,
isen eall ðurhgleded.   Hine ðær esnas mænige
wurpon wudu on innan,   swa him wæs on wordum
                                gedemed;

245 bæron brandas on bryne   blacan fyres,
    (wolde wulfheort cyning   wall onsteallan,
    iserne ymb æfæste),   oðþæt up gewat
    lig ofer leofum   and þurh lust gesloh
    micle mare   þonne gemet wære.

250 Ða se lig gewand   on laðe men,
    hæðne of halgum.   Hyssas wæron
    bliðemode,   burnon scealcas
    ymb ofn utan,   alet gehwearf
    teonfullum on teso.   Ðær to geseah

255 Babilone brego.   Bliðe wæron
    eorlas Ebrea,   ofestum heredon
    drihten on dreame,   dydon swa hie cuðon
    ofne on innan,   aldre generede.
    Guman glædmode   god wurðedon,

260 under þæs fæðme   þe geflymed wearð
    frecne fyres hæto.   Freobearn wurdon
    alæten liges gange,   ne hie him þær lað gedydon.
    Næs him se sweg to sorge   ðon ma þe sunnan scima,
    ne se bryne beot mæcgum   þe in þam beote wæron,

265 ac þæt fyr fyr scyde   to ðam þe ða scylde worhton,
    hwearf on þa hæðenan hæftas   fram þam halgan cnihton,
    werigra wlite minsode,   þa ðe ðy worce gefægon.
       Geseah ða swiðmod cyning,   ða he his sefan ontreowde,
    wundor on wite agangen;   him þæt wræclic þuhte.

270 Hyssas hale hwurfon   in þam hatan ofne,
    ealle æfæste ðry;   him eac þær wæs
    an on gesyhðe,   engel ælmihtiges.
    Him þær on ofne   owiht ne derede,
    ac wæs þær inne   ealles gelicost

275 efne þonne on sumera   sunne scineð,

246 onsteallan] onstealle   255 Bliðe] biliðe   264 þe] þen   265 þe] we
266 hwearf on] hweorfon   268 cyning] cynig   273 on ofne] *Not in MS.*

and deaw dryge   on dæge weorðeð,
winde geondsawen.   þæt wæs wuldres god
þe hie generede   wið þam niðhete.
  Ða Azarias   ingeþancum
280 hleoðrade halig   þurh hatne lig,
dreag dæda georn,   drihten herede,
wer womma leas,   and þa word acwæð:
  "Metod alwihta, hwæt!   þu eart mihtum swið
niðas to nergenne.   Is þin nama mære,
285 wlitig and wuldorfæst   ofer werðeode.
Siendon þine domas   in daga gehwam
soðe and geswiðde   and gesigefæste,
swa þu eac sylfa eart.
Syndon þine willan   on woruldspedum
290 rihte and gerume,   rodora waldend.
Geoca user georne nu,   gasta scyppend,
and þurh hyldo help,   halig drihten,
nu we þec for þreaum   and for ðeonydum
and for eaðmedum   arna biddað,
295 lige belegde.   We ðæs lifgende
worhton on worulde,   eac ðon wom dyde
user yldran;   for oferhygdum
bræcon bebodo   burhsittende,
had oferhogedon   halgan lifes.
300 Siendon we towrecene   geond widne grund,
heapum tohworfene,   hyldelease;
is user lif   geond landa fela
fracoð and gefræge   folca manegum,
þa usic bewræcon   to þæs wyrrestan
305 eorðcyninga   æhta gewealde,
on hæft heorugrimra,   and we nu hæðenra
þeowned þoliað.   þæs þe þanc sie,
wereda wuldorcyning,   þæt þu us þas wrace teodest.
  Ne forlet þu usic ane,   ece drihten,
310 for ðam miltsum   ðe ðec men hligað,

276 dryge] drias   281 dreag] *Not in MS.*   292 hyldo] *Not in MS.*
293 we] *Added above the line between* nu *and* þec   298 burhsittende]
burhsittendum   304 usic] us ec   309 ane] ana

and for ðam treowum þe þu, tirum fæst,
niða nergend, genumen hæfdest
to Abrahame and to Isaace
and to Iacobe, gasta scyppend.

315 Þu him þæt gehete þurh hleoðorcwyde,
þæt þu hyra frumcyn in fyrndagum
ican wolde, þætte æfter him
on cneorissum cenned wurde,
and seo mænigeo mære wære,

320 had to hebbanne swa heofonsteorran
bebugað bradne hwyrft, oððe brimfaroþes,
sæfaroða sand, geond sealtne wæg
in eare grynde,ð þæt his unrim a
in wintra worn wurðan sceolde.

325 Fyl nu frumspræce, ðeah heora fea lifigen!
Wlitiga þinne wordcwyde and þin wuldor on us!
Gecyð cræft and miht þæt þa Caldeas
and folca fela gefrigen habbað,
ða þe under heofenum hæðene lifigeað,

330 and þæt þu ana eart ece drihten,
weroda waldend, woruldgesceafta,
sigora settend, soðfæst metod!"
    Swa se halga wer hergende wæs
metodes miltse and his mihta sped

335 rehte þurh reorde. Ða of roderum wæs
engel ælbeorht ufan onsended,
wlitescyne wer on his wuldorhaman,
se him cwom to frofre and to feorhnere
mid lufan and mid lisse. Se ðone lig tosceaf,

340 halig and heofonbeorht, hatan fyres,
tosweop hine and toswende þurh þa swiðan miht,
ligges leoman, þæt hyra lice ne wæs
owiht geegled, ac he on andan sloh
fyr on feondas for fyrendædum.

345 Þa wæs on þam ofne, þær se engel becwom,

320 had] hat   321 oððe] oð þ *for* oð þæt   brimfaroþes] brim faro . þæs
323 in] me   eare] are   unrim a] unrima   327 þæt þa] þ þ   342
leoman] leoma   hyra] hyre

windig and wynsum, wedere gelicost
þonne hit on sumeres tid sended weorðeð
dropena drearung on dæges hwile,
wearmlic wolcna scur. Swylc bið wedera cyst,
350 swylc wæs on þam fyre frean mihtum
halgum to helpe. Wearð se hata lig
todrifen and todwæsced þær þa dædhwatan
geond þone ofen eodon, and se engel mid,
feorh nerigende, se ðær feorða wæs,
355 Annanias and Azarias
and Misael. Þær þa modhwatan
þry on geðancum ðeoden heredon,
bædon bletsian bearn Israela
eall landgesceaft ecne drihten,
360 ðeoda waldend. Swa hie þry cwædon,
modum horsce, þurh gemæne word:
    "Ðe gebletsige, bylywit fæder,
woruldcræfta wlite and weorca gehwilc!
Heofonas and englas, and hluttor wæter,
365 þa ðe ofer roderum on rihtne gesceaft
wuniað in wuldre, ða þec wurðiað!
And þec, ælmihtig, ealle gesceafte,
rodorbeorhtan tunglu, þa þe ryne healdað,
sunna and mona, sundor anra gehwilc
370 herige in hade! And heofonsteorran,
deaw and deor scur, ða ðec domige!
And þec, mihtig god, gastas lofige!
Byrnende fyr and beorht sumor
nergend hergað! Niht somod and dæg,
375 and þec landa gehwilc, leoht and þeostro,
herige on hade, somod hat and ceald!
And þec, frea mihtig, forstas and snawas,
winterbiter weder and wolcenfaru,
lofige on lyfte! And þec ligetu,
380 blace, berhtmhwate, þa þec bletsige!
Eall eorðan grund, ece drihten,
hyllas and hrusan and hea beorgas,

352 dædhwatan] *With second* a *altered from* e   365 ofer] of

sealte sæwægas,   soðfæst metod,
eastream yða   and upcyme,
385 wætersprync wylla,   ða ðec wurðiað!
Hwalas ðec herigað,   and hefonfugolas,
lyftlacende,   þa ðe lagostreamas,
wæterscipe wecgað!   And wildu deor
and neata gehwilc   naman bletsie!
390 And manna bearn   modum lufiað,
and þec Israela,   æhta scyppend,
herigað in hade,   herran sinne!
And þec haligra   heortan cræftas,
soðfæstra gehwæs   sawle and gastas,
395 lofiað liffrean,   lean sellende
eallum eadmodum,   ece drihten!
Annanias ðec   and Adzarias
and Misael   metod domige
breostgeðancum!   We þec bletsiað,
400 frea folca gehwæs,   fæder ælmihtig,
soð sunu metodes,   sawla nergend,
hæleða helpend,   and þec, halig gast,
wurðiað in wuldre,   witig drihten!
We ðec herigað,   halig drihten,
405 and gebedum bremað!   Þu gebletsad eart,
gewurðad wideferhð   ofer worulde hrof,
heahcyning heofones,   halgum mihtum,
lifes leohtfruma,   ofer landa gehwilc!"
    Ða þæt ehtode   ealdor þeode,
410 Nabochodonossor,   wið þam nehstum
folcgesiðum: "þæt eower fela geseah,
þeode mine,   þæt we þry sendon,
geboden to bæle   in byrnende
fyres leoman.   Nu ic þær feower men
415 geseo to soðe,   nales me sefa leogeð."
    Ða cwæð se ðe wæs   cyninges ræswa,
wis and wordgleaw: "þæt is wundra sum

392 sinne] þinne   396 eadmodum] *Not in MS.*   403 wurðiað] wurðað
406 wideferhð] ferhð   409 ealdor] ealde   410 nehstum] nehstam
412 þeode] þeoden   sendon] syndon   415 sefa] selfa

þæt we ðær eagum   on lociað.

Geðenc, ðeoden min,   þine gerysna!

420 Ongyt georne   hwa þa gyfe sealde

gingum gædelingum!   Hie god herigað,

anne ecne,   and ealles him

be naman gehwam   on neod sprecað,

þanciað þrymmes   þristum wordum,

425 cweðað he sie ana   ælmihtig god,

witig wuldorcyning,   worlde and heofona.

Aban þu þa beornas,   brego Caldea,

ut of ofne.   Nis hit owihtes god

þæt hie sien on þam laðe   leng þonne þu þurfe."

430   Het þa se cyning to him   cnihtas gangan.

Hyssas hearde   hyrdon lare,

cyrdon cynegode   swa hie gecyðde wæron,

hwurfon hæleð geonge   to þam hæðenan foran.

Wæron þa bende forburnene   þe him on banum lagon,

435 laðsearo leoda cyninges,   and hyra lice geborgen.

Næs hyra wlite gewemmed,   ne nænig wroht on hrægle,

ne feax fyre beswæled,   ac hie on friðe drihtnes

of ðam grimman gryre   glade treddedon,

gleawmode guman,   on gastes hyld.

440   Ða gewat se engel up   secan him ece dreamas

on heanne hrof   heofona rices,

heh þegn and hold   halgum metode.

Hæfde on þam wundre gewurðod   ðe þa gewyrhto ahton.

Hyssas heredon drihten   for þam hæðenan folce,

445 septon hie soðcwidum   and him sædon fela

soðra tacna,   oðþæt he sylfa gelyfde

þæt se wære mihta waldend   se ðe hie of ðam mirce

generede.

Gebead þa se bræsna   Babilone weard

swiðmod sinum leodum,   þæt se wære his aldre scyldig,

450 se ðæs onsoce   þætte soð wære

mære mihta waldend,   se hie of þam morðre alysde.

Agæf him þa his leoda lafe   þe þær gelædde wæron

---

421 gædelingum] gædelinge   434 bende] benne   444 heredon] heredo

445 septon] stepton

on æht ealdfeondum,   þæt hie are hæfdon.

Wæs heora blæd in Babilone,   siððan hie þone bryne
                                                fandedon,
455 dom wearð æfter duguðe gecyðed,   siððan hie drihtne
                                                gehyrdon.

Wæron hyra rædas rice,   siððan hie rodera waldend,
halig heofonrices weard,   wið þone hearm gescylde.

   þa ic secan gefrægn   soðum wordum,
siððan he wundor onget,
460 Babilone weard,   þurh fyres bryne,
hu þa hyssas þry   hatan ofnes,
færgryre fyres,   oferfaren hæfdon.

Wylm þurhwodon,   swa him wiht ne sceod
grim gleda nið,   godes spelbodan,
465 frecnan fyres,   ac him frið drihtnes
wið þæs egesan gryre   aldor gescylde.

   Ða se ðeoden ongan   geðinges wyrcan;
het þa tosomne   sine leode,
and þa on þam meðle   ofer menigo bebead
470 wyrd gewordene   and wundor godes,
þætte on þam cnihtum   gecyðed wæs:

   "Onhicgað nu   halige mihte,
wise wundor godes!   We gesawon
þæt he wið cwealme gebearh   cnihtum on ofne,
475 lacende lig,   þam þe his lof bæron;
forþam he is ana   ece drihten,
dema ælmihtig,   se ðe him dom forgeaf,
spowende sped,   þam þe his spel berað.

Forðon witigað   þurh wundor monig
480 halgum gastum   þe his hyld curon.

Cuð is þæt me Daniel   dyglan swefnes
soð gesæde,   þæt ær swiðe oðstod
manegum on mode   minra leoda,
forþam ælmihtig   eacenne gast
485 in sefan sende,   snyttro cræftas."

453 on æht] 7 nahte   464 godes] ac godes   477 dema] *Not in MS.*
482 soð] soðe   oðstod] oðstod, *a letter erased and deleted, and* o *written
above*

Swa wordum spræc   werodes ræswa,
Babilone weard,   siððan he beacen onget,
swutol tacen godes.   No þy sel dyde,
ac þam æðelinge   oferhygd gesceod,
490 wearð him hyrra hyge   and on heortan geðanc
mara on modsefan   þonne gemet wære,
oðþæt hine mid nyde   nyðor asette
metod ælmihtig,   swa he manegum deð
þara þe þurh oferhyd   up astigeð.
495   Þa him wearð on slæpe   swefen ætywed,
Nabochodonossor;   him þæt neh gewearð.
Þuhte him þæt on foldan   fægre stode
wudubeam wlitig,   se wæs wyrtum fæst,
beorht on blædum.   Næs he bearwe gelic,
500 ac he hlifode   to heofontunglum,
swilce he oferfæðmde   foldan sceatas,
ealne middangeard,   oð merestreamas,
twigum and telgum.   Ðær he to geseah,
þuhte him þæt se wudubeam   wilddeor scylde,
505 ane æte   eallum heolde,
swylce fuglas eac   heora feorhnere
on þæs beames   bledum name.
Ðuhte him þæt engel   ufan of roderum
stigan cwome   and stefne abead,
510 torhtan reorde.   Het þæt treow ceorfan
and þa wildan deor   on weg fleon,
swylce eac þa fugolas,   þonne his fyll come.
Het þonne besnædan   seolfes blædum,
twigum and telgum,   and þeh tacen wesan,
515 wunian wyrtruman   þæs wudubeames
eorðan fæstne,   oðþæt eft cyme
grene bleda,   þonne god sylle.
Het eac gebindan   beam þone miclan
ærenum clammum   and isernum,
520 and gesæledne   in susl don,
þæt his mod wite   þæt migtigra

491 mara on] maran   500 hlifode] hlfode   511 wildan deor] wildeor
515 wyrtruman] wyr trumam

wite wealdeð   þonne he him wið mæge.
   Þa of slæpe onwoc,   (swefn wæs æt ende),
eorðlic æðeling,   him þæs egesa stod,
525 gryre fram ðam gaste   ðe þyder god sende.
Het þa tosomne   sine leode,
folctogan feran,   frægn ofer ealle
swiðmod cyning   hwæt þæt swefen bude,
nalles þy he wende   þæt hie hit wiston,
530 ac he cunnode   hu hie cweðan woldon.
   Ða wæs to ðam dome   Daniel haten,
godes spelboda.   Him wæs gæst geseald,
halig of heofonum,   se his hyge trymede.
On þam drihtenweard   deopne wisse
535 sefan sidne geþanc   and snytro cræft,
wisne wordcwide.   Oft he wundor manig,
metodes mihta,   for men ætbær.
Þa he secgan ongan   swefnes woman,
heahheort and hæðen   heriges wisa,
540 ealne þone egesan   þe him eowed wæs.
Bæd hine areccan   hwæt seo run bude,
hofe haligu word   and in hige funde
to gesecganne   soðum wordum
hwæt se beam bude   þe he blican geseah,
545 and him witgode   wyrda geþingu.
   He ða swigode,   hwæðere soð ongeat,
Daniel æt þam dome,   þæt his drihten wæs,
gumena aldor,   wið god scyldig.
Wandode se wisa,   hwæðre he worde cwæð,
550 æcræftig ar,   to þam æðelinge:
   "Þæt is, weredes weard,   wundor unlytel,
þæt þu gesawe   þurh swefen cuman,
heofonheane beam   and þa halgan word,
yrre and egeslicu,   þa se engel cwæð,
555 þæt þæt treow sceolde,   telgum besnæded,
foran afeallan,   þæt ær fæste stod,
and þonne mid deorum   dreamleas beon,
westen wunian,   and his wyrtruman

227 feran] *Not in MS.*   536 Oft] eft   550 æcræftig] ar cræftig

foldan befolen, fyrstmearc wesan
560 stille on staðole, swa seo stefn gecwæð,
ymb seofon tida sæde eft onfon.
Swa þin blæd lið. Swa se beam geweox,
heah to heofonum, swa þu hæleðum eart
ana eallum eorðbuendum
565 weard and wisa. Nis þe wiðerbreca,
man on moldan, nymðe metod ana.
Se ðec aceorfeð of cyningdome,
and ðec wineleasne on wræc sendeð,
and þonne onhweorfeð heortan þine,
570 þæt þu ne gemyndgast æfter mandreame,
ne gewittes wast butan wildeora þeaw,
ac þu lifgende lange þrage
heorta hlypum geond holt wunast.
Ne bið þec mælmete nymþe mores græs,
575 ne rest witod, ac þec regna scur
weceð and wreceð swa wildu deor,
oðþæt þu ymb seofon winter soð gelyfest,
þæt sie an metod eallum mannum,
reccend and rice, se on roderum is.
580 Is me swa þeah willa þæt se wyrtruma
stille wæs on staðole, swa seo stefn gecwæð,
and ymbe seofan tide sæde onfenge.
Swa þin rice restende bið,
anwalh for eorlum, oðþæt þu eft cymst.
585 Gehyge þu, frea min, fæstlicne ræd.
Syle ælmyssan, wes earmra hleo,
þinga for ðeodne, ær ðam seo þrah cyme
þæt he þec aworpe of woruldrice.
Oft metod alæt monige ðeode
590 wyrcan bote, þonne hie woldon sylfe,
fyrene fæstan, ær him fær godes
þurh egesan gryre aldre gesceode.''
    No þæs fela Daniel to his drihtne gespræc
soðra worda þurh snytro cræft,

---

570 gemyndgast] gemydgast   584 anwalh] anwloh   590 bote] *Not in*
MS.

595 þæt þæs a se rica   reccan wolde,
      middangeardes weard,   ac his mod astah,
      heah fram heortan;   he þæs hearde ongeald.
      Ongan ða gyddigan   þurh gylp micel
      Caldea cyning   þa he ceastergeweorc,
600 Babilone burh,   on his blæde geseah,
      Sennera feld   sidne bewindan,
      heah hlifigan;   þæt se heretyma
      werede geworhte   þurh wundor micel,
      wearð ða anhydig   ofer ealle men,
605 swiðmod in sefan,   for ðære sundorgife
      þe him god sealde,   gumena rice,
      world to gewealde   in wera life:
          "Ðu eart seo micle   and min seo mære burh
      þe ic geworhte   to wurðmyndum,
610 rume rice.   Ic reste on þe,
      eard and eðel,   agan wille."
          Ða for ðam gylpe   gumena drihten
      forfangen wearð   and on fleam gewat,
      ana on oferhyd   ofer ealle men.
615 Swa wod wera   on gewindagum
      geocrostne sið   in godes wite,
      ðara þe eft lifigende   leode begete,
      Nabochodonossor,   siððan him nið godes,
      hreð of heofonum,   hete gesceode.
620 Seofon winter samod   susl þrowode,
      wildeora westen,   winburge cyning.
      Ða se earfoðmæcg   up locode,
      wilddeora gewita,   þurh wolcna gang.
      Gemunde þa on mode   þæt metod wære,
625 heofona heahcyning,   hæleða bearnum
      ana ece gast.   Þa he eft onhwearf
      wodan gewittes,   þær þe he ær wide bær
      herewosan hige,   heortan getenge.
      Þa his gast ahwearf   in godes gemynd,
630 mod to mannum,   siððan he metod onget.
      Gewat þa earmsceapen   eft siðian,

599 ceastergeweorc] ceastre weold   615 wod] woð

nacod nydgenga,   nið geðafian,
wundorlic wræcca   and wæda leas,
mætra on modgeðanc,   to mancynne,
635 ðonne gumena weard   in gylpe wæs.
　　Stod middangeard   æfter mandrihtne,
eard and eðel   æfter þam æðelinge,
seofon winter samod,   swa no swiðrode
rice under roderum   oðþæt se ræswa com.
640 þa wæs eft geseted   in aldordom
Babilone weard,   hæfde beteran ðeaw,
leohtran geleafan   in liffruman,
þætte god sealde   gumena gehwilcum
welan swa wite,   swa he wolde sylf.
645 Ne lengde þa   leoda aldor
witegena wordcwyde,   ac he wide bead
metodes mihte   þær he meld ahte,
siðfæt sægde   sinum leodum,
wide waðe   þe he mid wilddeorum ateah,
650 oðþæt him frean godes   in gast becwom
rædfæst sefa,   ða he to roderum beseah.
Wyrd wæs geworden,   wundor gecyðed,
swefn geseðed,   susl awunnen,
dom gedemed,   swa ær Daniel cwæð,
655 þæt se folctoga   findan sceolde
earfoðsiðas   for his ofermedlan.
Swa he ofstlice   godspellode
metodes mihtum   for mancynne,
siððan in Babilone   burhsittendum
660 lange hwile   lare sægde,
Daniel domas.   Siððan deora gesið,
wildra wærgenga,   of waðe cwom,
Nabochodonossor   of niðwracum,
siððan weardode   wide rice,
665 heold hæleða gestreon   and þa hean burh,
frod, foremihtig   folca ræswa,
Caldea cyning,   oðþæt him cwelm gesceod,
swa him ofer eorðan   andsaca ne wæs

643 gehwilcum] gehlilcum *with* w *written over the first* l

gumena ænig   oðþæt him god wolde
670 þurh hryre hreddan   hea rice.
Siððan þær his aferan   ead bryttedon,
welan, wunden gold,   in þære widan byrig,
ealhstede eorla,   unwaclice,
heah hordmægen,   þa hyra hlaford læg.
675   Ða in ðære ðeode awoc   his þæt þridde cneow.
Wæs Baldazar   burga aldor,
weold wera rices,   oðþæt him wlenco gesceod,
oferhyd egle.   Ða wæs endedæg
ðæs ðe Caldeas   cyningdom ahton.
680 Ða metod onlah   Medum and Persum
aldordomes   ymb lytel fæc,
let Babilone   blæd swiðrian,
þone þa hæleð   healdan sceoldon.
Wiste he ealdormen   in unrihtum,
685 ða ðe ðy rice   rædan sceoldon.
Ða þæt gehogode   hamsittende,
Meda aldor,   þæt ær man ne ongan,
þæt he Babilone   abrecan wolde,
alhstede eorla,   þær æðelingas
690 under wealla hleo   welan brytnedon.
Þæt wæs þara fæstna   folcum cuðost,
mæst and mærost   þara þe men bun,
Babilon burga,   oðþæt Baldazar
þurh gylp grome   godes frasade.
695   Sæton him æt wine   wealle belocene,
ne onegdon na   orlegra nið,
þeah ðe feonda folc   feran cwome
herega gerædum   to þære heahbyrig
þæt hie Babilone   abrecan mihton.
700 Gesæt þa to symble   siðestan dæge
Caldea cyning   mid cneomagum,
þær medugal wearð   mægenes wisa.
Het þam æðelum beran   Israela gestreon,

675 ðeode] *Preceded by a letter erased*   681 ymb] ym   691 cuðost] s
altered from c *or* t   694 frasade] frea sæde   700 symble] y *altered*
from u   703 æðelum] *Not in MS.*

huslfatu halegu,   on hand werum,
705 þa ær Caldeas   mid cyneðrymme,
cempan in ceastre,   clæne genamon,
gold in Gerusalem,   ða hie Iudea
blæd forbræcon   billa ecgum,
and þurh hleoðorcyme,   herige genamon
710 beorhte frætwe.   Ða hie tempel strudon,
Salomanes seld,   swiðe gulpon.

Ða wearð bliðemod   burga aldor,
gealp gramlice   gode on andan,
cwæð þæt his hergas   hyrran wæron
715 and mihtigran   mannum to friðe
þonne Israela   ece drihten.
Him þæt tacen wearð   þær he to starude,
egeslic for eorlum   innan healle,
þæt he for leodum   ligeword gecwæð,
720 þa þær in egesan   engel drihtnes
let his hand cuman   in þæt hea seld,
wrat þa in wage   worda gerynu,
baswe bocstafas,   burhsittendum.
Ða wearð folctoga   forht on mode,
725 acul for þam egesan.   Geseah he engles hand
in sele writan   Sennera wite.
Þæt gyddedon   gumena mænigeo,
hæleð in healle,   hwæt seo hand write
to þam beacne   burhsittendum.
730 Werede comon   on þæt wundor seon.
Sohton þa swiðe   in sefan gehydum,
hwæt seo hand write   haliges gastes.
Ne mihton arædan   runcræftige men
engles ærendbec,   æðelinga cyn,
735 oðþæt Daniel com,   drihtne gecoren,
snotor and soðfæst,   in þæt seld gangan.
Ðam wæs on gaste   godes cræft micel,
to þam ic georne gefrægn   gyfum ceapian
burhge weardas   þæt he him bocstafas
740 arædde and arehte,   hwæt seo run bude.

712 Ða] ð *with a added above the line*   739 burhge weardas] burh geweardas

Him æcræftig   andswarode,
godes spelboda,   gleaw geðances:
    "No ic wið feohsceattum   ofer folc bere
drihtnes domas,   ne ðe dugeðe can,
745 ac þe unceapunga   orlæg secge,
worda gerynu,   þa þu wendan ne miht.
þu for anmedlan   in æht bere
huslfatu halegu,   on hand werum.
On þam ge deoflu   drincan ongunnon,
750 ða ær Israela   in æ hæfdon
æt godes earce,   oðþæt hie gylp beswac,
windruncen gewit,   swa þe wurðan sceal.
No þæt þin aldor   æfre wolde
godes goldfatu   in gylp beran,
755 ne ðy hraðor hremde,   ðeah ðe here brohte
Israela gestreon   in his æhte geweald,
ac þæt oftor gecwæð   aldor ðeoda
soðum wordum   ofer sin mægen,
siððan him wuldres weard   wundor gecyðde,
760 þæt he wære ana   ealra gesceafta
drihten and waldend,   se him dom forgeaf,
unscyndne blæd   eorðan rices,
and þu lignest nu   þæt sie lifgende,
se ofer deoflum   dugeþum wealdeð.''

748 halegu] halgu *with* e *added above the line after* l

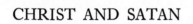

CHRIST AND SATAN

CHRIST AND SATAN

Þæt wearð underne   eorðbuendum,
þæt meotod hæfde   miht and strengðo
ða he gefestnade   foldan sceatas.
Seolfa he gesette   sunnan and monan,
5 stanas and eorðan,   stream ut on sæ,
wæter and wolcn,   ðurh his wundra miht.
Deopne ymblyt   clene ymbhaldeð
meotod on mihtum,   and alne middangeard.
He selfa mæg   sæ geondwlitan,
10 grundas in geofene,   godes agen bearn,
and he ariman mæg   rægnas scuran,
dropena gehwelcne.   Daga enderim
seolua he gesette   þurh his soðan miht.
Swa se wyrhta   þurh his wuldres gast
15 serede and sette   on six dagum
eorðan dæles,   up on heofonum,
and heanne holm.   Hwa is þæt ðe cunne
orðonc clene   nymðe ece god?
Dreamas he gedelde,   duguðe and geþeode,
20 Adam ærest,   and þæt æðele cyn,
engla ordfruman,   þæt þe eft forwarð.
Ðuhte him on mode   þæt hit mihte swa,
þæt hie weron seolfe   swegles brytan,
wuldres waldend.   Him ðær wirse gelamp,

1 wearð] ð *over* þ *erased*   eorðbuendum] eorð buendum *with a final* e *erased in* eorð   2 meotod hæfde] him *added above the line between these* *words*   6 wolcn] e *added above the line between* c *and* n   7 ymblyt] ybmlyt   9 sæ] æ *altered from* e?   10 geofene] heofene *corrected to* heofenon *with final* e *changed to* o *and* n *added above the line*   17 and] *Not in* MS.   heanne] henne *with* a *added above the line*   holm] holme   18 clene] *Corrected to* clæne *by altering* e   nymðe] *With a gloss* buton *added* *above the line*   19 gedelde] æ *above second* e   21 forwarð] *With* e *added* *above the line after* w   22 him] him *with* eo *above* i   23 weron] e *altered* *to* æ   seolfe] y *written above* eo   24 wirse] wise *with* ors *added above* *the last three letters*   gelamp] o *written above* a

25 ða heo in helle ham staðeledon,
an æfter oðrum, in þæt atole scref,
þær heo brynewelme bidan sceolden
saran sorge, nales swegles leoht
habban in heofnum heahgetimbrad,
30 ac gedufan sceolun in ðone deopan wælm
niðær under nessas in ðone neowlan grund,
gredige and gifre. God ana wat
hu he þæt scyldige werud forscrifen hefde!
  Cleopað ðonne se alda ut of helle,
35 wriceð wordcwedas weregan reorde,
eisegan stefne: "Hwær com engla ðrym,
þe we on heofnum habban sceoldan?
þis is ðeostræ ham, ðearle gebunden
fæstum fyrclommum; flor is on welme
40 attre onæled. Nis nu ende feor
þæt we sceolun ætsomne susel þrowian,
wean and wergu, nalles wuldres blæd
habban in heofnum, hehselda wyn.
  Hwæt, we for dryhtene iu dreamas hefdon,
45 song on swegle selrum tidum,
þær nu ymb ðone æcan æðele stondað,
heleð ymb hehseld, herigað drihten
wordum and wercum, and ic in wite sceal
bidan in bendum, and me bættran ham
50 for oferhygdum æfre ne wene."
  Ða him andsweradan atole gastas,

---

26 þæt] *The abbreviation, with a letter erased after it*   27 sceolden] sceoden
corrected to sceoldon *with* l *above the line before* d *and* o *above* e   28 swegles]
sweogles *with* o *erased*   29 habban] haban *with a second* b *above the line*
31 under] undęr   32 gredige] æ *above first* e   33 scyldige] scyldi *followed
by* ge *above the line*   hefde] hęfde   34 cleopað] cleopad   alda] e *before
first* a *above the line*   35 wordcwedas] cwedas *with* word *added above the
line*   37 þe] ða þe   38 ðeostræ] þe ðeostræ *with* þe *erased*   42 wergu]
wergum   nalles] nelles *with* a *above the deleted* e   wuldres] wulres
46 æcan] æ *altered to* e   47 heleð] *The first* e *altered to* æ   ymb] ym *with* b
added above the line   48 wordum] wordun   wercum] węrcum *with* io
above the deleted e   49 bættran] ættran *with* b *erased*   ham] for ham
with for *crossed out*

swarte and synfulle,   susle begnornende:
    "Þu us gelærdæst   ðurh lyge ðinne
þæt we helende   heran ne scealdon.
55 Ðuhte þe anum   þæt ðu ahtest alles gewald,
heofnes and eorþan,   wære halig god,
scypend seolfa.   Nu earttu sceaðana sum,
in fyrlocan   feste gebunden.
Wendes ðu ðurh wuldor   ðæt þu woruld ahtest,
60 alra onwald,   and we englas mid ðec.
Atol is þin onseon!   Habbað we alle swa
for ðinum leasungum   lyðre gefered.
Segdest us to soðe   þæt ðin sunu wære
meotod moncynnes;   hafustu nu mare susel!"
65   Swa firenfulle   facnum wordum
heora aldorðægn   on reordadon,
on cearum cwidum.   Crist heo afirde,
dreamum bedelde.   Hæfdan dryhtnes līht
for oferhygdum   ufan forleton,
70 hæfdon hym to hyhte   helle floras,
beornende bealo.   Blace hworfon
scinnan forscepene,   sceaðan hwearfedon,
earme æglecan,   geond þæt atole scref,
for ðam anmedlan   þe hie ær drugon.
75   Eft reordade   oðre siðe
feonda aldor.   Wæs þa forht agen,
seoððan he ðes wites   worn gefelde.
He spearcade,   ðonne he spreocan ongan
fyre and atre;   ne bið swelc fæger dream
80 ðonne he in witum   wordum indraf:

---

52 swarte] *With* e *above the line before* a   begnornende] begrorenne   54
helende] *With* æ *above the first* e   scealdon] *With* o *above* a   57
sceaðana sum] earm sceaða *followed by* na sum, *erased*   63 Segdest] *With* æ
above the first e   66 on] un   68 bedelde] *The second* e *erased and* æ *written
above*   līht] *With* i *erased and* eo *written above*   69 ufan] f *over an erasure,
perhaps originally* uppan   forleton] e *altered to* æ *and* o *to* e   71 hworfon]
With e *above the line after* w   72 hwearfedon] hwearfdon   74 anmedlan]
medlan *with* an *added above the line*   76 forht] for worht   77 ðes] e
erased and æ *written above*   78 spearcade] swearcade *with* c *corrected to* t
79 atre] *A second* t *above the line after* a   ne] n *altered from* h   80
wordum] word

"Ic wæs iu in heofnum   halig ængel,
dryhtene deore;   hefde me dream mid gode,
micelne for meotode,   and ðeos menego swa some.
þa ic in mode   minum hogade
85 þæt ic wolde towerpan   wuldres leoman,
bearn helendes,   agan me burga gewald
eall to æhte,   and ðeos earme heap
þe ic hebbe to helle   ham geledde.
Wene þæt tacen sutol   þa ic aseald wes on wærgðu,
90 niðer under nessas   in ðone neowlan grund.
Nu ic eow hebbe to hæftum   ham gefærde
alle of earde.   Nis her eadiges tir,
wloncra winsele,   ne worulde dream,
ne ængla ðreat,   ne we upheofon
95 agan moten. Is ðes atola ham
fyre onæled.   Ic eom fah wið god.
Æce æt helle duru   dracan eardigað,
hate on reðre;   heo us helpan ne magon.
Is ðæs walica ham   wites afylled;
100 nagan we ðæs heolstres   þæt we us gehydan mægon
in ðissum neowlan genipe.   Hær is nedran swæg,
wyrmas gewunade.   Is ðis wites clom

---

82 dryhtene] dryhtẹne *the final* e *crowded in*   85 ic wolde] *A letter erased
between the words*   towerpan] io *above* e   wuldres] wulres   86 helendes]
æ *above first* e   gewald] e *above the line before* a   87 ðeos] *Made by
altering* ðes *to* ðeos   88 geledde] *The second* e *altered to* æ   89 Wene]
wene *with* ge *added above* ne   þa ic aseald wes on wærgðu] 7 wærgðu
þa ic *of* aseald wes   90 nessas] nẹssas *with* æ *above* e   ðone] ðonne
with the first n *erased*   91 gefærde] geferde *with the second* e *made by erasing
the first half of* æ *and with* e *added above the line after* r, *i.e.,* geferede   92
alle] *With* e *above the line before* a   93 winsele] y *above* i *and final* e *altered
to* a   94 ængla] *The first half of* æ *erased*   ðreat] ð *perhaps altered
from* d *(Gollancz)*   we] *Added above the line*   upheofon] up heofon *with a
second* p *above the line after* p   95 agan moten] ne *above the line between
these words*   ðes] s *over erased* os   96 fyre] fyr *with* e *crowded in before
the next word*   97 Æce] æce *with* æ *altered to* e   98 heo] hẹọ *with* y
written above   99 ðæs] *The first half of* æ *erased*   100 nagan] Nagan
with N *over an erasure (of same large capital, Gollancz)*   mægon] *The second
part of* æ *erased*   101 Hær] *The first half of* æ *erased*   swæg] *The first half
of* æ *erased*

feste gebunden.   Feond seondon reðe,
dimme and deorce.   Ne her dæg lyhteð
105 for scedes sciman,   sceppendes leoht.
Iu ahte ic gewald   ealles wuldres,
ær ic moste in ðeossum atolan   æðele gebidan
hwæt me drihten god   deman wille,
fagum on flora.   Nu ic feran com
110 deofla menego   to ðissum dimman ham.
Ac ic sceal on flyge   and on flyhte ðragum
earda neosan,   and eower ma,
þe ðes oferhydes   ord onstaldon.
Ne ðurfon we ðes wenan,   þæt us wuldorcyning
115 æfre wille   eard alefan,
æðel to æhte,   swa he ær dyde,
ecne onwald;   ah him alles gewald,
wuldres and wita,   waldendes sunu.
Forðon ic sceal hean and earm   hweorfan ðy widor,
120 wadan wræclastas,   wuldre benemed,
duguðum bedeled,   nænigne dream agan
uppe mid ænglum,   þes ðe ic ær gecwæð
þæt ic wære seolfa   swægles brytta,
wihta wealdend.   Ac hit me wyrse gelomp!"
125   Swa se werega gast   wordum sæde

103 feste] *The first* e *altered to* æ   104 and] *The abbreviation written over* on *erased*   lyhteð] lyh *with* teð *added above the line*   106 Iu] nu   ic] *Added above the line before* gewald   107 ær] þær   æðele] *The first half of* æ *erased*   108 wille] y *written over* i   111 Ac] ac *with* c *over* h *erased*   113 onstaldon] *With* e *added above the line before* a   114 ðes] *With* e *altered to* æ   115 alefan] *With* y *written over* e   116 æðel] *The first half of* æ *erased* (*Clubb, Gollancz*)   117 ecne] ece *with* n *added above the line after* c   onwald] *With* e *added above the line before* a   alles] *With* e *added above the line before* a   gewald] *With* e *added above the line before* a   118 wuldres] wulres *with* d *added above the line after* l   waldendes] *With* e *added above the line before* a   119 sceal] *Added above the line*   earm] earm ma *with the* m *of* earm *added by the corrector and* ma *canceled by him*   hweorfan] hweọrfan *with* y *written above* eo   widor] *A second* d *after* d *above the line*   122 ænglum] *The first half of* æ *erased*   þes] *with* e *altered to* æ   123 swægles] *The first half of* æ *erased*   124 wihta wealdend] ihta wealdend *over an erasure, by second scribe?*   Ac] ac *with* c *over* h *erased*   me] him   gelomp] gelọmp *with* a *above* o

his earfoðo ealle ætsomne,
fah in fyrnum, (fyrleoma stod
geond þæt atole scræf attre geblonden):
"Ic eom limwæstmum þæt ic gelutian ne mæg
130 on þyssum sidan sele, synnum forwundod.
Hwæt, her hat and ceald hwilum mencgað;
hwilum ic gehere hellescealcas,
gnornende cynn, grundas mænan,
niðer under næssum; hwilum nacode men
135 winnað ymb wyrmas. Is þes windiga sele
eall inneweard atole gefylled.
Ne mot ic hihtlicran hames brucan,
burga ne bolda, ne on þa beorhtan gescæft
ne mot ic æfre ma eagum starian.
140 Is me nu wyrsa þæt ic wuldres leoht
uppe mid englum æfre cuðe,
song on swegle, þær sunu meotodes
habbað eadige bearn ealle ymbfangen
seolfa mid sange. Ne ic þam sawlum ne mot
145 ænigum sceððan,
butan þam anum þe he agan nyle;
þa ic mot to hæftum ham geferian,
bringan to bolde in þone biteran grund.
Ealle we syndon ungelice
150 þonne þe we iu in heofonum hæfdon ærror
wlite and weorðmynt. Ful oft wuldres sweg
brohton to bearme bearn hælendes,
þær we ymb hine utan ealle hofan,
leomu ymb leofne, lofsonga word,
155 drihtne sædon. Nu ic eom dædum fah,
gewundod mid wommum; sceal nu þysne wites clom
beoran beornende in bæce minum,
hat on helle, hyhtwillan leas."
    Þa gyt feola cwiðde firna herde,

133 gnornende] *With* i *added above the line between second* n *and* e   135
ymb] *With* e *added above the line*   140 wyrsa] *With* a *altered to* æ   143
eadige] eadigne   146 agan] to agan   151 sweg] *Not in MS.*   159
cwiðde] cwide *with* dum *written above, i.e.,* cwidum, *as alternative reading*
herde] herede *with a "faint letter above first* e," *possibly* a *erased* (Gollancz)

160 atol æglæca, ut of helle,
     witum werig. Word spearcum fleah
     attre gelicost, þonne he ut þorhdraf:
         "Eala drihtenes þrym! Eala duguða helm!
     Eala meotodes miht! Eala middaneard!
165 Eala dæg leohta! Eala dream godes!
     Eala engla þreat! Eala upheofen!
     Eala þæt ic eam ealles leas ecan dreames,
     þæt ic mid handum ne mæg heofon geræcan,
     ne mid eagum ne mot up locian,
170 ne huru mid earum ne sceal æfre geheran
     þære byrhtestan beman stefne!
     Ðæs ic wolde of selde sunu meotodes,
     drihten adrifan, and agan me þæs dreames gewald,
     wuldres and wynne, me þær wyrse gelamp
175 þonne ic to hihte agan moste.
     Nu ic eom asceaden fram þære sciran driht,
     alæded fram leohte in þone laðan ham.
     Ne mæg ic þæt gehicgan hu ic in ðæm becwom,
     in þis neowle genip, niðsynnum fah,
180 aworpen of worulde. Wat ic nu þa
     þæt bið alles leas ecan dreamas
     se ðe heofencyninge heran ne þenceð,
     meotode cweman. Ic þæt morðer sceal,
     wean and witu and wrace dreogan,
185 goda bedæled, iudædum fah,
     þæs ðe ic geþohte adrifan drihten of selde,
     weoroda waldend; sceal nu wreclastas
     settan sorhgcearig, siðas wide."
         Hwearf þa to helle þa he gehened wæs,
190 godes andsaca; dydon his gingran swa,

162 þorhdraf] þorh draf *with* u *above* o   165 leohta] o *altered from* d
(*Clubb*)   169 up] *Followed by* g̃ *erased* (*Clubb, Gollancz*)   171 beman]
With y *above* e   178 becwom] becwom   179 niðsynnum] mid synnum
180 ic] *At end of line; corrector adds abbreviation for* þæt   181 ecan]
ęcan   dreamas] *The second* a *altered to* æ   183 morðer] morðre   188
sorhgcearig] *The final* g *possibly added by the corrector*   siðas] sidas   190
swa] *Followed by* some *above the line as a variant, i.e.,* swa some

gifre and grædige,   þa hig god bedraf
in þæt hate hof   þam is hel nama.
Forþan sceal gehycgan   hæleða æghwylc
þæt he ne abælige   bearn waldendes.
195 Læte him to bysne   hu þa blacan feond
for oferhygdum   ealle forwurdon.
Neoman us to wynne   weoroda drihten,
uppe ecne gefean,   engla waldend.
He þæt gecydde   þæt he mægencræft hæfde,
200 mihta miccle,   þa he þa mænego adraf,
hæftas of ðæm hean selde.   Gemunan we þone halgan
                                                    drihten,
ecne in wuldre   mid alra gescefta ealdre;
ceosan us eard in wuldre   mid ealra cyninga cyninge,
se is Crist genemned;
205 beoran on breostum   bliðe geþohtas,
sibbe and snytero;   gemunan soð and riht,
þonne we to hehselde   hnigan þencað,
and þone anwaldan   ara biddan.
Þonne behofað   se ðe her wunað
210 weorulde wynnum   þæt him wlite scine
þonne he oðer lif   eft geseceð,
fægere land   þonne þeos folde seo;
is þær wlitig and wynsum,   wæstmas scinað,
beorhte ofer burgum.   Þær is brade lond,
215 hyhtlicra ham   in heofonrice,
Criste gecwemra.   Uta cerran þider
þær he sylfa sit,   sigora waldend,
drihten hælend,   in ðæm deoran ham,

---

191 hig] hę *with* ig *above* e   194 abælige] abælige *with the first half of* æ
erased   197 Neoman] neoman *with* i *above* eo   198 uppe] upne   202
ealdre] *Not in MS.*   207 hnigan] nigan *at beginning of a line, with* h *added
in margin;* h *perhaps transferred from end of preceding line, where there
is an erasure*   208 þone] þonne *with the first* n *partly erased*   anwaldan]
With eal *above* an *as a variant reading*   ara] *Final* a *changed to* æ   212
fægere] fægre *preceded by* .s. mycele, *i.e.,* scilicet mycele, *above the line*
213 is þær wlitig] is wlitig *with* .s. þær *above* is, *i.e.,* is þær wlitig   215
hyhtlicra] hyhtlicran *with the* n *erased*   216 Uta] uta *with* on *above the line
between* t *and* a, *and* a *connected by dash with* cerran, *i.e.,* uton acerran

and ymb þæt hehsetl   hwite standað
220 engla feðan   and eadigra,
halige heofenþreatas   herigað drihten
wordum and weorcum.   Heora wlite scineð
geond ealra worulda woruld   mid wuldorcyninge.
    Ða get ic furðor gefregen   feond ondetan;
225 wæs him eall ful strang wom and witu; hæfdon wuldor-
                                        cyning
    for oferhigdum   anforlæten;
    cwædon eft hraðe   oðre worde:
        "Nu is gesene   þæt we syngodon
    uppe on earde.   Sceolon nu æfre þæs
230 dreogan domlease gewinn   drihtnes mihtum.
    Hwæt, we in wuldres wlite   wunian moston
    þær we halgan gode   heran woldon,
    and him sang ymb seld   secgan sceoldon
    þusendmælum.   Þa we þær wæron,
235 wunodon on wynnum,   geherdon wuldres sweg,
    beman stefne.   Byrhtword aras
    engla ordfruma,   and to þæm æþelan
    hnigan him sanctas;   sigetorht aras
    ece drihten,   ofer us gestod
240 and gebletsode   bilewitne heap
    dogra gehwilcne,   and his se deora sunu,
    gasta scyppend.   God seolfa wæs
    eallum andfeng   þe ðær up becom,
    and hine on eorðan   ær gelefde.
245   Þa ðæs ofþuhte   þæt se þeoden wæs
    strang and stiðmod.   Ongan ic þa steppan forð
    ana wið englum,   and to him eallum spræc:
        'Ic can eow læran   langsumne ræd,

---

219 ymb] *With* e *crowded in after* b   220 eadigra] eadigre   221 halige]
haligre *with* r *erased* (*Clubb, Gollancz*)   223 wuldorcyninge] *The final*
e *added by corrector* (*Gollancz*)   224 feond] feonda   227 oðre worde]
With um *as variant reading above each* e, *i.e.,* oðrum wordum   228
syngodon] ge *added before above the line*   231 in] *Added above the line before*
wuldres   234 wæron] *Added above the line before* wunodon   244 gelefde]
y *written above first* e

gif ge willaõ minre   mihte gelefan.
250 Uta oferhycgan   helm þone micclan,
weroda waldend,   agan us þis wuldres leoht,
eall to æhte.   Þis is idel gylp
þæt we ær drugon   ealle hwile.'
    Ða gewearð usic   þæt we woldon swa
255 drihten adrifan   of þam deoran ham,
cyning of cestre.   Cuð is wide
þæt wreclastas   wunian moton,
grimme grundas.   God seolfa him
rice haldeð.   He is ana cyning,
260 þe us eorre gewearð,   ece drihten,
meotod mihtum swið.   Sceal nu þeos menego her
licgan on leahtrum,   sume on lyft scacan,
fleogan ofer foldan;   fyr bið ymbutan
on æghwylcum,   þæh he uppe seo.
265 Ne mot he þam sawlum   þe ðær secað up,
eadige of eorþan   æfre gehrinan,
ah ic be hondum mot   hæþenre sceale
gripan to grunde,   godes andsacan.
Sume sceolon hweorfan   geond hæleða land
270 and unsibbe   oft onstyrian
monna mægðum   geond middaneard.
Ic her geþolian sceal   þinga æghwylces,
bitres niðæs   beala gnornian,
sic and sorhful,   þæs ic seolfa weold,
275 þonne ic on heofonum   ham staðelode,
hwæðer us se eca   æfre wille
on heofona rice   ham alefan,
eðel to æhte,   swa he ær dyde."
    Swa gnornedon   godes andsacan,
280 hate on helle.   Him wæs hælend god

---

249 gif] *Followed by* w *erased*   minre] mire *with* n *added above the line after* i
mihte] mihtą *with* e *written above* a   250 Uta] uta *with* n *added above the
line*   261 swið] swilc   262 scacan] *With* e *above the line after the first* c
266 gehrinan] gerinan *with* h *above the line before* r   267 sceale] sceal
273 niðæs] in ðæs   274 sic] i *altered to* e *and* o *added above the line, i.e.,* seoc
278 eðel] eðle

wraðð geworden for womcwidum.
Forþon mæg gehycgan, se ðe his heorte deah,
þæt he him afirre frecne geþohtas,
laðe leahtras, lifigendra gehwylc.
285 Gemunan symle on mode meotodes strengðo;
gearwian us togenes grene stræte
up to englum, þær is se ælmihtiga god.
And us befæðman wile freobearn godes,
gif we þæt on eorðan ær geþencað,
290 and us to þam halgan helpe gelefað.
Þonne he us no forlæteð, ah lif syleð
uppe mid englum, eadigne dream.
Tæceð us se torhta trumlicne ham,
beorhte burhweallas. Beorhte scinað
295 gesælige sawle, sorgum bedælde,
þær heo æfre forð wunian moten
cestre and cynestol. Uton cyþan þæt!
Deman we on eorðan, ærror lifigend,
onlucan mid listum locen waldendes,
300 ongeotan gastlice! Us ongean cumað
þusend engla, gif þider moton,
and þæt on eorðan ær gewyrcað.
      Forþon se bið eadig se ðe æfre wile
man oferhycgen, meotode cweman,
305 synne adwæscan. Swa he sylfa cwæð:
"Soðfæste men, sunnan gelice,
fægre gefrætewod in heora fæder rice
scinað in sceldbyrig." Þær heo sceppend seolf
friðe befæðmeð, fæder mancynnes,
310 ahefeð holdlice in heofones leoht,
þær heo mid wuldorcyninge wunian moton
awa to aldre,
agan dreama dream mid drihtne gode,
a to worulde a buton ende.
315 Eala hwæt! Se awyrgda wraðe geþohte

290 gelefað] gelefąð *with* e *above* a   308 seolf] *At the end of a line; followed
by two letters erased?*   309 friðe] *Not in MS.*   mancynnes] mancyn
with nes *added above the line*   315 Eala] ala *with space for a capital, and*
e *noted at the edge of the margin*

þæt he heofencyninge heran ne wolde,
fæder frefergendum. Flor attre weol,
hat under hæftum; hreopan deofla,
wide geond windsele wean cwanedon,
320 man and morður. Wæs seo menego þær
swylce onæled; wæs þæt eall full strong,
þonne wæs heora aldor, þe ðær ærest com
forð on feþan, fæste gebunden
fyre and lige. Þæt wæs fæstlic þreat;
325 ec sceoldon his þegnas þær gewunian
atolan eðles, nalles up þanon
geheran in heofonum haligne dream,
þær heo oft fægerne folgað hæfdon
uppe mid englum. Wæron þa alles þæs
330 goda lease, ah nymþe gryndes ad
wunian ne moten and þone werigan sele
þær is wom and wop wide gehered,
and gristbitungc and gnornungc mecga.
Nabbað he to hyhte nymþe cyle and fyr,
335 wean and witu and wyrma þreat,
dracan and næddran and þone dimman ham.
Forðon mihte geheran, se ðe æt hylle wæs
twelf milum neh, þæt ðær wæs toða geheaw,
hlude and geomre. Godes andsacan
340 hweorfan geond helle hate onæled
ufan and utan (him wæs æghwær wa),
witum werige, wuldres bescyrede,
dreamum bedælde. Heofon deop gehygd,
þa heo on heofonum ham staðelodon,
345 þæt hie woldon benæman nergendne Crist
rodera rices, ah he on riht geheold
hired heofona and þæt halige seld.

318 hreopan] hreowan 319 windsele] winsele *with* d *added above the line after* n wean] wea 320 seo] ðær 330 lease] leas *with* e *added by a different hand* ah] *Underlined (for canceling?) according to Clubb, but with scarcely visible underlining in the collotype* ad] *Not in MS.* 331 ne] *Not in MS.* 333 gristbitungc] gristbitunge gnornungc] gnornunge 334 he] we 339 hlude] lude *with* h *before* l *above the line*

Nis nænig swa snotor   ne swa cræftig,
ne þæs swa gleaw,   nymþe god seolfa,
350 þæt asecgan mæge   swegles leoman,
hu scima þær   scineð ymbutan
meotodes mihte,   geond þæt mære cynn,
þær habbað englas   eadigne dream,
sanctas singað   (þæt is se seolfa) for god.
355 Þonne beoð þa eadigan   þe of eorðan cumað,
bringað to bearme   blostman stences,
wyrte wynsume   (þæt synd word godes),
þonne hie befæðmeð   fæder mancynnes,
and hie gesegnað   mid his swiðran hond,
360 lædeð to lihte,   þær hi lif agon
a to aldre,   uplicne ham,
byrhtne burhstyde.   Blæd bið æghwæm
þæm ðe hælende   heran þenceð,
and wel is þam   ðe þæt wyrcan mot.
365 Wæs þæt encgelcyn   ær genemned,
Lucifer haten,   leohtberende,
on geardagum   in godes rice.
Þa he in wuldre   wrohte onstalde
þæt he oferhyda   agan wolde.
370 Þa Satanus   swearte geþohte
þæt he wolde on heofonum   hehseld wyrcan
uppe mid þam ecan.   Þæt wæs ealdor heora,
yfeles ordfruma.   Him þæt eft gehreaw,
þa he to helle   hnigan sceolde,
375 and his hired mid hine,   in hynðo geglidan,
nergendes nið,   and no seoððan
þæt hi mosten in þone ecan   andwlitan seon
buton ende.   Þa him egsa becom,

351 scima] sunnu   354 se] *Written by the scribe and partly erased*   357
wyrte] e *altered to* a   360 lædeð] lædæð, *probably first written* lædað *and
changed to* lædæð   362 byrhtne] y *canceled and* eo *written above*
burhstyde] y *canceled and* e *written above*   363 heran] heran *with* y
written above e   364 wyrcan] *Not in MS.*   368 wrohte] wroht *with* e
crowded in before the next word   onstalde] *With* e *above the line before* a
370 þa] *Not in MS.*   373 ordfruma] ordfruman   375 hynðo] to   377
seon] *Not in MS.*

dyne for deman,   þa he duru in helle
380 bræc and begde.   Blis wearð monnum
þa hi hælendes   heafod gesawon.
Þonne wæs þam atolan   þe we ær nemdon
*   *   *

Þa wæron mid egsan   ealle afyrhte,
wide geond windsele   wordum mændon:
385 "Þis is stronglic,   nu þes storm becom,
þegen mid þreate,   þeoden engla.
Him beforan fereð   fægere leoht
þonne we æfre ær   eagum gesawon,
buton þa we mid englum   uppe wæron.
390 Wile nu ure witu   þurh his wuldres cræft
eall toweorpan.   Nu ðes egsa com,
dyne for drihtne,   sceal þes dreorga heap
ungeara nu   atol þrowian.
Hit is se seolfa   sunu waldendes,
395 engla drihten.   Wile uppe heonan
sawla lædan,   and we seoððan a
þæs yrreweorces   henðo geþoliað."
    Hwearf þa to helle   hæleða bearnum,
meotod þurh mihte;   wolde manna rim,
400 fela þusenda,   forð gelædan
up to eðle.   Þa com engla sweg,
dyne on dægred;   hæfde drihten seolf
feond oferfohten.   Wæs seo fæhðe þa gyt
open on uhtan,   þa se egsa becom.
405 Let þa up faran   eadige sawle,
Adames cyn,   ac ne moste Efe þa gyt
wlitan in wuldre   ær heo wordum cwæð:
    "Ic þe æne abealh,   ece drihten,
þa wit Adam twa   eaples þigdon

---

384 windsele] winsele *with* d *added above the line after* n   387 fægere] fæger
with final e *added by corrector*   398 to] *Above the line after* þa   403
fæhðe] fæhðẹ, *indicating that the final* e *is to stand*   405 sawle] e *altered to* a
406 ac] and, *in the usual abbreviated form*   Efe] efe *with the first* e *altered
from* æ *and the second over* re *erased; i.e.,* efe *from* æfre (*Clubb*)   407 heo]
he *with* o *crowded in*

410 þurh næddran nið,   swa wit na ne sceoldon.
    Gelærde unc se atola,   se ðe æfre nu
    beorneð on bendum,   þæt wit blæd ahton,
    haligne ham,   heofon to gewalde.
    Þa wit ðæs awærgdan   wordum gelyfdon,
415 namon mid handum   on þam halgan treo
    beorhte blæda;   unc þæs bitere forgeald
    þa wit in þis hate scræf   hweorfan sceoldon,
    and wintra rim   wunian seoððan,
    þusenda feolo,   þearle onæled.
420   Nu ic þe halsige,   heofenrices weard,
    for þan hirede   þe ðu hider læddest,
    engla þreatas,   þæt ic up heonon
    mæge and mote   mid minre mægðe.
    And ymb þreo niht com   þegen hælendes
425 ham to helle;   is nu hæftum strong,
    witum werig,   swylce him wuldorcyning
    for onmædlan   eorre geworden.
    Segdest us to soðe   þætte seolfa god
    wolde helwarum   ham gelihtan.
430 Aras þa anra gehwylc,   and wið earm gesæt,
    hleonade wið handa.   Þeah hylle gryre
    egeslic þuhte,   wæron ealle þæs
    fægen in firnum   þæt freodrihten
    wolde him to helpe   helle gesecan."
435   Ræhte þa mid handum   to heofencyninge,
    bæd meotod miltse   þurh Marian had:
       "Hwæt, þu fram minre dohtor,   drihten, onwoce
    in middangeard   mannum to helpe.
    Nu is gesene   þæt ðu eart sylfa god
440 and ece ordfruma   ealra gesceafta."
       Let þa up faran   ece drihten;
    wuldre hæfde   wites clomma
    feondum oðfæsted,   and heo furðor sceaf

421 hider] "der *over an erasure?*" (*Gollancz*)   433 freodrihten] heora
drihten   435 Ræhte] rihte *with æ above* i   437 minre] mire   439 god]
Written twice, the second time canceled   440 and] *The abbreviation, partly*
erased

in þæt neowle genip,   nearwe gebeged,
445 þær nu Satanus   swearte þingað,
earm aglæca,   and þa atolan mid him,
witum werige.   Nalles wuldres leoht
habban moton,   ah in helle grund,
ne hi edcerres   æfre moton
450 wenan seoððan.   Him wæs drihten god
wrað geworden,   sealde him wites clom,
atole to æhte,   and egsan gryre,
dimne and deorcne   deaðes scuwan,
hatne helle grund,   hinsiðgryre.
455   Þæt, la, wæs fæger,   þæt se feða com
up to earde,   and se eca mid him,
meotod mancynnes   in þa mæran burh!
Hofon hine mid him   handum halige
witigan up to eðle,   Abrahames cynn.
460 Hæfde þa drihten seolf   deað oferwunnen,
feond geflemed;   þæt in fyrndagum
witegan sædon   þæt he swa wolde.
Þis wæs on uhtan   eall geworden,
ær dægrede,   þæt se dyne becom,
465 hlud of heofonum,   þa he helle duru
forbræc and forbegde;   ban weornodon
þa hie swa leohtne   leoman gesawon.
    Gesæt þa mid þære fyrde   frumbearn godes,
sæde soðcwidum: "Snotre gastas,
470 ic eow þurh mine   mihte geworhte,
Adam ærest   and þæt æðele wif.
Þa hie begeton   on godes willan
feowertig bearna,   þæt forð þonon
on middangeard   menio onwocon,
475 and wintra feola   wunian moston,
eorlas on eðle,   oððæt eft gelamp
þæt hie afyrde eft   feond in firenum;

453 dimne] dimme   454 hinsiðgryre] in sið gryre   461 feond] *Followed*
by three or four letters erased   462 swa] sawla   474 on] *Not in MS.*
middangeard] *With a final* e *added by corrector*   onwocon] on węocon
477 hie] he   afyrde] afyrhte

fah is æghwær.

Ic on neorxnawonge   niwe asette
480 treow mid telgum,   þæt ða tanas up
æpla bæron,   and git æton þa
beorhtan blæda,   swa inc se balewa het,
handþegen helle.   Hæfdon forþon hatne grund,
þæs git ofergymdon   hælendes word,
485 æten þa egsan.   Wæs se atola beforan,
se inc bam forgeaf   balewe geþohtas.

   Þa me gereaw   þæt min handgeweorc
þæs carcernes   clom ðrowade.
Næs ða monna gemet,   ne mægen engla,
490 ne witegena weorc,   ne wera snytero,
þæt eow mihte helpan,   nimðe hælend god,
se þæt wite ær   to wrece gesette.
Ferde to foldan   þurh fæmnan had
ufan from eðle,   and on eorþan gebad
495 tintregan fela   and teonan micelne.
Me seredon ymb   secgas monige
dæges and nihtes,   hu heo me deaðes cwealm,
rices rædboran,   hrefnan mihten.
Þa wæs þæs mæles   mearc agangen
500 þæt on worulde wæs   wintra gerimes
þreo and þritig geara   ær ic þrowode.
Gemunde ic ðæs mænego   on þam minnan ham
lange þæs ðe ic of hæftum   ham gelædde
up to earde,   þæt heo agan sceolon
505 drihtnes domas   and duguðe þrym;
wuniað in wynnum,   habbað wuldres blæd
þusendmælum.   Ic eow þingade
þa me on beame   beornas sticedon,
garum on galgum.   Heow se giunga þær,
510 and ic eft up becom   ece dreamas
to haligum drihtne."

---

487 handgeweorc] handgeweorc *with* g *partly erased*   488 þæs] *Not in MS.*
495 fela and] and fela   498 rædboran] boran   502 on] *Abbreviation for*
and   þam] þa   minnan] minan *with second* n *above the line after* i
504 sceolon] *Not in MS.*   509 galgum] *With* e *added above the line before* a

Swa wuldres weard   wordum sæde,
meotod moncynnes   ær on morgen
þæs þe drihten god   of deaðe aras.

515 Næs nan þæs stronglic   stan gefæstnod,
þeah he wære mid irne   eall ymbfangen,
þæt mihte þam miclan   mægne wiðhabban,
ah he ut eode,   engla drihten,
on þæm fæstenne,   and gefatian het

520 englas eallbeorhte   andleofan gingran,
and huru secgan het   Simon Petre
þæt he moste in Galileam   god sceawian,
ecne and trumne,   swa he ær dyde.

þa ic gongan gefregn   gingran ætsomne
525 ealle to Galileam;   hæfdon gastes bled,
ongeton haligne   godes sunu
swa heo gesegon   hwær sunu meotodes
þa on upp gestod,   ece drihten,
god in Galileam.   To ðæs gingran þider

530 ealle urnon,   þær se eca wæs.
Feollon on foldan,   and to fotum hnigon;
þanceden þeodne   þæt hit þus gelomp
þæt hi sceawodon   scyppend engla.

þa sona spræc   Simon Petrus:
535 "Eart þu þis, drihten,   dome gewurðad?
We ðe gesawon   æt sumum cyrre,
þec gelegdon   on laðne bend
hæþene mid hondum;   him þæt gehreowan mæg
þonne heo endestæf   eft gesceawiað."

540 Sume hie ne mihton   mode oncnawan
þæt wæs se deora   (Didimus wæs haten)
ær he mid hondum   hælend genom
sylfne be sidan   þær he his swat forlet;

512 Swa] wa *with space for* s   514 þe] *Above the line after* þæs   515
stan] satan   518 ah] aḫ *with* c *above* h   519 gefatian] gefætian *with* æ
altered from a (*Gollancz*)   521 and] winum and   526 ongeton] *Not in
MS.*   528 þa on] þa gingran on   gestod] stod   531 and to fotum]
"*Blurred but still visible*" (*Gollancz*)   532 þæt hit] *Written twice, the second
time underscored*   537 þec] þeç   538 hæþene] hæþenne   540 mode] mod

feollon to foldan   fulwihtes bæðe.
545   Fæger wæs þæt ongin   þæt freodrihten
geþrowode,   þeoden ure.
He on beame astah   and his blod ageat,
god on galgan,   þurh his gastes mægen.
Forþon men sceolon   mæla gehwylce
550 secgan drihtne þanc   dædum and weorcum,
þæs ðe he us of hæftum   ham gelædde
up to eðle,   þær we agan sceolon
drihtnes domas,
and we in wynnum   wunian moton.
555 Us is wuldres leoht
torht ontyned,   þam ðe teala þenceð.
    Þa wæs on eorðan   ece drihten
feowertig daga   folgad folcum,
gecyðed mancynne,   ær he in þa mæran gesceaft,
560 burhleoda fruma,   bringan wolde
haligne gast   to heofonrice.
Astah up on heofonum   engla scyppend,
weoroda waldend.   Þa com wolcna sweg,
halig of heofonum.   Mid wæs hond godes,
565 onfeng freodrihten,   and hine forð lædde
to þam halgan ham   heofna ealdor.
Him ymbflugon   engla þreatas
þusendmælum.   Þa hit þus gelomp,
þa gyt nergende Crist   gecwæð þæt he þæs
570 ymb tene niht   twelf apostolas
mid his gastes gife,   gingran geswiðde.
Hæfde þa gesette   sawla unrim
god lifigende.   Þa wæs Iudas of,
se ðe ær on tifre   torhtne gesalde,
575 drihten hælend;   him seo dæd ne geþeah,
þæs he bebohte   bearn wealdendes
on seolfres sinc;   him þæt swearte forgeald
earm æglæca   innon helle.

548 galgan] *With* e *added above the line before* a   552 sceolon] *Not in MS.*
557 Þa] a *with space for a capital*   559 mancynne] man cynnes   569
gecwæð] *Not in MS.*   570 tene] ane   572 gesette] ge sette *with a letter
erased after* ge

Siteð nu on þa swiðran hond   sunu his fæderes;
580 dæleð dogra gehwæm   drihten weoroda
help and hælo   hæleþa bearnum
geond middangeard.   Þæt is monegum cuð
þæt he ana is   ealra gescefta
wyrhta and waldend   þurh his wuldres cræft.
585 Siteð him on heofnum   halig encgel,
waldend mid witegum.   Hafað wuldres bearn
his seolfes seld   swegl betolden.
Leaðað us þider to leohte   þurh his læcedom,
þær we moton seolfe   sittan mid drihtne,
590 uppe mid englum,   habban þæt ilce leoht,
þær his hired nu   halig eardað,
wunað in wynnum,   þær is wuldres bled
torht ontyned.   Uton teala hycgan
þæt we hælende   heran georne,
595 Criste cweman.   Þær is cuðre lif
þonne we on eorðan mægen   æfre gestreonan.
Hafað nu geþingod to us   þeoden mæra,
ælmihtig god,
on domdæge   drihten seolfa.
600 Hateð hehenglas   hluddre stefne
beman blawan   ofer burga geseotu
geond foldan sceatas.
Þonne of þisse moldan   men onwecnað;
deade of duste arisað   þurh drihtnes miht.
605 Þæt bið daga lengust,   and dinna mæst
hlud gehered,   þonne hælend cymeð,
waldend mid wolcnum   in þas woruld færeð.
Wile þonne gesceadan   wlitige and unclæne

---

587 betolden] betalden *with* t *partly erased, and* he *substituted above the line
i.e.,* behealden   588 Leaðað] lẹaðað *with* ẹ *erased; see l.* 630   591 his]
is *with* h *added before* i *above the line*   593 teala] *Not in MS.*   595
cweman] a *altered from* æ (*Gollancz*)   599 on] *Written twice, at the end and
at the beginning of a page*   600 hehenglas] heh englas *with* a *above line after
e in* heh   601 beman] *With* y *above* e   603 onwecnað] *With* i *added above
the line before* a   605 dinna] dimma   606 gehered] *With* y *above the
second* e   608 gesceadan] gesceawian

on twa healfe, tile and yfle.
610 Him þa soðfæstan on þa swiðran hond
mid rodera weard reste gestigað.
Þonne beoð bliðe þa in burh moton
gongan in godes rice,
and heo gesenað mid his swiðran hond
615 cynincg alwihta, cleopað ofer ealle:
"Ge sind wilcuman! Gað in wuldres leoht
to heofona rice, þær ge habbað
a to aldre ece reste."
Þonne stondað þa forworhtan, þa ðe firnedon;
620 beoð beofigende hwonne him bearn godes
deman wille þurh his dæda sped.
Wenað þæt heo moten to þære mæran byrig
up to englum swa oðre dydon,
ac him bið reordende
625 ece drihten, ofer ealle gecwæð:
"Astigað nu, awyrgde, in þæt witehus
ofostum miclum. Nu ic eow ne con."
Sona æfter þæm wordum werige gastas,
helle hæftas, hwyrftum scriþað
630 þusendmælum, and þider leaðað
in þæt sceaðena scræf, scufað to grunde
in þæt nearwe nið, and no seoððan
þæt hie up þonan æfre moton,
ah þær geþolian sceolon earmlic wite,
635 clom and carcern, and þone caldan grund
deopne adreogan and deofles spellunge,
hu hie him on edwit oft asettað
swarte suslbonan, stæleð feondas

612 þa] *Followed by* þe *above the line* 613 gongan] o *altered to* a (*Gollancz*)
618 reste] *The first* e *altered to* æ 620 hwonne] þonne *with* þ *altered to* w
and h *prefixed above the line* 624 Ac] *With* c *altered from* h (*Gollancz*)
reordende] reodi de *with two letters erased between* i *and* d, en *above erasure,*
and r *between* e *and* o; *one or two letters erased after this word* 625 gecwæð]
gecwæð *with* y *above* æ 630 þider] "*A word erased before* þider; *probably*
he" (*Gollancz*) leaðað] lę dað (*for* lædað), *a letter erased between* e *and* d,
and d *altered from* ð 638 feondas] *Not in MS.*

fæhðe and firne,   þær ðe hie freodrihten,
640 ecne anwaldan,   oft forgeaton,
þone þe hie him to hihte   habban sceoldon.
Uton, la, geþencan   geond þas worulde,
þæt we hælende   heran onginnen!
Georne þurh godes gife   gemunan gastes bled.
645 hu eadige þær   uppe sittað
selfe mid swegle,   sunu hælendes!
Þær is geat gylden   gimmum gefrætewod.
wynnum bewunden,   þæm þe in wuldres leoht
gongan moten   to godes rice,
650 and ymb þa weallas   wlitige scinað
engla gastas   and eadige sawla,
þa ðe heonon ferað.
Þær martiras   meotode cwemað,
and herigað hehfæder   halgum stefnum,
655 cyning in cestre.   Cweþað ealle þus:
    "Þu eart hæleða helm   and heofendema,
engla ordfruma,   and eorðan tudor
up gelæddest   to þissum eadigan ham."
    Swa wuldres weard   wordum herigað
660 þegnas ymb þeoden,   þær is þrym micel,
sang æt selde,   is sylf cyning,
ealra aldor,   in ðære ecan gesceft.
Þæt is se drihten,   seðe deað for us
geþrowode,   þeoden engla.
665 Swylce he fæste   feowertig daga,
metod mancynnes,   þurh his mildsa sped.
Þa gewearð þone weregan,   þe ær aworpen wæs
of heofonum   þæt he in helle gedeaf,
þa costode   cyning alwihta.
670 Brohte him to bearme   brade stanas,

---

639 firne] in firne   freodrihten] drihten   641 þone] þonne *with the first* n *erased*   þe] *Added above the line*   643 heran] y *above* e   646 selfe] y *above the first* e   sunu] torht sunu   647 gylden] gyldenne *with final* ne *erased*   656 heofendema] heofen deman   657 ordfruma] ordfruman *with the* n *erased*   658 up gelæddest] *Not in MS.*   662 aldor] aðor *with* ð *altered to* d *and with* e *above the line before* a *and* l *after*   668 he] *Inserted above the line*

bæd him for hungre   hlafas wyrcan—
"gif þu swa micle   mihte hæbbe."
    þa him andswarode   ece drihten:
"Wendest þu, awyrgda,   þæt awriten nære,
675 nymþe me ænne

          *   *   *

ac geseted hafast,   sigores agend,
lifigendum liht,   lean butan ende,
on heofenrice,   halige dreamas."
    þa he mid hondum genom
680 atol þurh edwit,   and on esle ahof,
herm bealowes gast,   and on beorh astah,
asette on dune   drihten hælend:
    "Loca nu ful wide   ofer londbuende.
Ic þe geselle   on þines seolfes dom
685 folc and foldan.   Foh hider to me
burh and breotone   bold to gewealde,
rodora rices,   gif þu seo riht cyning
engla and monna,   swa ðu ær myntest."
    þa him andswarode   ece drihten:
690 "Gewit þu, awyrgda,   in þæt witescræf,
Satanus seolf;   þe is susl weotod
gearo togegnes,   nalles godes rice.
Ah ic þe hate   þurh þa hehstan miht
þæt ðu hellwarum   hyht ne abeode,
695 ah þu him secgan miht   sorga mæste,
þæt ðu gemettes   meotod alwihta,
cyning moncynnes.   Cer ðe on bæcling!
Wite þu eac, awyrgda,   hu wid and sid
helheoðo dreorig,   and mid hondum amet.
700 Grip wið þæs grundes;   gang þonne swa
oððæt þu þone ymbhwyrft   alne cunne,

---

680 esle] *With* h *above the line after the first* e   681 herm] her *with* m *added above the line*   bealowes] bealowe *with* s *added by scribe* (Clubb) *or corrector* (Gollancz)   683 londbuende] lond b wende *with a letter erased after* b *and with* u *written above the erasure;* w *underscored as mark of deletion*   684 on] *Not in MS.*   seolfes dom] seoferdum   686 to] *Added above the line*   692 gearo] geara *with* o *above second* a   697 Cer] cer *with* y *above* e

and ærest amet ufan to grunde,
and hu sid seo se swarta eðm.
Wast þu þonne þe geornor þæt þu wið god wunne,
705 seoððan þu þonne hafast handum ametene
hu heh and deop hell inneweard seo,
grim græfhus. Gong ricene to,
ær twa seondon tida agongene,
þæt ðu merced hus ameten hæbbe."
710 Þa þam werigan wearð wracu getenge.
Satan seolua ran and on susle gefeol,
earm æglece. Hwilum mid folmum mæt
wean and witu. Hwilum se wonna læg
læhte wið þes laþan. Hwilum he licgan geseah
715 hæftas in hylle. Hwilum hream astag,
ðonne he on þone atolan eagum gesawun.
Hæfdon gewunnon godes andsacan

    * * *

blac bealowes gast, þæt he on botme stod.
Þa him þuhte þæt þanon wære
720 to helleduru hund þusenda
mila gemearcodes, swa hine se mihtiga het
þæt þurh sinne cræft susle amæte.
Ða he gemunde þæt he on grunde stod.
Locade leas wiht geond þæt laðe scræf,
725 atol mid egum, oððæt egsan gryre
deofla mænego þonne up astag.
Wordum in witum ongunnon þa werigan gastas
reordian and cweðan:
"La, þus beo nu on yfele! Noldæs ær teala!"
    Finit Liber II. Amen.

703 seo] *Follows* eðm *in MS.* 708 seondon] seond *with* on *added above*
the line (*Clubb, Gollancz*) 710 þa] þa *with* a *on an erasure* (*Gollancz*)
þam] a *altered from* e *and* þ *from* s? (*Gollancz*) werigan] werga *with* i *above*
the line before g *and with* n *after* a wracu] wrecę *with the first* e *altered to* a *and*
with v *above the second* e 711 ran] ra *with* n *added above the line* 712
æglece] æglęce 713 læg] *The first half of* æ *erased* 715 hream] ream *with*
h *added above the line before* r astag] *With* h *above* g 718 bealowes]
bealowe *with* s *added above the line* 722 sinne] synne 723 þæt] þa
727 ongunnon þa] ongunnon þa on þa

NOTES

ABBREVIATIONS IN THE NOTES

An. Andreas   Ap. Fates of the Apostles   Az. Azarias   Beow.
Beowulf   Dan. Daniel   El. Elene   Ex. Exodus   Gen. Genesis   Guth.
Guthlac   Jul. Juliana

For Bouterwek, Grein, Junius, Thorpe, Wülker, see Bibliography, Part II. For Behaghel, Blackburn, Clubb, Holthausen, Klaeber, Piper, Schmidt, Sievers, see Bibliography, Part III. For Bright, Ettmüller, Greverus, Kluge, Körner, Rieger, Sedgefield, Sweet, see Bibliography, Part IV.

Anglia Beibl.   Beiblatt zur Anglia.
Anz. fdA.   Anzeiger für deutsches Altertum.
Archiv.   Archiv für das Studium der neueren Sprachen und Literaturen.
Beitr.   Beiträge zur Geschichte der deutschen Sprache und Literatur.
Bonner Beitr.   Bonner Beiträge zur Anglistik.
Bos.-Tol.   Bosworth-Toller, Anglo-Saxon Dictionary.
Bouterwek, Erläut.   Erläuterungen (in Vol. I of his edition).
Dietrich.   Zu Cädmon, in ZfdA. X, 310–367.
Eng. Stud.   Englische Studien.
Gollancz.   The Cædmon Manuscript.
Graz.   Die Metrik der sog. Cædmonschen Dichtungen.
Grein, Dicht.   Dichtungen der Angelsachsen.
Grein, Spr.   Sprachschatz der angelsächsischen Dichter.
Grein-Köhler.   Sprachschatz der angelsächsischen Dichter, revised ed. by Köhler.
Groth.   Composition und Alter der altenglischen (angelsächsischen) Exodus.
Indog. Forsch.   Indogermanische Forschungen.
JEGPh.   Journal of English and Germanic Philology.
Johnson.   Translation of the OE. Exodus, in JEGPh. V, 44–57.
Kock, JJJ.   Jubilee Jaunts and Jottings.
Kock, PPP.   Plain Points and Puzzles.
Lye-Manning.   Dictionarium Saxonico- et Gothico-Latinum.
Mason.   Genesis A (translation).
MLN.   Modern Language Notes.
MLRev.   Modern Language Review.
Mürkens.   Untersuchungen über das altenglische Exoduslied, in Bonner Beitr. II, 62–117.
Rieger, Verskunst.   Die alt- und angelsächsische Verskunst, in ZfdPh. VII, 1–64.
Schubert.   De Anglosaxonum arte metrica.
Sievers, Angels. Gram.   Angelsächsische Grammatik, 3d ed., 1898.
ZfdA.   Zeitschrift für deutsches Altertum.
ZfdPh.   Zeitschrift für deutsche Philologie.

NOTES ON GENESIS

1–100

Genesis] For the title, see Introd., p. xviii.   **6 cymþ**] Holthausen changes
to *cymeð* to gain a metrical syllable, and so also in l. 2321.   For similar
emendations, see note on *sprycest*, l. 2528, and also on *gan*, l. 870, *doþ*, l.
1206, *Noes*, l. 1240, and *Sarran*, l. 1854.   **7 ecean**] Holthausen has *ēcęan*,
i.e. *ēcan*, the second *e* being deleted for metrical reasons. He also deletes
the *e* in *weccean*, l. 31, *secean*, l. 927, *geiceað*, l. 1514, and similar words.
These emendations will not be noted hereafter.   **9 swiðfeorm**] All edd.
read *-feorm*, as in l. 1770, but *-from* is also possible, see Bos.-Tol., under
swiðfrom. Holthausen suggests *-freom*.   **10 wide and side**] Holthausen,
following Graz, Festschrift für Schade, p. 68, reads *side ond wide*, for
metrical reasons.   **13 and**] Holthausen changes to *mid*. But *ordfruman*
may be taken as a genitive dependent on *blisse*.   **15–18**] Grein,
Spr. I, 208, proposes *dryhten-nes* for *drihtenes*, l. 17, a noun, "majesty,"
as obj. of *demdon*, with a genitive, "of god," to be supplied, or as
alternative, *drihtenes* [æ], "the law of the lord."   For the phrase *æ deman*,
see An. 1194, 1403, Ap. 10.   But the addition of *æ* does not remove the
difficulties in the passage any more satisfactorily than punctuation will do.
Translate, "The valiant thanes honored their prince, said his praise gladly,
glorified their life-lord, in the strength of the were very happy."
Holthausen has a comma after *liffrean* (for which he reads *liffregan* for
metrical reasons, as similarly in ll. 868, 1808, 1822, 1852, 2141, 2231
note, 2239, and 2784), no punctuation after *lof*, and a semicolon after
drihtenes.   **22 weard**] Holthausen, Anglia XLVI, 62, reads *wearð*,
and so previously Zupitza, Anz. fdA. I, 121, note.   **23 dwæl**] Grein,
Spr. I, 187, assumes a verb *delan*, not otherwise recorded, "labi," translating "lapsus est in errorem," but with hesitation. Bouterwek reads
dweal for *dæl*, from the verb *dwelan*, "to go astray," "to err," the explanation followed in the text. Wülker would read *dælde gedwilde*, "engaged in
error." The verbal echo in *dwæl* and *gedwilde* is nothing against the reading *dwæl*, see ll. 291, 564, 599, 657, 1825, 2216, etc.   Reading *wearð*, l. 22,
Holthausen takes *dæl* as a noun, "portion," and so also Grein-Köhler, p.
114.   **51 hehste**] Holthausen changes to *hehsta*, appositive to *waldend*,
l. 49. Kock, PPP., p. 10, suggests *hæste*, "with violence." But *hehste* can
agree with *honda*. Mason translates, "lifted up his almighty hand against
the throng," following Grein, Dicht., p. 2, "seine Hand erhub die höchste
wider die Heerschaar."   **58 tire**] Holthausen *fire*, corrected in Anglia
XLVI, 60.   **60 styrne mod**] Holthausen *styrnemod* (and so Kluge), but
changed to *styrne mod*, Anglia XLVI, 60. Kock, PPP., p. 10, also reads

styrne mod, "He had a stern spirit."   **63** yrre] Holthausen reads *yrre*, the usual form of the adjective, but the other edd. retain the MS. reading.   The word stands at the end of a line in the MS. and this position may have determined the form *yr*.   æðele] Subject of *bescyrede*, and referring to *se mæra*, l. 53.   But Junius and Grein read *eðele*, inst. of *eðel*, and Holthausen, notes, approves this reading, though he does not incorporate it in his text.   **65** Sceof] So Holthausen, as a Northumbrian form for *sceaf*. Greverus reads *sceof* or *sceaf*, Bouterwek *sceop* in his text, but *sceof* in Erläut., p. 294.   Grein, Wülker retain *sceop*, translated by Grein, Dicht., p. 3, "schaffte," and Spr. II, 400, "relegavit."   The *þ* in the MS. reading *sceop* may have been written in anticipation of *scyppend*, l. 65b.   **72** siðe] Wülker reads *seomodon swearte siðe*. *Ne þorfton*, etc. Sievers, Beitr. X, 512, and Holthausen read as in the text, except a colon after *swearte*. Cosijn, Beitr. XIX, 444, would rearrange to read:

> heo on wrace seomodon
> swearte siðe; syððan ne þorfton, etc.

82 buað] The edd. retain the MS. reading *buan*, except Holthausen, who reads *budan* (for *budon*), or as alternative, *buað*. The form *buan* might stand if there were need for a subjunctive here.   **98** roderas] Genitive singular in *-as*, see ll. 148, 485, and Sievers, Angels. Gram., §237, Anm. 1.

101–200

107 stiðfrihþ] The usual form is *stiðferhð*, as in ll. 241, 1406, 1683, and Bouterwek and Greverus alter the text here to agree. For examples of similar metathesis, see Sievers, Angels. Gram., §179. See l. 1142, note. **116** gyta] Holthausen reads *gyta*, which seems to have been the original form and is better metrically than *gyt*. The other edd., and Jovy, Bonner Beitr. V, 29, prefer *gyt*. See l. 155.   **117** græs] Bouterwek, Erläut., p. 297, supported by Holthausen, Anglia XLVI, 60, though not in his edition, reads *græse*, "with grass."   But *græs* may be taken as appositive to *Folde*. Grein, Spr. I, 623, calls *græs* an instrumental accusative, see l. 812, note. **118** synnihte] Subject of *þeahte*, *garsecg* and *wægas* being objects. See Genesis i. 2. So also Cosijn, Beitr. XIX, 445.   **131** gesceaft] Junius, Kluge, Wülker retain *gescaft*.   **135** timber] Grein retains *tiber*, but Spr. II, 530, alters to *timber*, and so Bouterwek, Erläut., p. 297, Dietrich, Greverus, Wülker, Holthausen.   **142** dydon] Holthausen, *dēdon*, and so also in l. 2600, following Sievers, Beitr. X, 498, who recommends *dǣdon* for metrical reasons.   **150** Flod] So Grein and later edd. See Genesis i. 7. **155** gyta] See l. 116, note.   **165** wide æteowde] Kock, PPP., p. 10, regards these words as parenthetical, "wide did it appear."   **167** onrihtne ryne] Holthausen changes to *ryne onrihtne* for the sake of alliteration, assuming that *onrihtne* must be stressed *ónrihtne*. But it is simpler to assume a pronunciation *onríhtne*. See Holthausen, Eng. Stud. XXXVII, 202–203. **168** and gefetero] The last words on p. 8, after which several pages have been lost from the manuscript, the matter on these pages corresponding to

Genesis i. 11 to Genesis ii. 18. Gollancz, p. li, believes that eight pages (four leaves) were lost here. The edd. since Bouterwek complete the word to read *gefeterode*. **182** liodende] From *leodan*, "grow." For the spelling, see *liodgeard*, l. 229, *niotað*, l. 235, etc. **183** wer unwundod] Holthausen, following Bouterwek, Erläut., p. 298, supplies *wæs* after *wer*. Kock, PPP., p. 11, takes *wer* as an uninflected dative appositive to *him*, l. 181, translating, "but out of his, the hale man's, body drew the angels' sovereign a bone that grew." Mason translates, "while the man was unwounded." This seems to be the intent of the passage, though perhaps it is unnecessary to supply *wæs*, and *wer unwundod* may be taken as appositive to *he*, l. 178. Cosijn, Beitr. XIX, 445, regards *ne þær...ban* as parenthetic. **184** freolice] Grein and the earlier edd. retain *freolicu*, but Grein, Spr. I, 345, *freolice*, and so Wülker, Holthausen. **186** Eve] Something is needed to complete the line and the sense here, and Holthausen supplied *Eve* after *wæs*. Grein supplied *þe god Eve nemde* after *bryd*, and Bouterwek, Erläut., p. 298, *Eue hatte*.

201–300

203 ða ðe land tredað] This clause modifies *wilde deor*, l. 202. In l. 203, *lifigende* goes with *feorheaceno cynn*, modified by *ða ðe flod wecceð*, "which the flood brings forth." Cosijn, Beitr. XIX, 445, reads *eall lifigende*. For l. 204*b*, Cosijn, Beitr. XIX, 526, suggests *ða ðe flod wecgað*, citing Dan. 388. **205** Inc hyrað eall] These are the last words on p. 10, only one half of which contains text, the other half being occupied by an illustration. Although there is no break in the syntax, Gollancz, p. li, thinks a leaf has been lost between p. 10 and p. 11, which contained a paraphrase of Genesis i. 29–30 and Genesis ii. 1–5, including the ordination of the first Sabbath. After that the poet returned, l. 206, to the paraphrase of Genesis i. 31, which he made to refer "directly to the Sabbath contemplation," although in the Bible, Genesis i. 31 refers only to the work of the first six days. With l. 210 the poet then continues with the matter of Genesis ii. 5 ff. Certainly the omissions are striking here, and since the physical state of the manuscript indicates the loss of one leaf at this place, the missing matter may thus be accounted for. **209** gastlic] Holthausen, following Greverus, *gæstlic*. But *gastlic* may be retained as a variant of the same word, "hospitable," "ready for guests," as defined in Bos.-Tol. Grein, Spr. I, 374, defines the word in this passage as "gastlich." Less probable is the interpretation of the word as *gāstlic*, "spiritual," or "good and holy," as *god and gastlic* is translated by Mason, p. 6. **210** leohte] "Flowed over," from *leccan*. **221** Þæra anne] The MS. reading *þære hatað* is not intelligible syntactically. Dietrich changed to *þæra anne*, followed by Grein and by Wülker. Holthausen reads merely *Hatað ylde*, but Holthausen, Anglia Beibl. XXX, 3, suggests *Ænne hatað ylde*. Kock, JJJ., p. 28, suggests *þæra ane*. Cosijn, Beitr. XIX, 446, suggests *þæne = þone*, citing l. 2645, taking the word as equivalent to *þone forman*. **222** se] Grein and later edd. read *se* for *sæ*. **224** Hebeleac] The MS. reads *hebeleac*, not *he beleac* as reported by Wülker and so interpreted by Junius and Thorpe. Grein changes to *Hebeleat*. Holthausen has *Hebeleað*. The Vulgate reads *Nomen uni Phison: ipse est qui circuit omnem terram Hevilath, ubi nascitur aurum*, Genesis ii. 11. **232 Assirie**] In the MS. the final letter of this word has a tag beneath it, like that used in various other places to indicate that *e* is to be taken as *æ*. Perhaps it should be also at this place so taken. See ll. 278, 661, 1235. **234 wide nemnað**] These are the concluding words on p. 12 of the manuscript. The page is only about two thirds filled with writing, the rest remaining blank, as an indication that "the artist was to give a full-page illustration on the next leaf, probably in this case a picture of the four rivers," Gollancz, p. li. But the leaf following that containing p. 12 has been lost, including this illustration and the paraphrase of matter dealing with the tree of knowledge and forming a transition to l. 235. **235 ac niotað**] With this line begins Gen. B, which is to a large extent an interruption of the orderly paraphrase of Gen. A. The work of the poet of Gen. A begins again with l. 852 with the paraphrase of Genesis iii. 8 ff. See Introd., p. xxv. For the text of the OS. fragment which corresponds to the passage in Genesis, see l. 791, note. **238 sædon ealles þanc**] For the sake of alliteration, Grein supplies *gode* before *ealles;* so also Sievers, but Sievers, Beitr. X, 195, retracts, noting with Rieger, Verskunst, p. 12, that *ea* alliterates with initial palatal *g*. But the confirmatory instances cited, Ex. 33, 190, 339, Christ and Satan 107, are all doubtful, except Ex. 339. Holthausen, Anglia XLIV, 335, suggests *sǽdon ěalles gōdes þanc*. Klaeber, Anglia XLIX, 361, remarks that nothing is needed to complete the meaning of the passage, but that one expects a *g* in the second half-line for alliteration. See l. 249 and note. **243 butan**] Bouterwek, Erläut., p. 299, alters to *butu* as subject of *læsten*, altered to *læston*. Grein suggests *hu* after *butan*, and Sievers, Piper, Behaghel supply *þæt* after *butan*. But *butan* must be taken here in some such sense as "on the condition that." **244 leof**] Uninflected because neuter plural, to refer to two subjects of different genders. So also *lað*, l. 630, *baru*, l. 838. **249 fyligan**] An appropriate word here, though it does not satisfy the demands of alliteration. Ettmüller, Grein, Rieger, Sievers, Klaeber alter to *fulgan*, Sweet, Körner to *fullgan*, and Piper, Behaghel to *fulgangan*, as in l. 782. Wülker retains the MS. reading. Grein, Spr. I, 356, records the word under *ful-gan*. See l. 238 and note. **258 leanes**] Grein suggests *lænes*, but Spr. II, 169, retains *leanes*. **leohte**] For this sense of *leoht*, see l. 310, and see Klaeber, Anglia XXXV, 455 f. for examples of *leoht = heofon*. See l. 401, note. **267 geongerdome**] "In d scipleship." **269 mægyn**] For *mægen;* see *engyl*, l. 262, *æfyn*, l. 313. **271 gespæc**] Piper, Behaghel, *gespræc*. **283 bugan**] Kock, PPP., p. 11, remarks that "Versification and phraseology both point to corruption" here. The sense of *bugan* seems not appropriate. Kock suggests a form *begean* (cf. OHG. *bijehan*), "avow." "The OE. scribe," continues Kock, "had before him a word common in the related dialects but more or less strange to him; no wonder that he turned it into a familiar OE. word." See also Sievers, Heliand, p. xxxiii, n., and Klaeber, Anglia XLIX, 361. Holthausen, Anglia XLIV, 355, proposes to replace *bugan* by *unnan*. It seems best to retain the form *bugan* in some such meaning as Kock suggests.   **287** folcgesteallan] A dative plural, see l. 657, note.

301–400

306 ufon] Omitted by Grein, Rieger, Sweet, but the other edd. retain the word.   **307** þurhlonge swa] The MS. has *þurh longe*, but the two parts of one word are often thus separated. Dietrich, Behaghel read *þurh longe þrage*, and Rieger, Kluge, *þurhlonge þrage*, taking *þurh, þurhlonge* as prepositions. Grein reads *þurh swa longe swa*, and so also Sievers, Piper, Sweet, Körner. Klaeber, Anglia XXXVII, 539, takes *þurhlonge* as an acc. pl. adj., citing the phrase *ondlangne dæg*, and Beow. 759, *uplang astod*. Kock, PPP., p. 12, takes *þurhlonge* as adv., like Latin *perlonge*, an adv. of extent of time, parallel to *þreo niht and dagas*. "As for *ða. . .swa*, it is simply a variant of *swa ða*, 'thus then' "; see Gen. 1669. Kock's interpretation seems the most acceptable.   **308** of heofnum] Grein, Rieger, and Sweet replace *of heofnum* by *ufon*, which they had omitted from l. 306.   **309** Forþon heo] Grein, Rieger, Sweet, Körner supply *þe* before *heo*.   **310** he] Grein, Rieger, Sievers, Sweet, Körner omit *he*, Thorpe, Bouterwek, Ettmüller, Greverus read *þe* for *he*.   **316** gar] Klaeber, notes, "Is *gar*, 'spear', meant for 'piercing cold'?" So also Klaeber, Anglia XXXVII, 539, and Anglia XLIX, 362. Holthausen, Anglia XLIV, 355, suggests *fær* (*fēr*) for *fyr* and *sār* for *gār*. Dietrich had suggested *gryre* for *gar*, Körner, *gal*. But *gar* may be taken literally, prodding with spears being commonly a part of the torments of hell.   **317** geswinc] Grüters, Bonner Beitr. XVII, 13, n., notes Grein's translation of this word as "Geschwing" (see Dicht., p. 10) and cites Jul. 337, *suslum swingen*.   **318** man] Behaghel omits, regarding *god*, l. 311, as the object of the verb. Klaeber, notes, "The indef. *man* (i.e. really 'God') serves as subj. of *fylde*."   **321** heofonrices hehðe] Graz, Festschrift für Schade, p. 69, transposes, *hehðe heofonrices*. Klaeber, *heofona rices hehðe*, citing l. 512, or as alternative, *heofones hehðe*. For ll. 320–322 Holthausen, Eng. Stud. XXXVII, 203, proposes to read:

Heoldon englas forð
hēhðe hĕofonrīces, þe ǣr hyldo godes,
lāre gelǣston: lāgon þā ōðre,
fŷnd on þam fŷre, etc.

331 hell] Ettmüller, Dietrich, Sweet, *helle*, but Klaeber, JEGPh. XII, 254, defends the form *hell* as a good OS. form, noting l. 792, where OS. *hell* has been made into AS. *helle*, to the detriment of the meter according to Graz. **334** fyres fær micel] Appositive to *oðer land*, Cosijn, Beitr. XIX, 446, but in the nominative on account of *þæt wæs*.   **344** cwæð se hehsta] Piper, Behaghel supply *þæt* before *se* from the corrector's reading.   **345** sweartan helle] Perhaps a comma should be placed after *helle*, making *sweartan helle* and *grundes* appositives, as urged by Kock, Anglia XLII, 122, though Klaeber, Anglia XLIX, 363, rightly points out that it is not always possible to dogmatise as to the poet's intention in passages like this. **356 þæs ænga styde**] The customary MS. form would be *þes enga stede*. The corrector's change of *ænga* to *æniga* seems to indicate that he did not understand the passage. On *æ* for *e*, see l. 564, note, and Bülbring, Altenglisches Elementarbuch, § 92, Anm. 1. Piper, Behaghel read *Is þes ænga stede*. **357 ham**] Rieger, note, supplies *hame*, Behaghel (1922), Klaeber, *ham* to complete the line. See Sievers, Angels. Gram., § 237, Anm. 2. **358 hean**] Grein suggests *heah*, but *hean*, for *heam*, is dative singular, agreeing with l. 357*a*; but as Klaeber, notes, points out, *heanne*, agreeing with *þe*, l. 357*b*, would also be possible. **362 helle þære hatan**] A dative parallel to *fyre*, see Kock, Anglia XLII, 122, and Klaeber, Anglia XLIX, 363. **370**] Thorpe, Bouterwek, Grein regard this passage as a rhetorical anacoluthon, and it is so taken here. Rieger, Sweet, Sievers, Klaeber assume a loss in the MS. after *werode*. Wülker assumes no gap and places a period after *werode*, joining the phrase *þonne...werode* with what precedes—but just how is not clear. **371 irenbenda**] Piper, Behaghel, *irenbendas*. **377 habbað**] Grein suggests, and Sweet accepts, *hafað;* but *gespong* is neuter and may be plural. **390 grimme, grundlease**] The first of these two adjectives is best taken as modifying *þrea*, the second *helle*, "But we suffer now torments in hell, (these are darkness and heat), torments grievous in hell the bottomless." **393 Ne**] Dietrich, Grein, Rieger, *nu* for *Ne*. **394 him**] Piper omits *him*.

401–500

401 Ne gelyfe ic, etc.] "I have now no more hope of that life (light), which he thinks long to enjoy to himself, of that happiness with his host of angels." See also Klaeber, Anglia XXXVII, 540. Grein, Sievers, Körner omit *nu*, Rieger changes *nu* to *na*. See l. 258, note. **406 ahwet**] "Rejects," "repudiates," if the word is from *ahwettan*. But Klaeber, citing Cosijn, ZfdPh. XXVIII, 149, thinks the word is *āhwēt* = *āhwǣt*, from an otherwise unrecorded *āhwātan*, "curse." But the simpler explanation is to be preferred. The word may of course be translated as a future. **410 þan**] Ettmüller, Greverus, Sievers change to *þam*, but see Sievers, Angels. Gram., § 187. **414 hwilc**] The MS. reads plainly *hwilc*, not *hwilc*, as given by Klaeber. **417 feðerhoman**] The scribe evidently wrote *fæder-* inadvertently as the first element of this word. His original may have had *fæðer-*. See l. 356, note, on *æ* for *e*. **431 gegarwod**] So Sievers, Klaeber, but other edd., *gegearwod*. **433 sefte**] Grein, Rieger, Sievers, Sweet, *softe*. **441 lare**] The last word on p. 22. Probably two leaves, i.e., four pages, have been lost between p. 22 and p. 23, containing sections IX and X of the manuscript. See Gollancz, p. cx. Various edd. complete the line in different ways, but no one has attempted to supply the whole of the missing sections. On the left-hand margin of p. 22 stand the letters *xm*, see Introd., p. xvii, misinterpreted by Wülker, Klaeber and others as XIII. **444 asette and þone**] Schröder, ZfdA. XLIII, 381, would omit these words. **hæleð-helm**] From *heoloðhelm*, "covering helmet," "helmet of invisibility," by

mechanical association of the first element with *hæleð*, "man," "hero."
445 spenn] Wülker correctly records the MS. reading as *speonn*, with *o*
above the line. Klaeber also gives *speonn* as a MS. reading. **446 wora**]
From *woh*, but the loss of the final consonant in the uninflected form evidently troubled some reader who wrote *wraþra* in the margin as a gloss.
464 on] Metrically stressed, therefore not a prefix, but adverbial, and to be
connected with *þær*, l. 464*a*. **465 godes and yfeles**] Behaghel supplies
gewand after *yfeles*, as in l. 481. **470 worulde**] Klaeber alters to *wuldre*,
but in Anglia XXXVII, 540, accepts *worulde* as permissible. **472 symle**]
Klaeber, *symble*. **475 habban**] Grein suggests omitting this word, but he
retains it in his text, placing it in l. 474, followed by a semicolon. So also
Wülker. This would make *wæron witode* a verb, "were decreed." But *to
wæron* is better regarded as an adverbial phrase, "in truth," and thus taken
makes unnecessary the various additions and emendations that have been
proposed. The interpretation in the text is that of Klaeber, following Graz,
Festschrift für Schade, p. 69. See also Klaeber, JEGPh. XII, 252. Kock,
JJJ., p. 29, takes *to wæron witod* as meaning "zugesichert." Piper, Behaghel
supply *tires* before *geþingþo*, following Grein, who later, Spr. I, 472, changed
to *wuldres*. Klaeber thinks the alterations prove that the original text was
different from the MS., and he restores thus: *habban him to wæron wuldor*
(or *wynne*, OS. *wunnia*) *geþinged | on þone hean heofon*. He thinks *witod*
might have been added as a gloss of *geþinged*. This is all possible, but if
this is what happened, the changes resulted in a surprisingly good substitute
for the original readings. It looks as though the scribe wrote *witod geþinge*,
"appointed destiny," which might well have been allowed to stand. The
corrector changed to *witode geþingþo*, "appointed honors." Holthausen,
Anglia XLIV, 355, would supply *sceolde* before *on þone hean heofon*, citing
the repetition of *sceolde* in ll. 479, 481, 484, 486, 488, but Klaeber, Anglia
XLIX, 365, thinks *moste* is more suitable, if any verb is supplied. **476
wende**] Subjunctive in a temporal clause, and better taken as a singular,
therefore *he* for *heo*, in accord with the rest of the passage. **481 gewand**]
Grein, Wülker read *gewanod*, following the MS. corrector. Grein, Spr. I,
475, translates the word "humiliatus," agreeing with the subject of *sceolde*.
Reading *gewand* as a noun, object of *witan*, the meaning would be a derived
sense of *windan*, "turning," "distinction," as suggested by Klaeber, notes.
Sweet, Student's Dictionary, gives "hesitation," "scruple" as meanings of
the word. **485 dreamas**] See l. 98, note. **486–488**] Behaghel, following
Graz, Festschrift für Schade, p. 69, makes two lines of these three, ending
his first half-line with *niotan*, the first full line with *sweartost* and a semicolon,
and the following half-line with *þeowian* and a colon. **487 on fyre**] Klaeber, notes, suggests that *fyre = fȳren*, and apparently he would translate
this half-line, "swartest, i.e., blackest in crime." But the combination of
sweart with *fyr*, "fire," is in keeping with the medieval conception of hell.

501–600

503 sceattes] "Property," "treasure," see l. 813, where the proper form of the word appears in the MS. Grein, Germania X, 417, Wülker retain *sceates*, "garment," but Grein, Spr. II, 405, *sceattes*, and so also Klaeber, Holthausen, Anglia Beibl. V, 228. **509** þis] Klaeber, *his*. **513** ufan] To be connected with *on*, l. 512. See *þær, on*, l. 464. **516** to þinre spræce] "For speech with thee." See l. 557, and Klaeber, Anglia XXV, 300, for other examples. **525** and me her stondan het] Sievers supplies *he* before *me*. Klaeber suggests omitting *and*. Grein suggests *stundum* for *stondan*. **546** geofian] Wülker wrongly records marks of deletion under *eo* in *geofian* in the MS. **555** swa] Klaeber puts *swa* in the second half-line, but logically it is closely connected with *hwilc*, "whatever." Grein, Germania X, 417, would supply a second *swa* before *hwilc*. The MS. has *hwilc ærende swa*, with a metrical point after *swa*. **561** his] "For it," "of it"—that the Lord will be angry. **564** Æt] An imperative, and altered by Ettmüller, Klaeber to *et*. But *æ* for *e* is frequent in the MS. Grein, Germania X, 417, suggests taking *æt* as an objective noun, "esum," "food," after *wisie*. Grein, Sievers read *ofætes* for *ofetes*, as in l. 599. **569** his willan] Klaeber, notes, takes *his* as gen. sg. neut., "if thou hast desire of this"—if you will agree to my plan. Kock, PPP., p. 14, translates "his good-will (and confidence)," that is, Adam's. But Klaeber, Anglia XLIX, 366, adequately defends his interpretation, supported also by Cosijn, Beitr. XIX, 446, who cites l. 733, *his sorge*, as parallel. **571** bisne] Klaeber suggests *blisse*. **573** an forlæteð] Grein, Wülker, *anforlæteð*. See ll. 643, 693. **574** him bu tu] Graz, p. 99, reads *bu tu him*, and Holthausen, Eng. Stud. XXXVII, 203, Klaeber read *swa wit him bu tu nu*, in order to make the first metrically stressed syllable of the second half-line fall on *bu*. But examples of alliteration on the second stressed syllable in the second half-line are not uncommon, see ll. 892, 966, 2762, 2770, Dan. 122, 202, 460, Christ and Satan 237, 513, 617. **575** an sped] For *on sped*, "successfully," "effectively." **581** teonum georn] Klaeber suggests *teona*, noting the similar syntax of *dæda georn*, Dan. 281. In Anglia XXXVII, 540, he suggests the possibility of reading *gearo* for *ᵹeorn*, noting Beow. 1813, *searwum gearwe*, etc. **592** lætan] Bouterwek, Erläut., p. 301, *lædan* for *lætan*. The use of *lætan* here is not customary Anglo-Saxon, but Sievers, note, points out a similar idiom in Heliand, l. 2517.

601–700

609 forhatena] Klaeber suggests *forhwatena*, "accursed." See l. 406, note. **613** getruwodest] Sievers, Beitr. X, 486, Graz, p. 97, read *getrēowdest*, for metrical reasons. Klaeber suggests *getrū(w)dest*, and Trautmann, Bonner Beitr. II, 162, Eng. Stud. XLIV, 336, suggests a short vowel in the word, *trŭwian*. **617** hwilce þu gesihðe, etc.] "What vision, what powers thou hast through my coming." In AS. *cræft* is usually masculine, but Klaeber, notes, points out that in OS. the word is masc., fem. or neut., the form here being influenced by OS. Grein, Spr. I, 168, gives *cræfta* as gen. pl. with a question. Greverus alters *minne* to *minre*, "through the power (effect) of my coming," but *cime, cyme* is masculine. **622 þæs fela]** The edd. take *þæs fela* as continuing the construction after *alætanne*, with *þæs fela* in the first half-line and no punctuation after *alætanne*. Kock, PPP., p. 14, thinks that "*þæs* belongs to the *b*-verse, and goes with *spræc*, whereas *alætanne* governs *his*." He places a colon after *alætanne*. Klaeber, Anglia XLIX, 367, approves. **623 hire]** Junius, Klaeber retain *hire*, but other edd. change to *his* in order to make *Swa hire*, etc., harmonize with and become a part of the preceding speech of Satan. But one scarcely expects the poet to derive wisdom from the words of Satan, and ll. 623–625 seem like an inept moral intrusion, not a part of Satan's speech. See also Klaeber, JEGPh. XII, 253. Klaeber, notes, suggests that *hire*, l. 623, is for *hira*. But this is unnecessary, since Satan is speaking directly to Eve. **633 hierran]** For *herran, hearran*, "the favor of the Lord." **634 monige hwile]** "For a long time." Unusual Anglo-Saxon, but Klaeber, notes, accounts for the phrase as OS. use. **636 Sum...sum]** Accusative sg. masc., referring to *æppel*, "One she bare in her hand, another lay at her heart," and the correct grammatical form would therefore be *sumne* for the first *sum*. **644 laðe treow]** Grein, Sievers, Wülker, Piper, *laðtreow*. **647 hie]** Bouterwek, Erläut., p. 301, changes to *he*, Satan, and deletes *and*, l. 648*b*. Holthausen, Anglia XLIV, 355, would agree, unless one takes *hie* as accusative sing. fem. referring to Eve. But it may also be plural, referring to both Adam and Eve and continuing the dative plural of *him*, l. 646, then changing in l. 648*b* to remarks about Eve alone. Holthausen would also change *and hyge* to *hygeþanc*. He had previously suggested *speon hyge* (*Evan*), Anglia Beibl. XVIII (1907), 203, and *hygesceaft*, Eng. Stud. LI (1917), 180, as substitutes for *and hyge*. **649 wac geþoht]** Sievers, Behaghel, *wacgeþoht*. Grein, Spr. I, 472, glosses this phrase as nominative singular, but it is better taken as appositive to *hyge*, l. 648. But one would expect *wacne geþoht*, unless *geþoht* is regarded as a neuter. The compound avoids the grammatical difficulty, but it creates others. **656 bliðe]** Klaeber, *bliðe*, citing l. 751. The earlier edd. follow the MS. **657 gearwan]** A dative plural with a late weakened ending, see l. 287, *folcgesteallan*. Grein, Spr. I, 495, takes it as a weak dat. sing., but he has no other examples of this word as a weak sing. **667 suð and east]** Thorpe and others read *suðeast*, and Cosijn, Beitr. XIX, 447, formally defends this reading on the ground that "gott sitzt doch nur an einer und derselben stelle," not in two places. But of course *suð and east* can be the equivalent of *suðeast*. **676 leohte]** Grein adds *swa* before *leohte*, and so also Sievers, Piper. **680 from]** Klaeber suggests *for* or *be*. **686 bræcon]** For *bræcen*, "should break," and Junius so gives it, but the other edd. follow the MS.

701–800

702 him] So Thorpe, notes, and later edd. except Grein, Germania X, 417, Wülker, Piper, who retain *hire* as a reflexive, an improbable construction. **703** to forlæranne] Similar incomplete lines occur elsewhere in the MS., see ll. 1125, 1199, 1602, and may have been so left by the poet. The editors have filled out this line in various ways. Grein, Piper supply *on laðlicne wroht* for l. 703*b*, Klaeber supplies *leofne mannan*. There is no indication of loss in the MS., but if anything has dropped out, this is more likely to have occurred after *handweorc godes*, which comes at the end of a line in the MS., than after *to forlæranne*, which begins a line. Klaeber's addition makes it possible to take *handweorc* as the subject of *wæs*, but in the text as it stands, *handweorc* is object of *forlæranne*.   **707** þe him þæt wif] Sievers assumes that something has been lost from the MS. after *wif*, and Klaeber, JEGPh. XII, 254, suggests as the original reading, *þe him þæt wif weðum | wordum sægde*, and so in his edition. Holthausen, Anglia XLIV, 355, supplies *wlitige* before *wif*, but Indog. Forsch. IV, 379, and Anglia Beibl. V, 228, *ofta* after *wif*. Behaghel supplies *wærlice*, and Graz, Festschrift für Schade, p. 70, reads *þe þæt wif to him*. But many lines of the same type as *þe him þæt wif* can be found in the MS. and no change is necessary.   **708** þær] Grein alters to *þæs*.   **719** ofetes] Wülker, Klaeber misreport the MS. as reading *ofætes* and so print in their texts.   **723** ofet unfæle] Appositive to *hit*, l. 720.   **725** begra] "He said thank for both (i.e. Adam and Eve) to his master." Or Klaeber suggests reference to l. 751, though this seems remote. **730** his] Sievers, Graz, p. 97, Piper place *his* in l. 731. But see l. 748 and l. 771.   **733** his] "For this," "of this," explained by l. 735*b* ff.   **748** eft] Klaeber, following Behaghel, places *eft* in l. 748*a*.   **752** heofonrice] Grein, Wülker, and the earlier edd., except Ettmüller, retain the MS. reading, but Ettmüller and Grein, Germania X, 417, read *heofonrice*.   **760** laðes] "With respect to the injury." So apparently Klaeber in his edition and in Anglia XLIX, 367. Kock, JJJ., p. 29, takes the construction as equivalent to *and eall þæt wit laðes*, "whatever of injury that we have long suffered." **765** simon] For *simum*, dat. pl. of *sima*.   **769** forstodon] Sievers, Behaghel assume a loss in the MS. after *forstodon*.   **771** hof] Ettmüller alters to *heaf*, Grein to *heof*, from *heafan*, "lament," as the sense requires, but Klaeber suggests OS. influence on the MS. form.   **772** þa heo, etc.] "When she saw that light depart elsewhere which he who had brought this affliction on them through his advice had showed to her deceptively as a token."   **774** geræd] For *gerēd*, preterite of a reduplicating verb, "brought about by advice," Sweet, Student's Dictionary. See l. 797. On *æ* for *e*, see ll. 258, 356, 417, 564.   **780** heofones waldend, etc.] Holthausen, Anglia Beibl. XVIII, 204, would supply *helpan* before *bædon*, alter *þæt*, l. 781, to *hwæt*, and supply *to* before *hearmsceare*. But as Klaeber points out, Anglia XXXVII, 541, the text can stand without alteration. Holthausen's readings are supported by l. 829.   **785** sælða] Ettmüller suggests *selda* for *sælða*, but the form in the MS. is probably influenced by OS. *seliða*, "dwelling," "habitation." With Grein, Spr. I, 455, *gesetena* is to be taken as participial adjective, modifying *sælða*. **788** forweard] "In future," "continually," the only occurrence of this sense, and perhaps the word should be *forðweard*. But see Kock, PPP., p. 14. **791** Hwæt, etc.] The text of the OS. fragment which corresponds to Gen. 791–817, is as follows:

"Uuela that thu nu, Eua, habas," quað Aðam, | "ubilo gimarakot ‖ unkaro selbaro sið. | Nu maht thu sean thia suarton hell ‖ ginon gradaga. | Nu thu sia grimman maht ‖ hinana gihorean. | Nis hebanriki ‖ gelihc sulicaro lognun. | Thit uuas alloro lando sconiust ‖ that uuit hier thuruh unkas herran thank | hebbian muostun, ‖ thar thu them ni hordis | thie unk thesan haram giried, ‖ that uuit uualdandas | uuord farbrakun, ‖ hebankuningas. | Nu uuit hriuuig mugun ‖ sorogon for them siða, | uuand he hunk selbo gibood ‖ that uuit hunk sulic uuiti | uuardon scoldin, ‖ haramo mestan. | Nu thuingit mi giu hungar endi thrust, ‖ bitter balouuerek, | thero uuaron uuit er beðero tuom. ‖ Hu sculun uuit nu libbian, | efto hu sculun uuit an thesum liatha uuesan, ‖ nu hier huuilum uuind kumit | uuestan efto ostan, ‖ suðan efto nordan; | gisuuerek upp dribit, ‖ kumit haglas skion | himile bitengi, ‖ ferið ford an gimang, | that is firinum kald. ‖ Huilum thanne fan himile | heto skinit, ‖ blikit thiu berahto sunna. | Uuit hier thus bara standat, ‖ unuuerid mið giuuadi. | Nis unk hier uuiht biuoran ‖ . . . . . te scura, | unk nis hier scattas uuiht ‖ te meti gimarcot. | Uuit ebbiat unk giduan mathigna god ‖ uualdand uureðan. | Te hui sculun uuit uuerdan nu? ‖ Nu mag mi that hreuuan, | that ik is io bad hebanrikean god, ‖ uualdand th. . ."

801–900

806 cymð] Graz, p. 100, Klaeber, *cymeð*, as an improvement in meter. **812** wædo] Grein, Spr. II, 642, calls this an "instrumentaler acc.," and Ettmüller alters to *wæde*. See l. 846, where *wæda* occurs as an accusative. Klaeber reads *wædon* from *wædum*, and so also JEGPh. XII, 254. It seems best to take the word as a dat. inst. with Klaeber, but if any change is made, to read *wæde* with Ettmüller. See l. 117, note. **813** sceattes] "Money"— a naive conception already present in the OS. original. Holthausen, Anglia Beibl. XIII, 266, suggests that a scribal error lies back of OS. *scattas*, miswritten for *scaftas*, gen. sing. of **scaft*, "creature," "something fashioned, prepared." This certainly improves the poetry of the passage. Trautmann, Bonner Beitr. XVII, 139, reads *scēates* in the sense "Gewand." Koegel, Geschichte d. deutschen Lit., I, Ergänzungsheft, p. 10, suggests that the word means something to eat and that *scattas* = Fries. *sket*, "Vieh." The word is discussed also by Braune, Beitr. XXXV, 272, and Siebs, ZfdPh., XXVIII, 139. **830** no sniomor] "None the quicker," or Klaeber, Anglia XXXVII, 542, suggests merely "never," connecting with l. 833, "you would never see...that ever my mind doubted of it." **835** niod] The MS. plainly has *niod*, not *mod*, as Thorpe, Bouterwek, Ettmüller, and Grein read. **856** dyde] For *dyden*, a plural; see *swice*, l. 954, for *swicen*. Similar forms occur so frequently in AS. manuscripts as to place them out of the class of accidents. See Bloomfield's article, JEGPh. XXIX (1930), 100–113. But Holthausen alters to *dyden*. **857** þam] Grein, Wülker retain the MS. reading *þa*, but Grein, note, suggests *þam*. **863** weard] Klaeber, notes, and Anglia XLIX, 369, and Holthausen, notes, take *weard* as accusative, referring to Adam, but Kock, PPP., p. 15, prefers to take it as nominative, accusative to *aldor*. Either is possible. **869** Scyldfull mine] Ettmüller supplies *sceame*, Grein *sceome* after *mine*, and Holthausen, Eng. Stud. XXXVII, 203, would supply *sceame* (see l. 942) before *mine*, or as alternative, replace *mine* by *sceame*. In his edition, Holthausen reads *scyldfull [scęame] mine*, with a colon after *mine*. Klaeber, JEGPh. XII, 257, rejects all this and would alter *sceaðen* to *sceande* (see l. 874), and he prints it so in his edition, with no punctuation after *þecce*, l. 868, and none after *mine*, but a comma after his *sceande*, l. 869. But the passage can stand on its own merits if *mine* is taken as a noun, and *sceaðen* also as a noun, appositive to *me*, "a guilty conscience is to me, a sinner, grievous, oppressive in spirit." Both *sare* and *frecne* may be taken syntactically as adverbs. **870** gan] Holthausen, *gangan*, for metrical reasons, and so also in ll.2236 and 2356. But see l. 1241, note. **871** eall eall] The MS. repeats *eall*, though Wülker mistakenly reports only one *eall*. Klaeber, Holthausen omit one *eall*, but the repetition may have been intentional for rhetorical emphasis. **877** gesyhst sorge] Grein, Spr. I, 453, "beholdest sorrow," Dicht., p. 26, "siehest Sorge." But *gesyhst* may be for *gesicst*, "sighest in sorrow." The order of the clause following is *sylf þecest þin lic*. **880** byrgde] Ettmüller, Grein, Wülker, Holthausen, *byrgdest*, but Klaeber, *byrgde*. The optative form is obviously permissible. **888** Hwæt druge þu, etc.] The Vulgate merely says *Quare hoc fecisti?*, Gen. iii. 13. Translate: "What madest thou, daughter, of the abundant blessings...when thou greedy," etc., and see Bos.-Tol., I, 423, under *genog*. Holthausen reads *Hwæt druge þu, dohtor? Dugeþa [wæs] genohra*, and remarks in his notes that he takes *Dugeþa* as a partitive genitive, citing Shipley, The Genitive Case in AS. Poetry, p. 94. But Shipley's examples do not make Holthausen's reading of this passage convincing. **892** me on teonan] Sievers, Beitr. X, 512, Holthausen, *on teonan me*. But see l. 885. **893** þa] Holthausen omits *þa*. **894** wæstme] For a plural *wæstme*, beside the more common *wæstmas*, see l. 990. **899** fægir] For the spelling, see *twegin*, l. 460. **900** feondræs] Bouterwek, Erläut., p. 304, suggests *feondræd*, Cosijn, Beitr. XIX, 447, *feondes ræd* for *feondræs*.

901–1000

906 werig] Bouterwek, Erläut., p. 304, reads *werged* for the MS. *werg*, Ettmüller, *wearg*, and Grein, Wülker retain *werg*, "accursed," though *werg þinum* does not make a complete half-line. Sievers, Beitr. X, 512, changes to *wērig*, "weary," and so Klaeber, Holthausen. But Kock, JJJ., p. 29, returns to the interpretation "cursed," and alters *bearm* to *bearme*, already accepted by Ettmüller, as appositive to *breostum*, therefore not connected with *bradre eorðan*, and he places *breostum* in l. 906b. The main objection to this reading, as Holthausen, Anglia Beibl. XXX, 3, points out, is that the resulting l. 907a, *bearme tredan*, is not acceptable metrically, a verse of this type with the second stressed syllable short normally having a rather heavy secondary stress in the first foot. Wülker accepts *bearm* as appositive to *breostum*, taking it as an instrumental without inflectional ending. By so doing he is able to retain the MS. reading *brade*, l. 907, as an accusative. **907** bradre] Wülker retains *brade*, see l. 906, note. **914** tuddor] Ettmüller, Klaeber, Holthausen alter to *tuddre*. But see l. 1613, where *tuddor* as an instrumental occurs. Holthausen has *tuddre* in his text, but in his notes he defends *tuddor* as a dative. **934** swatig hleor] Dietrich, Grein, Wülker read *swatighleor*. So also Kock, JJJ., p. 29, who also would read *wegan swatighleor ‖ þinne hlaf, etan*. This would make *wegan* and *etan* parallel and *hlaf* object of both. **954** swice] Holthausen, *swicen*, but see l. 856, note. **959** gehwilcre] So Klaeber in his text (not *gehwilce*, as reported by Holthausen), but he suggests *gehwilce* as a possible reading. The MS. reading must be taken as a dat. fem. after *het*, the gender being determined by *teohha*. Translate, "He commanded each of procreating generations of sea and land to produce fruits for the benefit of this married pair." **964** æfter] Holthausen, *after*, corrected to *æfter*, Anglia XLVI, 60. of] Klaeber places *of* in l. 964b, but in Anglia XLIX, 370, places it in l. 964a. **966** bebead metod] Dietrich, Grein, Holthausen read *bebead metod*, but see l. 574, note. **972** elnes] Dietrich, *ætes*, see l.1557. But the change is unnecessary, Cosijn, Beitr. XIX, 447. **974** forð] Holthausen, *ford*, corrected in Anglia XLVI, 60, to *forð*. **980** Hygewælm asteah] A better form for the verb would be *astah*, from *astigan*, and Wülker assumes that *asteah* is for *astah*, and so also Holthausen, though other examples of this variation are not recorded. Thorpe reads *wælm ofteah* for the MS. *wælmos teah*, translating, "rage him of thought bereft." Bouterwek makes a compound of *hyge* and *wælm* and omits the *-os* of the MS. In his text he reads *hygewelm ofteah*, in Erläut., p. 305, *hygewelm upteah*. Grein reads *hygewælmas teah*, defining *teah*, Spr. II, 528, as "produced," "brought forth," as Wülker points out, a meaning otherwise unrecorded. Grein, Dicht., p. 28, translates, "es zog Herzwallen auf in der Brust dem Helden." See l. 2237. **986** þæs] Thorpe, Bouterwek, Grein, Holthausen alter to *þes*. But see l. 356, and note.

1001–1100

1010 Hwæt, befealdest þu, etc.] Grein, Wülker, Holthausen take this as a question, with no punctuation after *Hwæt* and question mark after *cigeð*, apparently taking *Hwæt* in the sense of "why." The Vulgate has *Quid fecisti?*, but the main part of the sentence in the Vulgate is not a question. **1022** ædre] Supplied by Graz, Festschrift für Schade, p. 70, for alliteration. See ll. 872, 2187. **1028** manscyldigne] "Guilty," the first element being *mān-.*   So also l. 1048.   **1040** þe] Holthausen supplies *þec*, Grein, note, *þe.*   The sense of the passage requires an object.   **1055** Enos] The Vulgate has *Henoch.*   See l. 1134, *Enos*, son of Seth.   **1056** fæsten] Supplied for alliteration.   Bouterwek altered *frumbearn* to *sunu.*   Grein, Holthausen supply *furðum*, and Holthausen notes ll. 1131, 1238, but these lines have *þa*, not *siððan.*   See l. 1058*b.*   **1062** burhstede] Holthausen wrongly states that *burh* is over *stede.*   But *burhstede* is the last word on p. 50, *burh* the last word on a line, followed by *stede*, widely spaced, on the next line. The page is about three-fourths full.   **1063** Iared] The Vulgate has *Irad*, and Cosijn, Beitr. XIX, 447, would read *Irad* here, *Irade* in l. 1067, because the alliteration in both is vocalic, but *Jared* in l. 1174, where the alliteration is consonantal.   Holthausen in his edition, *Īąred*, but Anglia XLVI, 60, *Ired.*   Grein reads *Iared*, l. 1063, *Iarede*, l. 1067, and *Jared*, l. 1174.   Wülker has *J* in all three passages.   Holthausen reads *Īąrede*, l. 1067, and *Jāred* in l. 1174.   The alliterative intention is clear, but the spelling need not be altered, since the scribe made no distinction between *I* and *J*.   **1066** Malalehel] For the Vulgate *Maviael.*   See l. 1160.   **1070** bearn æfter bearne] Holthausen, notes, thinks that *bearn* is for *bearne*, "to one man after another," with the inflectional vowel omitted on account of the *æ* following.   He would also place a comma after *bearne.*   But Kock, PPP., p. 15, takes *bearn æfter bearne* more naturally as meaning practically "in his turn," "as his father had done before him."   Cosijn, Beitr. XIX, 447, takes *bearn* as object of *dælde*, which he assumes has the double sense required by the two different objects *bearn* and *gestreon*—a forced construction, as Cosijn himself acknowledges.   **1084** smiðcræftega] Bouterwek, Wülker, *smið cræftega.*   But Cosijn, Beitr. XIX, 447, defends *smiðcræftega.*   So Thorpe, in his translation, Grein, Holthausen.   **1088** æres] See the Vulgate, *faber in cuncta opera aeris et ferri*, Genesis iv. 22.   **1098** ic] Something is necessary metrically, and *ic* is supplied by Graz, Festschrift für Schade, p. 70, and Holthausen.

1101–1200

1106 Seth] The MS. has *seth*, and so elsewhere for this name.   But l. 1133 the MS. has *sedes* for *sethes.*   **1109** Adames and Euan] Genitive after *frofre*, not appositive to *fæder and meder*, as Holthausen takes it, changing *Adames* to *Adame.*   See l. 2176.   **1111–1112** sunu sealde] The transposition of the MS. reading *sealde sunu* was suggested by Graz, Festschrift für Schade, p. 71, and is followed by Holthausen in order to regularize the meter of l. 1112*a.*   But it also improves the order of words in the passage. The object of *sealde* is *sunu*, and *ece* goes with *waldend*, and so also *selfa.*   As an alternative, Graz suggests *me ece god sealde sunu selfa.*   **1118** eðelstæfe] Grein, Wülker, *eðulstæfe*, Holthausen, *eðelstæfe.*   **1125** nigenhund wintra].   Grein supplies *niðða fæder* before *nigenhund*, Holthausen *niðða ordfruma*, to complete the line.   Wülker gives *nigenhund wintra* as a second half-line, indicating the loss of a first half-line.   But if anything has been lost, there is nothing to show that what has dropped out preceded *nigenhund wintra.* See l. 703, note. **1128** leod] The reading *leod* was suggested by Grein and accepted by Holthausen, thus giving *weardode* an object. Holthausen, Anglia XLVI, 60, alters *eafora* to *eaforan,* but it is better taken as an appositive to *Seth.* See l. 1070, note. **1133** Sethes] See l. 1106, note. **1136–1137** stop on grene græs] Holthausen, notes, "since he died," but Kock, PPP., p. 15, more plausibly, "since Adam trod on the earth's green grass endowed with a living soul." **1142** friðgedal] Grein, Spr. I, 348, defines the first element of this compound as meaning "peace," the whole as *divortium a pace = obitus.* So also Holthausen in the glossary to his edition. Klaeber, JEGPh. XIX, 412, would change *frið-* to *ferhð-,* and Thorpe, notes, Bouterwek had previously made a similar suggestion. There can be no question that the first element must mean the same as *ferhð-,* but the form *frið-* may stand, see l. 107, note. **1143** worulde] Replaced by *earde* by Holthausen for the sake of alliteration. **1145** sædberendes] An appropriate description of Seth, Cain and Abel being dead. Moore, MLRev. VI, 199ff., sees in this adjective a reference to the legend of Seth and the Cross. **1154** fyrnwita] Grein, Wülker read *fyrnwited,* "experienced of old," as for a MS. *fyrn witet.* Thorpe, notes, Bouterwek change *witet* to *wintrum.* Cosijn, Beitr. XIX, 448, reads *fyrnwita,* and so also Holthausen. **1162** feowertig] Shipley, Genitive Case in Anglo-Saxon Poetry, p. 102, reads *feowertig,* and so Holthausen. Earlier edd. follow the MS., and Grein, Spr. I, 296, takes *eahta hund and feowertigum feorum,* "with 840 lives"! But Grein, Dicht., p. 33, "achthundert und vierzig Jahre mit vielen Kindern." **1172** meowle] Holthausen omits as not needed for sense and as making the half-line too full metrically. **1174** Iared] See l. 1063, note, and *Geared,* ll. 1181, 1195. **1184** fyore] For *feore,* from *feorh.* **1188** Enoc] Holthausen alters to *Enoch,* the Vulgate form being *Henoch.* See l. 1197. **1191** eahtahund] Supply *wintra* in thought to complete the meaning of *eahtahund,* and take *eaforan* as appositive to *cneorim.* Grein, Wülker retain *eafora,* Bouterwek, Holthausen read *eaforan.* Thorpe replaces *eafora* by *wintra.* **1193** nihtgerimes] Cosijn, Beitr. XIX, 448, accounts for *nihtgerimes* instead of *wintergerimes* or *geargerimes* by the requirements of alliteration and as a translation of the Vulgate *sunt omnes dies Iared CMLXII anni,* Genesis v. 20. **1194** frod wintres] Holthausen alters to *wintrum frod.* **1198** wisa] Sievers, Beitr. XII, 475, omits *wisa* as being metrically superfluous. So also Holthausen. **1199** dom and drihtscipe] Dietrich supplies *dæge sine,* Grein, Holthausen, *dædrof hæle* to complete the line. See l. 703, note.

1201–1300

1206 doþ] Holthausen, following Sievers, Beitr. X, 477, alters to *doaþ* to gain a metrical syllable, as similarly for *don* and *onfon (onfoð)* in ll. 1759, 1789, 1918, 1938, 2040, 2332, 2413 *(doen),* and 2919. **1208** æhta and ætwist] "Goods and residence," as translated by Kock, Anglia XLIII, 307,

the first element of *ætwist* being the adverb *æt*.   **1209** on genimeð] Holthausen, Eng. Stud. LI, 184, Anglia XLVI, 60, would supply *ān* after *on*, i.e.
on ān, "straightway," because he thinks l. 1209*a* is too short.   But *on* is
needed as a preposition to govern *him*, l. 1207, "unto himself," and *on
genimeð* is by no means without parallels metrically, nor does the addition
of *ān* essentially change the metrical structure of the half-line.   **1211**
feran] So Grein, Wülker, and Holthausen.   **1217** eac III hund] Holthausen, *III hund eac*, as an improvement in alliteration.   **1219** þissa] Grein,
Wülker retain *þisse*, presumably as modifying *lichoman*, Mason, "in this
body."   But Grein suggests *þissa*, and so Holthausen in his text.   **1224**
to] "In addition."   See Cosijn, Beitr. XIX, 448.   æfter] Holthausen,
after, corrected Anglia, XLVI, 60.   **1232** and] Supplied for metrical reasons; so Graz, Festschrift für Schade, p. 71, Holthausen.   **1234** eaforan]
The earlier edd. retain *eafora*, which would then be a genitive, but better
with Holthausen, *eaforan*, appositive to *byras*.   **1235** Noe] Thorpe prints
this *Noæ*, and perhaps it should be so taken, see l. 232, note.   **1240** Noes]
Holthausen, following Sievers, Beitr. X, 480, reads *Nōēes*, as also in ll.
1323, 1423, and 1551, for the sake of meter.   The half-line must be so read,
whether or not one alters the spelling.   See l. 1241, note.   **1241** oðer Cham]
Holthausen supplies *wæs* before *oðer* to complete the half-line metrically.
But if *Noes*, l. 1240, can be read as a trisyllable, *Cham* can be read as a
dissyllable, and the reading without *wæs* is better stylistically.   See l. 1736,
Carran, and l. 1854, *Sarran*.   **1256** cneorisn] Dietrich, Grein, Wülker
read *cneoriss*, the more usual form of this word, see l. 1274.   But Cosijn,
Beitr. XIX, 448, defends *cneorisn*.   Grein, Germania X, 417, suggests *cneorim*,
as in l. 1190.   **1260** þær] The syntax would be improved by reading *þæra*,
Holthausen, Anglia XLVI, 60.   **1264** bisgodon] Wülker misreports the
MS. as reading *bisgŏdon*, hence *bisgedon* in his text, and so also Holthausen.
Cosijn, Beitr. XIX, 448, suggests *basnedon*, see l. 2419, for *bisgodon*.   As the
text stands *bisgodon* must be taken as an intransitive, "suffered," and *wræce*
as instrumental.   **1270** sigoro] So Holthausen, the earlier edd. altering to
sigora.   But see Sievers, Angels. Gram., § 237, Anm. 4, on -*o* as a gen. pl.
ending.   **1280** aæðan] Holthausen, *aeðan*, but see l. 356, note.   **1296**
acwellan] Wülker, Holthausen incorrectly report the MS. as reading
æcwellan.   **1298** fedað] Holthausen, text, *felað*, notes, *fedað*.

1301–1400

1308 and] Supplied by Holthausen to complete the line metrically, following
Sievers, Beitr. X, 512.   **1309** and] Holthausen, text, places this word in
the first half-line, but Anglia XLVI, 60, suggests placing it in the second half-
line and supplying *þinra* before *elngemeta*, or reading *elna gemetenra*.   But
no change is necessary, see l. 1209, note.   gewyrc] Bouterwek, Erläut., p.
306, suggested *gewyrþe*, and so also Holthausen, notes, citing An. 306, *ofer
waroða geweorþ*.   But see An. 466, 932.   **1316** þæt hof] The MS. has the
usual abbreviation for *þæt* before *hof*.   Grein, Holthausen alter to *yþ-*,

reading *yþhof.* See ll. 1345, 1489. **1330** and] Holthausen changes to *mid.* This is perhaps a slight improvement but not necessary. The subject of *nimest* is both *þu* and *feora fæsl,* "the progeny of living creatures." **1337** to mete] Holthausen, *mete to,* as a metrical improvement, and Anglia XLVI, 61, he suggests a more elaborate reconstruction, *þara þe mannum to mete lifige.* **1338** twa] Holthausen, following Sievers, Beitr. X, 512, changes *twa* to *twegen* to secure a metrical syllable. **1355** sweart racu] Holthausen and the earlier edd., *sweartracu,* except Thorpe, Bouterwek, *sweart racu.* Dietrich, *stearc racu* or *streamracu,* and Grein, *streamracu,* for the sake of alliteration. stigan] Holthausen alters to *swogan,* to alliterate with *sweart-,* citing l. 1375. For the sense of *stigan,* see l. 1406. **1358** wægþæl] Junius, *-þæl,* the later edd., *-þel.* On *æ* for *e,* see l. 356, note. Holthausen incorrectly states that *a* has been erased after *þel* in the MS., but the erasure is after *þ* in the word. **1374** gehwære] Holthausen, *gehwæm,* citing Beow. 25, where some editors also read *in mægða gehwam,* as a metrical correction of the MS. reading *gehwære,* suggested by Sievers, Beitr. X, 485. See also Sievers, Angels. Gram., § 341, Anm. 4. **1378** manfæhðu] A genitive after *bearn;* see Cosijn, Beitr. XIX, 448. **1380** hof] Holthausen alters to *hofu.* **1387** hea beorgas] Graz, Festschrift für Schade, p. 71, reads *hēahe beorgas.* **1394** fære] This may be taken as a dative of **fær,* "ship," with Grein, Spr. I, 270, Holthausen, notes, or perhaps better as an instrumental case of *fǣr,* "with terror," parallel to *hæste,* l. 1396. See Kock, JJJ., p. 30. **1398** se] Thorpe, Ettmüller, Lexicon, p. 656, Bouterwek retain the MS. reading *sæ,* making a compound *sǣdrence,* but Dietrich and the later edd. alter *sæ* to *se.* **1400** þam æt niehstan] For *æt þam niehstan,* "thereupon"? See Kock, Anglia XLIV, 253. Holthausen places *wæs* in the first half-line. Or should one read *þa* for *þam?* Or *þam* may be demonstrative, "for them," "to them," i.e. the victims of the flood. nan to gedale] Taking *nan* in the sense "nothing," Grein, Spr. II, 274, and *to gedale* in the sense "for a portion," "for a lot," with Kock, Anglia XLIV, 253, the sense of this phrase seems to be "Then nothing else was granted." This implies also the change of *heo* to *heof* in l. 1401.

1401–1500

1401 heof] Sievers, Beitr. XIX, 448, suggested *heof,* "lamentation," for the MS. *heo,* which otherwise would seem to stand for *earce,* a difficult interpretation, as Cosijn, ibid., points out. Holthausen accepts *heof* in his text. Mason translates, "there was nothing at hand for [the Ark] but destruction, except that it was raised," etc. But this does not correspond to the text. Translate literally, "There was nothing to them for a portion, except lamentation was raised," etc., freely, "Then naught was their portion except lamentation raised," etc. **1404** hine] The antecedent is *egorhere,* l. 1402. **1405** edmodne] Dietrich altered the MS. *ed monne* to *edniowe,* "continually renewing itself," connecting it with *tuddor,* l. 1402. Grein, Germania X,

417, improved this by reading *edniowne*, referring to *egorhere*. As this would make a short line metrically, Cosijn, Beitr. XX, 98, suggested *a edniowne*, and Holthausen reads *edniowne flod*. Holthausen, Indog. Forsch. IV, 380, had previously proposed *e[acne an]d wonne*. Wülker suggested, but did not place in his text, the reading *edmodne*, "obedient," i.e. obedient to the commands of the Lord, a reading to be preferred both on the side of sense and because it calls for only the change to *n* to *d*. It should be noted that the reading *edniowne* supposes that an original runic symbol for *w* was read as *n* by the scribe. **1407** gemunde god] Holthausen, Eng. Stud. XXXVII, 203, would replace *god* by *se mæra*. In his text he prints *gemyndgode*, but Anglia XLVI, 61, retracts this in favor of the MS. reading. **1416** torhtne] Wülker prints merely *torht ryne*. To complete the line metrically Grein read *rodortorht*, referring to *metod*, l. 1414, and so also Holthausen. But *torhtne ryne* is adequate, lines of this metrical type being not uncommon. Perhaps the inflectional ending of the adjective was lost in anticipation of the final *-ne* of *ryne*. **1417** L and C] To be resolved as *fiftig and hundteontig*. **1428** þæra] See l. 1522. Perhaps one should supply *þe* after *þæra*. **1447** se feonde] Cosijn, Beitr. XIX, 449, Holthausen read *feonde*, "but it [the raven] rejoicing," following a suggestion by Grein. Holthausen, Anglia Beibl. XXIII, 88, alters *feond* to *feorh*, appositive to *hreaw*, but not in his text. **1491** liðe] Bouterwek, Erläut., p. 307, reads *lide* for the MS. *hliðe*, but Grein and the later edd. read *liðe*. **1492** þrymme geþeahte þriddan eðyl] Holthausen in his text reads *þrymme geþeahte*, but in his notes he suggests either *mid þrymme geþeaht*, or *þrymme geþeahtne*. Dietrich, Grein, Wülker take *geþeahte* as a verb, parallel in syntax to *hæfde*—an awkward construction. Grein, Wülker, Holthausen alter *þridda* to *þriddan*, and this is necessary if *eðyl* is accusative, and not appositive to *lago*. Kock, PPP., p. 15, reads *þrymme geþeahtne þriddan eðyl*, suggesting that the poet had in mind heaven (air), earth, and ocean (water), not heaven, earth, and hell, as Holthausen, notes, states. But in any case *þriddan eðyl* seems to refer here to the earth. Mason, p. 59, would read *ðryðe*, "strength," "in place of the meaningless *ðridda* = 'third,' in the MS., and at the same time making *þrymme* the object of *hæfde* (reading *þrymmas*, if necessary)." He translates, "while the deluge held sway [and] covered your home with its abundance." But Bos.-Tol., I, 454, translates more closely, "water had covered the country." For the spelling of *eðyl*, see l. 962. **1498** reðran] Not otherwise recorded as a verb. Bouterwek, Erläut., p. 307, suggested *renian* for *reðran*, and Dietrich *reðian* or *ræran*. Grein, Wülker, Holthausen, *reðian*, but Holthausen, Anglia XLVI, 61, *redian*. So also Bos.-Tol., under *redian*. The meaning is obviously "prepare," but one hesitates to change such a clear reading in the MS., especially since *reðian* and *redian* are very unusual forms, though *aredian* as a compound is more frequent. Sweet, Student's Dictionary, p. 140, records a word *gerēþre* in the sense "ready," from which perhaps one may infer a verb *rēðran*, "to make ready." The word *gerēðre*, as thus defined by Sweet, occurs in *Gregory's Pastoral Care*, ed. Sweet, p. 306, l. 15, where it is used as a synonym of *arod*. "prepared."

1501–1600

1504 þa he Noe] Holthausen adds *þær* after *Noe* to fill out the line metrically. But see ll. 1240, 1241, notes, on this word as a possible trisyllable. **1508** þæt] The change of the MS. *þa* to *þæt*, suggested by Grein, seems necessary, since *þæt him ealra*, etc., is an object clause after *geearnod*. **1511** wuldris] For the spelling, see *twegin*, l. 460, *fægir*, l. 899, *eðyl*, ll. 962, 1492, and Sievers, Angels. Gram., § 44, Anm. 2, § 237, Anm. 1. **1512** tiedrað] Holthausen, Anglia XLVI, 61, *tydrað*, but in his edition, *tiedrað*. **1515** and] Added to supply a metrical syllable by Sievers, Beitr. X, 512, and Holthausen. **1520** sawl] Metrically a dissyllable, and Holthausen alters to *sawul*, following Graz, Festschrift für Schade, p. 72, who reads *sawol*. **1522** þæra] See l. 1428. **1524** modgeþance] The MS. has *mod-*, not as Grein and Wülker read, *mode-*, and the change of *mode-* to *mod-* by Holthausen is unnecessary. **1525** sece] Thorpe, Grein retain the MS. reading *seðe*, which Grein takes as a verb, "avenge," citing Beow. 1106. So also Spr. II, 423. Wülker, Holthausen read *sette* for *seðe*. Bouterwek suggested *asece* (but Erläut., p. 307, *sece*), Dietrich, *sece*, and Sievers, Beitr. X, 512, Kock, JJJ., p. 31, also *sece*. This would correspond to *requiram*, in Genesis ix. 5, *et de manu viri et fratris ejus requiram animam hominis*, and *to slagan*, "from the slayer" (Bouterwek, Kock), would correspond to *de manu viri*. **1526** to broðor banan] The edd. print as a compound, but Kock, JJJ., p. 31, points out that the phrase should translate the Vulgate *et fratris ejus*, "and from the brother of the slayer." **1528** Monn wæs] Holthausen reads *Wæs monn*, as a metrical improvement. **1539** and] Needed both for meter and for sense. **1543–1549**] The simplest and most satisfactory explanation of these lines is that given by Gollancz, pp. lxii–lxvii. The matter printed in parentheses in the text is obviously unmetrical, and *wif* should agree in syntax with *eaforum þrim*. The suggestion of Gollancz is that the reference to the names of the wives of Noah's sons was a late marginal comment which some scribe copied as part of the text. Gollancz notes that in this passage the poet was versifying Genesis ix. 18, where the wives are not mentioned. They are mentioned in Genesis viii. 18, but their names are not given there or elsewhere in the Bible. On the origin and occurrence of these names in medieval literature, see Gollancz, pp. lxiv–lxvii. It is perhaps idle to speculate how this bit of legendary lore got into the manuscript, but it may be pointed out that this is just the kind of information that Ælfwine of Newminster (see Introd., p. x) seems to have been interested in. Grein alters *Percoba* to *Phercoba*, making one line of *and heora feower wif nemde wæron Phercoba*, then one line of the following three proper names, after which he supplies a line of his own, *þa wið flode nerede frea ælmihtig*. Grein, Germania X, 417, recasts to read:

> and heora feower wif Phercoba,
> Olla, Olliua, Olliuani
> nemde wæron, þa genered hæfde
> wærfæst metod wætra lafe.

Holthausen follows this reading except that he adds *þa* before *Phercoba* and *ond* before *Olliuani*.   **1549** wærfæst metode] The manuscript reading *metod* makes the word a nominative and appositive to *sunu Lamehes*, but *metod* would not be an appropriate term for Noah.   Gollancz, p. lxiv, would read *wærfæst metodes*, calling attention to Gen. 2169, which he would translate, "observant of thy will."   But it seems a little simpler to read *metode* and to translate, "faithful to the Lord."   **1551** Noes] Holthausen, *Noees*, following Graz, Festschrift für Schade, p. 72, but see l. 1240, note   Graz also adds *samod* before *Sem*.   and] Holthausen, Eng. Stud. XXXVII, 204, and in his text, *oðer* for *and*.   But *Cham* may be taken as a dissyllable, see l. 1241, note.   **1553** folc] Holthausen, following Graz, Festschrift für Schade, p. 72, supplies *eal* before *folc*.   **1560** þa] Grein alters to *þæt*. **1564** symbelwerig] Holthausen, *sumbęlwerig*, i.e. *sumblwerig*.   **1572** wryon] Grein, *wrion*.   The usual form of the verb is *wreon*.   **1579** ferhðe] Holthausen adds *se wæs* before *ferhðe*, for metrical reasons.   Graz, Festschrift für Schade, p. 72, reads *forstolen ferhðe*.   **1582** hlihende] Holthausen, *hlihhende*.   **1585** bewrigenum] Holthausen, following Grein, Spr. I, 98, takes *andwlitan bewrigenum* as dative or inst. absolute, "with countenances concealed."   Both *in* and *listum* are adverbial.   Perhaps it would be better to emend to *bewrigene*.   The *-um* ending of *bewrigenum* might easily have been anticipated from the dative endings in the following line.   Cosijn, Beitr. XIX, 450, would unite *in* with *stopon*, therefore remove the comma after *stopon*, but Sievers, ibid., rightly objects that this would be a very difficult order of words.   **1587** gefremede] Bouterwek, Holthausen, *gefremeden*, but see l. 856, note.

1601–1700

1601 freomen æfter flode, etc.] Grein suggests deleting *freomen* in order to shorten the line, which in his text includes *freomen...gewat*.   Wülker also prints all this as one line.   Holthausen would read *freom æfter flode ond fiftig eac* as one line, *freom* modifying *Noe*, l. 1598, and the following line he constructs to read *fæder on laste, oð þæt he forð gewat*.   Cosijn, Beitr. XIX, 450, also assumes a loss in the MS., and Holthausen, Anglia XLVI, 61, offers two new readings, *þa he forð gewat*, *fæder of life* or *feran of life*.   See Sievers, Altgermanische Metrik, § 98, and l. 703, note.   **1607** rice] "Kingdom," see Kock, Anglia XLIII, 308, and Holthausen, Anglia XLVI, 61. The other possibility would be to take *rice* as an adjective, in which case there would be no comma after it.   **1610** Geomor] For the Vulgate *Gomer*. **1613** tuddor] See l. 914, note.   **1615** Chames] Bouterwek, Erläut., p. 308, Dietrich, Grein, Holthausen read *Chame*, slightly better syntax, as Wülker remarks, though *Chames* is permissible.   **1617** Chus and Chanan] The MS. has *chus* and *cham* for the Vulgate *Chus* and *Chanaan*.   **1619** æðelum] Holthausen, following Rieger, Verskunst, p. 16, *hæleðum* for *æðelum*. **1623** gesceod] Dietrich (see Beitr. X, 485), Grein, Wülker, *gesceode*, but Cosijn, Beitr. XIX, 450, calls attention to Dan. 667, 677, and the frequent other occurrences of *gesc(e)od*. Holthausen has *gescẹ̄od*, and so also in Anglia Beibl. V, 229.   lice] Holthausen, Eng. Stud. XXXVII, 204, reads *life* for *lice*, but in his text retains *lice*.   **1628** Nebroðes] Grein reads *fæderne hreðer* for the MS. *nebreðer*, "er suchte den Schoos Gottes des Vaters." Wülker reads *Fæderne breðer*, with a point after *lif*, l. 1627.   Cosijn, Beitr. XIX, 450, calls attention to Genesis x. 8, where the form *Nemrod* occurs as the name of the son of Chus, and suggests *fæderne Nebrod, Nebrod* as subject of *weold*, and *fæderne* an adjective modifying *yrfestole*.   Sievers in a note to this reads *fæder Nebroðes*, appositive to *rinc*, l. 1626, with a period following. So also Holthausen in his text, but in Grein-Köhler, p. 887, he reads *fæder Nembroðes*.   **1629** weold] Graz, Festschrift für Schade, p. 72, reads *yrfestol heold*, see l. 1129.   **1638** widfolce] The MS. reading *wid folc* leaves the line lacking one syllable metrically.   Holthausen, following Sievers, Beitr. X, 513, reads *of þam wide folc*, but the syntax of this is awkward, *wide* being taken as an adverb.   The compound *widfolc* is like *widland*.   **1642** frod] The MS. reading *forð* might be retained, as it is by Grein, Wülker, and the earlier edd., but Grein, Germania X, 417, suggests *frod*.   The alliteration supports this, and *wintrum* would then go with *frod*.   Holthausen reads *frod*.   See l. 1743a.   **1650** Folc wæs, etc.] Kock, PPP., p. 15, would place ll. 1650b–1651 within parentheses.   **1656** leofum mannum] A dative plural to be construed with *wæron*, l. 1659.   Holthausen, in his text, places a colon after *mannum*, and no punctuation after *ræswan*.   In his notes, he moves the colon forward to follow *foldan*, l. 1658.   **1661** be] Cosijn, Beitr. XIX, 450, would omit *be* and would alter *þæs*, l. 1663, to *þæt*.   Holthausen so prints in his text.   But as Kock, PPP., p. 16, points out, *biddan be his mægwine* is good idiom, and the construction of *þæs* is not unusual, see El. 962.   **1664** bearm] Grein, Wülker, and the earlier edd. retain the MS. *bearn*, which might stand as a kind of plural amplification of the singular *mengeo*.   But Grein, Germania X, 417, accepts *bearm*, as suggested by Lye-Manning, and so also Holthausen.   **1666** geworhte] Holthausen, *geworhten*, but see l. 856, note.   Holthausen also reads *arærden*, l. 1667.   **1676** stænenne] So Grein, Wülker, Holthausen.   **1687** hie] Kock, PPP., p. 16, takes *hie* as reflexive object of *gemitton*, the phrase meaning "gathered together," with *spedge, teoche*, and *wisan* as appositive subjects of *gemitton*. "When they came together...with their many tribes," etc.   **1688** teoche] For *teohhe*.   **1693** tohlocon] Grein, Wülker, and the earlier edd. retain the MS. *tohlodon*, derived by Grein, Spr. II, 545, from an otherwise unrecorded *tohladan*, "scatter."   So also Bos.-Tol., p. 999, Sweet, Student's Dictionary, p. 174.   Cosijn, Beitr. XIX, 450, suggested *tóhtodon = tótodon*, for *to-eodon*, "went apart," "separated."   Sievers in a note to Cosijn proposes *tohlocon*, citing a verb *hlecað*, "assemble," from which might be assumed a strong verb *tohlacan*, "disperse."   Holthausen follows Sievers, but in his notes suggests *tohleopan* also as a possibility.   **1694** oðerre] Grein, Wülker retain *oðere*, but Rieger, Verskunst, p. 51, Sievers, Beitr. X, 462, Cosijn, Beitr. XIX, 451, Holthausen alter to *oðerre*, to the improvement of grammar and meter.

1701–1800

1701 samod samworht] Holthausen, following Sievers, Beitr. X, 513, reads *samworht samod* for metrical reasons. **1704** rim] Bradley, MLRev. XI, 213, would read *sum* for *rim*, but Kock, PPP., p. 16, correctly interprets *þære cneorisse* and *cynebearna* as parallel genitives after *rim*, object of *on*. **1705** þeawum hydig] Bradley, MLRev. XI, 213, would replace these words by *þare wæs haten*, assuming that the poet would not let the *þancolmod wer* go unnamed. The name in the Vulgate is *Thare*. But poets are sometimes heedless. **1708** freolicu] Holthausen, Anglia XLVI, 61, would supply *ful* before *freolicu*, citing l. 1618. **1715** unforcuðlice] Holthausen, following Sievers, Beitr. X, 513, reads *unfracoðlice*, for metrical reasons. **1718** drihtfolca bearn] Holthausen, following Dietrich and Grein, reads *bearn* for *bearnum* construing *bearn* as subject of *demað*, *hie* as object. In order to complete the line metrically, Holthausen then alters *drihta* to *drihtfolca*, and suggests as an alternative reading *drihta eaforan*. Some such change seems necessary, since *demað* cannot be taken as a passive, see Cosijn, Beitr. XIX, 451. Kock, JJJ., p. 32, takes *dugeðum deman* as a set phrase, "praise highly." Wülker retains *bearnum*, citing Christ and Satan 299 in support, but Wülker's *lifigendon* in this line is a misinterpretation of the MS. and the line therefore offers no parallel. **1736** Carran] For the Vulgate *Haran*. Holthausen, following Rieger, Verskunst, p. 56, reads *Carrane* for metrical reasons. But perhaps the metrical reading may have been as though the word were *Cárráan*. See l. 1747, *Cárrán ofgíf*, and l. 1778, and see ll. 1240–1241, notes. **1755** hine...on] The pronoun is object of the preposition, *werðo* the object of *sette*, and *mine* modifies *werðo*. **1759** eorðbuende] Holthausen, following Dietrich, *eorðbuend*, as a metrical improvement, citing l. 1648, and Graz, Festschrift für Schade, p. 73. So also Jovy, Bonner Beitr. V, 30. But the half-line as it stands is metrically acceptable. **1765** fromcyme] Holthausen, following Dietrich, changes to *fromcynne*. **1768** of Egipta] Grein replaces *Egipta* by *Assyria*, remarking that *Egipta* is an obvious error. Wülker changes *of* to *on*, "nach Ægypten hin," the journey of Abraham towards Egypt being referred to here, see Genesis xii, and from Egypt in l. 1873ff. But Abraham did not go from Haran to Egypt, but *in terram Chanaan*, as the poet says, l. 1772, and if any change is made, Grein's reading is to be preferred. **1783** Sicem] The Vulgate has *Sichem*. Dietrich, Grein, Holthausen read *Sicem*. Wülker retains the MS. reading as *Siem*, on the ground that *siem* = *sigem*, for *Sichem*. **1784** Cananeis] Holthausen, following Grein's suggestion, alters to *Cananea*. Grein retained *Cananeis* in his text, but translated, Dicht., p. 50, as a genitive plural. The MS. reading may be retained as a genitive singular, corresponding to the Vulgate, Genesis xii. 6, *Chananaeus autem tunc erat in terra*. On *i* for *e*, see l. 899, note, also *y* for *e*, l. 269, note. hine] Holthausen transfers *hine* to the beginning of l. 1785a, for metrical reasons, or as alternative, suggests adding *þær* after *Abrahame*. **1789** gewlo] Holthausen, following Sievers, Beitr. X, 458, *gewloe*, for metrical reasons. **1795** landa] So Grein and later edd. **1795–1797** lisse...gecyðde] Grein, Wülker, Holthausen enclose within parentheses. **1799** Bethlem] For the Vulgate *Bethel.*

1801–1900

1805*a*] Holthausen adds *git* after *þa,* to complete the line metrically, taking *Abraham* as a dissyllable. **1809** metend] Cosijn, Beitr. XIX, 452, would change to *me(o)tud* and Holthausen prints *metud.* Grein, Wülker retain *metend* as a synonym for "God," and there is no reason why this should not stand. Cosijn places ll. 1808*b*–1809 within parentheses, and so also Holthausen, but Grein, Wülker print without parentheses. **1810** gledstyde] On *y* for *e,* see l. 269, note. **1813** brohþrea] Holthausen, following Sievers, Beitr. X, 479, *brohþręawu,* as a metrical improvement. **1818***a*] Holthausen, following Graz, Festschrift für Schade, p. 73, adds *se wæs* before *drihtne* for metrical reasons. **1829** onegan] Thorpe, notes, and the later edd. alter the MS. *on agen* to *onegan.* So also Cosijn, Beitr. XIX, 451. **1831** freondmynde] Thorpe, notes, suggested *feondmynde* for *freondmynde,* "through hostile mind." But Grein, Wülker retain *freond-,* "through loving intent," i.e. love of Abraham's wife. Cosijn, Beitr. XIX, 451, would read *freondmyne,* "love of a friend (woman)," and so Holthausen. Perhaps *-myne* for *-mynde* is an improvement, but *freond-,* "woman," "wife," raises doubts. The whole word might be reconstructed to read *freomyne,* see l. 1861, *wifmyne.* **1840** an] From *unnan,* "grant." **1842** sceolde] Holthausen, *scęolden.* See l. 856, note. **1849–1850** him drihtlicu, etc.] Translate "To them, many a valiant one, the woman seemed noble in countenance." For *drihtlicu* as applied to *mæg,* see l. 2782. Kock, PPP., p. 16, would rearrange to read *him drihtlicu on mægwlite.* Holthausen, Anglia XLVI, 61, suggests *on wlite modgum wlancum,* citing l. 1825. In his text, Holthausen reads *modgum wlite on,* and suggests *wynsum* as a substitute for *mænegum.* Cosijn, Beitr. XIX, 451, has *mægwlite,* anticipating Kock. If one reads *on mægwlite,* l. 1850*b* should read *modgum mænegum* and ðuhte should go with l. 1851. **1852** þæt] Perhaps *and* might stand, but *þæt* provides a closer logical connection. Holthausen, following Sievers, Beitr. X, 352, prints *þæt.* fægerro] A genitive plural, see *Egipto,* l. 1866, parallel to *idesa,* l. 1853. For the meaning of *sunnon,* "go," "walk," or perhaps "seek for," see Sievers, Beitr. XI, 352–353. The use of *lyt* is the familiar Anglo-Saxon figure of litotes. Grein alters *fægerro* to *fægerra.* Wülker would take *fægerro* as standing for *fægerrō = fægerran,* translating, "und wenig gedachten sie...einer lieblichern frau," Mason, "few women did they repute fairer before the king." Jovy, Bonner Beitr. V, 30, takes *sunnon* in the sense "desired," translating, "und begehrten wenig eine schönere frau für den fürsten." **1853** idesa] Wülker retains *idese* as a genitive singular. Dietrich took *idese* as standing for *idesa,* and Grein, Holthausen print *idesa.* **1854** Sarran] Holthausen, following Rieger, Verskunst, p. 56, assumes an indeclinable trisyllabic form *Sarrai,* which he reads instead of *Sarran* here and in ll. 2216, 2243, 2267, 2390, 2715, and 2728, and also

instead of *Sarra* in ll. 2342 and 2356.   But see l. 1241, note.   The MS. has
Sarrai in ll. 2743 and 2761.   **1863–1868**] The subject of *Ongæt* is *aldor*, i.e.
Pharaoh, of *heht* is *brego*, and after *heht* a verb of motion, "come," is to be
understood; *wine* is object of *heht*, l. 1867, *æðelingas* is appositive to *wine*,
and *oðre duguðe* is a dependent genitive according to Holthausen, notes,
or better, with Kock, PPP., p. 17, and Grein-Köhler, p. 132, an accusative
plural, appositive to *æðelingas*.   **1866** Egipto] Grein changes to *Egipta*.
It is possible that the final *-o* of *Egipto* is an echo of the *-o* of *brego*, but see
fægerro, l. 1852, note.   **1873a**] Holthausen adds *his* after *Abraham*.   See
l. 1805a, note.   **1876** Bethlem] Holthausen, following Rieger,Verskunst,
p. 56, *Bethleme*.   See l. 1240, note.   **1879** on] Thorpe, notes, Bouterwek,
Cosijn, Beitr. XIX, 451, Holthausen read *on willan*, but Grein retains *and*
suggesting that it is a preposition, and Wülker retains *and*, taking *willan* in
the sense "desirable things," appositive therefore to *ceapas*, etc.   But the
phrase merely means "then they led *on willan*,"—"according to their desire," "as they wished."   **1880** bytlian] Holthausen,.*bytlįan*, i.e. *bytlan*,
and so also l. 2177, following Sievers, Beitr. X, 484.   **1884** þa westan com]
Grein reads *þa he west ancom*.   **1898** hearmplega] Dietrich alters to
hearmplegan as an instrumental, and so Holthausen.   But Grein rightly
takes *hearmplega* as appositive to *teonan*, and *heardum* as appositive to
weredum.

1901–2000

1905 eall tela] Holthausen, notes, makes a compound, *ealltela*, following
Grein, Germania X, 417.   **1909** Feretia] Dietrich, Grein alter to *Feresita*,
as closer to the Vulgate *Pherezaeus*, Genesis xiii. 7.   **1910** Ne willað]
Supply *wesan*.   **1911** lædan] Cosijn, Beitr. XIX, 452, doubts *lædan* as an
intransitive, but finds no word to take its place.   Kock, PPP., p. 17, defends
lædan as an intransitive, and such a use seems highly probable here.   Jovy,
Bonner Beitr. V, 30, emends *lædan* to *leoran*, "depart," previously considered
and rejected by Cosijn.   Holthausen changes *lædan* to *læfan*, with *landriht*
to be supplied in sense.   For the use of *lædan* intransitively in the sense of
"venture forth," see Fates of the Apostles, ed. Krapp, l. 43, note.   Jovy
and Holthausen place a period after *sculon*, l. 1911, and Kock places the
teon wit of þisse stowe of the MS. within parentheses as an exclamation.   But
see l. 1912, note.   **1912** teon of] The presence of *wit* in the MS. after *teon*
is accounted for as an echo of the *wit* of l. 1911.   But *lædan* and *teon* are
best taken as infinitives parallel in syntax.   Dietrich, Grein, Wülker read
teonwit, "contention," in Mason's translation, "Therefore shall we remove
our differences from this place," p. 32.   **1916** life] "Grant," "permit."
1917 and geþancmeta] Kock, PPP., p. 18, questions the existence of an
Anglo-Saxon verb *geþancmetian*, accepted by the edd. and Cosijn, Beitr.
XIX, 452.   He would read *and* as *on*, and take *geþanc* as object of the preposition, *meta* alone being the verb.   What Kock proposes is possible, but
geþancmetian is also possible to a poet.   **1923** leoht] Past participle of

leccan, "lave." **1929** ealle lædde] Something must be supplied to satisfy meter and to give a verb governing the objects. Grein reads *lædde eall þider,* and Holthausen *lædde ealle* for l.1929a, placing *æhte sine* in the second half-line. Kock, PPP., p. 19, supplies *lædde eadig* as l. 1929a. **1945** eðeleardum] Holthausen, following Schröder, ZfdA. XLIII, 370, *eðelgeardum,* to avoid double alliteration in the second half-line. **1951** foldwonga] Thorpe, Grein, Wülker retain the MS. reading as *fullwona,* which Thorpe translates "of the baptized," Grein, Dicht., p. 54, "des Taufbades," Mason, p. 33, "children of baptism." Bouterwek, Erläut., p. 309, suggested *fulwodra bearn,* "children of the baptized," or *foldwuna bearn* or *foldan bearn.* Holthausen reads *foldwonga bearn,* and some such change seems necessary for the sake of meaning, though it is doubtful if *foldwonga* really arrives at the original intention of the poet. **1952** he] Holthausen, following Cosijn, Beitr. XIX, 452, reads *her*—an improvement, but not a necessity. **1953** *hleowlora*] Dietrich, Grein, Wülker, Holthausen, *hleowlora,* "unprotected," for the MS. *hleor-,* in which the *r* was probably written in anticipation of the *r* in the second syllable. **1954** æt edwihtan] "In any way," or perhaps "at all," but no other occurrences of *edwihtan* which might determine the meaning of the word are recorded. æfre] Holthausen, following Grein, Germania X, 417, *ænig,* on which *feorhberendra,* genitive plural, would depend. With *æfre* retained, a similar syntax for *feorhberendra* must be assumed, with some such word as *ænig* implied. The *æfre* of l. 1954 may be an echo of *næfre,* l. 1953. **1956** æfter a] Grein supplies *mundbyrde* after *æfter,* and Holthausen supplies *miltse,* to the improvement of the meter but not of the sense. Wülker indicates a loss after *æfter* but supplies nothing. This whole passage, from l. 1953 to l. 1959, seems a bit suspicious, as possibly a hortatory interpolation, and perhaps the line never did alliterate. The phrase *æfter a* may be taken as adverbial, "always," "ever," like *symles a, a forð,* etc., or *a* may be taken as a noun, "according to the law," i.e. the Bible. **1957** mode] Thorpe and the later edd. read *mode.* **1963** Sennar] Holthausen, following Rieger, Verskunst, p. 56, reads *Sennare.* But see l. 1241, note. Holthausen, Anglia XLVI, 61, proposes *Sennaar.* side worulde] Bouterwek, Erläut., p. 310, Dietrich, Grein, Holthausen read *worude* for *worulde.* **1964** for] Holthausen alters to *foron,* and assumes a gap in the narrative between ll. 1963–1964, to account for the fact that only two of the four kings are named. **1975** suðon] Grein alters to *suðan.* **1986** þryðge] The edd. except Holthausen retain *þrydge,* which Grein, Spr. II, 602, would connect with the verb *þreodian, þrydian,* "deliberate." But Holthausen, following Bos.-Tol., p. 1075, reads *þryðge,* "resolute," and so also Grein-Köhler, p. 727. Thorpe, note, suggests *þryste.*

2001–2100

2007 ahyðdan] Bouterwek, Grein, *ahudon,* Wülker, *ahudan.* Grein, Spr. I, 25, supposes an infinitive *ahuðan,* "despoil," but no such strong verb is recorded. Grimm, Andreas und Elene, p. 141, alters to *ahyðdon,* from

ahyðan, of the same meaning as Grein's *ahuðan*. So also Dietrich, and
Holthausen, Grein-Köhler, p. 376, *ahyðdan*.   hordburh] Holthausen,
Eng. Stud. LI, 184, Anglia XLVI, 61, reads *hordbyrh*, a plural, but in his
text retains *hordburh*.   Grein, Spr. II, 97, suggests that *hordburh* is to be
taken as an accusative plural, but this meticulous logical consistency may
not have been in the mind of the poet.   2027 Manre] The Vulgate has
Mambre, Holthausen *Mamre*.   2032 ahreded] Grein,Wülker, and earlier
edd. retain *ahred*, except Bouterwek, *ahreded*.   Holthausen reads *ahreded*,
and see l. 2085.   2038 feollan] Grein, Wülker, and the earlier edd. retain
feallan, but Grein, Germania X, 417, suggests *feollan*.   Holthausen has
feollan and the word is obviously preterite.   Perhaps one should emend
further to *feollon*, see *gewræcon*, l. 2038*a*.   2042 þeodenholdra] Grein,
þeoden holdra, taking *þeoden* as an uninflected dative.   But Grein, Germania
X, 417, and later edd., *þeodenholdra*.   2046-2047] Though these two lines
are complete in sense, l. 2046 is defective in alliteration and l. 2047 is only a
half-line.   There is also a difficulty with the MS. *folce getrume*.   Grein retains as two words, translating, Dicht., p. 57, "mit ihrem Volk dem starken."
Wülker also prints as two words.   Dietrich reads *folcgetrume*, as in l. 1987,
which makes a practicable compound.   So also Grein, Spr. I, 308, where
Grein says that the alliteration in this line rests upon *t* (rather *tr*).   Otherwise the passage can be emended only by extensive alteration.   Wülker
supposes a gap between *getrume...wolde*, which he does not supply.   Cosijn, Beitr. XIX, 453, proposed *þe him ær wære sealdon mid heora wigena
getrume*, or *wera getrume*.   Holthausen, in his edition, reads *þe him tornum
ær | treowe sealdon, || mid heora mægnes getrume*.   Kock, PPP., p. 19, would
read *micle getrume* for Holthausen's *mægnes getrume*.   Holthausen, Anglia
XLVI, 61, proposes for l. 2047 *mid heora folces getrume | wolde his freond
huru*.   The disturbance seems too deep-seated for any plausible emendation,
and there still remains the possibility that the alliteration was never more
perfect in l. 2046 and that l. 2047 was never completed, see l. 703, note.
2049 wæron] Wülker retains *waron*, but since the whole passage indicates
careless writing, it seems better to emend with Grein and Holthausen to
wæron.   2054*b*-2057] Grein, Wülker, Holthausen place *him...hand-
plegan* within parentheses.   2055] Holthausen, following Grein, adds
tirlice after *hie*, placing *on twa healfe* in the second half-line.   See l. 703,
note.   2057 him se halga] Cosijn, Beitr. XIX, 453, Holthausen read *se
halga him*.   2058 eaðe] As a comparative *eað* might stand, but a comparative is not needed here, see Sievers, Beitr. X, 513, and the extra syllable
of the positive is needed for meter.   Grein, Wülker retain *eað*, Holthausen,
following Bouterwek, Erläut., p. 310, *eaðe*.   2066 hlihende] Holthausen,
hlihhende.   2080 wæron] Supplied by Thorpe, notes, and later edd., and
needed both grammatically and metrically.   2082 Domasco] Holthausen,
following Grein, *Damasco*.   2085 Loth wæs ahreded] Holthausen, *Loth
ahreded wæs*.   2091 oðle nior] The MS. has *oð leni*, at the end of a line,
followed on the next line by *or*.   The earlier edd. found this troublesome,
but Grein and the later edd. read *oðle nior*, *oðle* being for *eðle*, or as Cosijn,

Beitr. XIX, 453, suggests, *œðle*. **2096** folce] The edd. retain the MS. reading *folc*, and Grein, Dicht., p. 58, translates, "Da gieng südwärts von dannen das Sodomvolk, dass sie die Kunde brachten," Mason, p. 37, "Then the people of Sodom was southward from there, to bear the news." Holthausen retains *folc*, but states that *wegan*, l. 2097, is an infinitive for a present participle. This syntax is unconvincing, and Kock, JJJ., p. 32, points out that the view that "the Sodomites brought the news" does not accord with the Vulgate. Kock changes *wegan* to *wegen* as a past participle. **2099** eorlum bedroren] Holthausen, following Graz, Festschrift für Schade, p. 74, adds *se wæs* before *eorlum* for metrical reasons.

2101–2200

2101 Solomia] A genitive plural, = Salem, "the keeper of the treasury of Salem." **2107** Wæs] Grein emends the MS. *wær* to *wære*, but suggests *wes*. Wülker retains *wær*, and Holthausen reads *Wæs*. On *æ* for *e*, see l. 356, note. **2111** læt] Grein, Holthausen, *let*, but Wülker retains *læt*. **2112** rancstræte] Dietrich altered to *randstræte*, Holthausen to *radstræte*, but Holthausen, notes, reverts to the MS. reading. A compound *rancstræte*, with which Cosijn, Beitr. XIX, 453, compares *herepað*, is otherwise unrecorded, and the meaning is debatable. Kock, PPP., p. 19, interprets as meaning "a bold path." **2114** on swaðe sæton] To account for the abruptness of this sentence, Cosijn, Beitr. XIX, 453, suggests that the words *þæt hie* may have fallen out before *on*. **2117** sceolde] From *scieldan*, "protect," "shield," therefore for *scielde*, *scylde*, as suggested by Dietrich. **2120** beorn] Holthausen reads *beornwiga* for metrical reasons, or as alternative, Anglia XLVI 61, *beorhta beorn*. **2141** and] Supplied by Grein, Wülker, Holthausen. **2142** woruldfeoh] Holthausen, *woruldfeos*, made a genitive to accord with his addition of *ænig on eorðan*, to complete l. 2143. **2143a**] Grein places *þe ic me agan wille* in l. 2142, and so also Wülker. Holthausen supplies *ænig on eorðan* for l. 2143a, placing *þe ic*, etc. in the second half-line. On incomplete lines, see l. 703, note. **2147** willgesteallum] Dietrich, Grein, Kock, JJJ., p. 33, read *willgestealdum*, "riches," as an appositive to *ærgestreonum*, l. 2148. But Grein, Spr. II, 706, suggests that the word may be from *willgestealla*, "faithful follower," and there is no reason why it should not be this as a dative after *cweðe*, or with *eadig*. **2149** rices] Grein, Wülker, Holthausen, and others read *rices* as required by the grammar of the passage. selfa] The MS. reads *ac þu most heonon*, with metrical pointing before *ac* and after *heonon*. Grein, Germania X, 417, supplied *selfa* after *þu*, but placed *heonon* in the following line. Holthausen follows this reading of Grein, except that, with Graz, p. 75, he omits *heonon* altogether. In his text, Grein assumed a greater loss in the MS., supplying *seolfre and golde* for l. 2149b, and placing all of *ac...gesloh* in the following line. Wülker follows Grein, except that he supplies nothing for l. 2149b. **2159** ac nefuglas] The MS. reading *eacne*, "gorged," might be retained except that it violates alliteration. Grein, Wülker, Holthausen read *nefuglas*, "carrion birds."   **2160** blodige] The edd. read *blodig*, but Holthausen, Eng. Stud. LI, 184, *blodige*.   **2161** wæle] Grein retained the MS. reading *wæl* as an uninflected instrumental with *sittaðˇ*, translating, Spr. II, 644, "sitzen auf den Leichen." Wülker also retains *wæl*. But Grein, Dicht., p. 60, translates, "gefüllet dicke mit der Volksheere Leichen." So also Cosijn, Beitr. XIX, 453, Holthausen, Grein-Köhler, p. 752, read *wæle* as instrumental.   **2173a**] Holthausen, *Him þa Abraham*.   **2176** freomanna] Holthausen, *freora*, following Graz, Festschrift für Schade, p. 74.   **2184** sie] Holthausen, *sin*. But *sie* may stand for *sien*, see l. 856, note.   **2189** eafora] Holthausen, following Thorpe, notès, reads *eaforan*.   **2191** Sceawa heofon, etc.] This makes a very light half-line, though Grein, Wülker print it so, with a full stop after *heofon*. Something may have dropped out after *heofon*, perhaps the second element of a compound, such as *heofonwerod*, *heofonleoma*. Of course the compound may have been *heofonhyrste*, but if so, an *h*- alliterating word must be supplied in the second half-line. So Holthausen, *Sceawa heofonhyrste ond hadre gerim*, following Schubert, p. 28. The Vulgate has *Suspice caelum et numera stellas, si potes*, Genesis xv. 5. and] Though not necessary for sense, *and* supplies a required metrical syllable.   **2195** mægburge] The edd. retain *mægburh*, but Grein suggests *mægburge*, and cites l. 2222. Holthausen, Eng. Stud. LI, 184, would read *mægbyrh*. The word obviously should be a genitive to agree with *þinre*, and it may have been written as a nominative by the scribe merely because it stands next to *biðˇ*.   **2197** asæled] All edd. print *asæled*, and the first *æ* of the MS. is probably there merely by anticipation of the second.

2201–2300

2203 feowera] Grein alters to *feawera*, and Holthausen, notes, remarks that *feowera* is equivalent to WS. *feawera*. Grein, Dicht., p. 61, translates, "mit wenigen Begleitern."   **2210** niðas] Holthausen, *niððas*, and so Sievers, Beitr. X, 505.   swa] Grein and later edd. read *swa* for the MS. *twa*. Holthausen places this *swa* at the end of l. 2210a.   **2211** Wendelsæ] Thorpe, notes, suggested *oð wendelsæ* for the MS. *eft wendeð sæ*. Grein, Wülker retain the MS. reading, and Grein, Spr. II, 660, construes *sæ* as subject of *wendeð*, *rice* as object. Holthausen prints *wendelsæ*, defined in his glossary as "Weltmeer," and so Grein-Köhler, p. 773. On *Wendelsæ* as the name of the Mediterranean, see Bos.-Tol., p. 1189. All the passage means to say is that Egypt is bounded by *Eufraten*, by *Nilus*, and by *Wendelsæ*. The Vulgate, Genesis xv. 18, has merely *Semini tuo dabo terram hanc a fluvio Ægypti usque ad fluvium magnum Euphraten*.   **2217** him] "To them," i.e. to her and Abraham, with Abraham then repeated in the dative. wearð] Holthausen, *wurde*.   **2225** eðylstæf] Holthausen, following Bouterwek, Erläut., p. 314, *æðˇylstæf*. The other edd. retain *seo eðˇylstæf*, though Grein, Spr. I, 232, mentions *se æðˇylstæf* as a possibility. The change to a masculine article seems necessary, but the proper form of *eðˇylstæf* is doubtful. The article *seo* stands at the end of a line in the MS. and *eðˇylstæf* be-

gins the next line. A form *oðylstæf* is suggested as a possibility by l. 2091.
2227] Holthausen, following Graz, Festschrift für Schade, p. 75, adds *Ea la*
before *Drihten.* **2228** freolecu mæg] Holthausen Anglia XLVI, 61, reads
ful freolecu mæg. See l. 1708, note. **2235]** Holthausen adds *þær* before
geðafode. **2236** larum] Grein reads *lastum,* "with the footsteps of a bride,"
and so also Mason, p. 60. See Holthausen, Eng. Stud. LI, 184. But
Grein, Germania X, 418, returned to the MS. reading, which would mean
"by the counsel of his wife." The phrase *bryde larum* may have been a
scribal echo of *idese larum,* l. 2234, and see l. 2716, *bryde laste,* and l. 2249,
idese laste. **2240** herian] "Scorn," and so Grein, Dicht., p. 62, "verhönen."
See Cosijn, Beitr. XIX, 453, who further defines *halsfæst* as "unfrei," *agendfrean* as "herrin." **2249** idese laste] "After (in the track, place of) thy
wife." See l. 2236, note. **2252** Agar] Apparently the scribe misread
agar as *agan,* and therefore omitted an infinitive to go with *sceal,* perhaps
agieldan, as given in the text. There is no indication of loss in the MS.
Holthausen indicates the loss of at least a line, but probably only one word
has dropped out. Thorpe, notes, suggested *Agar* for *agan,* and so Holthausen, but Grein, Wülker retain the MS. reading. Kock, PPP., p. 19,
retains *agan,* translating, "I shall have that owing," "I shall claim compen-
sation for that," assuming also that *sceal = ic sceal.* The whole passage,
ll. 2251–2255, indicates careless writing. **2253** mine wealdan] Grein,
Dicht., p. 63, translates, "wenn ich meiner Magd vor dir noch mag gebieten,"
Mason, p. 41, "if I may still control mine own." See l. 2787. It is possible
that *mennen* has dropped out after *mine,* see l. 2260, but this would require
min, singular or plural, for *mine.* **2256** drihtna] So Thorpe and the later
edd. **2278** wulf] Holthausen, *wulfas,* or Anglia Beibl. XVIII, 205, *se hara
wulf,* both for metrical reasons. **2279** abregde] Holthausen, *abregden.*
See l. 856, note. **2290** and] Supplied by Sievers, Beitr. X, 453, Cosijn,
Beitr. XIX, 454, and Holthausen for metrical reasons. Kock, JJJ., p. 33,
would supply a more significant word, e.g. *wrað* or *wlonc.* **2293** frum-
garan] Grein, Wülker retain *frumgarum,* but Grein, Germania X, 418, suggests *frumgaran.* Holthausen, *frumgaran.* This permits taking *frumgaran* as object of *awæcniað* and accords with the reference here to *Ismahel,*
l. 2288. The dative plural *frumgarum* was an easy mistake after *þam,*
"from that one." awæcniað] The MS. reads plainly *apæcniað,* but all
edd. read *awæcniað,* except Holthausen, following Sievers, Beitr. X, 486,
awæcnað. **2297** hire hlafordum] Grein suggests supplying *to* before *hire,*
"to her masters," and so Holthausen in his text. But Grein, Spr. II, 69,
takes *hire = heore,* in this passage, as an adjective, "submissive to her
masters," and with this interpretation, as Holthausen, note, remarks, *to* is
unnecessary.

2301–2400

2305] Holthausen puts *wið* in the first half-line, but in his notes he places
the word in the second half-line and alters *Abrahame* to *Abraham,* citing
l. 2407. **2322** seofon] Kock, PPP., p. 20, would read *seofona* to gain a

metrical syllable. Holthausen, following Schubert, p. 35, supplies *symble* before *ymb*, but as Kock points out, this would mean "every seventh night," i.e. day. **2323** oððe of eorðan] Cosijn, Beitr. XIX, 454, adds *beon* after *eorðan*, and so Holthausen. But the infinitive can be supplied from *wesan*, l. 2320, and on *oððe* as an emphatic word, see Introd., p. xx. **2332** fremum] Kock, Anglia XLIV, 253, interprets as a noun, "by means of benefits," not as an adjective modifying *magorince*, l. 2330. **2338** Abraham ða] Holthausen transposes and supplies *his*, reading *His ða Abraham*, or as alternative, Anglia XLVI, 61, *ða Abraham his*. **2339** hucse] Junius has *hucse*, but not "aus versehen," as Wülker says, for the MS. has here *hucse*, though *husce*, l. 2384. In l. 2339, all edd. have *husce*, except Junius and Thorpe, *hucse*. **2346** C] To be resolved as *hundteontig*. **2362** tanum tudre] Grein, Dicht., p. 65, translates, "mit wachsender Familie," Mason, p. 43, "with spreading progeny." This assumes that *tanum* is an adjective and *tudre* a noun. But an adjective *tan* is dubious, Kock, JJJ., p. 34, and it is better to take *tudre* as a verb, equivalent to *tydre*, and *tanum* as a noun, "with branches." So also Holthausen, Anglia XLVI, 61. **2364** gen] Holthausen, following Sievers, Beitr. X, 484, *gena*. **2368** gelæstan] Grein retains *gelætan*, supplying *wesan* in meaning. He translates, Dicht., p. 66, "bleiben lassen." So also Wülker. Thorpe, Bouterwek, Holthausen read *gelæstan*. **2369** higetreowa] Wülker and the earlier edd. retain *-treawa*, except Dietrich, Grein, Holthausen, *-treowa*. **2372** wegan] Dietrich, Grein, Wülker, Holthausen, *wegan*, as demanded by the sense. **2380** fære] Cosijn, Beitr. XIX, 454, alters to *on feore*, "during his life," but acknowledges that *on fære*, from *faru*, "journey," "life's journey," is possible. Grein had previously made the same suggestion. Holthausen alters to *on feore*. Kock, JJJ., p. 34, takes *fære* as derived from *fēore*, through *fēre*. On *æ* for *e*, see l. 356, note. **2381** willan fremman] These are the concluding words on p. 108 of the manuscript, which contains only four lines of writing, the rest left blank for illustration. Between p. 108 and p. 109 a leaf has been cut out of the manuscript, on which must have been the paraphrase of Genesis xviii. 1–11. **2382** wereda drihtnes] Cosijn, Beitr. XIX, 454, suggests *be worde drihtnes* for *wereda drihtnes* to avoid the unusual construction of a genitive after *ahloh*. Kock, PPP., p. 20, defends the genitive object. Jovy, Bonner Beitr. V, 31, avoids the syntactical difficulty by taking *wereda drihtnes* as limiting *wif*, "the wife of the lord of hosts," i.e. of Abraham. **2396** wordgehat] Grein retains *worngehat*, defining it, Spr. II, 736, as meaning "promise of multitudes," "promise of abundant offspring," and he translates, Dicht., p. 66, "dann ist mein Wort erfüllt, das vielen Samen dir verheisst." Wülker also retains *worngehat*. Bouterwek, Erläut., p. 315, Dietrich, Holthausen, Grein-Köhler, p. 820, *wordgehat*.

2401–2500

2402 Lothes] Grein, Wülker retain *leohtes*, but Grein, Germania X, 418, reads *Lothes*, and so Holthausen. **2408** þisse byrig] Holthausen, *byrig þisse*.

2412 folces] The earlier edd. suggested a compound *folcefirena* or *folcfirena*, but Grein altered to *folces*, suggesting *folca* as alternative. Wülker, Holthausen, *folces*. It is appositive to *wærlogona*. **2416** fyr] An alliterating syllable is needed and *fyr* was supplied by Cosijn, Beitr. XIX, 455, who notes ll. 2543–2544. Holthausen also supplies *fyr*. **2418** hæðnum folce] The last words on p. 110, which is left blank for illustration, except for a little over one line of writing. A leaf has been cut out of the manuscript between p. 110 and p. 111 which must have contained the matter of Genesis xviii. 23–33. **2419** witelaces] Dietrich suggested *witelaces* for the MS. *wite loccas*, and so Grein, as appositive to *wean*. Holthausen prints *witelacas*, taking *-as* a genitive singular ending. Wülker reads *witeloccan*, taking *-locan* as a genitive singular or accusative plural of *-loca*, "stronghold," and Cosijn, Beitr. XIX, 455, rejects this interpretation in favor of Dietrich's. See *witelac*, l. 2556. **2436** ærendracan] Dietrich, Holthausen, *ærendrecan*. **2439** sunnan] So Holthausen. The word is sometimes masculine and sometimes feminine, but always weak. **2440** forlæt] Holthausen, following Jovy, Bonner Beitr. V, 23, *forlet*. **2441** þa to fotum Loth] These words begin p. 112 in the MS., with no indication that anything has been omitted. To complete the line, Holthausen, following Grein, reads *þa to fotum feoll | on foldan Loth*. The Vulgate has *adoravitque pronus in terram et dixit*. Wülker indicates the loss of a second half-line after *þa to fotum Loth* but does not attempt to fill the gap. See l. 703, note. **2451** Lagustreamas] Holthausen, notes, takes this as genitive, dependent on *þrym*. It seems simpler to take it as object of *wreah*, and also *þrym...þisses lifes*, "the glory of this life with darkness," as object. **2482** wineþearfende] All the edd. except Holthausen retain the MS. reading, with great difficulties of interpretation. Cosijn, Beitr. XIX, 455, alters to *wineþearfende*, citing Guth. 1321, An. 300. Holthausen follows Cosijn. **2487** þa] All edd. place *þa* in l. 2487, the metrical stresses then falling on *gromra* and *þa*. It may be taken as an adverb, or better as a demonstrative, "these (men)," appositive to *cuman*. **2496** gistmægen] Grein prints as two words, translating, Dicht., p. 69, "die Gäste hatten Macht," and so also *styrnde* is treated as a plural. But Grein, Germania X, 418, makes a compound, *gist-mægen* (defined in Spr. I, 374, as "Schaar der Gäste?"), with an alternative *gæst* as collective singular and *mægen* as object. Wülker prints *gistmægen*, and so also Holthausen, who defines the word in his glossary as meaning "Macht der Gäste," "mächtige Gäste." It seems best to take the word as a compound, though the two angels scarcely make a troop, except by poetical exaggeration. **2497** styrnde] Cosijn, Beitr. XIX, 455, would alter to *styrde*, and Bouterwek, Erläut., p. 316, had previously suggested *styrede*, "directed," "restrained." Holthausen prints *stŷrnde*, i.e. *stŷrde*. Grein, Spr. II, 492, defines *styrnan*, recorded only for this passage, as meaning "severum esse," and he translates, Dicht., p. 69, "straften." Grein-Köhler, p. 644, retains *styrnan*. As this gives a possible meaning, it seems best to retain *styrnde*.

2501–2600

2506 Unc hit] Cosijn, Beitr. XIX, 455, would read *Uncit,* citing l. 2530, *wit.*
2509 cwealmþrea] Holthausen, following Sievers, Beitr. X, 480, *cwealmþręawe*
= *-þrawe.*　　**2512** frea milde] The concluding words on p. 116, which contains only ten lines of writing. A leaf has been cut out of the manuscript between p. 116 and p. 117, on which was the matter of Genesis xix. 14–17. Most of the missing leaf must have been left blank for illustration, and this was probably the reason why it was cut out.　　**2522** Sigor] Holthausen, *Segor,* Vulgate, *Segor.* See *Sægor,* ll. 2533, 2540.　　Perhaps *Sigor* here has been affected by the noun *sigor.*　　**2528** sprycest] So Holthausen, following Sievers, Beitr. X, 473.　　Grein, without comment, *sprycst,* Wülker, *sprycst.* The form *sprycest* supplies a needed metrical syllable, and in any case, the MS. form *spryst* seems to be wrong.　　**2538** gelædde] Holthausen, Eng. Stud. XXXVII, 204, adds *hie* after *gelædde;* in his ed. he adds *þær.* As it stands in the text, *he* must take a metrical stress.　　**2545** on ærdagum] Grein alters to *on dagum ær,* the other edd., *ærdagum,* and see l. 2577.　　Holthausen changes *drihten,* l. 2545*b,* to *ecne* to improve the alliteration.　　**2547** heahþrea] Holthausen, following Sievers, Beitr. X, 480, *heahþręawu* = *-þrawu.*　　**2559** leg, geador] The MS. reading *swogende forswealh eall eador* cannot be divided to give an alliterating syllable in the second half-line. Grein, Wülker follow the MS., and Grein, Dicht., p. 71, translates *swogende ...eador* by "zusammen sausend." Dietrich, Holthausen read *geador* for *eador,* and this may be accepted as an orthographical improvement. Holthausen, following Schubert, p. 41, supplies *leg* after *swogende.* So also Sievers, Beitr. X, 513.　　Kock, PPP., p. 20, *swogende forswealh | samod eall eador.*　　Jovy, Bonner Beitr. V, 31, reads *swogende feor, swealh eall eador,* or *swogende forð,* etc.　　For *swogende leg,* see Beow. 3145.　　**2596** be hliðe] Holthausen adds *steapum* after *hliðe,* or Nachträge, p. 132, *ānum,* to improve the meter, but Anglia XLVI, 61, suggests *bliðe* for *be hliðe* and no addition.　　Kock, PPP., p. 21, assumes a form *hlīð,* with long vowel, remarking that "the O. Sax. original [Was there an OS. original for this part of the poem?] thus evidently had *hlīðu,* which gave a perfect verse." But *hie* may take a metrical stress and no change is necessary.　　**2599** dohtor twa] The last words on p. 122, which contains only four lines of writing. A leaf has been cut out between p. 122 and p. 123, on which must have been the matter of Genesis xix. 31–32.　　**2600** Hie dydon swa, etc.] The earlier edd. suppose an omission in the MS. here and supply variously, e.g. Grein reads *Hie dydon swa druncnum were.* Wülker supposes an omission after *druncnum* but supplies nothing. Holthausen arranges as in the text, but alters *dydon* to *dēdon.*

2601–2700

2603–2604] Grein reconstructs to read *hwonne him fæmnan to fæðme eodon ‖ and bryde laste him bi wæron.* Wülker assumes a loss of two half-lines between *to* and *bryde* but supplies nothing. Holthausen reads *hwonne him*

fæmnan to | foron on reste, ‖ bearn to bryde | him bu wæron. There is no
indication of loss in the MS., and no change is necessary, except possibly
the omission of *him* in l. 2603a. **2604** genearwod] So Grein and later edd.
2614 hire] Grein, Wülker place *hire* at the end of l. 2613, but this leaves
l. 2614a too short. Sievers, Beitr. X, 513, transfers *hire* to l. 2614, and so
also Holthausen, Indog. Forsch. IV, 380, and in his edition. Holthausen
also adds *ides* after *hire* to fill l. 2613b metrically. The alternative would be
to take *gingre* as metrically a trisyllable. **2616** folces unrim] Grein retains
folc unrim, though this is metrically incomplete. Wülker reads *folca unrim,*
following Sievers, Beitr. X, 513, who suggested *folca unrim* or *folc unrimu.*
Holthausen reads *folc unrimu.* But it seems better to read *folces unrim,*
with Schubert, p. 41, since only two tribes or nations are in question.
2625–2626] Holthausen and the earlier edd. read *bearh his aldre þy ‖.* In the
MS. the metrical pointing puts *þy* in l. 2626a. In l. 2626, Holthausen reads
wiste he, following Graz, Festschrift für Schade, p. 76. **2629** heht hie,
etc.] Grein, following Bouterwek, Erläut., p. 316, reads *heht bringan to him
selfum bryd Abrahames,* all as one line. In his text, Bouterwek had supplied
Sarran sciene, but replaced this in the Erläut., p. 316, by *bryd(e)Abrahames.*
Wülker indicates an omission after *selfum* but supplies nothing. Holt-
hausen, Indog. Forsch. IV, 380, *heht beornes wif | bringan to him selfum,* and
so in his edition. But an accusative feminine *hie* is all that is needed.
2631 Abrahames] Thorpe, Grein, and later edd., *Abrahames* for the MS.
abrames. **2641** him] Holthausen, Anglia XLVI, 61, suggests placing *him*
before *þurh,* l. 2642. **2642** sinces] Grein, Wülker retain *synna.* Thorpe,
notes, Bouterwek, Holthausen, *sinces.* See l. 2728. **2645** beheowan]
Grein reads *beheopian* and records this incorrectly for the MS. *beheopan,*
translating, Dicht., p. 73, "behauen." Wülker reads *beheopan.* But as
Cosijn, Beitr. XIX, 455, maintains, *beheopan* (otherwise unrecorded) is
probably merely a miswriting of *beheowan = beheawan.* For the phrase
aldre...beheowan, "deprive of life," see l. 2702. Holthausen reads *beheowan.*
þæne] Wülker retains *þære,* but Grein, Cosijn, Beitr. XIX, 456, Holthausen,
þæne. **2647** miltse him] The transposing of the MS. *him miltse* makes the
alliteration regular. For a similar metrical use of a pronoun, see l. 2649a.
The edd. assume a loss here in the MS. and Grein supplies *sylfum,* placing
to þe in l. 2647b, and reading *sylfum seceð* for l. 2648a. So also Holthausen,
except *simle* instead of *sylfum.* Wülker indicates an omission here but does
not supply anything. The metrical pointing in the MS. is · *and him miltse·
to þe seceð.* **2658** wið god] Supplied by Grein, Holthausen, to the improvement of syntax and meter. Wülker indicates an omission after *self* but
supplies nothing. Thorpe, notes, suggested omitting *self* and supplying
wið god. This makes the smoothest reading but *self* seems to be authentic.
2662 ærendu] Thorpe, notes, Bouterwek, Grein, *ærende.* Grein, Germania
X, 418, changes to *ærendu,* and so Holthausen. Wülker retains the MS.
ærenda as an accusative plural, but the customary form would be *ærendu.*
2668 gesprecan] Grein, Wülker, and the earlier edd. follow the MS. *sprecan.*
Sievers, Beitr. X, 453, gains a metrical syllable by reading *gesprecan.* So

also Holthausen.   2669 egesan geðread] Graz, Festschrift für Schade, p. 76, reads *se wæs egesan geðread.*   2691 Abraham þa] Holthausen, *Him þa Abraham.*   2694 guðbordes sweng] Cosijn, Beitr. XIX, 456, suggests *guðsweordes sweng.* Holthausen reads *guðbrordes sweng,* "stroke of the battle point," i.e. spear. But Kock, PPP., p. 22, takes *guðbordes sweng* as equivalent to "a blow on the shield"—as suitable a meaning as any other that has been proposed.   2695 lare gebearh] The difficulty in this passage is metrical. As the text stands, l. 2695*b* does not correspond to the usual types of verse as defined in the Sievers system of scansion. But for a defense of this metrical form, see Kock, Anglia XXVII, 219–220, and Anglia XLVI, 187–188. Holthausen emends *lare* to *on lade,* citing Beow. 1987, Ap. 92, and An. 276. Grein, Dicht., p. 74, translates, "durch die List," Cosijn, Beitr. XIX, 456, translates, "rat," device, counsel, citing l. 1671, Kock, PPP., p. 22, "by my lore," "by my words." The notion of cunning is not necessarily contained in *lare.*   2696 hyrde] Bouterwek, Erläut., p. 316, suggests *hirede frea, frea* going with *se halga.* Grein retains *hyrde = heorde,* "land," "earth," translating, Dicht., p. 74, "vom Grund und Boden." But Grein, Spr. II, 68, takes the word in the sense "family," with Bouterwek's *hirede* as alternative reading, and with *frean* carried over to l. 2697*a.* So also Grein-Köhler, p. 331. Holthausen glosses as "Hürde," "Tür," and cites Kluge, Zft. für vergl. Sprachforschung XXVI, 100.   2697 mines fæder] Holthausen, Indog. Forsch. IV, 380, adds *eðle* after *fæder* to complete the line metrically, and so in his edition.   alædde] So Thorpe, notes, and later edd.

2701–2800

2707 mid wealandum] As it stands this compound at first suggests *wea,* "woe," and *land,* and Thorpe translates "hostile nations." Bouterwek, Erläut., p. 316, suggests *weallændum wunian,* "dwell among foreign (peoples)." Dietrich retains *winnan* as equivalent to *dreogan,* and *wealand* as for *wealland = wealhland* "foreign lands," though he also suggests *mid wealdendum.* Grein follows the MS. with Dietrich's interpretation, but Grein, Germania X, 418, changes *winnan* to *wunian.* Wülker retains the MS. reading. Holthausen reads *mid weallendum wunian,* following Bouterwek, regarding *weallendum* as similar in formation to *ellende.* So also Klaeber, Anglia Beibl. XXXVIII, 357. Kock, PPP., p. 23, would take *wealandum* as appositive in meaning to *wigsmiðum,* l. 2704, connecting the word, though not convincingly, with the name of Weland, the smith. It seems best to take *wealandum* as equivalent to *weal-landum,* "foreign lands," and to retain *winnan* as equivalent to *dreogan,* though *wea-lende = wealh-lende* is also plausible.   2714 Sarra] Holthausen, *Sarrai,* following Rieger (see l. 1854, note) and Sievers, Beitr. X, 480. Cosijn, Beitr. XIX, 456, suggested *þæt Sarra me,* but withdrew this in favor of *Sarrai.* See l. 1241, note. Grein reads *Sarrah,* Dietrich, Wülker, *Sarra.*   2721 weorcþeos] The MS. reading *feos* seems to be an echo of *feoh* in l. 2720. Grein reads *weorc-*

þeos, noting Genesis xx. 14, *servos et ancillas.* Wülker retains the MS. reading, but does not indicate how he would construe a form like *weorcfeos.* Cosijn, Beitr. XIX, 456, Holthausen follow Grein. **2725** þe ic agan sceal] Grein takes this as an independent clause, translating, Dicht., p. 75, "ich will dich haben." Mason, p. 52, "I must have thee." So Wülker, Holthausen, but Holthausen, Anglia XLVI, 61, notes this unusual use of *agan* and suggests changing to *ecan,* "endow," "make rich." But it is better to take *þe* as a relative, with *wic* as antecedent, in the sense "any habitation," as the context of the passage implies. **2730** flettpaðas] So Holthausen and all edd. since Bouterwek. **2732** ac] Grein suggests *i c* for *ac.* **2733** deope] Grein alters to *deore* and suggests *bette* for *bete.* ceara] Grein alters to *cearað,* and translates, Dicht., p. 75, "Sorgt ihr beide nicht." But Grein, Spr. I, 158, returns to the MS. reading, taking *incit* as accusative with following infinitive, and so Grein-Köhler, p. 85. The direct address to Sarah in the preceding passage favors a singular here, changing to the plural *wuniað* in l. 2735 because of *incit.* Wülker retains the MS. reading. Holthausen reconstructs to read *Ne cearað duguða inc.* Sievers, Beitr. X, 513, reads *duguða inc[it],* transposing *duguða* to improve the alliteration. **2743** Sarrai] Bouterwek, Erläut., p. 317, Grein, *Sarran.* **2747** þeowe] Holthausen, following Sievers, Beitr. X, 492, *þeos.* See l. 2754*b.* **2748** bregoweardas] A genitive singular, see Cosijn, Beitr. XIX, 457. ecan] Bouterwek, Erläut., p. 317, *ecean,* Grein, Germania X, 418, *ecan* for the MS. *agan,* and so Holthausen, but the other edd. retain *agan* in the very doubtful meaning "endow," or "beschenken," Grein, Dicht., p. 76. See l. 1122. **2749** monrim mægeð] The object of *meahton...ecan* is *monrim,* and *mægeð* is appositive to *freo ne þeowe.* Retaining the MS. reading *agan* as meaning "endow," Kock, Anglia XLIII, 308, would take *bregoweardas* as object, and *monrim* as appositive to *bregoweardas,* with *mægeð* appositive to *freo ne þeowe.* **2751** arna] The earlier edd. followed the MS., but Grein altered to *arna.* Wülker returned to the MS. reading, but Cosijn, Beitr. XIX, 457, Holthausen, *arna.* **2754** þeowra] Grein alters to *þeowna,* but see l. 2747, note. **2758** weard] So all edd. **2762** hæfde wordbeot] Holthausen, following Schubert, p. 51, *wordbeot hæfde,* but see l. 574, note. **2768** mid] Supplied by Cosijn, Beitr. XIX, 457, citing Guth. 274, and Holthausen. Cosijn and Holthausen read *agne* for *agene.* Grein retained the MS. reading as instrumental, translating, Dicht., p. 76, "mit eigener Hand." **2770** hine on woruld] Holthausen, following Schubert, p. 50, *on woruld hine,* but see l. 574, note. **2772–2773** cynde, æðele] Holthausen alters *cynde* to *cynn,* declaring *cynde* to be metrically impossible, and *æðele* to *æðelo,* the first a noun, the second an adjective. Grein retains *cynde* but reads *æðelo,* the latter a noun and *cynde* an adjective. But Grein, Spr. I, 178, suggests *cynde* as a nominative plural feminine and *æðele* as adjective modifying *cynde.* This is the simpler reading, "as his qualities were excellent." Wülker follows the MS. **2774** hundteontig] Wülker retains *hunteontig,* but Thorpe and the other edd. *hundteontig* **2777** dægwillan] Grein, Wülker take as two words, see Grein, Spr. II, 708, "day of joy." But Grein suggests also *dægwillan*, and translates, Dicht., p. 77, "den Freudentag." So Holthausen, and see Cosijn, Beitr. XIX, 457. 2781 halig on hige] Holthausen reads *on hige halig*, and so previously Graz, Festschrift für Schade, p. 77.   2790 þu of lice] Holthausen, following Graz, Festschrift für Schade, p. 77, reads *of lice þu*. So also Cosijn, Beitr. XIX, 456.   2795 cearum] Cosijn, Beitr. XIX, 457, suggests *cearium*, taking the word as an adjective, for *cearigum*, but *cearum* as adj. is doubtful and the word is best taken as inst. pl. of *cearu*.

2801–2900

2806 agen bearn] The last words on p. 134. Between p. 134 and p. 135 a leaf has been cut out which contained the matter of Genesis xxi. 15–21. 2809 snytru] The earlier edd. follow the MS., but Cosijn, Beitr. XIX, 457, and Holthausen, *snytru*, as a genitive. The proper adjectival form would be *snottrum*. But Kock, Anglia XLVI, 87, takes *snytrum mihtum* as an example of asyndetic paratexis, i.e. as parallel instrumental nouns, citing several other examples, which scarcely prove that this is one. See l. 1084. 2810*b*] The lack of a half-line is supplied by Holthausen, *mago Ebrea*, following Grein. There is no indication of loss in the MS. See l. 703, note. 2814 on] Grein in his text follows the MS., taking *forðwegas* as an adverbial genitive, and so Wülker. But Grein, Spr. I, 320, supplies *on*, and so Holthausen.   2819 þina] Grein alters to *þine*, but see l. 2709.   2832 Ða Abraham] Holthausen, *His ða Abraham*.   2838 þæt] So Grein and later edd.   2839 lond] So Thorpe and the later edd.   2843 glædstede] Grein alters to *gledstede*, and so Holthausen. See l. 1810, and on *æ* for *e*, l. 356, note.   2844 geneahe] Holthausen, *geneahhe*.   2844*b*] Holthausen, following Cosijn, Beitr. XIX, 457, supplies *him* before *lif*, and Cosijn suggests omitting *þam*.   2857*b*] Holthausen, *ond hine blotan sylfa*.   2861 frean] So Holthausen, following Thorpe and the later edd.   2862 waldend] Thorpe and later edd., *waldend*, but Bouterwek, Erläut., p. 317, would read *hæs waldendes* for *his waldende*.   2869 men] Holthausen, *mannan*, and so previously Schmitz, Anglia XXXIII, 32.   2900 stowe] Bouterwek, Erläut., p. 317, and the later edd. supply *stowe*, except Wülker who indicates an omission after *þære* but does not supply it.

2901–2936

2907 scencan] Thorpe retains the MS. reading here, translating, "the fire quench with the youth's gore." Bouterwek, Erläut., p. 317, reads *gesencan*, and *fyr* as object. Grein follows the MS., translating, Dicht., p. 80, "die Brandglut dämpfen mit des Sohnes Blute." But Grein also suggests *sengan* and *dreor*, "burn, consume the blood of his son with fire." Kock, JJJ., p. 34, would let *sencan* stand as equivalent to *sengan*, but suggests *mæg on dreore* for *mæges dreore*. The meaning thus would be, "consume with fire his son in his own blood." Jovy, Bonner Beitr. V, 31, suggested *swencan* for *sencan*, and Holthausen follows, reading *fyre swencan* ‖ *mæg his deorne*, "with fire afflict his dear son." So also Grein-Köhler, p. 597. Bright, Anglo-Saxon Reader, p. 221, proposed *scencan*, "to pour out liquor for drinking," translating literally, "to give drink to the fire (by means of) kin's blood." Klaeber, Anglia Beibl. XXV, 295, approves Bright's reading, and Anglia Beibl. XXXVIII, 358, defends the syntax of *dreore* as an instrumental after *scencan*. Bright's interpretation offers the least difficulty, though so violent a metaphor is not in the tone of Genesis, and *scencan* may be taken merely in the sense "pour out." Other suggestions, *swelgan* for *sencan* by Körner, *besprengan* by Zupitza, Übungsbuch, notes, call for the substitution of an entirely new word for *sencan*.   **2921** leofre] Grein follows the MS., but suggests *leofre*. Wülker, Holthausen, *leofre*.   **2932** onhread] Cosijn, Beitr. XIX, 457, suggests *onread*, citing Corpus Gloss. 1129, *onreod*, "stained." So Bos.-Tol., p. 756. The form *onhread* would be from *onhreodan*, "adorn." Grein altered to *onhreað*, from *onhreoðan*, "adorn," Spr. II, 347, but Grein-Köhler, p. 358, gives the infinitive as *onhreodan*.   **2933** reccendne] Grein, Holthausen, *recendne*.   **2935** and ealra þara sælða] Grein, Körner, Zupitza, in his Übungsbuch, Bright supply *sælða* after *þara*. Wülker indicates an omission but does not supply it. Holthausen omits *and* and reads *ealra þara* for l. 2935a as of the same syntax as *leana*.   sið and ær] Holthausen, *ær ond sið*.

NOTES ON EXODUS

1–100

Exodus] For the title, see Introd., p. xxvii.   **3** wræclico wordriht] Bouterwek, Erläut., p. 318, reads *wrætlicu word dryhtnes*. But *wordriht* is an acc. pl. neuter noun, appositive to *domas*. Sedgefield reads *wrætlico*.   **4–5**] Cosijn, Beitr. XIX, 457, would place these two lines within parentheses. **8** weroda] So all edd., except Blackburn, who assumes a gen. pl. *werode*. See Bright, MLN. XXVII, 13.   **14** freom] A variant form of *from*, "valiant." Blackburn, in his glossary, unnecessarily assumes a word *frēom*, "strenuous." See Klaeber, Eng. Stud. XLI, 109, Bright, MLN. XXVII, 13.   **15** andsacan] All edd. alter to *andsacan*, except Blackburn, who assumes that *andsaca* is a Northumbrian form for *andsacan*, either a genitive appositive to *Faraones*, or an accusative, appositive to *cyn*. But a Northumbrian *andsaca = andsacan* is very improbable in this text, and *andsacan* seems to be the necessary reading. Grein, Germania X, 418, sought to retain this word as a nominative by emending to *andraca*, taking this as a variant of *ærendraca*, "messenger," and as referring to Moses. So also Grein-Köhler, p. 24, but see Holthausen, p. 874.   **17** magoræswan] Grein, Körner read *magoræswan*, the other edd. follow the MS. A dative plural is possible here, but the context strongly demands a dative singular, as Mürkens, p. 113, points out. Cosijn, Beitr. XIX, 458, approves *magoræswan*, calling attention to a similar scribal error in *frumgaran*, l. 2293.

18 onwist] Bouterwek, Erläut., p. 318, reads *ondwist*, as in An. 1540.　But the word occurs only once in each of these two forms.　**20 gesealde wæpna**] Körner inserts *him* between these two words.　**22 feonda**] All edd. after Junius omit one *feonda*, except Körner, who emends the second to read *freonda*, and also omits *folcriht*.　This makes *feonda* object of *ofercom* and *freonda* appositive to *cneomaga*.　**folcriht**] Cosijn, Beitr. XIX, 458, suggests *feonda folcdriht*, but *folcriht* is supported by Beow. 2608.　**27 sigerice**] Grein, Spr. II, 448, takes *sigerice* as an adj., here and in l. 563, and Klaeber, JEGPh. XIX, 412, defends this interpretation, citing Beow. 94, *sigehreþig*.　But Kock, JJJ., p. 24, more plausibly takes the word in both passages as a noun.　**28 yldo**] A genitive plural, see l. 437.　**33 ingere**] The MS. reads *ingere*, as one word.　Bouterwek, Erläut., p. 318, suggests *iugera*, and Grein, Wülker read *iu gere*.　Blackburn reads *ingere*, glossed "unexpectedly?", but suggests *ungere*, "not long before," in his notes, in accord with Klaeber, Archiv CXIII, 146.　Sedgefield reads *ungera*.　The emendation *iu* does violence to the alliteration, and though *ungere* is possible, there seems to be no reason why a reference should be made just at this moment either to remote or near past time.　It is better to retain the MS. reading, interpreting it, with Mürkens, p. 92, as an emphatic adverb, the second element as in l. 291, and *in-* an intensive prefix, as in the adj. compound *infrod*, Beow. 1874, 2449.　The meaning then would be "altogether," "completely," and the metrical structure of this half-line would be parallel to that of l. 291.　**ealdum witum**] Cosijn, Beitr. XIX, 458, suggests changing to *geald unwitum*, with *werodes aldor* to be supplied in sense, and *geald unwitum* to be treated as a parenthesis.　This would preserve the alliteration with *iu* for *in* in the first half-line.　**34 gedrenced**] The word *gedrenced* is an alteration of some earlier reading, probably made by an early reader of the MS. to cause this passage to refer definitely to the passing of the Red Sea.　Groth, p. 15, would read *gedemed* for *gedrenced*, and Blackburn, notes, surmises *gedrecced*, *gedrefed*, or *gedemed* as the original form of the word. Cosijn, Beitr. XIX, 458, Bright, MLN. XXVII, 13, Klaeber, Archiv CXIII, 146, favor *gedrecced*.　The reading *gedrecced* undoubtedly improves the sense, the phrase *ealdum witum*, "with terrible afflictions," referring to the threefold punishment of the Egyptians, loss of treasure, death of the first born, and the overthrowing of the idols, according to Bright.　**36 berofene**] In intent *berofene* goes with *hordwearda*, but grammatical agreement would require a genitive.　A plural *wæron* may be supplied in sense from *wæs*, l. 35, "they were deprived of treasure."　Blackburn takes *since berofene* as an instrumental phrase, "through plundered treasure," but this seems improbable.　**37 mansceaðan**] Bouterwek, Erläut., p. 318, Mürkens, p. 113, and Bright, MLN. XXVII, 13, would read *mansceaða* as subject of *hæfde*.　Otherwise *mansceaðan* is retained as an accusative, e.g. Grein, Dicht., p. 82, "er hatte die Meinschädiger furchtbar gefället, viele der Erstgebornen," or as dative plural, Blackburn, notes, referring to the Egyptians, the subject of *hæfde* being Jehovah, to be supplied from l. 30.　This third is the least and the second the most plausible interpretation.

39 abrocene] Cosijn, Beitr. XIX, 458, would read *abrotene*, and so Sedgefield.
40 drysmyde] Dietrich, Grein, Wülker read *drysmyde*, see Beow. 1375, but if the second *r* of *dryrmyde* is a scribal echo of the first, the second *y* may be similarly an echo of the first *y*, and perhaps one should emend to read *drysmede* or *drysmode*. Sedgefield has *drysmode*. 44 alyfed laðsið] As Kock, JJJ., p. 24, points out, *wæs* is to be supplied in sense before *alyfed* and also before *folc*, l. 45. gretan] Sedgefield reads *grǣttan*. 45 folc ferende] The *folc* are the Egyptians, *ferende* "departing," "perishing," with *hergas*, l. 46, appositive to *folc*, and *on helle* supplementing *ferende*. feond] Thorpe, note, Bouterwek, Erläut., p. 318, Grein, Körner, Wülker read *feond*, and so Blackburn in his notes. But the interpretation of *feond* varies, Mürkens, p. 70, assuming that the word refers to the Egyptians, Bright, MLN. XXVII, 13, that it refers to Satan. Blackburn, notes, comments as follows: " 'The devil and the hosts of hell were robbed' is an expression quite in keeping with the style of our poet, who thinks of the escape of the Hebrews as a rescue from bondage to Satan"—a far-fetched interpretation. One might retain *freond* as *freonda*, "was deprived of its friends," but this is improbable. 46 hergas on helle] Taking *hergas* as appositive to *folc*, *feond*, it would mean "hosts," "armies," Grein, Dicht., p. 82, "die Heere in der Hölle." But Kock, PPP., p. 6, would place a full stop after *bereafod* and take *hergas* as appositive to *deofolgyld*, in the sense "altars." So also Bright, MLN. XXVII, 13. Kock would also take *on helle* as equivalent merely to an adjective, "hellish," modifying *hergas*, as in Beow. 101, *feond on helle*, an interpretation given by Klaeber, Archiv CXIII, 147. Mürkens, p. 70, taking *hergas* in the sense "hosts," would alter *on helle* to *on healle*, "in the hall," and so previously Holthausen, Anglia Beibl. V, 231. Cosijn, Beitr. XIX, 458, proposes *hergas onælde*, for *hergas onhælde*, from *onhæled* for *onæled*. Heofung] Grein makes a compound *heofon-þider*, taking the second element in the sense "service," and translating, Dicht., p. 82, "Himmelsdienst," but Grein, Germania X, 418, separates and takes *heofon* in the sense "lamentation." But Blackburn, notes, more probably assumes that *heofon* is a scribal error for *heofung*. Kock, PPP., p. 6, would retain *heofon* in the sense "heaven," making *heofon þider becom* parenthetic, but it is not clear what this should mean. Thorpe had previously translated, "heaven thither came." 49 Swa] Thomas, MLRev. XII, 343, would take *swa* as a relative, "who," "which," and *ealdwerige* and *folc* as accusatives parallel to *fæsten*, translating, "That was a famous day when the Israelites fared forth, who had endured for many years captivity, the perverse folk of the Egyptians, because they (the Egyptians) had determined for ever to refuse to Moses' kinsmen their desire for the cherished expedition"—a very forced interpretation. fæsten] Mürkens, p. 113, would reconstruct to read *swa þæs (þas ?) fæhðan dreah*, "obwol fehde (feindschaft) unterhielt viele jahre." 50 ealdwerige] Grein, Spr. I, 243, took this word as *eal-dwerig*, "very wicked," translating, however, Dicht., p. 83, "altelenden," and Körner, "das altverdammte," Johnson, p. 45, "accursèd of old." Grein-Köhler, p. 146, retains the explanation of the second

element as -*dwerig*, and so Thomas, MLRev. XII, 343. Cosijn, Beitr. XIX, 459, would read *þæt ealwerige* or *ealwērige* for *ealdwerige*. For *eald* as an intensive, see *ealdum witum*, l. 33. Sievers, Beitr. X, 461, suggests the possibility of an original *ealdwerigra*, in the same case as *Egypta*. 53 on langne] Grein, Wülker, Blackburn read *onlangne*. Bouterwek, Erläut., p. 318, proposes *ondlangne*. Kluge, Bright, MLN. XXVII, 14, read *on langne*. It seems better to take *on langne lust*, meaning freely, at their pleasure, as long as they wished, and continuing the meaning of *wideferð*, l. 51. This improves the meter and makes it possible to take *wyrnan* in the usual construction with genitive of the thing, *siðes*, and dative of the person, *magum*. 57 leodweard] Grein suggests *leodgeard*, and Sedgefield prints the word so. 59 Guðmyrce] Taken by Grein, Spr. II, 786, as meaning the Ethiopians, "die kampfgeübten Schwarzen." Cosijn, Beitr. XIX, 459, would define as "grenzbewohner," noting Exodus xiii. 20, *in extremis finibus solitudinis*. Gollancz, p. lxxx, takes *Guðmyrce* to mean "the war-negroes," the Nubians, and sees in the word *lyfthelme*, l. 60, a play on the word *nubes*, "cloud," and the fictitious etymology of *Nubae*, "Nubians," from *nubes*, "cloud." gearwe] Sedgefield, MLRev. XVI, 59, and in his Verse Book, reads *geatwe*, "armor." But *gearwe* may be retained in the same meaning, and see l. 193. 61 mearchofu morheald] The meaning and form of *morheald* is in question. Blackburn glosses the word "near or by the moors, on the moors," but accepts this meaning only doubtfully. He construes *mearchofu* as object of *ofer*, and *þa* as adverb, citing l. 362 in support of this unusual syntax. For Blackburn's translation, see l. 62, note. Gollancz, p. lxxxi, would change *morheald* to *marheald*, the first element meaning "rope" (see AS. *mærels*, *mærels-rap*), the second meaning "safe," "secure." The whole phrase would mean "desert habitations, rope-secure," or in Gollancz's phrase, "desert dwellings securely moored," i.e. tents, this being the poet's interpretation of the Hebrew word Succoth (see Exodus xiii. 20), the first stopping place of the Israelites after their setting out. The Hebrew word means "tents," see Genesis xxxiii. 17. A word *mar*, "rope," is not found in AS., nor does *heald* occur in the sense "secure," though related forms of these words do occur with appropriate meanings. According to this interpretation *mearchofu* would refer to the dwellings of the Israelites, and this seems the best way to take the word, whether or not it is an allusion to Hebrew Succoth. Johnson translates, p. 45, "their march-dwellings on the hillside." Bright, MLN. XXVII, 14, would take *heald* as a verb = *heold*, and interprets, "a damp waste (*mōr*) extended its reach (*hēald* = *hēold*) over the marches (*mearchofu*)." 62 fela meoringa] The meaning of *meoringa* is doubtful. A word of this form does not occur elsewhere in AS., but it may possibly be related to *gemearr*, "hindrance," and other similar forms. This is the sense in which it is taken by Grein, Spr. II, 240. This would give Blackburn's translation, "Moses then led the army past the border-dwellings of the moors, [past] many hindrances." Gollancz, p. lxxxi, supposes here a scribal corruption and that the poet originally wrote *"fele Mering = fæle Mæring*, the trusty Amramite (cf. Numbers iii. 27, etc.), the

description of Moses which one would expect in this passage, and which
poetically balances the lines... Now Amram was taken to mean 'the exalted
people,' from the Hebrew meaning of its component syllables, and for an
Amramite no happier equivalent could perhaps be found in Old English
than the term *mæring*, i.e. 'one of an illustrious family.' " Gollancz supposes that the scribe misunderstood *Mæring*, therefore changed *fele* = *fæle*,
"trusty," into *fela*, and *Mæring* into a genitive plural to follow *fela*. But if
so, he would seem to have changed from an unknown word to one no better
known, for *meoringa* surely is not self-explanatory. Gollancz's theory is
ingenious, but only slightly probable. A simpler reconstruction would be
fæle magorinc, which also would balance *Moyses*, l. 61. Mürkens, p. 88,
would read *meorringa* = *mearringa* for *meoringa*, citing Gothic *marzjan*,
an emendation approved by Bright, MLN. XVII, 424, who translated,
"Moses then led the host over many obstacles," and followed also by Sedgefield.   63 ymb twa niht] The camp at Etham, see Genesis xiii. 20, was the
third camp, as is stated in l. 87, made after the Hebrews had been on the
way two days. The second camp was the one at Succoth, not definitely
named in the poem, unless *mearchofu morheald*, l. 61, is an allusion to it.
The first camp was presumably at Rameses, see Genesis xii. 37, but this also
is not definitely mentioned. The fourth and last camp, l. 133, was at the
shore of the Red Sea, see Genesis xiv. 2, where the news that the Egyptians
were pursuing was brought to the Hebrews.   tirfæste] All edd. except
Körner and Sedgefield retain *tirfæstne*, but Bouterwek, Erläut., p. 318,
suggests *tirfæste*, and so Körner, Cosijn, Beitr. XIX, 460, Mürkens, p. 113,
and Sedgefield. The MS. reading could be retained only if one provided a
subject for *heht*, but the natural subject for *heht* is not God, who has not
been mentioned, but Moses, see l. 61.   66 ælfere] The MS. has *ælf* at the
end of a line and *ere* on the following line, hence Thorpe and Bouterwek
read *ælf ere*, but Grein, Spr. I, 57, makes the proper compound, *æl-faru*,
"the whole army," citing *eal-mægen* as a similar compound. In his text
Grein had explained the first element as *el-*, "foreign," as in *el-þeod*. Sedgefield reads *ælfare*.   68 genyddon] Grein, following Dietrich, *geneðdon*, but
Grein, Germania X, 418, returns to the MS. reading. Grein, Dicht., p.
83, translates, "Mit Nachdruck eilten sie," Johnson, p. 45, "Straitly they
pressed on the northern roads." But Napier, MLRev. VI, 168, rejects this
and translates, "the difficulties facing them (*nearwe*, i.e. the heat, if they
took a southerly direction) forced them to the north."   69 Sigelwara]
Mürkens, p. 113, changes to *Sigelwarena* for metrical reasons.   70 burh-
hleoðu] Thorpe, notes, Bouterwek, *beorhhleoðu*. Grein retains the MS.
reading, but defines the word, Spr. I, 148, as though the first element were
beorh-, "mountain." So also Napier, MLRev. VI, 168, and Kock, Anglia
XLV, 124.   73 bælce] Holthausen, Archiv CXV, 163, would read *bælge*,
"covering," "canopy," citing *sances*, l. 309, as another instance of *c* for *g*.
But it is doubtful if a word *bælg* was intended here, though the meaning
"canopy" may very well have been, see Grein, Spr. I, 77, Bos.-Tol., p. 66,
Cosijn, Beitr. XIX, 460. See also l. 94, where the cloud is referred to as

beam. **78** hate] Grein reads *hat*, and he translates, Dicht., p. 83, "das heisse himmelsklare." Bouterwek, Erläut., p. 318, reads *hæte*, and *acwanc* for *adranc*, l. 77. It seems best to take *hate* as a noun, though it may be merely an instrumental of *hat*, "heaven-bright with heat." **79** Dægsceades] The MS. reads *dæg* at the end of a line, followed by *scealdes* in the next line. The edd. retain *dægscealdes*, but with insuperable difficulties of interpretation. Lye-Manning, Supplement, proposed *dægsceades*, referring to the cloud by day. The passage would thus mean "The protection of the day-shadow coursed *ofer wolcnum*, across the skies," and with *ofer wolcnum*, compare the common phrase *under wolcnum*, "on earth." Holthausen, Anglia Beibl. V, 231, proposed *dægstealdes*, "des tagbesitzers"; in Archiv CXV, 163, Holthausen proposed *dægsweol(o)ðes hleo*, "protection against the heat of the day," but in Anglia Beibl. XXIX, 283, he returns to the MS. reading, taking *dægsceald* as for *dægsceld* and as referring to the sun as the "day-shield," *dei clipeus*, noting Ovid., Met. XV, 192 f. This is likewise Cosijn's interpretation, Beitr. XIX, 460. But the subject of *wand* is not a hypothetical *dægsceld*, but *hleo*, and "the protection of the day-shield" for "sun" is too tortured and unpoetical a figure of speech to be credible, even if *sceald* = *sceld* = *scield*, *scyld* were credible. Blackburn, notes, and Thomas, MLRev. XII, 343, also take *dægsceald* as meaning "day-shield," though they refer it to the pillar of cloud. Bright, MLN. XXVII, 14, suggests *dæges-cealdes hleo* "protection against, or deliverance from, the day-cold"—i.e. the sun. Grein, Spr. I, 184, takes the word as certainly referring to the sun and notes the usual interpretation as "day-shield," but suggests as to be preferred the meaning "Tagbeherscherin." But he translates, Dicht., p. 83, "Der Schirm des Tagschiffes wand sich über die Wolken," with variants "Des Sonnen-schiffs oder Sonnenwagens." Perhaps the *l* in the MS. *scealdes* was written by the scribe in anticipation of the *l* in *hleo*. **81** segle] Junius and Bouterwek follow the MS., but Thorpe, note, and the later edd. read *segle*, as the sense demands. See ll. 83, 89. **95** efngedælde] Cosijn, Beitr. XX, 98, suggests *efne gedælde*, "divided equally," assuming that *efngedælde* would mean "shared." But *efngedælde* may be taken in the former sense, with Grein, Spr. I, 218. Kluge reads *efn gedælde*.

101–200

104 latþeow] Sedgefield alters to *latteow*. lifweg] Dietrich proposed *liftweg*, i.e. *lyftweg*, for *lifweg*, followed by Grein, Kluge, Wülker, Cosijn, Beitr. XIX, 460, and Sedgefield. Bouterwek, Erläut., p. 319, proposed *liðweg* or *lidweg* for *lifweg*. Gollancz, p. lxxxiii, sees in *lifweg* an allusion to the journey of the children of Israel as an allegory of "the way of life." But if the poet had this allegory in mind, he made remarkably slight use of it. He might well call the journey which was to save the lives of the children of Israel a "life-way" without any hidden meaning. **105** swegl] Bouterwek, Erläut., p. 319, Grein, Wülker, Sedgefield alter to *segl*. **106** flodwege] Grein suggests *fold-* for *flod-*; Blackburn, notes, translates, "by (on, along) the road to the sea," Grein, Dicht., p. 84, "auf dem Flutwege nach," Johnson, p. 46, "toward the waters." **109** sunne] Bright, MLN. XVII, 425, reads *sunne* as subject of *beheold* and *setlrade* as object, punctuating as follows: *Heofonbeacen astah* || *æfenna gehwam,* | *oðer wundor,* || *syllic, æfter sunne* | *setlrade beheold,* || *ofer leodwerum* | *lige scinan,* || *byrnende beam.* Napier, MLRev. VI, 168, thinks the difficulty in the passage lies in *beheold* and suggests changing to *ongann,* as improving the sense. Blackburn, notes, takes *beheold . . . scinan* in the sense "took heed to shine" with *wundor* as the subject. Holthausen, Eng. Stud. LI, 182, rejects this interpretation and suggests merely supplying "one," impersonal, as the unexpressed subject of *beheold.* Or one may take the subject as carried over from *Folc,* l. 106, see Bos.-Tol., Supplement, p. 74. This interpretation involves putting *byrnende beam,* l. 111, in the accusative case. Thomas, MLRev. XII, 344, takes *sunnan* as object of *æfter,* translating, "Another wonder, a strange one following upon the sun, observed the sun's setting, shining over the people with flame." Bright's interpretation presents the fewest difficulties. **110** lige scinan] Cosijn, Beitr. XIX, 460, suggests *liges sciman.* **113** sceado] Junius retains *sceaðo,* but Thorpe, notes, and later edd. read *sceado,* except Blackburn, who thinks *sceaðo* may be an orthographic variant of *sceado.* swiðredon] Sedgefield alters to *sweðredon.* **115** heolstor] Accusative, with *nihtscuwan* as subject, see Grein, Spr. II, 67, Bright, MLN. XXVII, 15. Johnson, p. 46, "The deep shades of night availed not to hide the dark retreats." Johnson fails to translate *neah,* which Grein, Dicht., p. 84, renders as "genugsam." **118** hæðbroga] Rieger, Verskunst, p. 46, suggested *hæðstapa,* as in Beow. 1368, and Bright, MLN. XVII, 425, supports this. But *hæðbroga,* suggested by Cosijn, Beitr. XIX, 460, is a better parallel to *westengryre.* Sievers, Beitr. X, 513, Kluge, Mürkens, p. 113, would read *hares hæðes,* but Graz, Eng. Stud. XXI, 2, *harre hæðe,* taking *hæð* as a feminine. **119** on ferclamme] Dietrich recognized in the MS. *ofer clamme* a noun and read *færclamme,* dropping the *o* and treating the noun as an instrumental. Grein, Wülker, Blackburn retain the *o* as adverb, "ever." Kluge reads *on* for *o,* a reading approved by Mürkens, p. 113, and Bright, MLN. XXVII, 15. Sedgefield reads *on færclamme.* getwæfde] Bouterwek in his glossary proposed *getwæfe,* but all edd. approve *getwæfde.* **121** bellegsan] "With fire terror," parallel to *hatan lige,* l. 122. Regarded thus, the first element is an irregular spelling for *bæl-, bel-.* Bouterwek, Erläut., p. 319, Grein read *bælegsan,* Sedgefield, *bælegesan.* The other possibility would be to regard *bell-* as having the sense of *bellan,* "roar," and according to Blackburn, notes, the poet may have "thought of the pillar of fire as gleaming with lightning and consequently bellowing with thunder." **122** in] Omitted by Grein, without comment. **124** hyrde] For *hyrden,* "hear," "obey," see Bright, MLN. XXVII, 15. See *gebohte,* l. 151. **126** rihte stræte.] This might be taken as accusative, appositive to *segn,* but better as an instrumental, as by Johnson, p. 47, "in a straight course." Grein alters to *rihtre* and then translates, Dicht., p. 85, "die Randkempen sahen der rechten Strasse Anzeichen über den Schaaren."

127 sweoton] Grein, Graz, p. 25, Mürkens, p. 113, *sweotum*.   **128** leod-mægne forstod] All edd. after Junius read *leodmægne*, but Blackburn, notes, defends *leode mægne*, translating, "protected the people by its might," the subject being *sæfæsten*. But the proper sense of *forstod* is indicated by Bright, MLN. XXVII, 15, as "opposed," "hindered," followed by the dative *leodmægne*. Translate, "until the seafastness, at the end of the land, stood opposed to this people-host." So also Klaeber, Eng. Stud. XLI, 110.   **129** fus on forðweg] Bouterwek, Erläut., p. 319, reads *fusne forðweg* as object of *forstod*. Mürkens, p. 114, alters *fus* to *fuse* and connects it with *leodmægne*. Cosijn, Beitr. XX, 98, Kock, JJJ., p. 25, accept this syntax, though they retain *fus* as an uninflected form. Klaeber, Eng. Stud. XLI, 110, proposed *fuson* = *fusum* for *fus on*, taking *forðweg* as object of *forstod*, and *fuson* as a dative, "to them eager (to proceed)." So also Napier, MLRev. VI, 168. Holthausen, Anglia Beibl. XXI, 14, and XXX, 3, proposes *fúson on*, for *fus on*. But the simplest and most convincing interpretation is that of Bright, MLN. XXVII, 15, who takes *fus on forðweg* as limiting *werod*, l. 125, noting as parallel l. 103*a*.   **131** beton] Grein alters to *bētan*, an infinitive. Mürkens, p. 114, would read *bētton*.   **134** þan] Grein alters to *þam*.   **139** onnied] The MS. has *on nied*, but the alliteration here is vocalic, and *on nied* can scarcely be a prepositional phrase. Grein, Kluge, Wülker, Sedgefield alter to *ohtnied*, but Cosijn, Beitr. XX, 99, rejects *ohtnied*. Blackburn reads *onnied*, "oppression," and so Kock, PPP., p. 7.   **141** ær ge] These syllables stand at the end of p. 148 in the manuscript. This is a full page of 26 lines, the first line of the page being the beginning of a section. The following page, p. 149, also begins a section. According to Gollancz, p. lxix, two leaves, that is four pages, have been lost between p. 148 and p. 149, which probably "contained an account of how Joseph got all the property of the Egyptians into Pharaoh's hands, Gen. xlvii. 20, and generally saved the country from famine. The *wære* in l. 140 seems to refer to the promise made by the elder Pharaoh that the Israelites should dwell in the land of Goshen. The attempts made by editors, notwithstanding the sectional division, to connect the last words of p. 148 with the opening words of p. 149 seem to me altogether futile." Dietrich, Grein read *getiþode*, Kluge, Graz, Eng. Stud. XXI, 2, Mürkens, p. 114, *gelyfde*, to complete l. 141*b*, and assume no further loss in the MS.   **142** þa wearð, etc.] Grein connects these words directly with what precedes as a temporal subordinate clause, so translating, Dicht., p. 85, and followed by Johnson, p. 47, "when with treasures he purchased the lordship of the native-born people, and so mightily prospered." But Johnson remarks that construction and meaning are doubtful here. Grein supplies *he* before *wearð*.   ingefolca] Dietrich suggested *yrre folce*, or *yrre folca herge*, or *heape*, for *ingefolca*. Kock, PPP., p. 7, also thinks that some word indicating the king's state of mind has dropped out after *wearð*, and he suggests *onmod*, "self-confident." Since the direct allusion to what preceded is missing, it seems best to let the text stand, in some such meaning as "Then he became guardian of the people, of the men after the treasure [had come into his

possession], so that he greatly prospered." **145** ymbe antwig] The MS.
has *ymb án twig*, which is metrically too short for a half-line and not clear
in meaning. Bouterwek, Erläut., p. 319, tried to connect *twig* with Aaron's
rod. Dietrich suggested *ymb an wig*, "über einen todtschlag." Grein
reads *andwig*, citing Guth. 147. But Grein, Germania X, 418, suggests
anwig, and so Wülker. Bright, MLN. XVII, 425, reads *ymbe anwig*.
Mürkens, p. 114, reads *ymb ane* (= *anne* = *ænne*) *wig*. Sedgefield, MLRev.
XVI, 59, proposes *ymb anes wig*, "concerning the attack of one man," i.e.
Moses, and so in his Verse Book. Cosijn, Beitr. XIX, 461, suggested *ymb
antwig seredon*, the Egyptians being the subject of the verb and *antwig* the
object. Kock, PPP., p. 7, proposed *antþigða*, "success," for *antwig*, the
ða coming from the next line, i.e. the Egyptians were angry on account of
the prosperity of the Israelites. Blackburn retains *antwig* as an orthographic
variant of *andwig*, and he interprets *ymb antwig* in a general sense, "in
regard to war," "in apprehension of warfare." It seems best to retain
antwig as a variant of *andwig*, though the reference may be more precise,
see Exodus ii. 11–15. Blackburn would read *antwige* to complete the line
metrically, but *ymb* takes the accusative. **147** fræton] Bright, MLN.
XVII, 425, would read *bræcon*. **149** manum treowum] Bright, MLN.
XXVII, 15, would alter to *mannum tweonum*, "to the two men," taking this
to be a reference to *ymbe anwig*, "which is accepted to mean the 'duel' in
which Moses slew the Egyptian." But it is better to take *manum treowum*
as an adverbial phrase, parallel to *facne*, l. 150, see Bright, MLN. XVII,
425. **151** hie] Grein suggested *hie* for the MS. *he*, but did not place *hie* in
his text. As Blackburn, notes, points out, the context requires a plural
here, and *gebohte* is to be taken as an optative plural without ending, see
Gen. 856, note. Cosijn, Beitr. XX, 99, retains *he*, and takes *leode* as genitive, *Moyses* as nominative in l. 152. But with *hie* as a plural, *leode* becomes appositive. **157** oferholt wegan] Parallel to *forð ongangan*, Cosijn,
Beitr. XX, 99. Thorpe, Bouterwek divided *ofer holt wegan*, and Kluge
proposed *ofer holtwegan* (-*wegan* for *wegum*). But *oferholt* is best taken as
meaning "shield," the covering or protecting wood. According to Sedgefield, *oferholt* "probably means the forest of spears rising above the Egyptian
army; but perhaps the original word was *eoferholt*, 'boar-spear.' " **160**
þufas þunian, etc.] Grein places this line after l. 157, and so also Sedgefield.
þeod mearc] Thorpe, Bouterwek, Graz, p. 25, Mürkens, p. 114, make a
compound, *þeodmearc*. **161** on hwæl] In the MS. *on hwæl* stands at the
beginning of a line, followed by *hwreopðn*, with metrical pointing before and
after this word. There is no indication of loss in the MS., but there was
evidently some confusion in the mind of the scribe, for he apparently wrote
the *hw* of *hwreopðn* as an echo of the *hw* of *hwæl*. The parallel of l. 168 indicates that the MS. *hwreopðn* is the beginning of a new sentence. Kluge,
Holthausen, Archiv CXV, 163, omit *on hwæl*. Mürkens, p. 114, proposes
on hræ hrēopon on here fugolas, for l. 161, and *hildegrædige hræfn sweart āgōl*,
for l. 162. Grein made *On hwæl...herefugolas* into one line, the following
line being *hilde grædige; hræfen gol*. He translates *On hwæl* by "Rings im

Kreisse," Dicht., p. 86, connecting it therefore with the word for "wheel." For l. 162, Bright, MLN. XVII, 425, reads *hilde grædige hræfn üppe gōl*, citing El. 52–53. Holthausen, Archiv CXV, 163, supplies a whole line between l. 163 and l. 164, *herge on lāste; hræfn üppe gōl.* 164 wonn wælceasega] Johnson, p. 47, "the black carrion-seeker." The change from the plural *herefugolas*, l. 162, to the singular here is avoided by some of the emendations recorded under l. 161, note. But it is a simple rhetorical device that may have been intended. Blackburn, notes, prefers to take *wonn* as preterite of the verb *winnan*, "the lover of carrion hastened [thither]." Holthausen, Anglia Beibl. V, 231, would change to a plural, *wonne wælceasge.* 167 fyl] Wülker retains the MS. *ful* as a variant orthography for *fyl*, but the other edd. since Dietrich change to *fyl* or *fyll*. Grein, Germania X, 418, suggested *fal* = *feall*, "Fall," and so Spr. I, 286. 169 gehæged] Grein reads *genæged*, translating, Dicht., p. 86, "angegriffen," but in Germania X, 418, Grein returns to the MS. reading. Bouterwek, Erläut., p. 319, proposed *gehnæged*, and Cosijn, Beitr. XX, 99, suggested *geæged*, "terrified." Blackburn, reading *gehæged*, translates, "hemmed in," the translation Grein gave for the MS. reading, but which he rejected in favor of *genæged.* 172 segncyning] Dietrich suggested *secga cyning*, Grein, Kluge alter to *sigecyning*. But Wülker, Blackburn, Sedgefield retain *segncyning*. For a similar verbal echo, see l. 93, and see Gen. 23, note. 176 wælhlencan] The alliteration and the sense require *wæl-*, as all later edd. read. Perhaps *hwæl*, l. 161, is a similar miswriting. 178 onsegon] Thorpe and Bouterwek retained *onsigon*, but Thorpe, note, suggested *onsawon*. Blackburn also retains *onsigon*, taking the word in the sense "approach," "draw near," with *cyme* as plural subject, "the advance of the men of the land moved toward the friends with hostile looks." The other edd. read *onsegon*, except Kluge, *on segon*, Sedgefield, *on sægon*. 180 wægon] Sedgefield, MLRev. XVI, 59, and so also in his Verse Book, reads *wæron*, since *wægon* would have no object. Cosijn, Beitr. XX, 100, also questions *wegan* in the sense "se movere." But the change to *wæron* enfeebles the line. See Cosijn's suggestion, l. 181, note. wigend] Sievers, Beitr. X, 511, Graz, Eng. Stud. XXI, 3, Mürkens, p. 115, alter to *wigan*. Sievers proposes as alternative the stressing *unfórhte*, with *wigend* retained. 181 heorawulfas] Thorpe, note, Bouterwek read *herewulfas*. Grein alters to *heorowulfas*, but Spr. II, 71, *heoruwulfas*, defined as "lupus sanguinarius," "bellator." In Dicht., p. 86, however, Grein translated this word as "Kampfwölfe," i.e. *herewulfas*. Sedgefield reads *heorowulfas*, glossed "sword-wolf," under *heoru-*. gretton] Cosijn, Beitr. XX, 100, would alter to *geatwe*, combining with the preceding word, and thus giving *wægon* an object. 183 alesen] Kluge, Graz, Eng. Stud. XXI, 3, Mürkens, p. 115, read *alesene* 184 twa þusendo] Bright, MLN. XXVII, 16, suggests *twa hund þusendo*. For further comment, see Cosijn, Beitr. XX, 100, Kock, PPP., p. 8. 186 on þæt eade riht] Thorpe suggested *eorðrice* or *eardrice* for *eade riht*. Kluge, Sedgefield read *ealde riht*, and Bright, MLN. XVII, 425, would change to *on þæs eades riht*, citing ll. 338–339, 353–354. Blackburn, notes, translates, " 'for that

NOTES ON EXODUS 207

honored duty,' i.e. for subordinate command, as the following verses show."
As an adjective *ead* is not frequent but may be defended. 190 ingemen]
The MS. has *ingemen* as a single word. It is so given by Thorpe, Bouterwek,
Kluge, but Bouterwek, Erläut., p. 319, suggests *incgemen*. Dietrich, Grein,
Wülker, Blackburn, Sedgefield read *inge men*, taking *inge* as equivalent to
ginge, "young," see Sievers, Beitr. X, 195. But as Mürkens, p. 93, points
out, it remains doubtful if *inge* is meant for *ginge*, not only because of the
alliteration, but also because a noun, something similar to *ingefolca*, l. 142,
or *ingeþeode* (Grein's reading), l. 444, is expected here. 191 oft] Bouterwek altered to *eft*, Grein to *-ost*, combining with *cuð* to give *cuðost*. ge-
bad] Grein, Sedgefield read *gebead*, and so Blackburn, notes. This seems to
be the intent of the word, though a meaning from *gebīdan*, "await," is not
impossible. 193 gearwe] Sedgefield, MLRev. XVI, 59, and in his Verse
Book, reads *geatwe*. See l. 59, note. 194 ecan] Grein takes *ecan* =
eacan in the sense "addition," "reënforcement," and so Kluge, Graz, Eng.
Stud. XXI, 3, Sedgefield. Blackburn, glossary, derives *ecan* from the
adjective *ece*, "eternal," translating, "continuous," "unending," in his
notes. Bright, MLN. XXVII, 16, changes to *eacan*, "increased," "great,"
"vast." It seems best to take *ecan* = *eacan* as a noun, appositive to *werod*.
Thorpe, Bouterwek, Grein, Germania X, 418, Spr. I, 229, and Wülker
read *ec anlæddon*. 197 to] Cosijn, Beitr. XX, 100, Bright, MLN. XVII,
425, omit this word. 200 in] Grein has *on* for *in*.

201–300

202 weredon wælnet] Cosijn, Beitr. XIX, 461, suggests *weredum wælned*,
citing ll. 136*b*-137*a*. Mürkens, p. 115, accepts *weredum* but retains *wælnet*,
translating, "angstgraus drohte, das netz des todes dem volke." Bright,
MLN. XXVII, 16, defends *weredon wælnet*, taking *weredon* from *werian*,
"wear." But it seems better to take *weredon* as meaning "defended," with
wælnet, simply "coat of mail," see Kock, JJJ., p. 25, as object, and *woma*
as meaning "war itself," see Kock, Anglia XLIV, 252. 204 wlance]
Grein suggests *wlence* but retains *wlance* in his text. 206 mid him] To be
united in sense with *tosomne*, l. 207, with *geseon* as reflexive, see Cosijn,
Beitr. XX, 100. Johnson, p. 48, translates, "so that no longer could the
foes gaze upon each other." 212 blacum] Bright, MLN. XXVII, 16, reads
blăcum, "black," and so Holthausen, in Grein-Köhler, p. 876, but the usual
interpretation is *blācum*, "bright," "shining." 216 bemum] Thorpe,
notes, and later edd. read *bemum*. 220 sande] Grein suggests *sunde* but
retains *sande* in his text. 222 burgum] Grein alters to *beorgum*. 226
moderofra] Bouterwek, Erläut., p. 320, Grein, note, Kluge, Graz, p. 25,
Mürkens, p. 115, Sedgefield read *mode rofra*. Blackburn would retain
-rofa as Northumbrian for *-rofan*, an adjective modifying *feðan*. But he
suggests *-rofra* and *-rofe* as alternatives. 227 æðelan] Grein alters to
æðeles. Holthausen, in Grein-Köhler, p. 873, proposes *æðel[est]an*. 233
wace] Grein and later edd. read *wace* to secure grammatical agreement.

237 feond] Sedgefield, notes, says *feond* is genitive sing., but he does not explain how this can be. It is accusative singular with the adjective *flane*, from *flah*, agreeing. Kluge reads *fane*, from *fah*, for *flane*. **239** swor] Grein retained *swor* = *sweor*, defining it as "dolor," but suggested also *spor*. Blackburn, Grein-Köhler, p. 627 accept *spor*, "trace," "mark." Sedgefield, MLRev. XVI, 60, and Verse Book, reads *licwunde swol*, "the burning of a wound." But see Kock, Anglia XLIII, 305, for an adequate defense of *swor*, "pain." **242** modheapum] Grein suggests *modneapum*, citing *nep*, l. 470, but does not place it in his text. He retains *modheapum* as derived from *modhæp*, "rich in courage," see Spr. II, 259. But Blackburn, Sedgefield take the word as a noun, defining it as "bold host," "gallant band." swiðrade] Sedgefield changes to *sweðrade*, translating, "had failed." But the usual form of this verb, meaning "grow less," "vanish," in this MS., has *i* and no change is necessary. See ll. 113, 309, 466. **243** on wig curon] Holthausen, Beibl. V, 231, suggested *him þa* before *wig* to complete the line metrically. Graz, Eng. Stud. XXI, 3, supplies only *him* before *wig*, citing Gen. 1803. Mürkens, p. 115, reads *wigende curon*, Bright, MLN. XXVII, 16, *on wig curon*. Sedgefield reads *wigheap* for *wig*. **245** aran] Wülker, *æran*, which he mistakenly reports as the reading of the MS. **246** garbeames feng] There is no indication of loss in the MS., and perhaps the line was never completed. Wülker, Sedgefield indicate a missing first half-line, which they do not supply. But there is nothing to show that a first half-line, rather than a second, has been lost. Grein supplied *gegan mihte* before *garbeames*, and Kluge, Graz, Eng. Stud. XXI, 3, Mürkens, p. 115, supply *gretan mihte* after *feng*. But it is possible to take *cræft*, l. 245, and *feng*, l. 246, as subjects of *wolde*, and as parallel to and amplifying *mod*. **248** forðwegas] Kluge altered to *fus on forðwegas*. But *forðwegas* is a gen. sg. in *-as*. gerad] Sievers, Beitr. X, 513, Graz, p. 25, Mürkens, p. 115, Sedgefield supply *ge* before *rad* to complete the line metrically. **249** beama] Cosijn, Beitr. XX, 100, alters to *beacna*. bidon] So Grein and all later edd. **251** bræc] Cosijn, Beitr. XX, 100, thinks an optative *bræce* would be more in keeping here, but see Bright, MLN. XXVII, 16. The suggestion *bræce* had previously been made by Grein. **253** beohata] Bouterwek, Erläut., p. 320, suggests *bodhata;* Dietrich reads *beahhata*, "treasure hater," i.e. one who gives away treasure gladly, a prince. Grein, following Ettmüller, Lexicon, p. 303, reads *beothata*, translated in Dicht., p. 88, "Verheissungbringer," but Grein, Germania X, 418, follows the MS. Bos.-Tol. follows Grein's first reading, taking *beo* as for *beot*, "command," "decree." Grein-Köhler, p. 44, records *beohata* as for *bihata*, and so Sedgefield, glossary, *bīhata*, "challenger," "champion." Blackburn, notes, suggests that *beohata* is Northumbrian for *bēah-hāta*, " 'promiser of treasure,' a prince, like *bēah-gifa*." The parallel to *hildecalla*, l. 252, and the context suggest *(ge)bod*, perhaps influenced by *beodan*, as the first element of the compound, but the formation of the word remains obscure. **255** monige] Cosijn, Beitr. XX, 101, translates, "die Volksmengen," citing l. 553. **265** ægnian] Bouterwek, Erläut., p. 320, would read *egian*, and Sedgefield, MLRev. XVI, 60, and Verse Book, reads *ognian*, from *oga*, "terror." Dietrich suggested *æglian* or *eglian*, and Holthausen, Anglia XLVI, 54, suggests *eglan*. See also Cosijn, Beitr. XX, 101. Kock, JJJ., p. 26, would read *ængian*, "oppress." Blackburn retains *ægnian* in the sense "vex," "torment," and Bright, MLN. XXVII, 17, regards *ægnian* as a variant of *āgnian*, "own," "control as a possession," and so also Holthausen, in Grein-Köhler, p. 873. A verb *ægnian* occurs only in this passage, but it seems best to retain it, in the sense of *egsian*, or if any change is made, to omit the first *n*, reading *ægian* = *egian*, with Bouterwek.   **269** on] From *unnan*. Dietrich, Kluge read *ræde*, as a verb. Cosijn, Beitr. XIX, 461, reads *ic con beteran ræd*, and Mürkens, p. 115, proposes *ræd ic on beteran*.   **277** leod] Gollancz, p. lxxi, suggests *þeodne* for the MS. *þeod*, regarding the line as suggested by Exodus xiv. 15, "when Moses raised a loud cry to the Lord of living men, then he spoke thus to the people." But this makes an unusual line metrically. Blackburn, notes, suggests *þeoden*, but against this the same objection holds. Bouterwek, Erläut., p. 320, proposed *leod*, and so Grein, Kluge, Wülker, Sedgefield. See l. 172, note. Bright, MLN. XXVII, 17, proposed *leoð* for *þeod*, "song of the living," citing ll. 308–309, but this seems remote. **278** to] Bright, MLN. XXVII, 17, Sedgefield, notes, would omit *to*. Blackburn, notes, suggests that *to* here may be an echo of *to* in the preceding line. **280** and] Bouterwek, Erläut., p. 320, *mid* for *and*, and *þas* for *þeos*.   **281** tacne] Dietrich proposed *tane* and the later edd. follow, except Blackburn, notes, who retains *tacne*, " 'with the green symbol' [of authority], i.e. Moses' rod." The reference is undoubtedly to Exodus xiv. 16, with which *tane* would more literally agree, but *tacne* may well have been the poet's unliteral modification.   **283** wæter wealfæsten] Grein retained *and* as a preposition, but Grein, Germania X, 418, following Thorpe, note, omits *and*. So also Graz, Eng. Stud. XXI, 4, Mürkens, p. 115, Bright, MLN. XXVII, 17, Sedgefield, *wæter* as subject, *wealfæsten* as object. Bright, MLN. XVII, 425, had previously proposed *in* for *and*, citing l. 296, and Cosijn, Beitr. XX, 101, would read *on* for *and*.   **288** in ece tid] The MS. *in ece* is incomplete. Grein, Wülker read *iu ece*, which is still incomplete metrically. Cosijn, Beitr. XX, 101, proposes *iu ær ece*. Kluge, Graz, Eng. Stud. XXI, 4, Mürkens, p. 115, read *in ecnysse*, Sedgefield, MLRev. XVI, 60, and Verse Book, *in ecnesse*. Holthausen, Anglia Beibl. V, 231, proposed *in ece tid* or *in ælce tid*.   **289** sælde] Thorpe suggested *sealte*, Cosijn, Beitr. XX, 101, *side* for *sælde*. Cosijn also suggests *sund wind* for *suð wind*, *sund* as object of *fornam* and *wind* as subject. This would make *blæst*, l. 290, appositive to *wind*. But the allusion in Exodus xiv. 21 seems to justify *suðwind*. Sedgefield follows Cosijn.   **290** brim] Thorpe and later edd., *brim* for *bring*.   **291** sand sæcir spaw] Dietrich suggested *spen*, "bound," with *sæcir*, "the sea's return," as object. Bouterwek, Erläut., p. 321, proposed *âspâv* = *āspāu*, and Grein reads *spav* = *spau*. Wülker follows Grein. Ettmüller, Lexicon, p. 656, gives *span*, and so Kluge. Blackburn, notes, retains *span*, and taking *sæcir* in the sense "ebb of the sea,"

he remarks, "have we here a strong metaphor, 'hath spun [a road of] sand'?"
Sedgefield, MLRev. XVI, 60, and Verse Book, reconstructs to read *sandsæ*
aspranc, "the sandy waters have started aside." The reading *spaw* is
supported by l. 450. For *sæcir* see *cyre*, "tide"? l. 466.   **295** agend]
Bouterwek, Erläut., p. 321, Mürkens, p. 115, Sedgefield read *agendfrea*.

301–400

305 anes modes] To supply a second half-line, Grein added *yða weall*, Kluge,
Graz, Eng. Stud. XXI, 4, Mürkens, p. 115, add *swylce him yða weall*, Bright,
MLN. XVII, 426, *him yða weall*, and Blackburn, notes, *hie yða weall*, taking
freoðowære, l. 306, as a dative. Though probably some such addition is to
be made, it is possible to read the passage as it stands if *gedriht*, l. 304, is
taken as subject of *heold*, l. 306.   **307** hige gehyrdon] "They disregarded,
scorned not in mind," taking *gehyrdon* as from *gehyrwan*. Grein reads
hige gehyrwdon, but Germania X, 418, *gehyndon*. Thorpe, notes, Bouterwek, Kluge, note, Graz, Eng. Stud. XXI, 4, Mürkens, p. 115, Sedgefield
change *hige* to *hie*, *hi*.   **309** sances] Dietrich, Grein, Kluge, note, Graz,
p. 25, Mürkens, p. 115, Sedgefield change to *sanges*.   **312** grenne] Not an
appropriate adjective here.   Perhaps one should read *ofer ginne grund*, "over
the wide abyss."   **313** on orette] Thorpe, Bouterwek read *anon onette*,
but Thorpe suggests *onette*, and Bouterwek, Erläut., p. 321, *an on onette*.
Grein, Wülker, Blackburn read *an onorette*. Cosijn, Beitr. XX, 101, sug-
gests *an ore onette*.   Sedgefield reads *an onette*.   But *orette* seems too genuine
lightly to be set aside for *onette*, and the main difficulty in the passage lies
apparently in the MS. reading *an on*. It seems best to take *orette* not as a
verb, but as a noun, see Chambers, Widsith, p. 203, after *on*, and to attach
an, for *on*, to *uncuð gelad*, making the line similar in structure to l. 311.   Or
an may be omitted and *uncuð gelad* taken as appositive to *grenne grund*.
318 cynericu] Cosijn, Beitr. XX, 102, suggests *cynrynu*, "supra gentes," for
cynericu.   **321** leon] Thorpe, note, and later edd. read *leon*.   **326**
þracu] Grein altered the MS. *praca* to *pracu*, a nominative, and so Kluge,
Mürkens, p. 115, Blackburn, in his glossary, Sedgefield, Holthausen, Eng.
Stud. LI, 182, but Wülker retains *praca*.   **327** hægsteald] The noun is
singular and *modige* is plural. Bright, MLN. XXVII, 17, suggests *hægstealda*
mod, citing l. 489. Cosijn, Beitr. XX, 102, reads *hægstealdas modge*. Blackburn, Sedgefield, Grein-Köhler, p. 295, take *hægsteald* as a plural, the former remarking in his notes that *hægsteald* is a singular for the plural "to
fit the metre."   **328** wælslihtes] Cosijn, Beitr. XX, 102, would read *wæl-*
slihtas, parallel in syntax to *handplega*, l. 327.   Otherwise the genitive must
be taken as dependent on *modige* (Sedgefield), or on *unforhte* (Bright, MLN.
XXVII, 17).   wigend] Sievers, Beitr. X, 511, Graz, Eng. Stud. XXI, 3,
Mürkens, p. 115, read *wigan*. See l. 180, note.   **329** blodige] Sievers,
Beitr. X, 461, note, Holthausen, Eng. Stud. LI, 182, read *blodig*.   **331**
flota modgade] Bright, MLN. XVII, 426, reads *feða modgode*.   **334** manna
menio] Sievers, Beitr. X, 513, Graz, Eng. Stud. XXI, 4, Mürkens, p. 115,

Blackburn, notes, Sedgefield read *manna menio*, but Mürkens suggests also *man-menio*, i.e. "man-multitude." micel angetrum] Kluge, note, suggests *micelan getrume*. 339 gearu] Dietrich, Grein read *earu*, "quick," "active," but Grein, Germania X, 418, returns to the MS. form, taking *gearu* as for *ge-earu*. But it is doubtful if there is such an adjective as *earu*, and *gearu*, of the same meaning, seems more probable, in spite of the alliteration. 340 forð] Grein supplied *forð* for alliteration, and so Cosijn, Beitr. XX, 102. Holthausen, Anglia Beibl. V, 231, would supply *fuse* after *him*, and Mürkens, p. 116, supplies *for*, from *faran*, before *þær*. Sedgefield supplies *foron* after *him* and changes *sunu*, l. 341, to *suna*. But *sunu* may be a plural, see Sievers, Angels. Gram. § 270. 343 guðcyste] This may be retained as an instrumental, "in a war-band," or less plausibly as a nom. pl. with sing. verb, see Spr. I, 534. Cosijn, Beitr. XX, 102, would read *guðcyston þrang*, *guðcyston* for *guðcystum*. Grein, Kluge read *guðcyst*, a nominative appositive to *þeodmægen*. 344 deawig] Sedgefield, MLRev. XVI, 60, and Verse Book, reads *deaðwigsceaftum*, "with deadly spears." 345 garsecge] The MS. *secges* may have been a scribal anticipation of the ending of *godes*. Bouterwek supplied *gin* after *garsecges*, Ettmüller, Lexicon, p. 434, supplied *begang*, Grein has *begong*. Kock, PPP., p. 8, supplies *begang*. Cosijn, Beitr. XX, 102, suggests *deop* or *stream*. Graz, Eng. Stud. XXI, 4, proposed *garsecge* or *geofones begang*. Mürkens, p. 116, Bright, MLN. XXVII, 17, Sedgefield read *garsecge*. Blackburn, notes, takes *ofer* as a noun, "shore," object of *becwom*, "came to." 346 mæretorht] Kluge suggests *meretorht* or *mære morgentorht*. Sedgefield reads *meretorht*, glossed as "gleaming over the sea." Cosijn, Beitr. XX, 102, defends *mæretorht*. 348 an wisode] Kock, PPP., p. 8, places l. 348*b* and the whole of l. 349 within parentheses. 349 mægenþrymmum] Bright, MLN. XVII, 426, alters to *mægenþrymma*. 350 on forðwegas] Grein adds *for*, from *faran*, before *on*, taking *folc* as the subject. wolcnum] Thorpe, Bouterwek, Sedgefield read *folcum* for *wolcnum*. Bright, MLN. XVII, 426, reads *folce*. 353 æðelo] Ebert, Anglia V, 409, proposes *æðel* = *eðel*, "der männer heimat." 358 onriht] Thorpe, Bouterwek read *on riht*. See l. 587, and Krapp, Andreas, l. 120, note. The chief objection to this division of the words is that in this passage the alliteration is vocalic. Sedgefield, MLRev. XVI, 60, and Verse Book, reads *ānriht*, " ' possessing alone the right,' i.e. the privileged one of God." Blackburne translates, "the peculiar people of Jehovah?" 362 oferlað] For the scansion, see Bright, MLN. XXVII, 18. Blackburn reads *ofer lað*, taking *ofer* as a preposition governing *flodas*. 364 drencefloda] Thorpe, note, Bouterwek, Grein, Wülker read *drencfloda*, which is incomplete metrically. Sievers, Beitr. X, 513, would add *þara* or *ealra* before *drencfloda*. Cosijn, Beitr. XX, 103, reads *drencefloda*, citing Gen. 1398, and so Graz, Eng. Stud. XXI, 5, Mürkens, p. 116. 370 ece lafe] Thorpe suggested *ecende* for *ece*, Grein reads *egelafe*, and Holthausen, Anglia Beibl. V, 231, proposed *eagorlafe*. Blackburn translates *ece* as " 'continuing,' lasting, surviving," as applied to those who survived the deluge. Graz, Eng. Stud. XXI, 5, supports the MS. reading.

371 gehwæs] All edd. accept *gehwæs*, but Blackburn, notes, suggests that *gehæs* may be a dialectal variant, not a scribal error for *gehwæs*.   **373** mismicelra] Grein suggests adding *ma* after this word.   Cosijn, Aanteekeningen, p. 1, suggests *mislicerra*.   Bright, MLN. XXVII, 18, defends *mismicelra* as the gen. pl. of the comparative, citing Sievers, Angels. Gram. § 231, 4.   **383** he on wræce lifde] Cosijn, Beitr. XX, 103, regards these words as a parenthesis.   **386** on Seone] Grein, Wülker print *Seone*, i.e. Zion, and so Bright, MLN. XXVII, 18.   But Mürkens, p. 116, reading *onseone beorh*, parallel to *heahlond*, sees here a reference to Genesis xxii. 12, *in terram visionis*.   **387** wuldor gesawon] Kock, JJJ., p. 16, regards these words as parenthetic.   **391** gode] Graz, Eng. Stud. XXI, 5, Mürkens, p. 116, alter to *dryhtne* to avoid a metrical stress on a short syllable.   **392** alh] Bouterwek, following Grimm, Deutsche Myth.², I, 58, and later edd. read *alh*.   **399** fyrst] Klaeber, Archiv CXIII, 147, suggests *fus* for *fyrst*. If *ferhðbana* refers to Abraham, as is most probable, then *fyrst* as an adj. seems inappropriate.   But *fyrst*, "first," as an AS. adj. is dubious in any case.   The only AS. example of *fyrst* as an adj. in the New English Dictionary is this passage, as of the year 1000, and the next is for 1220.   It seems best to take *fyrst* as adverb, "At the first the life-destroyer was not the more joyful [though all turned out happily in the end]."   fægenra] All edd. read *fægra*, deriving the word from *fæge* (Blackburn, notes, Grein-Köhler, p. 171) or from the adjective which appears in Beow. 915 as *gefægra* (Thomas, MLRev. XII, 344).   Cosijn, Beitr. XX, 103, suggested *fægenra*, a reading approved by Klaeber, Archiv CXIII, 147, and Bright, MLN. XXVII, 18. Whether one interprets the first half-line as referring to the devil, to Cain or to Abraham will depend on what word one employs here.

401–500

401 beorna] Barnouw, Textkritische Untersuchungen, p. 87, suggests *bearna*.   **404** forð gebad] Wülker begins a new sentence with *ða* and takes *forðgebad* as a verb.   But *ða* is better taken as a relative, referring to *frofre*, see Cosijn, Beitr. XX, 103, Blackburn, notes.   **405** lafe] Bouterwek, Grein read *lare*.   **411–412** Grein, Wülker make one line of these two, with no additions to the MS. reading.   **413** ecgum] Thorpe and later edd. read *ecgum*, but Grein, Spr. II, 374, notes *eagum reodan* as a possible instrumental phrase, "with red eyes."   Blackburn reads *ecgum*, but takes *reodan* as an adj., "with red blade."   **414** metod] Grein, Cosijn, Beitr. XX, 103, Graz, Eng. Stud. XXI, 5, Mürkens, p. 116, Blackburn, notes, read *metod*, but Wülker follows the MS.   **415** ætniman] Sievers, Beitr. X, 454, suggests *æt niman*, *æt* governing *him*, l. 415*a*, and so Graz, p. 26.   **423** freoðo] Graz, Eng. Stud. XXI, 6, reads *freode*, Holthausen, Eng. Stud. LI, 182, proposes *furðor* for *freoðo*, or *freolic*, in Grein-Köhler, p. 882.   **429** mæge] A plural, see Bright, MLN. XXVII, 18, and Bos.-Tol., Supplement, p. 75, under *behwylfan*.   The singular *mæg*, l. 427, has *heofon and eorðe* as subject as two closely coordinated ideas.   sceattas] Dietrich, Grein read *sceatas*.

431 geomre lyft] Cosijn, Beitr. XX, 104, suggests *eormen-lyft.* This would
make a compound like *eormengrund,* Beow. 859.   **432** He] Thorpe, note,
and later edd. read *he* for *ne,* but Kock, JJJ., p. 27, Holthausen, Anglia
Beibl. XXX, 3, prefer *þē,* "to thee," and Bright, MLN. XXVII, 18, reads
nu.   **434** soðfæst sigora] Dietrich, Grein add *weard* after these words.
437 yldo] Grein alters to *ylde.*   **442** sand] Thorpe and later edd. read
sand.   **444** oð Egipte incaðeode] Blackburn, notes, and Gollancz, p.
lxxiii, retain the MS. reading *incaðeode,* defined by Blackburn "hostile
nation," by Gollancz "culprit folk." This is the only occurrence of the
compound in Anglo-Saxon. Grein, Wülker alter to *ingeðeode,* see *ingefolca,*
l. 142, and so Grein-Köhler, p. 389. *Egipte* is genitive plural.   **446** folca
selost] The last words on p. 163, which is about three-fourths full. Page 163
is followed by two blank pages, numbered 164 and 165, and p. 166 begins a
new section in the manuscript. One leaf has been lost between p. 164 and
p. 165, according to Gollancz, p. lxx, which contained Section XLVIII and
which dealt with the matter of Exodus xiv. 23–24.   **453** forhtigende]
Sievers, Beitr. X, 482, Mürkens, p. 116, read *forhtende.*   **455** genap] Grein,
gehnap, but Grein, Germania X, 418, returns to *genap.*   **457** behindan]
Grein, *hie hindan,* but Grein, Germania X, 418, returns to *behindan.*   **461**
herewopa mæst] Bright, MLN. XXVII, 18, takes these words as object of
cyrmdon, therefore no punctuation after *mæst.*   **463** stæfnum] Grein
suggests *flæscum* for *stæfnum.* Sedgefield reads *stefnum.*   **466** cyre
swiðrode] Dietrich, Grein read *cyrr,* but Grein, Germania X, 418, returns to
cyre. See l. 291, note. Cosijn, Beitr. XX, 104, suggests *cyrm,* and so Sedgefield
in his text. Sedgefield reads *swiðrode,* "grew strong," Grein, Spr. II, 512,
swiðrode, "diminished," "ceased." Cosijn places l. 466b within parentheses.
Imelmann, Forschungen zur ae. Poesie, p. 403, reads *cyre,* "Kür, Wahl," "Ihre
Chance verminderte sich."   **467** sæs] Grein, Kluge, Graz, Eng. Stud. XXI,
6, Mürkens, p. 116, alter to *wæges* for alliteration.   **470** forðganges weg]
Grein retained *nep,* but Spr. II, 281, found no plausible explanation for the
word. Wülker also retained *nep,* without explanation, and so Blackburn,
notes. Sedgefield, MLRev. XVI, 60, and Verse Book, alters to *forðgang
esnes,* translating, "The advance of the warrior(s) was impeded by their
armour." Thomas, MLRev. XII, 344, would retain *nep* in the sense "lacking," citing possible Icelandic but no Anglo-Saxon connections for the word.
Mürkens, p. 76, reads *forðgange neh.* Bright, MLN. XXVII, 18, alters
nep to *weg,* which gives a reasonable meaning for the passage.   **471**
æsæled] Grein, Wülker, Sedgefield read *asæled.*   sand basnodon] Bouterwek, Erläut., p. 322, suggested *berenod on witodre fyrde.* Similar is Sedgefield's reading, MLRev. XVI, 60, and Verse Book, *sand hie renedon witodre
wyrde,* "The sands prepared for their appointed destiny," with *fyrde* altered
to *wyrde.* Grein reads *basnode,* "awaited," but Dietrich, Grein, Germania
X, 418, Klaeber, Eng. Stud. XLI, 110, read *basnodon.* The edd. begin a
new sentence with *sand,* but a punctuation which permits connecting the
clause beginning with *hwonne* not only with *sand basnodon* but also with
what precedes gives a more coherent structure in keeping with the style of

214 NOTES ON EXODUS

this writer.   472 fyrde] Dietrich, Wülker, Klaeber, Eng. Stud. XLI, 110,
Sedgefield alter to *wyrde*.   474 æflastum gewuna] Bouterwek suggested
æglastum, or *ægflotum*, and Erläut., p. 322, *ealastum* or *wæglastum gewunad*,
for this phrase.   Cosijn, Beitr. XX, 104, proposed *æflastungewuna*, "der
noch nie hinweggeströmt war." Retaining the MS. reading, Sedgefield,
notes, translates, "now accustomed to its changed course."   476 geneop]
Dietrich reads *gehneop*, Sedgefield, MLRev. XVI, 60, and Verse Book, reads
gehweop, "menaced." Grein, note, suggests a possible connection of this
verb, which is of uncertain origin, with the MS. *nep* in l. 470. See l. 455.
480 modge rymde] The MS. reads *mod gerymde*, and so Thorpe, Bouterwek,
Graz, Eng. Stud. XXI, 6, Blackburn, the last translating, notes, "loosed
its fury." Grein and later edd., except Blackburn, read *modge rymde*,
translated by Johnson, p. 54, "removed the valorous."   482 famgode]
Cosijn, Beitr. XX, 105, suggests *famgende*.   483 lagu land] Dietrich,
Grein, Kluge, Graz, p. 26, Mürkens, p. 116, read *laguland*, but Grein, Germania X, 418, Wülker, Cosijn, Beitr. XX, 105, Blackburn, Sedgefield read
lagu (subject) and *land* (object).   487 on werbeamas] The MS. reading
lacks one metrical syllable in this half-line. Holthausen, Anglia Beibl. V,
231, proposes *werbeama sweot*, Mürkens, p. 116, *wraðe werbeamas*. Bright,
MLN. XXVII, 19, alters to *on wægstreamas*. Grein-Köhler, p. 782, would
read *werge beornas*. Sedgefield, MLRev. XVI, 60, reads *werbeamas on*,
translating, "When the Almighty...struck the barriers," with *wer-beam*
taken as meaning "weir-bar," "flood-gate." Sedgefield, Verse Book, reads
on werbeamas, with the same interpretation. Blackburn, notes, would
read *engel werbeamas*, or *weard werbeamas* (replacing *weard*, l. 486b, by *god*),
werbeamas as a genitive singular, = *wærbēam*, "the protecting column, i.e.
the pillar of cloud." Thomas, MLRev. XII, 345, reads *on werbeamas*, "the
protecting columns." Grein, Dicht., p. 95, takes *werbeamas* and *ðeode*
(with a period after *ðeode*) as appositives, "die Wehrbäume, das verwegene
Volk." Grein, Spr. II, 661, suggested "baumstarker Mann," as a defini-
tion of *werbeam*. Johnson, p. 55, translates, "those warriors of oak." It
seems most natural to take *werbeamas* as continuing the thought expressed
by *meretorras*, l. 485, but the precise meaning remains debateable.   488
helpendra pað] Bouterwek, Erläut., p. 322, suggested *halwendne* for *helpendra*. Grein suggested *helpenda*, as a form of *elpend*, "elephant," here
for walrus. Kock, Anglia XLIII, 305, proposed *hleopandra pað*, "path of
the sea-leopards." Holthausen, Anglia XLIV, 353, would read *hwelpendra
pað*, the first element related to *hwilpe*, "water-fowl," see Seafarer 21, and
so Bright, MLN. XVII, 426, translating, "the path of the sea-dogs, or sea-
monsters = the sea." In Grein-Köhler, p. 885, Holthausen suggests *hel-
warena* for *helpendra*. Sedgefield, MLRev. XVI, 60, and Verse Book, reads
helpendra fæðm, "Neither the proud people (the Egyptians) nor the hand
(lit. embrace) of helpers could check the fury of the sea." Mürkens, p.
116, proposes *helpendra paða*, "sie konnten nicht zurückhalten (*forhabban*)
von den (ihnen sonst) helfenden (sie schützenden) pfaden die wütende meer-
flut (*merestreames mod*)." In the lack of any convincing emendation, it

seems best to retain the MS. reading. Bouterwek's *halwendne* suggests a plausible emendation to *hal-*, *hælwendra*, but as between *helpendra* and *hælwendra* there is little to choose. **492** wælbenna] Sisam, MLN. XXXII, 48, takes the second element as a form of *bend*, "bond," and translates, "the death-bonds (i.e. the enveloping waves) seethed." Witrod] Thorpe, note, alters to *witod*, "fated," Bouterwek to *wite-rod*, "rod of punishment." Dietrich proposed *wit-rod* = *wit-rad*, "zauberstrasse," and so Grein. But Grein, Germania X, 418, interpreted as *wig-trod*, and so Spr. II, 703, meaning "battle-way." Kock, JJJ., p. 27, translates, "the passage, God's handiwork, broke down from high aloft." Bright, MLN. XVII, 426, reads *wīgrād*. Sedgefield, MLRev. XVI, 60, and Verse Book, reads *wīgrōd*, " 'the war-pole,' i.e. the mighty thunderbolt which God hurls down upon the Egyptians." Sisam, MLN. XXXII, 48, gives *wipertrod* as a suggestion of Napier's, and translates, "God's handiwork (the sea) fell upon their ways of retreat." Cosijn, Beitr. XX, 105, cites l. 483 as indicating that *witrod* is accusative. This seems the best interpretation of the syntax, though the form and meaning of *witrod* are debateable. See Gen. 2084. **494** sloh] Cosijn, Beitr. XX, 105, suggests *flod weard gesloh*, with a full stop after *famigbosma*. **498** flodblac] See *wigblac*, l. 204. **499** siððan hie, etc.] Grein, Wülker read *onbugon* for *on bogum*. Blackburn, notes, reads *buge* for *bogum* and translates, "when on them fell the hugest of wild waves, dark [*brun*] with its towering mass [*yppinge*, as an instrumental]." Bright, MLN. XVII, 426, reads *onbrugdon* or *onbrudon* for *on bogum*, "after the brown floods struck them." Holthausen, Eng. Stud. LI, 182, changes *brun* to *brēcun*, with *yppinge* as subject. Bright, MLN. XXVII, 19, suggests *brim-yppinge* or *brim yppende* for *brun yppinge*. Sedgefield, MLRev. XVI, 60, and Verse Book, reconstructs to read, *siððan hie on hogum hran yrringa modwæga mæst*, "when the greatest of angry waves furiously seized them by the heels." Mürkens, p. 116, reads *siððan hie on bugon ypping brunne*, "nachdem sie eingebogen waren in die offene braune flut." Thomas, MLRev. XII, 345, reads *siððan hie on bugon brun yppinge*, "after the dark masses fell on them," explaining *brun* for *brune* as due to loss of the final *e* by elision. This last seems the most plausible interpretation, though perhaps one should read *brune* with Dietrich. As a possible substitute for *yppinge*, see *ypung*, "inundation," Bos.-Tol., Supplement, p. 753. **500** modewæga] Grein, Graz, Eng. Stud. XXI, 6, Mürkens, p. 117, read *mōdwæga*, but Grein, Spr. II, 259, as in the MS.

501–590

501 ða gedrencte wæron] The MS. reads *ða þegedrecte*, probably for *ða þe gedrecte*. Bouterwek, Grein, Mürkens, p. 117, read *he* for *þe*. Thorpe and later edd., except Blackburn, read *gedrencte*, "drowned." Blackburn retains *gedrecte* = *gedrehte*, translating, notes, "when it (i.e. the great sea-wave mentioned just before) overwhelmed the hosts of Egypt." But this forces the meaning of *gedrehte*. Sedgefield, MLRev. XVI, 60, and Verse Book, reads *deaþe*, see l. 34, for *ða þe*, and takes *gedrencte* as participial adjective modifying *mægen*, "submerged in death." For *dugoð* as a plural, see l. 547, and Krapp, Andreas, l. 693, note. 502 onfond] Thorpe, notes, Grein and later edd. read *onfond*, but Blackburn, notes, thinks *onfeond* may be a variant, not an error, for *onfond*. 503 grund] Grein, Kluge, Graz, p. 26, Mürkens, p. 117, Blackburn, notes, supply *grund*. Sedgefield supplies *he grund*. gestah] Dietrich alters to *geseah*. 504 wæs] Grein alters to *þær*. 505 heorufæðmum] Grein reads *heorofæðmum*, Kluge, Wülker, Sedgefield read *heorufæðmum* for the MS. *huru fæðmum*. Blackburn, notes, retains the MS. reading and translates *fæðmum* by " 'embraces,' the whelming of the hosts by the sea," with *huru* as adverb, "certainly." But the reference here seems to be more general and merely to sword warfare. 509 ungrundes] Bouterwek, Erläut., p. 323, suggested *ungerimedes*, Kock, PPP., p. 10, *ungerimes*. Graz, Eng. Stud. XXI, 6, defends the MS. reading. 510 heora] Thorpe, note, and later edd. read *heora*, except Blackburn, who retains *heoro* as a variant of *heora*. 514 spelbodan eac] The MS. reading *spelbodan* is metrically deficient. Grein, Graz, Eng. Stud. XXI, 6, Mürkens, p. 117, supply *spilde* before *spelbodan*. Sedgefield supplies *swa eac* before, and Blackburn, notes, *eac* after *spelbodan*. Rieger, Verskunst, p. 46, proposed *hyrde* before *spelbodan*. 517 Moyses sægde] That the lines following were not intended as a formal speech is indicated by the informality of this phrase. But in l. 549, the address of Moses to the army is introduced by *Swa reordode*. Thorpe and later edd. read *Moyses*, a nominative, except Bouterwek, who retains the MS. form. 519 Dægword] The edd. retain *dægweorc*, interpreting it as meaning either the Decalogue, or the comment of Moses, as indicated in Deuteronomy i. 3 (Cosijn, Beitr. XX, 105). But Gollancz, p. lxxvii, ingeniously surmises that the poet wrote *dægword = dierum verba*, the Latin name of Chronicles, which in turn is a translation of the Hebrew name of Chronicles. But the Hebrew name for Deuteronomy is similar, and "old glossaries confused the Hebrew for Chronicles, written as one word, with the name for Deuteronomy, and this seems to explain the present crux. The poet's intention was to refer to Deuteronomy." There is nothing in Exodus xiii or xiv to account for *dægword* or for *dægweorc*, but this whole passage is an elaboration not contained in the Vulgate. 521 doma gehwilcne] Cosijn, Beitr. XX, 105, calls attention to Deuteronomy vi. 1. 524 weard] Holthausen, Anglia XLIV, 353, reads *hord* for *weard*. 525 ginfæstan] Bouterwek, Grein read *ginfæst*, but Grein, Germania X, 418, reads *ginfæstan*, a weak adjective modifying *gōd*. See Beow. 2182, *ginfæstan gife*. Blackburn retains the MS. spelling with the same value. Cosijn, Beitr. XX, 105, also reads *ginfæstan* as a weak adjective. Sievers, Beitr. X, 514, suggests *ginfæsta*. Mürkens, p. 117, reads *ginfæste god*, which he interprets as meaning the soul. Kock, Anglia XLIII, 306, retains *ginfæsten* as meaning "stronghold," translating, "If, with the Spirit's keys, Life's herald will unlock the body's ward, the stronghold good, that shines within his breast"—i.e., if the prophet will speak. 526 gæð] Mürkens, p. 117, reads *gangeð* to gain a metrical syllable. 529 gesne]

So in the MS., though all edd., except Blackburn, print *gesine* as the MS. reading, interpreting the word, however, as for *gesne, gæsne*. 532 lifwynna] Thorpe, Grein, Wülker read with the MS., *lyft wynna*, and Grein, Spr. II, 198, interprets *lyft* as meaning "grant," "gift." Thorpe suggested *lif wynna*, and Cosijn, Beitr. XX, 106, reads *lifwynna*, Blackburn, notes, *lyfwynna*. Grein-Köhler, p. 426, glosses the word under *līf-wyn*. 535 healdað] Grein, Kluge, notes, Wülker read *healdað*. Blackburn reads *healdeð* but glosses this form as a plural. 539 rice dælað] "Share dominion," see Klaeber, Archiv CXIII, 147, Eng. Stud. XLI, 110. The words *yldo ðððe ærdeað* are appositive to *regnþeofas*. 540 cymð] Sievers, Beitr. X, 473, Graz, Eng. Stud. XXI, 7, Mürkens, p. 117, read *cymeð*. 546 is] Grein, Kluge, Graz, p. 26, Mürkens, p. 117, supply *is* before *leoht*, but Wülker, Blackburn have no verb. 556 us on] Bouterwek, Erläut., p. 323, Grein, Kluge, Wülker, Sedgefield read *us on*, but Blackburn retains *ufon*, "from his home in the heavens (lit. from above)." 563 sigerice] See l. 27, note. 567 fægerne] Mürkens, p. 93, suggests *fægenne* for *fægerne*. 570 gefegon] Dietrich, Grein and later edd. read *gefegon* for the MS. *gefeon*, except Kluge, who retains *gefeon*. 574 þam herge] Grein, Kluge, Graz, Eng. Stud. XXI, 7, Mürkens, p. 117, Blackburn, notes, supply *herge* before *wiðforon*. Sedgefield changes *þam* to *ham*, reading *siððan hie ham wiðforon*. herge wiðforon] Bouterwek replaces by *hildefrumum* followed by no punctuation. 576] Cosijn, Beitr. XX, 106, would inclose this line within parentheses. 578 golan] Grein reads *golon*, Wülker has *golan*. Thorpe, Bouterwek, Kluge, Graz, p. 26, retain the MS. reading. 580 Afrisc neowle] The MS. reading *afrisc meowle* would mean "an African maiden," i.e. Egyptian maiden. But there is no reason to suppose that the Egyptians had maidens with them in their army, and no reason for referring to them here if they had. Cosijn, Beitr. XX, 106, assumes that the reference is to the Hebrew women, and Holthausen, Anglia Beibl. XXI, 14, Bright, MLN. XXVII, 19, Gollancz, p. lxxv, take *afrisc* as a scribal error for *ebrisc*. Klaeber, Eng. Stud. XLI, 111, would explain *afrisc* as referring to the Hebrew women as "expressing an accidental relation rather than a permanent quality." Routh, Two Studies, p. 54, retains *afrisc* as referring to captive maidens in the Egyptian army. Gollancz further proposes that the phrase originally read *ebrisc neowle* (*neowle* probably adverb), and that it referred to the Hebrews prostrate in prayer, see Exodus iv. 31. This assumes that the Hebrews stopped to pray before they began to plunder. Reading *Afrisc neowle* with Blackburn, notes, the passage becomes consistent and credible: "Then an African [Egyptian] was easily found prostrate on the shore of the sea, adorned with gold," referring to Exodus xiv. 31. As Cosijn, Beitr. XX, 106, points out, *þa wæs eðfynde* is equivalent to "in great numbers," and *neowle* may be taken as logically a plural adjective. The sentence beginning *Handa hofon* then refers to the Hebrews who plundered the dead Egyptians of the gold with which they were adorned, not to an operatic chorus of Jewish maidens. A reference to Miriam, see Exodus xv. 20–21, is too remote to be plausible. 581 hand] Holthausen, in Grein-Köhler, p. 884,

reads *handum*. **586** on yðlafe] "On the shore," Cosijn, Beitr. XX, 106.
In l. **585** *sælafe* is appositive to *madmas*, and *segnum* means "by standards,"
Blackburn, notes, Sedgefield, notes, i.e. among the divisions of the army.
Bouterwek, Erläut., p. 323, suggested *secgum* for *segnum*, and Klaeber,
Archiv CXIII, 147, would read *lædan* for *dælan*, but both changes are unnecessary. **587** Heo on riht sceodon] Grein, Kluge, Wülker, Sedgefield
read *heom* for *heo*, and *sceode* for the MS. *sceo*, "rightly to them [the Hebrew
women, on the assumption that the preceding lines also refer to a chorus of
Hebrew women] fell." Thorpe, note, suggested *sceodon*, and so Blackburn,
notes, and see Bright, MLN. XVII, 426, for *sceadan* in the sense "divide,"
"distribute." **590** mæst] All edd. agree that *mæ* is incomplete for *mæst*.

NOTES ON DANIEL

1–100

Daniel] For the title, see Introd., p. xviii. **5** wig] Cosijn, Beitr. XX, 106,
suggests *wigsped*. **9** wealdan] All edd. retain *weoldon*, but the context
indicates *wealdan*, parallel to *rædan*. **16** heriges helmum] Cosijn, Beitr.
XX, 107, suggests *hæleð under helmum* or *hergas under helmum* for this half-
line. Schmidt reads *heapum* for *helmum*. þara] Schmidt would omit.
22 hweorfan] Grein reads *lifgan* for *hweorfan*. Holthausen, Eng. Stud. LI,
181, would arrange the first half-line to read, *þa ic þa gedriht geseah*. Cosijn,
Beitr. XX, 107, suggests *gefreah* for *geseah*, citing *gefrægn*, l. 1. **25** to
lare] Cosijn, Beitr. XX, 107, suggested the addition of *to*. **27** þa þam]
Schmidt, *þa þe þam*. **29** hie] All edd. read *hie*. **30** eorðan dreamas]
Kock, JJJ., p. 12, places a comma after *beswac* and takes *eorðan dreamas* as
a nominative appositive to *langung*. Otherwise it must be taken as a modifier of *langung*, "until the desire of the joy of earth," *dreamas* being a gen.
sing. in -*as*. Schmidt suggests but does not adopt *dreama*. Cosijn, Beitr.
XX, 107, rearranges ll. 30*b*-31 to read *þæt hie ece rædas ‖ æt siðestan sylfe
forleton*. **34** þeodum] The MS. *þeoden* appears to be an echo of *ðeoden*,
l. 33. Blackburn retains *þeoden* as a careless writing for *þeodum*. Schmidt,
Kock, JJJ., p. 12, read *þeodum*. Cosijn, Beitr. XX, 107, would replace
þeoden, l. 34, by *drihten*. Thorpe proposed *þeodne*, Bouterwek, Erläut.,
p. 324, *þeode*. þe] Grein, Wülker read *he* for *þe*. **35** Wisde him æt
frymðe] Schmidt retains *wisðe* = *wiste*, "knew," and changes *æt frymðe* to
ætfremde, "estranged." Cosijn, Beitr. XX, 107, reads *wisðe him fremðe*,
"sibi alienos." Holthausen, Anglia Beibl. XXX, 2, takes *wisðe* as for *wiste*,
acc. pl. of *wist*, parallel to *æhte*, but Anglia Beibl. XXXII, 137, retracts this
in favor of *wisde*, a verb. Thorpe, Grein, Wülker, Blackburn, notes, read
wisde, "directed," Bouterwek has *wisode*, and Bouterwek, Erläut., p. 324,
fysde. **37** dugoða dyrust] The repetition of *dyrust* in this line is dubious.
Grein reads *drymust*, but Grein, Germania X, 419, returns to the MS.
reading. Cosijn, Beitr. XX, 107, suggests *demend* for *dyrust*, and Kock,

JJJ., p. 12, suggests *dryhta*.   **38** herepað tæhte] All edd. read *herepað* for the MS. *-poð*, except Blackburn, who retains *-poð* as a scribal variation, and Schmidt, who has *-pæð*. As the word is too short for a half-line, Hofer, Anglia XII, 199, adds *laðne* before it, Holthausen, Indog. Forsch. IV, 381, adds *rihtne* or *hæleða*, Cosijn, Beitr. XX, 107, Schmidt, Kock, JJJ., p.12, add *tæhte*, and Blackburn, notes, adds *heora*.   **41** witgan] Sievers, Beitr. X, 514, Graz, Eng. Stud. XXI, 7, Schmidt read *wigan*, "warriors," for metrical reasons, and Cosijn, Beitr. XX, 107, defends *wigan* on the ground that a city is besieged by warriors, not by *magi*. But *witgan*, in the sense "false worshippers," may very well have been in the poet's mind as applicable to the Chaldeans, see Wülker, l. 41, note.   **51** guman] Cosijn, Beitr. XX, 107, suggests *Gudan* or *Giuðan*, for *guman*, calling attention to the phrase *regem Juda*, Daniel i. 2.   **52** Gesamnode þa] Schmidt reads *þa gesamnode* as a metrical improvement.   Kock, JJJ., p. 13, takes *gesamnode* as an intransitive verb.   **53** and west foran] Körner reads *foran*, pret. pl., for the MS. *faran*, and so Kock, JJJ., p. 13.   Thorpe suggested *het* after *faran*, and Blackburn, notes, would supply *het* before *west*.   Schmidt supplies *eode* before *west*, and Cosijn, Beitr. XX, 108, supplies *gewat;* both read *hæðencyning*, l. 54, as subject of the verb supplied.   But with *herige* as inst., *hæðencyninga* may remain, "with their host of heathen kings."   **55–56** Israela... lifwelan] Cosijn, Beitr. XX, 108, connects *Israela* with *byrig* as a genitive modifier.   Kock, JJJ., p. 13, takes *eðelweardas* as a genitive, and *lufan*, *lifwelan* of the MS. as datives going with *byrig*, regarding this as an instance of asyndetic parataxis.   Kock, Anglia XLVI, 89, suggests *eðelwearda* for *eðelweardas*.   Grein, note, regarded *lufan*, the MS. reading in l. 56a, as a verb, "loved," but supplied no evidence to justify such a verb.   Cosijn, Beitr. XX, 108, suggested *lifdan* for *lufan*, with *lifwelan* = *lifwelum*.   Hofer, Anglia XII, 200, proposed *lucon*, "maintained," "preserved," and Schmidt reads *lucan* for *lufan*.   Blackburn, notes, following Bos.-Tol., p. 631, proposed *hæfdon* before *lufan*, and Klaeber, Eng. Stud. XLI, 111, would supply *brucon* before *Israela*, retaining *lufan*, *lifwelan* as asyndetic objects.   It seems necessary to supply a verb, but the choice is even between the proposal of Blackburn and that of Klaeber.   Körner supplied *ðær* before *Israela*, Schmidt supplied *þa* after this word.   The MS. has metrical pointing before and after *israela*, and the poet may well have regarded this word as sufficient for a half-line.   **57** ic] Grein, Wülker, Schmidt, Blackburn, notes, read *ic*.   **58** gelyfdon] Kock, Anglia XLIV, 250, proposes *gældon*, "the warriors did not hesitate," for *gelyfdon*, and later, Anglia XLVI, 184, *geyldon*, "delayed."   Holthausen, Anglia Beibl. XXXII, 137, suggests *gelæfdon*, intransitive or with *wuldor* as object.   Trautmann, in Schmidt, p. 31, reconstructs the passage to read for ll. 58b–59, *wigan beræddon* ‖ *þa receda wuldor│readan golde.*   Cosijn, Beitr. XX, 108, retains *gelyfdon* as equivalent to "believed in God," citing l. 106b.   This is also Blackburn's interpretation, "The warriors [of the Chaldeans] believed not (*i.e.* were heathen)."   Schmidt would omit *þa* before *wigan*.   **59** readan golde] Graz, Eng. Stud. XXI, 7, would omit these words to shorten the line metrically.   **61** stanhliðum] Schmidt reads *stanhlidum*. **66** feoh and frætwa] Ettmüller proposed *feo* = *feoh* for the MS. *fea*. For the MS. *freos* Grein proposed *fleos*, "Vlies, kostbares Pelzwerk." Körner reads *feoh and frætwa*, see Gen. 2130, and Cosijn, Beitr. XX, 108, approves this reading. Kock, Anglia XLIII, 305, retains the MS. *fea and freos* as genitives, "of cattle and its breed," citing Icelandic but no Anglo-Saxon justifications for these meanings. Holthausen, Anglia XLIV, 353, reads *featu* (= *fatu*?) for *fea* and *feos* = *feoes* for *freos*, or *fata freolicra*, omitting *and*. Holthausen, Anglia Beibl. V, 231, had suggested *feoh and freafatu*. Blackburn retains *fea* as a Northumbrian form of *feo(h)*, and retains *freos* also as a variant of *frean*, translating, "the wealth and the lords." Schmidt reads *feo and freosigl*, "money and jewels," and cites Trautmann as proposing *feo and freosinc*. Körner's reading presents the fewest difficulties, though *frætwa* is merely a substitution for, not an explanation of the MS. *freos*. **73** ofer ealle lufen] For the MS. *otor*, Bouterwek reads *uton*. Grein, Körner, Schmidt read *ofer*, Wülker *ofor*. Kock, Anglia XLVI, 89, suggests *ofer ealle lufne*, "'without any tenure,' i.e. without any privilege bestowed on free men." Schmidt reads *lufan* for *lufen*. Blackburn retains *lufen* in the sense "hope." **77** leoda] Blackburn retains *leode* as a gen. pl. form. See Ex. 8, note. Grein and later edd. read *leoda*. **79** þa] Schmidt alters to *þonne*. **82** boca bebodes] Graz, Eng. Stud. XXI, 7, would read *in bebodum boca* for metrical reasons. Schmidt reads *bebodes boca*, and Blackburn, notes, proposes *in bocum bebodes*. **85** he] Schmidt would omit *he*. Schmidt, notes, says this passage, ll. 85–87, is unintelligible and probably corrupt. But the meaning is clear: Nebuchadnezzar wanted to profit personally by the wisdom of the youths (taking *mihte*, l. 84, as a plural), and was not interested in their wisdom as a gift of God for which he should be grateful. **88** þær fundon] Bouterwek, Erläut., p. 324, proposed *þreo feredon* for *þær fundon*. þry] Schmidt alters *to* to *þry*, and so Cosijn, Beitr. XX, 108, though Cosijn would place *þry* after *freagleawe*. Thorpe, note, Bouterwek read *frean gleawe*. **90** godsæde] Thorpe, Bouterwek read *god sæde*, Dietrich and later edd., *godsæde*. Cosijn, Beitr. XX, 108, notes Daniel i. 3, *de semine regio et tyrannorum*. Trautmann, see Schmidt, suggested *godspede* for *godsæde*. **94** and] Schmidt would omit *and*. **95** corðres] Klaeber, Eng. Stud. XLI, 112, suggests *morðres* for *corðres*. Cosijn, Beitr. XX, 109, calls attention to Daniel i. 5. **97** cyðan] Thorpe, note, and later edd., *cyðan*, except Wülker, Schmidt, *cyðon*.

101–200

101 þæt þa, etc.] Schmidt, note, declares this line to be unintelligible and reconstructs to read *þe þa frumgaras befeormode*. But *dæde* is for *dyden*, and *be feore* means "on penalty of life," i.e. loss of life. See Cosijn, Beitr. XX, 109. **102** gengum] Blackburn reads this word in the MS. as *geagum*, but what he reads as *a* is clearly not a normal *a* and is probably merely *n* with an accidental stroke connecting the two lower points of the letter. In his glossary, Blackburn suggests that *geagum* is an error for *gengum*. **104** Þa wæs breme] Schmidt reads *þa breme wæs*. **106** ylda bearnum] Schmidt reads *yldum* and omits *bearnum*. **111** geteod] Graz, Eng. Stud. XXI, 8, alters to *geteohhod*. **114** gelimpan] Holthausen, Anglia Beibl. V, 231, Graz, Eng. Stud. XXI, 8, omit *gelimpan*. **115** dreamas] A gen. sing. in -*as*. **118** woma] Grein reads *woman*, which would make the word a modifier, not an appositive of *sorh*. So also Cosijn, Beitr. XX, 109. **119** him meted wæs] Grein, Germania X, 419, would alter *wæs* to *wæf*, thus making *metod* a noun. Holthausen, Anglia Beibl. V, 231, reads *hine gemæted wæs*, Graz, Eng. Stud. XXI, 8, reads *him gemæted wæs*. Schmidt has *meted*, for *metod*, as suggested by Dietrich. **122** hwæt hine gemætte] Holthausen, Anglia Beibl. V, 231, adds *ær* after *gemætte*. Graz, Eng. Stud. XXI, 8, reads *him gemæted wæs*, but Holthausen, Eng. Stud. XXXVII, 204, *hwæt gemætte hine*, for the sake of alliteration. **125** word] Kock, JJJ., p. 2, notes a similarity to An. 555–556, and Cosijn, Beitr. XX, 109, connects *angin* with *or*, l. 133. The alliteration forbids *ord* for *word*. **138** þæt ge cuðon] Graz, Eng. Stud. XXI, 8, Cosijn, Beitr. XX, 109, supply *wel* after *cuðon*. Holthausen, Anglia Beibl. V, 231, supplies *geare*. Schmidt alters *þæt* to *þætte*. Grein, Wülker place *mine* of l. 139 at the end of l. 138. But it seems best to take the line as a bit of mechanical versifying with a stress on *þæt* in each half-line. **139** æfter] Grein alters to *æfre*. **141a** Nu] Grein, Cosijn, Beitr. XX, 109, Schmidt read *nu* for the MS. *ne*. **142** berað] Bouterwek, Erläut., p. 324, Hofer, Anglia XII, 200, Cosijn, Beitr. XXI, 13, read *berað*. Blackburn retains *bereð*, but takes it to be a plural. **147** ne ahicgan] Holthausen, Indog. Forsch. IV, 381, would supply *hraðe*, *huru* or *auht* after *ahicgan*. Schmidt supplies *na*. But the scansion may again be mechanical. þa hit, etc.] Schmidt changes *þa* to *na*. and places it in the first half-line, with a dash before and after the second half-line. But translate, "when it was denied that they should tell," etc. **159** reccan] Sievers, Beitr. X, 514, Schmidt read *areccan*. **160** wereda] Thorpe, note, Bouterwek, Cosijn, Beitr. XX, 109, read *wyrda* for *wereda*, and Blackburn, note, takes this as possible, but if this reading is not accepted, "the meaning of the phrase is 'the destiny of nations.'" The reference may well be to Daniel ii. 36ff. **170** weoh] Dietrich, Grein, Schmidt read *weoh*, "idol," and Wülker retains *woh* in the same sense. Blackburn retains *woh*, "to work wrong," but notes the other interpretation. **172** ðe swa hatte] Grein added *þrymlice* after *swa*, but Sievers, Beitr. X, 514, regards this as "metrisch falsch." Holthausen, Indog. Forsch. IV, 381, Graz, Eng. Stud. XXI, 8, Cosijn, Beitr. XX, 109, change *swa* to *þus*, and Cosijn also suggests *þa* for *swa*. Schmidt reads *þa* for *swa*. But there is no telling how mechanically some of the verses of the poem may have been made, see ll. 138, 147, and notes. **176** þe] Bouterwek, Grein, Wülker alter *þe* to *he*. **177** riht] The last word on p. 180. A page has been cut out of the manuscript between p. 180 and p. 181, see Gollancz, p. lxxxv, containing the matter of Daniel iii. 2–6. Bouterwek adds *ne cuðe*, and Grein reads *rihtes ne gymde*, to complete the line. **185** Fremde] Cosijn, Beitr. XX, 110, Schmidt read

fremede for this word.   **189** þæt hie] In the MS. appears the usual abbreviation for *þæt*, which Blackburn says may stand here for *þe*.   Schmidt
replaces *þæt* by *þe*.   Thorpe, note, Bouterwek read *þa ðe* for these two
words.   **192** on herige] Thorpe, note, Grein altered to *on byrig*, Dietrich
to *on byrige*.   Cosijn, Beitr. XX, 110, reads *on berig*, Schmidt, *on berige*,
"on the mount."   Blackburn, notes, suggests *hornas* for *byman*, and Grein,
Germania X, 419, proposed *herebyman*.   Wülker left a gap before *byman*.
There are many ways in which the line might be regularized, but it is not
improbable that it slipped by without ever having alliteration.   See l. 710.
194 wæron] Cosijn, Beitr. XX, 110, proposed *weras* for *wæron*.   But *wæron*
is for *wærum*, "faithful in their covenants."   An objection to this is the
repetition in *wærfæste*, but the Daniel poet is fond of puns and etymological
echoes, see ll. 5, 36, 90, 175, 204, 264, 265, 295, 344, 521–522, 550.   **195**
ælmihtigne] Grein retains the MS. *ælmihtne*, but Thorpe, Bouterwek, Wülker, Schmidt read *ælmihtigne*, and Sievers, Beitr. X, 514, approves this
reading.   Blackburn, notes, suggests that *ælmihtne* may be a correct form,
some word for "Lord" being lost after it, but that more probably the scribe
merely omitted a syllable.   **196** gedydon] Sievers, Beitr. X, 498, Schmidt
read *gedædon*.   **197** gold] Thorpe, note, Bouterwek alter to *gyld*, "idol,"
and Schmidt reads *goldgyld*.

201–300

202 mihte gebædon] Wülker, Schmidt, Blackburn, notes, retain *gebædon* as
infinitive, the other edd. read *gebædan*.   Grein reads *gebædan mihte*, and
Holthausen, Anglia Beibl. XVIII, 206, would put *mihte* in the first half-line
and supply *æfre* after *gebædon*.   But see Gen. 574, note.   **203** hæðen
heriges] Thorpe, Bouterwek read *hæðenheriges*.   **205** þæt] Schmidt would
omit *þæt*.   **206** hæftas hearan] As appositive to *þegnas*, *hæftas* means the
servants of the king, see l. 266, and *hearan*, for *hearran*, is appositive to
þeodne, see Cosijn, Beitr. XX, 110.   Blackburn takes *hæftas hearan* as
referring to the three children, "the higher captives in this lofty city, who
will not do this or worship," etc.   Schmidt leaves *hearan* unglossed and
unexplained.   Grein changed *hearan* to *heran*, "obey," but Grein, Germania
X, 419, returned to the MS., taking *hearan* as the comparative of *heah*.
Bouterwek, Erläut., p. 324, also proposed a verb for *hearan*, i.e. *heanan*,
hynan or *hangan*.   **207** þa þis, etc.] Grein changed *þa* to *þæt*, supplied
hæðengyld after *þis*, and changed *hegan* to *hergan*, his l. 207 then ending
with *willað*.   He compressed ll. 207*b*–208 into one line.   Wülker follows
Grein, except that he merely indicates an omission where Grein read *hæðengyld*.   In Germania X, 419, Grein changed his earlier reading *hergan* to the
MS. *hegan*.   Schmidt follows Grein's text, except that he retains *þa*.
Cosijn, Beitr. XX, 110, suggests *heremæðl* as better than *hæðengyld*.   As a
strong demonstrative *þa* means "those (men)."   **208** to wuldre] If *hæðengyld* or some other word is not supplied in l. 207, something is needed here
to complete this line and for alliteration.   Blackburn, notes, suggests

wuldre after *to*, and this also gives the personal pronoun *þe*, "as honor to thyself," more significance.   **214** wolde] A plural, see Gen. 856, note, and so *gelæste*, l. 219.   **216** he] Schmidt omits *he*.   **219** æ] Cosijn, Beitr. XX, 110, would supply *hie* before *æ*.   **221** ne þan mæ gehwurfe] The MS. has *neþan* (or *ne þan*) *mæ*, then the end of a line and *gen hwyrfe* on the next line, with metrical pointing after *hwyrfe* and before *ne*.   Thorpe, Bouterwek made a compound *mægenhwyrfe*, translated "high course" by Thorpe. Bouterwek, Erläut., p. 324, suggested *mægen hwyrfden*.   Grein reads *ne heanmægen hwyrfe*, Grein, Germania X, 419, has *mæ* (= *ma*) *gen hwyrfe*. Wülker, Blackburn, Schmidt follow the MS. with the reading *ne þan mægen hwyrfe*.   Cosijn, Beitr. XX, 110, reads *ne þan ma gehwurfe*, which gives the best reading, though *mæ* = *ma* may stand.   Taking *gehwurfe* as a plural, the passage means, "nor the more would they turn towards heathendom."   **224** Þa wearð, etc.] Grein, Wülker, Schmidt make two half-lines of l. 224*a*, and to make a full line of l. 224*b*, Grein inserts *egeslice*, Hofer, Anglia XII, 201, inserts *egeslicor*, Holthausen, Anglia Beibl. V, 231, *esnas* or *iserne*, Cosijn, Beitr. XX, 110, *eft sona*, and Schmidt *ofestlice* before *ofn*.   But the metrical pointings in the MS. come after *cyning, onhætan, feorum, onsocon*, and these pointings indicate the best reading with no additions necessary.   **226** gegleded] Bouterwek, Erläut., p. 324, suggested *þæt* for *þa* and *gleded* for the MS. *gelæded*.   Grein, Wülker read *gegleded*.   Blackburn, notes, thinks *gelæded* is a careless spelling of *glæded* = *gleded*.   Schmidt alters to *gefeded* and supplies *gledum* before this word.   **232** him] Schmidt omits. grome] Schmidt changes to *grimme*.   **233** fæðm fyres lige] Thorpe, note, suggested *fyrliges*, Hofer, Anglia XII, 201, proposes *fæðmfyres*. Schmidt reads *fyres and liges*.   But the phrase should be taken as it stands, literally, "in the embrace to the flame (*lige*) of the fire."   hwæðere] Blackburn misreports the MS. as *hwæðre*.   **234** metodes] Schmidt alters to *man-werodes*. One expects something like *manna weard*, see *gumena weard*, l. 236.   **235** halige] Thorpe, note, Bouterwek read *haliga*, Bouterwek, Erläut, p. 324, *halig* or *se haliga*.   Schmidt reads *halig him þær helpe*.   But take *halige* as modifying *help*, "a holy help," i.e. *gast þone halgan*, l. 236.   **237** in þone ofn innan] Sievers, Beitr. XII, 476, would omit *innan*, Schmidt would omit *þone*.   **239–240**] Grein supplied *ne him wroht oðfæstan* after *gewemman* as l. 239*b*.   Schmidt supplies *ne nænig wloh of hrægle*, and also omits *þeah* in l. 239*a*.   Hofer, Anglia XII, 201, transfers *þeah* to a place after *gewemman*, making *gewemman þeah* serve as l. 239*b*.   Cosijn, Beitr. XX, 110, reads *gewemman owiht*, citing l. 343.   **241** bærnan] Schmidt reads *forbærnan*.   **246–247**] The parenthesis was suggested by Cosijn, Beitr. XX, 110.   For the MS. *onstealle*, Thorpe, note, proposed *onsteallan*, Bouterwek reads *onstellan*.   Grein reads *onsweallan*, but Germania X, 419, *on stealle*. Wülker also has *on stealle*.   Schmidt reads *onstealle* as an infinitive.   Blackburn, notes, favors *onswælan*, "make hot."   Perhaps *on stealle*, "at the place," is the proper reading here, but if so, an infinitive to complete *wolde* must be found, and the most probable place to look for it would be in *iserne*. The reference in this passage is not to the oven, but to a wall of fire, and perhaps some general word meaning "to construct" lies hidden in *iserne*. But if so it is so deeply hidden as not to be readily discovered. Perhaps a simple substitution, e.g. *wyrcan*, should be made for *iserne*. To accord with his reading *on stealle*, Grein, Germania X, 419, supplies a full line after *æfaste: eall þurhgledan ‖ þurh ældes leoman.* Schmidt prints *iserne* as the last word of a line and thinks the rest of this line has disappeared. He does not attempt to restore the supposed missing parts.   249 þonne] Schmidt reads *þon* for *þonne.*   253 alet] Holthausen, Eng. Stud. XXXVII, 204, supplies *ond* or *for*, Schmidt supplies *þa*, before *alet*, for metrical reasons. 257 dydon] Cosijn, Beitr. XX, 110, reads *dyrdon*, "glorified." 258 aldre generede] Grein, Dicht., p. 105, translates, "unversehrt am Leben," "preserved in life." Blackburn, notes, less plausibly takes the whole phrase as instrumental, "because of saved life."   260 þe] Schmidt reads *þa* for *þe.* 262 gange] Grein changes to *ganga*, a gen. pl., and Blackburn retains *gange* but regards it as gen. pl.   Schmidt alters to *fenge.*   gedydon] Schmidt alters to *gedædon.*   263 sweg] Bouterwek, Erläut., p. 325, and Schmidt read *swol* for *sweg.*   264 beot mæcgum] Schmidt supplies *wæs* after *beot*, which makes *beot* a noun. Holthausen, Eng. Stud. XXXVII, 204, reads *beorhtum* for *beot*, in Grein-Köhler, p. 876, he reads *beotmæcgum* as a compound.   þe] Grein, Wülker, Schmidt read *þenden* for the MS. *þen.* beote] Schmidt alters to *bæle*, and so Holthausen, as above. For the wordplay in *beot*, verb, and *beote*, noun, see l. 194, note.   265 fyr fyr scyde] The MS. writes *fyrscyde* as one word. Thorpe, Bouterwek, Dietrich, Grein, Wülker omit the second *fyr*. Holthausen, Eng. Stud. XXXVII, 204, reads *fyrsode*, following Lye-Manning, Supplement, which read *fyrsyde*, for *fyr scyde*, and supplies *frecnan* before *scylde*, l. 265*b*, for alliteration. Cosijn, Beitr. XX, 110, suggests *þæt fyr þa scynde.* Bradley, Archiv XCIX, 127, proposed *ac þæt fyr fysde to ðam firen-wyrhtum*, an entirely unjustified rewriting of the text. Blackburn retains *fyrscyde* as a "careless writing" for *forscyde*. Schmidt reads *ac þæt fȳr fyr scynde to ðam, þe ða fyrene worhton, fyr*, "fire," and *fyr*, "further." The retention of *fyr*, noun, and *fyr*, adverb, seems required, but *scyde* may remain, see Gen. 1103, and the change of *scylde* to *fyrene* is unnecessary. For *fyr* as a comparative, see Beow. 143, 252.   266 hwearf on] Napier, Archiv XCVIII, 397, reads *hwearf on* for *hweorfon*, and all later edd. and commentators follow, though Blackburn, notes, keeps *hweorf* as a variant spelling of *hwearf.*   267 þa] Grein alters to *þara*, and *gefægon*, l. 267*b*, to *gefegon.*   269 wræclic] Schmidt alters to *wrætlic.*   270 in þam] Schmidt supplies *on* after *in.* 271 æfæste ðry] Grein supplies *unforbærned* after *ðry*, and begins a new line with *him eac.* Schmidt takes *him...gesyhðe* as l. 271*b*, for l. 272*a* he reads *engel ælmihtiges godes*, and *him...derede* constitutes his l. 272*b*. The supplying of *on ofne*, l. 273*a*, is a simpler solution of the difficulty.   275 þonne] Schmidt reads *þon* for *þonne.*   276 deaw dryge] For the MS. *drias* read *dryge*, when the dew becomes dry in the day, i.e. in the morning sunlight. Thorpe, note, suggested *deawdripas* for *deaw drias*, Bouterwek reads *deawdropan*. Grein prints *deaw-drias* in his text, in his note suggests *deaw drias,* "the dew of the magician," the dew on the grass being regarded as the work of the fairies. In this Grein followed Dietrich. In Germania X, 419, Grein proposed *deaw-drias* = *-dreas,* and Blackburn, Schmidt retain *deaw-drias,* defining it as "dew-fall." Cosijn, Beitr. XX, 110, proposed *deawdriarong,* "dew-falling." Besides the uncertainty of *-drias* or *-driarong,* the objection to this interpretation is that the dew-fall does not come in the day. In l. 277, *winde gesawen* also refers to the scattering of the dew by the breeze. For Cosijn's *-driarong,* see l. 348*a.* **281** dreag] Cosijn, Beitr. XX, 110, Schmidt supply *dreag* before *dæda,* following Az. 3. **283** þu] Schmidt omits. **284** niðas to nergenne] Schmidt reads *niððas to nergan,* following Sievers, Beitr. X, 482. **288***b*] Grein completes the line by adding *sigores waldend,* Cosijn, Beitr. XX, 111, Schmidt add *soðfæst metod,* see l. 332. **291** nu] Schmidt omits, following Graz, Eng. Stud. XXI, 10. See Az. 12. **292** hyldo] Supplied by Thorpe, Bouterwek, Grein, Schmidt, after Az. 13. **293** þreaum] Bouterwek, Erläut., p. 325, reads *þearfum,* after Az. 14, and in l. 293*b,* his text has *preanydum* for *ðeonydum.* **298** bræcon bebodo] Schmidt reads *þin bebodo bræcon,* following Graz, Eng. Stud. XXI, 10. burhsittende] All edd. read *burhsittende.*

301–400

301 hyldelease] Schmidt reads *hylda lease.* **302** is user lif] Holthausen, Eng. Stud. LI, 181, Schmidt read *is lif user.* **304** usic] Grein, Schmidt read *usic,* Wülker *usec,* but Grein, Germania X, 419, as the MS. See l. 309*a.* **305** æhta gewealde] Thorpe, note, Bouterwek read *æhtgewealde.* **308** þu] Schmidt omits. **309** ane] Hofer, Anglia XII, 201, changes to the plural *ane* to agree with *usic.* Schmidt would omit *ana,* and Blackburn, notes, retains *ana* as referring to *drihten,* "thou only, eternal Lord." **310** hligað] On the meaning of *hligað,* "attribute," see Cosijn, Beitr. XX, 111. **312** niða] Schmidt reads *niðða,* following Sievers, Beitr. X, 505. **316** þæt þu, etc.] Cosijn, Beitr. XX, 111, proposes *in fyrndagum* (as going with *gehete) þæt þu frumcyn hira.* **319** seo mænigeo] Cosijn adds *þæt* before *seo,* Holthausen, Indog. Forsch. IV, 381, adds *manna* before *mænigeo.* **320** had to hebanne] Bouterwek, Wülker, Schmidt, Blackburn, notes, read *had,* after Az. 37. Grein reads *hat to hebbanne,* translated, Dicht., p. 107, "Verheissung zu haben," but Grein, Germania X, 419, has *had to hebanne.* Blackburn, notes, translates, "a race to be exalted." **321** bebugað] Cosijn, Beitr. XX, 111, reads *þe bugað,* a relative clause limiting *heofonsteorran.* oððe brimfaroþes] Grein, Germania X, 419, suggested *oððe brim faroðes* instead of the MS. reading, and Wülker prints *brim faroþæs,* and so Schmidt. Cosijn, Beitr. XX, 111, reads *oððe brimfaroþæs,* and so Blackburn, notes and glossary. **322** sæfaroða] Grein, Germania X, 419, Wülker, Schmidt read *sæwaroða,* an unnecessary change, since Anglo-Saxon texts regularly show an interchange of *faroð* and *waroð.* **323** in eare] Fulton, MLN. XVI, 122, would supply a relative *þe* before *in eare.* Bouterwek read *in eargrynde* for the MS. *me are gryndeð.* Grein and later edd. and commentators read *in eare*. The meaning of *gryndeð* seems best derived from the noun *grund*, "foundation," "bottom," i.e. "is founded," "under-lies" (Blackburn).   **326** þinne] Schmidt omits.   **327** þæt þæt] The abbreviation for the second þæt may stand for þa, according to Blackburn, in which case *and* of l. 330 must be omitted.   Cosijn, Beitr. XX, 111, suggests *þec* for the second *þæt*, and omits *and*, l. 330.   Schmidt also omits *and*. But the clause beginning with *and*, l. 330, may be parallel in syntax with the clause beginning with *þæt*, l. 327*b*.   **341** hine] Schmidt omits.   to-swende] Probably for *toswengde*, and perhaps so to be altered, see Cosijn, Beitr. XX, 111.   **342** leoman, hyra] So Thorpe, note, and later edd.   **347** hit] Thorpe, note, Schmidt omit *hit*.   **349** cyst] Cosijn, Beitr. XX, 111, would place a period after *cyst* and alter *swylc* of l. 350 to *se*, after Az. 65. **365** ofer] Bouterwek, Grein, Kock, PPP., p. 3, read *on* for the MS. *of*.   riht-ne] Grein, Wülker, Kock, as above, Schmidt read *rihtre*.   **368** tunglu] Schmidt reads *tungl*, following Graz, Eng. Stud. XII, 11.   **372** mihtig god] Grein, Schmidt read *god mihtig*.   **379** ligetu] Schmidt reads *ligettu*. **391** Israela] For *Israela* as a nom. pl., see l. 750.   **392** herran sinne] Thorpe, note, suggests *hyra* for the MS. *þinne*.   Bouterwek, Erläut., p. 325, alters to *heora þeodne*.   Grein, Wülker read *herran sinne*.   Schmidt, following Hofer, Anglia XII, 201, alters to *hēran þīne*, a nom. pl., "thy serv-ants."   **396** eadmodum] Grein, Schmidt supply *æfæstum* after *eallum*. Blackburn, notes, suggests *eadmodum* as corresponding more closely to the Latin *humiles corde*.

401–500

403 wurðiað] Grein, Wülker, Schmidt read *wurðiað*.   **404** ðec herigað] Schmidt reads *herigað ðec*.   **406** wideferhð] Thorpe, note, Bouterwek read *ferhðe* for the MS. *ferhð*.   Bouterwek, Erlaut., p. 325, replaces his *ferhðe* by *werode*.   Grein, Schmidt read *wideferhð*.   **409** ehtode] Trans-lated "uttered" by Kock, JJJ., p. 13.   ealdor] Grein and later edd. read *ealdor*, and Blackburn, notes, takes *þeode* as gen. pl.   **410** nehstum] Holt-hausen, Anglia Beibl. V, 231, supplies *spræc* after this word to gain a metri-cal syllable.   In Anglia Beibl. XXX, 2, he suggests reading *nēistum* instead of *nehstum*, with no addition.   **412** þeode] Bouterwek, Erläut., p. 325, reads *þeode wisan* for *þeoden mine*.   Grein, Wülker, Schmidt read *þeode*.   Cosijn, Beitr. XX, 111, retains the MS. *þeoden*.   Blackburn, notes, suggests *þeod-nas*.   Hofer, Anglia XII, 201, reads *þeodend*.   þæt we þry sendon] Bou-terwek, Erläut., p. 325, reads *þe* for *we* and retains *sindon* for *syndon*. Grein reads *sendon* for *syndon*, but Grein, Germania X, 419, and Wülker follow the MS.   Schmidt, Blackburn, notes, read *sendon*.   **413** geboden] Bouterwek, Erläut., p. 325, suggests *gebunden*, and Cosijn, Beitr. XX, 111, Schmidt read *gebundne*, see ll. 228, 434.   Cosijn also reads *byrnendes*, in l. 413*b*.   **415** sefa] Bouterwek, Erläut., p. 325, Grein and later edd. read *sefa*.   **421** gædelingum] Thorpe, note, Grein and later edd. read *gædel-ingum*.   **423** on neod sprecað] Cosijn, Beitr. XX, 112, would place these lines within parentheses. **428** Nis hit owihtes] Grein reads *þæt* for *hit*, and Sievers, Beitr. X, 485, Schmidt read *ohtes* for *owihtes*. **429** hie] Schmidt omits, and alters *þonne*, l. 429*b*, to *þon*, following Graz, Eng. Stud. XXI, 11. **430** se] Schmidt omits. **432** swa hie gecyðde wæron] Cosijn, Beitr. XX, 112, Schmidt reconstruct to read *swa him gecyðed wæs*. **434** bende forburnene] Thorpe, note, suggested *bendas* for the MS. *benne*, Bouterwek, Grein read *bendas*, but Grein, Germania X, 419, and later edd., *bende*. Blackburn, notes, proposes *forburnen* for *forburnene*. **436** wroht] Cosijn, Beitr. XX, 112, reads *wloh*, citing An. 1471. **440** up] Schmidt reads *uppe*. **442** heh þegn] Schmidt reads *heh-þegn*. **444** heredon, for] All edd. read *heredon*, Schmidt *fore* for *for*. **445** septon hie] Grein reads *sewton*, Zupitza, Cynewulf's Elene p. xi, Cosijn, Beitr. XX, 112, Hofer, Anglia XII, 202, Schmidt read *septon*, "instructed," after El. 530. Blackburn retains *stepton*, "raised," "lifted," "edified," with *hie* as subject and some word referring to the king to be supplied. Schmidt omits *hie*. Thorpe, Bouterwek changed *hie* to *hine*, a necessary change according to Holthausen, Anglia Beibl. V, 232, unless one reads *septon*. **449** his] Schmidt omits. **450** se] Grein reads *þe* for *se*. **453** on æht] Dietrich proposed *rahte* for the MS. *nahte*, and Blackburn approves, deriving the verb from the infinitive *ræcan*, "extend," "reach." Grein, note, suggested *hnahte*, "bowed." Holthausen, Anglia Beibl. V, 232, Cosijn, Beitr. XX, 112, Schmidt read *on æht* for *and nahte*. **459***b*] Grein supplies for this half-line *worden in ofne*. Cosijn, Beitr. XX, 112, supplies *wyrd gewordne*, after l. 470. Schmidt adds *wyrd on ofne*. **460** Babilone] Grein reads *Babilones*. þurh fyres bryne] Cosijn, Beitr. XX, 112, suggests *bælbryne* or *bælblyse* (see l. 231) for *fyres bryne*. Schmidt satisfies the requirements of alliteration by reading *þurh bryne fyres*, following Grein. But see Gen. 574, note. **464** godes] Bouterwek, Grein and later edd. omit *ac* before *godes*. **467** geðinges] Schmidt reads *ðinges*. **469** bebead] Cosijn, Beitr. XX, 112, reads *abead*. **475** lacende] Grein, note, suggested *lacendne*, and Schmidt so reads. Cosijn, Beitr. XX, 112, cites Gen. 1081 (see also Gen. 1407) as in part justifying *lacende*. **476–477**] This passage is most simply regularized by inserting *dema*, with Blackburn, before *ælmihtig*. Grein reads *ece ælmihtig* ‖ *dugoða drihten*. Wülker follows the MS. but indicates an omission after *ælmihtig*. Hofer, Anglia XII, 202, reads *ece ealra gesceafta* ‖ *drihten ælmihtig*. Holthausen, Anglia Beibl. V, 232, Schmidt read *ece waldend* ‖ *drihten ælmihtig*. Cosijn, Beitr. XX, 112, reads *ece ælmihtig god*, ‖ *dugoða drihten*. **479** monig] Grein reads *monige*. **482** soð] Cosijn, Beitr. XX, 112, Schmidt read *soð* for the MS. *soðe*. **484** for þam] Cosijn, Beitr. XX, 112, Schmidt add *him* after *þam*. **491** mara on modsefan] Dietrich, Schmidt read *mara modsefa*, or as second reading Dietrich proposed *geðah* for *geðanc*, l. 490*b*. Holthausen, Anglia Beibl. V, 232, proposed *mara on modsefan*, and Kock, PPP., p. 3, defends this reading. Blackburn translates, "in the thought of his heart greater pride [grew up]," which implies *mara modsefa*. **492** oðþæt] Schmidt reads *oð*. **497** þæt] Schmidt omits. **499** he] Thorpe, note, suggested *him* for *he*.

501–600

504 þæt] Schmidt omits. **505 ane æte]** Dietrich proposed *ana* for *ane*, and so Cosijn, Beitr. XX, 112, citing Daniel iv. 9, *et esca universorum in ea.* But the same general intent is expressed by *ane* as adjective with *æte*. **507 þæs]** Schmidt reads *þisses.* **511** wildan deor] For the MS. *wildeor*, Graz, Eng. Stud. XXI, 12, Schmidt read *wildu deor*, Cosijn, Beitr. XX, 112, *wildan deor.* **512** eac] Cosijn, Beitr. XX, 112, transposes after *fugolas.* **517** sylle] Thorpe, note, suggested *wille.* **522** þonne] Schmidt reads *þon.* **527** folctogan feran] Rieger, Verskunst, p. 46, completed the line by supplying *frome* before *folctogan.* Sievers, Beitr. X, 514, Cosijn, Beitr. XX, 113, Schmidt supply *feran* after *folctogan*, and Cosijn also changes *folctogan* to *folctoga.* **529** hit wiston] Sievers, Beitr. X, 514, Schmidt read *wiston hit.* **536** Oft] Cosijn, Beitr. XX, 113, Schmidt read *oft* for the MS. *eft.* **550** æcræftig] Grein, note, Cosijn, Beitr. XX, 113, Schmidt read *æcræftig.* See l. 741. **558** westen] Grein, Germania X, 419, suggested *weste* for *westen.* wyrtruman] A nom. pl., Kock, JJJ., p. 14, who translates, "and that its roots should for some time be hidden in the earth," *befolen* being an uninflected predicate adjective. **559** befolen] Sievers, Beitr. X, 489, suggests, and Schmidt reads, *befolene*, but see l. 558, note. Graz, Eng. Stud. XXI, 12, reads *befolen in foldan.* **562** lið] Thorpe, note, Bouterwek read *bið*, Sievers, Beitr. X, 473, Schmidt read *liged* for *lið.* **571** wildeora] Sievers, Beitr. X, 486, Cosijn, Beitr. XX, 113, Schmidt read *wildra.* **573** hlypum] Schmidt, note, suggests *heorta mid heapum* for *heorta hlypum.* Bouterwek, Erläut., p. 325, had previously suggested *hypum.* **574** þec] Schmidt reads *þe.* mælmete] Dietrich, Grein, Wülker read *mæl mete.* **576** weceð] Cosijn, Beitr. XX, 113, defines as "benetzen," from an infinitive *weccan.* Grein-Köhler, p. 749, derives the word from *wæcan, wēcan*, "weaken, afflict." **581** wæs] Thorpe, note, suggests *wære* for *wæs.* **582** ymbe] Grein reads *ymb.* **583** Swa] Schmidt adds *eac* after *Swa.* **584** anwalh] Cosijn, Beitr. XX, 113, Schmidt read *anwalh*, "safe," glossed by Grein-Köhler, p. 535, under *on-walg.* Blackburn retains *anwloh* as meaning the same as *gewloh*, " 'adorned,' hence here, 'without loss of beauty,' unharmed." cymst] Sievers, Beitr. X, 473, Cosijn, Beitr. XX, 113, Schmidt read *cymest.* **588** aworpe] Grein alters to *aweorpe.* **590** wyrcan bote] For this defective line, Grein read *wean and wyrcan.* Grein, Germania X, 419, read *witeleaste wyrcan.* Hofer, Anglia XII, 202, Cosijn, Beitr. XX, 113, Schmidt read *wommas wyrcan.* Holthausen, Indog. Forsch. IV, 381, proposed *weorðmynd wyrcan*, which fits the context better than *wommas.* Blackburn, notes, suggests *wyrcan bote*, citing the Latin *forsitan ignoscet delictis tuis.* Kock, JJJ., p. 14, suggested *wending wyrcan*, accomplish a turn, change (of heart), and Holthausen, Anglia Beibl. XXX, 2, would read *wyrþ gewyrcan.* Kock, PPP., p. 4, suggests *weldæde wyrcan.* **591** fyrene fæstan] Cosijn, Beitr. XX, 113, proposes *ætfæstan*, the passage in this interpretation meaning "when they would establish themselves in sin." But it seems better to take *fyrene fæstan* as appositive to *wyrcan bote* and to translate, "expiate their

sins by fasting," see Kock, JJJ., p. 14. Blackburn, notes, suggests taking
fæstan as an adjective agreeing with *ðeode*, l. 589. **595** reccan] Grein
reads *rēcan*. **599** ceastergeweorc] For the MS. *ceastre weold*, Bouterwek,
Erläut., p. 325, proposed *ceastre weorc*, and so Schmidt. Grein reads *ceastre
weall*, Cosijn, Beitr. XX, 113, proposed *ceastra geweorc*.

601–700

602 þæt] Grein, note, suggests *þe* for *þæt*, and so Schmidt. **608** ic] Cosijn,
Beitr. XX, 114, Schmidt supply *me* after *ic*. **615** wod] Dietrich, Grein,
Wülker, Blackburn, notes, Schmidt, notes, read *wod*, and Schmidt also
proposes adding *aldor* after *wera*. **617** ðara] Schmidt omits. **619**
hreð] Holthausen, Anglia Beibl. V, 232, Schmidt read *hreðe* for *hreð*. **621**
wildeora] Graz, Eng. Stud. XXI, 12, Schmidt read *wildra* here and in l. 623.
Cosijn, Beitr. XX, 114, reads *on wildra westen* in l. 621, *wildra* in l. 623, and
wildrum in l. 649. Sievers, Beitr. X, 486, reads *wildrum* in l. 649. See
l. 571, note. **627** þær] Grein, Schmidt read *þæs*. he] Schmidt omits.
632 nið geðafian] Thorpe, note, suggested *geþolian* for *geðafian*. Bouterwek, Erläut., p. 325, alters to *niðum gedefe*, and Grein to *niðgeþafa*. But
Grein, Germania X, 419, returns to the MS. Klaeber, Eng. Stud. XLI, 112,
retains *nið geðafian*, "suffering distress," i.e. the general humiliation of
having to return naked and *wæda leas*. **634** modgeðanc] Grein, note,
suggests *modgeðance*. **637** þam] Schmidt omits. **645** lengde] Bradley,
MLRev. XI, 213, suggests *lēgnde* = *līgnde*, "denied," for *lengde*. Retaining
lengde, the meaning must be "deferred." **646** witegena] Schmidt reads
witena. **647** þær] Grein, *þæs*, but Grein, Germania X, 419, returns to
the MS. **650** frean godes] Grein, Germania X, 419, proposed *gumfrean*
for *him frean*. Schmidt reads *ongean* for *frean*. Kock, PPP., p. 4, proposes *from gode* for *frean godes*. But take as genitive after *sefa*, "the spirit
of the Lord God." **657** Swa he ofstlice] Dietrich, Grein, Schmidt read
geornlice to provide alliteration. Holthausen, Anglia Beibl. V, 232, reads
giffæstlice. Cosijn, Beitr. XX, 114, suggests *swylce* for *swa* to avoid repetition of this word, and so also *þenden* for *siððan*, l. 659, to avoid repetition of
siððan. godspellode] Thorpe, Bouterwek, Grein read *god spellode*, but
Grein, Germania X, 419, reads *godspellode*. Hofer, Anglia XII, 202, has
god ecne spellode. **667** gesceod] Grein, note, proposes *gesceode*, and so
also in l. 677. **675** ðære] Schmidt omits. **681** ymb] Grein, note,
suggests *unlytel* for the MS. *ym lytel*, but in his text he reads *ymb litel* (mistake for *lytel*?), and all edd. read *ymb*, first suggested by Thorpe, except
Blackburn, who thinks *ym* may be a genuine form. **683** hæleð] Graz,
Eng. Stud. XXI, 13, Schmidt read *hæleðas* to gain a metrical syllable.
Holthausen, in Grein-Köhler, p. 884, reads *þa hæleð[a bearn]*. **684** he]
Schmidt omits. **692** bun] Sievers, Beitr. X, 476, Cosijn, Beitr. XX, 114,
read *buen*. Schmidt omits *þara* in this half-line. **693** Babilon burga]
Bouterwek, Erläut., p. 325, Cosijn, Beitr. XX, 114, read *Babilone burh*.
But take *burga* as appositive to *fæstna*, l. 691, and Babilon as a nominative

appositive to the subject of *wæs*. **694** frasade] Thorpe, Bouterwek retained the MS. reading *frea sæde*, but Bouterwek, Erläut., p. 325, suggested
freolsade. Dietrich reads *freasæde* as for *freasede, frasade*. Wülker also
has *freasæde*. Grein has *freasade*, Schmidt has *frasade*, and Blackburn,
notes, explains *freasæde* as careless spelling for *frasade*. **697** na] Grein,
note, suggests *a* for *na*. **698** heahbyrig] Sievers, Beitr. X, 478, alters to
hean byrig.

701–764

703 þam æðelum] The half-line is defective in the MS., and Grein changed
þam to *þa* and added *on æht* after *þa*. Hofer, Anglia XII, 202, reads *het
in æht þam beran*. Cosijn, Beitr. XX, 114, reads *þa inn ætberan*, Schmidt
has *þa inne beran*. Holthausen, Indog. Forsch. IV, 381, Klaeber, Eng.
Stud. XLI, 112, propose *þa in beran*, and Holthausen also suggests omitting
gestreon, l. 703*b*. Blackburn supplies *æðelum*, a reading to be preferred
because it permits retaining *þam*, and because it finds a parallel in *on hand
werum*, l. 704*b*. **704** halegu] Sievers, Beitr. X, 461, note, reads *halig*, and
so also in l. 748*a*. **709** hleoðorcyme] For this Thorpe, note, suggested
hleoðorcwyde, and Cosijn, Beitr. XX, 115, *hleoðorhlynn*. Schmidt reads
þurh hloða cyme. Blackburn reads *hleoðor cyme*, taking *cyme* as an adj.,
"glad," modifying *hleoðor*. Kock, Anglia XLIV, 250, retains *hleoðorcyme*
as parallel to *herige*, translating, "and took with boisterous onset, with a
host, the brilliant ornaments"—the best interpretation. **710** beorhte]
Thorpe, note, and later edd., except Wülker and Blackburn, read *torhte* for
alliteration. But see l. 192, note. **715** friðe] Graz, Eng. Stud. XXI, 13,
reads *frofre* for *friðe*, Schmidt alters to *wræce*. **717** þæt] Grein, Schmidt
read *þæs*. **719** þæt] Dietrich reads *þær*, and *þæt* for *þa*, l. 720*a*. **729** to
þam beacne] Cosijn, Beitr. XX, 115, Schmidt read *to beacne þam*, i.e. *þam*
going with *burhsittendum*, l. 729*b*. **731** in sefan gehydum] Schmidt reads
sefan in gehydum. Graz, Eng. Stud. XXI, 13, omits *in*. **735** drihtne]
Graz, Eng. Stud. XXI, 13, Schmidt supply *se wæs* before *drihtne*, citing
l. 150. **739** burhge weardas] Thorpe, Bouterwek, Wülker, Schmidt read
burhgeweardas = burh-geweardas. Grein reads *burge weard*, Hofer, Anglia
XII, 202, Cosijn, Beitr. XX, 115, read *þære burge weard*. Blackburn, notes,
retains *burhge*, as a genitive, and for the spelling, he cites Sievers, Angels.
Gram. § 214, 1, Anm. 5. Blackburn also retains the plural *weardas*, as including the king and his followers. In the speech that follows, l. 743ff.,
Daniel addresses the king in the singular, but such slight logical inconse-
quences are not improbable in the style of this poet. **745** ac þe] Schmidt
omits. **747** in æht bere] Cosijn, Beitr. XX, 115, suggests *in(n) ætbere*. **753**
þæt] Bouterwek, Erläut., p. 326, suggested *þæs* or *þus* for *þæt*. Perhaps
þær? **755** ne] Thorpe, note, Bouterwek read *he*. **764** dugeþum weal-
deð] These are the last words on p. 212, a full page. Between p. 212 and
p. 213, according to Gollancz, p. lxxxviii, a leaf has been lost which contained
the end of the poem, and on this missing sheet was indicated "the conclusion of Liber I, even if merely by a scribal addition of the word 'Finit.' "

NOTES ON CHRIST AND SATAN

1–100

Christ and Satan] For the title, see Introd., p. xxxiv.   5 stream ut on sæ]
Cosijn, Beitr. XXI, 21, suggests *streamas and utsæ*.   7 Deopne ymblyt]
For *ymblyt*, Grein reads *yðmyð*, but in Germania X, 419, and Spr. II, 772,
Grein returns to the MS. reading.   Holthausen, Anglia Beibl. V, 232, proposes *ymbhwyrft* for *ymblyt*.   Bright, MLN. XVIII, 129, reads *ymblyhte*,
followed by a period.   He places a semicolon after *eorðan*, l. 5, and takes
stream as object of *ymblyhte*, and *deopne* as adjective qualifying *stream*.
Clubb retains *ymblyt*, defining it as "expanse," "circuit."   clene ymb-
haldeð] Unless *ymb-* in *ymbhaldeð* be taken as alliterating with *ymb* in l. 7*a*,
this half-line provides no alliteration.   Though this alliteration supposes
an unusual stressing of the verb compound, it may nevertheless have been
the poet's intention.   See l. 294, ll. 343–344 for similar verbal echoes.
Grein, note, suggests *dene*, a noun appositive to his *yðmyð*, for *clene*, and
Grein-Köhler, p. 852, suggests *derne*, an adverb.   Holthausen, Anglia
Beibl. V, 232, proposes *dēre*, and Cosijn, Beitr. XX, 21, suggests *dryhten*
for *dene* (*clene*).   Thorpe, note, avoids the repetition of *ymb* by reading
uphaldeð, and Ettmüller has *uphealdeð*.   Clubb, notes, acceptably translates, "The Creator in his might wholly embraces the deep expanse (i.e.
the ocean which surrounds the world) and all the earth."   10 geofene]
Grein, Graz, Eng. Stud. XXI, 14, Cosijn, Beitr. XXI, 21, Clubb read
geofene, as the sense demands.   Wülker reads *heofenen*.   11 rægnas scuran]
Cosijn, Beitr. XXI, 21, reads *regna scura*, "each of the drops of the showers
of the rains," citing Dan. 575.   The same syntax could be retained with
scuran and *rægnas* taken as genitive singular, or *scuran* may be accusative.
14 Swa se wyrhta] Holthausen, Anglia Beibl. V, 232, adds *eac* after *wyrhta*.
16 eorðan dæles] Thorpe, note, suggested *dalas*, "valleys," but he translates,
"the parts of earth."   Grein retained *dæles* as a genitive of *dæl*, "valley,"
translating in Dicht., p. 129, by "drunten," beneath.   Wülker retains
dæles but does not explain.   Clubb, notes, more plausibly retains *dæles* as
plural of *dæl*, "region," "part," with the late ending *-es* for *-as*, see Sievers,
Angels. Gram. § 237, Anm. 3.   up on heofnum] Thorpe, note, suggested
and upheofon or *upheofonas*, and Ettmüller, Cosijn, Beitr. XXI, 21, Bright,
MLN. XVIII, 129, Clubb read *and upheofon*.   This may have been the
original reading, but to secure it, one must rewrite a passage which is quite
clear as it stands.   17 heanne holm] Cosijn, Beitr. XXI, 21, suggests
heanne ofer holme, or as less plausible, *heahe holmas* for l. 17*a*.   Ettmüller,
Grein read *heahne* for *heanne*.   Holthausen, Anglia Beibl. V, 232, Bright,
MLN. XVIII, 129, and Clubb add *and* before *heanne*, to supply a metrical

syllable. Ettmüller, Grein, Wülker, note, and later commentators read *holm* for *holme*. **19** duguðe and geþeode] Both objects of *gedelde*, "Joys he appointed, men and nations, Adam first," etc. Thorpe, note, suggested *geteode*, "created," for *geþeode*, and Kock, JJJ., p. 69, would retain *geþeode* in the same sense, with *Adam* as object and *dreamas* and *duguðe* as objects of *gedælde*. Ettmüller, note, Graz, Eng. Stud. XXI, 14, Bright, MLN. XVIII, 129, read *duguðe and geogoðe*. **24** ðær] Grein ðæs, but in Germania X, 419, he returns to the MS. wirse] The earlier edd. read *wors*. Grein, Clubb read *wirse*, Wülker, *wirs*. **29** heahgetimbrad] Bouterwek, Erläut., p. 326, suggested *heahgetimber* for this word. Grein, note, suggests *heahgetimbra* as appositive to *swegles*, l. 28. Holthausen, Anglia XLIV, 354, suggests *heahgetimbru*, citing Guth. 556, or *heofnes heahgetimbrum*. Clubb reads *heahgetimbra*, as acc. pl., appositive to *leoht*. Kock, Anglia XLIII, 311, retains *heahgetimbrad* as qualifying *heofnum* and in antithesis to *wælm*, *grund*, ll. 30, 31. It is quite possible that this passage and the one in Guthlac are related, but they may be so without being syntactical duplicates. See *folgad*, l. 558 and note. **30** sceolun] Ettmüller, Grein, Wülker, Cosijn, Beitr. XXI, 22, read *sceoldun*. **37** þe] The MS. has ða þe, but since ða cannot have the singular ðrym as its antecedent, Clubb properly omits it. One might read ðone þe. **40** Nis] Grein changes to *is*. **41** sceolun ætsomne] Cosijn, Beitr. XXI, 22, reads *ætsomne sceolun*. **42** wean and wergu] Bouterwek and the earlier edd. retain the MS..*and wergum*, but Bouterwek, Erläut., p. 326, suggests *mid wergum*. Wülker also retains *and wergum* without explanation. Grein read *wergung*, "curse," but Grein, Germania X, 419, changes to *wergun*, with the same meaning. Dietrich, Cosijn, Beitr. XXI, 22, also read *wergun* = *wergung*. Frings and v. Unwerth, Beitr. XXXVI, 559, propose an abstract noun *wergum*, for *wergm*, "stranglement." Sperber, Beitr. XXXVII, 148, Williams, Short Extracts, p. 81, read *an* (*on*) *wergum*, "among the accursed." Sievers, Beitr. XXXVII, 339, Grein-Köhler, p. 782, Clubb read *wergu*, which Clubb glosses "misery." Kock, JJJ., p. 71, considers it an even choice between *wean and wergu* and *wean on wergum*. wuldres blæd] Clubb retains the MS. *wulres* here and in l. 85. Grein changes *blæd* to *leoht* without comment. **52** susle begnornende] "Lamenting in torment." See l. 134. For the MS. *begrorenne*, Ettmüller, Wülker, Clubb read *begrorene*. Dietrich, Grein change to *begrowene*. Holthausen, Anglia Beibl. V, 232, proposes *behrorene*, and so Sievers, Beitr. XXI, 22. Cosijn, ibid., suggests *susl begnornedon*. Clubb, notes, translates his reading *susle begrorene* by "horrified by," or "in terror at their torment," deriving *begrorene* from an unrecorded *begrēosan*, "be terrified." Grein-Köhler, p.275, also records a verb *begrēosan* on the evidence of *begrorene*. But a single form in a carelessly written manuscript can scarcely carry such heavy weight. The changes required by *begnornende* are slight, and the improvement in meaning is great. **57** sceaðana sum] Thorpe, Ettmüller, Grein, Wülker read with the MS., *earm sceaða*, and Bouterwek reads *earmsceaða*. Grein, note, suggests *sceaða earm*. Bright, MLN. XVIII, 129, reads *nu, sceaða, eartu*, or *nu eartu, sceaða earma*. Clubb omits *earm* as a scribal echo after *eart* and restores the erased letters, reading *earttu sceaðana sum*. It seems most probable that this was the original reading.   64 meotod] Clubb, notes, rightly rejects the interpretation of this passage which makes *meotod* subject of *wære*, "that the ruler of mankind was thy son," i.e. thy subject. Gollancz, p. civ, notes "in the *Gospel of St. Bartholomew* a direct reference to Satan taking counsel with his son Salpsan (*Apocryphal New Testament*, ed. M. R. James, 1924, p. 178)."   hafustu] Ettmüller reads *hafas tu*, Grein *hafastu*.   66 on reordadon] The earlier edd. retain the MS. *unreordadon*, except Ettmüller, who reads *onreordadon*, as Bouterwek suggests in a footnote.   Grein, Germania X, 419, Kock, PPP., p. 24, Clubb read *an reordadon*.   But *an* would be a very unusual form for *on* in this text.   67 cearum] The edd. all follow the MS. *cearum*, except Clubb, who reads *cearium*, with Cosijn, Beitr. XIX, 457.   Sievers, Beitr. X, 456, suggested *ceargum*, from *cearig*, and so Holthausen, Anglia Beibl. V, 232, and in Grein-Köhler, p. 877.   In these interpretations *cearum*, *ceargum*, *cearium* is an adjective.   Kock, PPP., p. 24, reads *on cearum = in cearum*, and takes *cwidum* as appositive to *wordum*, l. 65.   This seems the most reasonable interpretation.   Graz, Eng. Stud. XXI, 14, retains *cearum* and changes *cwidum* to *cwiðdum*.   See Gen. 2795, note.   68 bedelde] Kock, JJJ., p. 30, would take *bedelde* as a finite verb, parallel to *afirde*, l. 67.   This is possible grammatically but awkward stylistically.   See l. 343.   72 hwearfedon] All edd. follow the MS. except Clubb, who reads *hwearfedon*, following Sievers, Beitr. X, 453, Holthausen, Anglia Beibl. V, 232, Graz, Eng. Stud. XXI, 14, Cosijn, Beitr. XXI, 22.   76 forht] All edd. follow the MS. except Grein, Clubb, who alter *forworht* to *forht* for the sake of alliteration. So also Graz, Eng. Stud. XXI, 14.   Grein, note, suggests *þy forhtor gen*, and Cosijn, Beitr. XXI, 22, reads *þa forhtra gen*.   Williams, Short Extracts, p. 23, reads *ða forworhta gen*.   78 spearcade] Ettmüller, note, suggested *spearcade*, and so Grein, Cosijn, Beitr. XXI, 21, Williams, Short Extracts, p. 23, Clubb.   Wülker reads *sweartade*.   80 wordum] All edd. read *word*, except Clubb, who reads *worde*, and so Kock, JJJ., p. 17.   But see l. 727. Holthausen, Indog. Forsch. IV, 382, proposes *word-gid* for *word*, and later, Anglia Beibl. XXX, 2, *þæt, þa* or *þas word*.   Bright, MLN. XVIII, 129, reads *þa* or *þas word*.   Graz, p. 60, proposes *in adraf*, but Eng. Stud. XXI, 15, prefers *ut adraf* or *ut þorhdraf*.   See l. 162.   85 wuldres] See l. 42, note. 89 Wene] All edd. read *wene ge*, except Clubb, who follows the uncorrected reading.   tacen] Grein-Köhler, p. 666, suggests *socen* for *tacen*.   þa ic, etc.] Thorpe, Bouterwek and Wülker assume a loss in the MS. after *wærgðu*.   For l. 89*b* Grein reads *and teon-wærgðu*, and for the following line he reads *þa ic of swegle aseald wæs*.   Wülker follows the MS. except that he indicates another omission after *of* which he does not supply.   Williams, Short Extracts, p. 23, follows Grein, except that he reads *wærgðu gesyne* instead of *teon-wærgðu*.   Holthausen, Indog. Forsch. IV, 382, reads *þa ic aseald wes of swegles wlite*.   Cosijn, Beitr. XXI, 22, proposes *þa ic of swegle adrifen and asæled wæs*.   The reading in the text is that of Clubb, and the simplest way of disposing of the confusion in the MS.   92 eadiges]

Thorpe, note, Grein, note, and Cosijn, Beitr. XXI, 22, suggest *eadigra* for *eadiges.* **94b** ne we] Cosijn, Beitr. XXI, 22, would read *nu* for this *ne*, which would enable one to retain the *ne* added above the line in l. 95. The addition of *we* is necessary for sense. Cosijn also reads *moton* for *moten*, l. 95. **97** Æce] Holthausen, Eng. Stud. XXXVII, 205, would omit this word. Klaeber, Anglia Beibl. XXXVIII, 359, would change to *ēc* and would make l. 96b parenthetic. All edd. follow the corrector's reading *ece*, except Wülker, Williams, Short Extracts, p. 24.

101–200

102 gewunade] Bouterwek, Erläut., p. 326, suggests *gewuniað*, also *wile-hus* for *wites* and *clommum* for *clom.*   ðis] Ettmüller, Grein, Williams, Short Extracts, p. 24, alter to *ðes.*   **105** sciman] Thorpe, note, suggests *scuwan*, and so Ettmüller in his text.   **106** Iu ahte ic] All edd. read *iu* for the MS. *nu*, and accept the corrector's *ic*, except Clubb, who retains *nu* and omits *ic*. Clubb also retains *þær* in l. 107, and translates, "But now had I possession of all glory; whereas I was forced to abide whatever God wills to condemn me to, his enemy on hell's floor." But the changing of the readings puts less constraint on the text.   **111** on flyge and on flyhte] Clubb, following Graz, Eng. Stud. XXI, 15, reads *on flyhte and on flyge* as a metrical improvement.   **117** ecne] All edd. accept the corrector's *ecne* as grammatically necessary.   **124** me] Ettmüller, Grein, Cosijn, Beitr. XXI, 23, read *me* for the MS. *him*, and Cosijn cites l. 174.   **131** Hwæt, her] The edd. read *hwæðer* or *hwæther* for the MS. *hwæt her*, but Holthausen, Anglia Beibl. V, 232, and Clubb treat as in the text.   **135** winnað] All edd. read *winnað*, except Clubb, who reads *windað*, following a suggestion of Thorpe, note, with *wyrmas* as subject and *men* object of *ymb*.   **143** eadige] All edd. read *eadigne*, except Clubb, who reads *eadige*, following Bouterwek, Erläut., p. 326, and Graz, Eng. Stud. XXI, 16, who reads *eadge*.   **145** ænigum sceððan] The missing half-line has been variously supplied. Ettmüller added *earmum atolum* before *þe*, l. 146. Grein supplied *eadigra* before *ænigum*. Grein, Germania X, 419, Graz, Eng. Stud. XXI, 16, supply *þara æfæstra* before *ænigum*. Barnouw, Textkritische Untersuchungen, p. 104, suggested *þe up of eorðan cumað* or *þe up to eðle (earde) cumað* before *ænigum*, and Clubb supplies *ðe of eorðan cumað* before *ænigum*.   **146** agan] The MS. has *to agan*, and Thorpe and Bouterwek made a compositional verb, *toagan*. Grein reads *to agen*, taking *agen* as a noun, "possession" (see Spr. I, 20, Germania X, 419, where he reads *to agan*, translating, "zu Eigen"), from an otherwise unrecorded nominative *age*. Cosijn,Beitr. XXI, 23, reads *āgen*, "own," but Sievers, ibid., rightly objects that one would expect a word for "have" to complete the sense. Sievers suggests that *to* be omitted as a scribal anticipation of *to* in l. 147a. Clubb reads *to agan* and calls it, notes, a "simple uninflected infinitive."   **151** sweg] Grein, Holthausen, Anglia Beibl. V, 232, Kock, JJJ., p. 69, Clubb supply *sweg* to complete the sense.   **152** bearn] Kock, JJJ., p. 69, would change to *bearne*, a dative, the idiom requiring in his opinion some such phrase as *bearne to bearme*. Otherwise *bearn* must be taken as subject of *brohton*. **154** leomu] Bouterwek, Erläut., p. 326, suggested *leoðu* for *leomu*. Kock, JJJ., p. 69, takes *leomu* as object of *hofan*, l. 153, and translates it as "wings." Much more plausible is Clubb's interpretation of *leomu* as appositive to *we*, "limbs," in the sense "members (of a group of people)," "servants." lofsonga word] Object both of *hofan* and *sædon*.   **159** cwiðde] The edd. read *cwide*, except Clubb, who reads *cwiðde*, following Rieger, Grein, Germania X, 419, Sievers, Beitr. X, 456, Cosijn, Beitr. XXI, 23, Graz, Eng. Stud. XXI, 16.   herde] For *hyrde*, as in Beow. 750; see Cosijn, Beitr. XXI, 23.   **166** upheofen] All edd. read *upheofon*, except Wülker and Clubb, who read *upheofen*.   **174** þær] Grein, note, suggests *þæs* for *þær*, and so Rieger and Graz, Eng. Stud. XXI, 16.   **175** þonne ic, etc.] Grein supplies *ær* after *.ic*. Bright, MLN. XVIII, 129, would read *þone þe* for *þonne*, the antecedent of *þone* being *sunu*, l. 172, and he would also treat *and agan...gelamp*, ll. 173*b*–174, as parenthetical. Holthausen, Anglia Beibl. V, 232, and Graz, Eng. Stud. XXI, 16, change *agan* to *habban*. As it stands, the alliteration in the line must be on *ic* and *agan*.   **178** in ðæm] Grein takes ðæm as a noun, in his text þæm, for þeam, "vapor," and Rieger reads *in þone ðæm*. Dietrich supposes a noun, *hof* or *ham*, has been lost, and Graz, Eng. Stud. XXI, 16, proposes *in þæt ham* or *in hæft*.   **179** niðsynnum] Bouterwek and later edd. read *nið-* for the MS. *mid*, as the alliteration demands. Thorpe and Ettmüller assumed a loss of two half-lines after *geniþ*, but the change of *mid* to *nið-* removes any irregularity. **180** worulde] Grein, Rieger, Graz, Eng. Stud. XXI, 17, read *wuldre* for *worulde*.   **183** þæt morðer] Thorpe, note, suggested *þæs morðres*, and so Ettmüller. Grein, Wülker read *þæs morðre* and Rieger has *þæs morðer*. Kock, JJJ., p. 70, reads *þæt morðor* and Clubb, *þæt morðer*, parallel in syntax to *wean*, etc.   **188** sorhgcearig] All edd. have *sorhg-*, except Ettmüller, Grein, who have *sorh-*, and all have *-cearig*, except Clubb, who has *-ceari*. **190** swa] Grein reads *swa some*.   **198** uppe] The edd. follow the MS. *upne*, except Clubb, who reads *uppe*, an adjective *upne* being highly improbable.   **199** gecydde] Bouterwek and later edd. read *gecyðde*, except Clubb, who reads *gecydde*.   mægencræft] Ettmüller, Grein, Holthausen, Anglia Beibl. V, 232, Graz, Eng. Stud. XXI, 17, Clubb omit *mægen* in order to regularize the alliteration.

201–300

203–205] These lines have been variously rearranged and rewritten. Ettmüller reads *ecne in wuldre ealdor; heran we þone ælmihtigan* ‖ *mid alra gescæfta mænego; ceosan us*, etc. Bouterwek supplies *eorðan*, but Bouterwek, Erläut., p. 326, and Grein supply *ordfruman* before *ceosan*, taking *eorðan* or *ordfruman ceosan* as a half-line following *gescefta*. Dietrich suggested *ealdre* or *ealdor* to be supplied before *ceosan*, and Holthausen, Indog. Forsch. IV, 382, proposes *or* or *ord*, "beginning." Clubb reads *ecne mid alla gescefta* ‖

ceosan us eard in wuldre, etc.   By reading *ecne...wuldre*, ll. 202–203*a*, as one expanded line, Graz, Eng. Stud. XXI, 17, is enabled to combine *mid...genemned* as a succeeding line.   Perhaps this should be done, but there is so much evidence of careless composition here that it seems best to let the text stand with the least possible change, which would be the addition of some noun, like *ealdre*, to account for the genitive plural *alra gescefta*.   A change of *cyninge*, l. 203, to *cyning* was suggested by Sievers, Beitr. XII, 476, and Cosijn, Beitr. XXI, 23, as a metrical improvement.   If this change is made, then *ealdre*, l. 202, should be *ealdor*.   **207** hnigan] So all edd. except Clubb, who reads *nigan*.   But in any case the alliteration demands *hnigan*.   **210** him wlite] Read *his wlite* here?   See l. 222.   **212** fægere] Thorpe and Bouterwek read *mycele fægre*, Ettmüller, Grein, Wülker, Sievers, Beitr. X, 499, read *mycele fægerre*.   Clubb reads *fægere*, omitting the corrector's addition.   **213** is þær wlitig] Thorpe, Bouterwek read *seo is wlitig*, etc., omitting *þær* and ending the preceding line with *folde*. Grein, Wülker read *folde seo:* ‖ *þær is wlitig*, etc.   Clubb reads *folde seo,* ‖ *is wlitig*, etc.   Graz, Eng. Stud. XXI, 17, omits both *is* and *þær*, *wlitig* and *wynsum* thus limiting *land*, l. 212.   **214** brade] Kock, JJJ., p. 70, reads *bradre*, to agree with the other comparatives in the passage. **216** Uta cerran] All edd. read *uton acerran*, except Clubb, who reads *Uta cerran*.   See l. 250.   For the form *uta* = *utan*, Clubb cites Brown, Language of the Rushworth Gloss to the Gospel of Matthew, I, 2, 43.   **220** eadigra] All edd. read *eadigra*, except Clubb, who retains *eadigre* as equivalent to *eadigra*.   **223** wuldorcyninge] Holthausen, Anglia Beibl. V, 232, would read *-cyning*.   See l. 203, note.   **224** feond ondetan] Thorpe reads *feond* for *feonda*, as a plural, and Bouterwek reads *feondas*.   Grein supplies *bearn* after *feonda*, Holthausen, Indog. Forsch. IV, 382, Graz, Eng. Stud. XXI, 17, supply *mænigu*.   Wülker indicates an omission after *feonda* but supplies nothing.   Clubb reads *feond*, and regards *ondetan* as used absolutely.   This is not altogether satisfactory, but it is probably as near to the original form of the passage as a more elaborate rewriting would make it.   But it seems better to take *feond* as a plural, as in ll. 103, 195, than as a singular, as Clubb does.   Grein also supplies *unriht* before *ondetan* and begins a new line with *unriht*.   Holthausen and Graz supply *yfel*.   This gives a half-line *unriht* or *yfel ondetan*, and for a succeeding half, *wæs him eall ful strang*.   **225** hæfdon] Clubb reads *hæfde* here and *Cwæð* in l. 227, to accord with his interpretation of *feond* as singular in l. 224.   On the confusion of numbers and pronouns in the passage ll. 224–281, see Clubb, notes, pp. 81–82.   **230** domlease] Sievers, Beitr. XII, 467, would read *domleas*, and Graz, Eng. Stud. XXI, 17, would omit *gewinn* for metrical reasons.   **234** þusendmælum] Bouterwek, Grein supply *þegnas ymb þeoden* before *þusendmælum*, the whole constituting one line.   Wülker indicates an omission before *þusendmælum* but supplies nothing.   For the succeeding line Bouterwek and Grein have *þa we...sweg*, omitting the corrector's *wæron*.   Wülker, Clubb read *þa we þær wæron,* ‖ *wunodon*, etc.   See ll. 507, 568, 630.   **236** Byrhtword] Cosijn, Beitr. XXI, 23, suggests *burgweard*, as appositive to *ordfruma*, for *byrht-*

word, an adjective glossed "clear-voiced" by Clubb, "voce clarus" by Grein, Spr. I, 152.   **237** to þæm æþelan] Holthausen, Indog. Forsch. IV, 382, Graz, Eng. Stud. XXI, 18, Clubb read *þæm æþelan to.* But see Gen. 574, note.   **241** gehwilcne] Cosijn, Beitr. XXI, 23, reads *gehwilce.*   **243** andfeng] Cosijn, Beitr. XXI, 23, suggests *andfenge* or *andfengea.*   **245** Þa ðæs] Grein, Wülker supply *me* after *þa.*   **249** minre] Clubb reads *mīre* = *minre*, and so in l. 437.   **250** Uta] All edd. read *utan*, except Clubb, who has *uta.* See l. 216, note.   **257** þæt] Grein, Wülker supply *we* after *þæt.* **258–259**] Grein, Wülker take *grimme...healdeð* as one line, and *he...drihten* as the succeeding line. Sievers, Beitr. XII, 477, supposes that two half-lines have fallen out after *haldeð*, or omitting *ece drihten*, he would take *he... gewearð* as one line. The main difficulty lies in the lack of alliteration in the MS. reading *he is ana cyning*, l. 259*b.* Graz, Eng. Stud. XXI, 18, corrected this by reading *riht* for *ana.* Cosijn, Beitr. XXI, 24, would read *an* or *on riht* for *ana.* Clubb reads *he is ana riht Cyning*, but even with this reading *ana* should alliterate. One may replace *ana* by *riht*, with Graz, or if one prefers, read *an* or *on riht* with Cosijn, but for other lines without alliteration, see ll. 296, 334, 450, 484, 634, 712, 717, 723, 726.   **261** swið] Bouterwek, Erläut., p. 326, and later edd. read *swið*, except Clubb, who retains *swilc* in the sense "so great."   **265** he] Grein changes to *ic.*   **266** gehrinan] So all edd. except Clubb, who retains *gerinan.*   **267** hæðenre sceale] Thorpe, note, suggested *hæðene scealcas.* Grein reads *mæg* for *mot*, l. 267*a*, and *hæðenra sceal* for l. 267*b.* But Grein, Spr. II, 403, changes to *hæðenne scealc*, and so Bouterwek, Wülker. Clubb reads *sceale*, "troop," "band," for *sceal.*   **272** þinga æghwylces] Graz, Eng. Stud. XXI, 18, proposes *þinga æghwylc* or *gehwylces* as a metrical improvement.   **273** bitres niðæs] The MS. reading *in ðæs* does not fit the context and might well be a careless scribal error for *niðæs* = *niðes.* The object of *geþolian* is *beala*, and *þinga æghwylces* and *niðæs* are dependent genitives. The edd. propose more elaborate reconstructions. Thorpe, note, suggested *bitre in þas bealu.* Grein has *bitre in þæs brynes beala*, Holthausen, Indog. Forsch. IV, 382, Graz, Eng. Stud. XXI, 18, as Grein, except *brandes* for *brynes.* Trautmann, see Wieners, Zur Metrik, p. 65, would read *bæles beala.* Clubb has *in ðæm bitran bryne.* Clubb places *in ðæm bitran...sorhful* within parentheses.   **276** hwæðer, etc.] Clubb treats *hwæðer...dyde* as a question.   **278** eðel] Thorpe, note, and later edd. read *eðel.*   **279** gnornedon] Clubb reads *gnornede*, and also *andsaca* to agree, in l. 279*b*, and *hat* in l. 280*a.* **294a** beorhte] For this *beorhte*, Holthausen, Eng. Stud. XXXVII, 205 would read *blāce.*   **296** æfre forð] Grein, Graz, Eng. Stud. XXI, 19, Clubb read *wideferð*, the other edd. follow the MS. despite the lack of alliteration. See l. 259, note.   **298** lifigend] The edd. all read *lifigendon*, except Clubb, who reads *lifigend*, with *on-* as prefix in the verb *onlucan*, l. 299*a.* This reading was suggested by Kock, JJJ., p. 70. Grein reads *lifigendon*, but also *onlucan.*

301–400

301 gif] Grein, Wülker supply *we* after *gif*.   **309** friðe] Grein, note, suggests *friðe* before *befæðmeð*, and so Wieners, Zur Metrik, p. 65.   Holthausen, Anglia Beibl. V, 232, transfers *heo* from l. 308*b* to the beginning of l. 309*a* and makes no addition.   Clubb follows Holthausen.   **311** wuldorcyninge] Sievers, Beitr. XII, 476, Holthausen, Anglia Beibl. V, 232, read *-cyning* for metrical reasons.   Graz, Eng. Stud. XXI, 19, reads *wuldr-*.   **312** awa to aldre] Bouterwek supplements the text by adding *unswiciende* after *aldre*.   Grein reads *agan sceolon* for l. 312*b*.   Holthausen, Indog. Forsch. IV, 382, would supply *æfre, fægre* or *wynne* instead of Grein's *sceolon*. Clubb, following Graz, Eng. Stud. XXI, 19, omits *a to worulde*, l. 314, and transfers *awa to aldre* from l. 312 to take the place of the omitted words. **314** buton ende] Rieger, Verskunst, p. 18, Holthausen, Anglia Beibl. V, 232, supply *forð* after *ende*.   **318** hreopan] Grein and the earlier edd. retained *hreowan*, but Grein, Germania X, 420, altered to *hreopan*, and so Wülker, Kock, JJJ., p. 71, Clubb.   Grein also changes *deofla* to *deoflu*.   **319** wean cwanedon] All edd. read *wea-cwanedon*, except Bouterwek, Clubb, who read *wea cwanedon*, and so Holthausen, Anglia Beibl. V, 232.   Kock, JJJ., p. 71, changes *wea* to *wean*, but Clubb retains *wea* as a northern equivalent of *wean*.   Kock treats *hreopan...morður* as parenthetical.   See Jul. 537, *sar cwanian*.   **320** seo] Thorpe, note, suggested *seo* for the MS. *ðær*, and so Bouterwek.   Grein, Wülker, Kock, JJJ., p. 72, Clubb emend *ðær* to *ðære* as a dative.   **321** swylce] Grein reads *swiðe*, Wülker *swyðe* for *swylce*. eall] Bouterwek, Erläut., p. 326, suggests *æled* for *eall*.   **324** þreat] Grein, note, suggests *þrea* or *þræd* for *þreat*.   **330** gryndes ad] Grein supplies *bealu* after *gryndes*.   Wülker would read *grynde* or *grundas* and supply nothing, but this leaves the half-line metrically imperfect.   For *gryndes* as a possible plural, see *stences*, l. 356.   Kock, JJJ., p. 73, omits *ah* and reads *nymðe grundas an*, "they might dwell only in the abysses."   Clubb retains *gryndes* and supplies *ād*, "flame," "fire," after this word.   **331** ne] Supplied by Thorpe and later edd.   **333** gristbitunge and gnornunge] All edd. follow the MS. except Clubb, who reads as in the text, wth Cosijn, Beitr. XXI, 24.   Reading *-unge* in both words, Graz, Eng. Stud. XXI, 20, omits *and* in l. 333*a* and *mecga* in l. 333*b* for metrical reasons.   **334** he] Bouterwek, Erläut., p. 326, Grein, Wülker read *hie* for *we*, Clubb reads *he* as a plural, see l. 716.   cyle and fyr] All edd. follow the MS. except Clubb, who reads *hat and cyle*, with Cosijn, Beitr. XXI, 24.   Graz, Eng. Stud. XXI, 20, reads *hat and ceald*.   See l. 259, note.   **339** hlude and geomre] Clubb retains *lude*, all other edd. read *hlude*.   Holthausen, Eng. Stud. XXXVII, 205, would read *geomre and hlude*, and take *hweorfan* as standing for *hwurfon*.   **348** cræftig] Grein reads *sundorcræftig*, Holthausen, Indog. Forsch. IV, 383, proposes *searocræftig*, and so Graz, Eng. Stud. XXI, 20.   **349** gleaw] Graz, Eng. Stud. XXI, 20, would add *and wis* after *gleaw*.   **351** scima] Thorpe, note, suggested that *sunnu* was an error for *sunne*.   Grein reads *scir sunnu*, and Cosijn, Beitr. XXI, 24, proposes *scir sunna* or *scir* *sunu.* Holthausen, Indog. Forsch. IV, 383, replaces *sunnu* by *scima*, and so Graz, Eng. Stud. XXI, 20, Clubb.   This provides the appropriate alliteration and preserves the sense, "how the gleam shineth thereabout by the might of the Lord."   354 þæt is se seolfa] All edd. read *þæt is seolfa for god*, except Clubb, who reads *þæt is se seolfa God*, and so Holthausen, Anglia Beibl. V, 233, except that Holthausen omits *se*. Holthausen, Eng. Stud. LI, 181, also proposed *þæt is for seolfan gode*. Clubb places *þær...singað* within parentheses.   But it seems better to take *þæt is se seolfa* as the parenthesis, and as exposition of the light that shines (whether one reads *scima* or *sunne* or *sunu*) as God.   Note the similar exposition in l. 357*b*. See l. 394.   356 stences] An acc. pl., see l. 330, note.   357 wyrte] All edd. read *wyrte*, except Clubb, who reads *wyrta*.   360 lædeð] Clubb reads *lædað*, but treats this form as a third singular.   364 wyrcan] All edd. read *ðe þæt mot*, except Clubb who supplies *wyrcan* before *mot*, following the suggestion of Dietrich. Holthausen, Anglia Beibl. V, 233, suggests *fon* after *mot*. Graz, Eng. Stud. XXI, 20, omits l. 364, as a prose addition by a pious scribe.   365–367] The text as it stands offers some difficulties. In the first place, Lucifer was not the name of an *encgelcyn*, "a race of angels." Clubb, notes, suggests *encgelcyning* for *encgelcyn*, but wisely rejects this suggestion.   It would also call for a further change of *þæt* to *se*. Apparently *encgelcyn* must stand, and Clubb concludes that it is "not unnatural that Lucifer should be called 'that angel-order' by a sort of synecdoche." Thorpe, note, suggested that there was a gap in the MS. after *genemned*. Gollancz, p. civ, thinks the scribe has omitted a line or two, and he rewrites as follows:

> Wæs þæt encgelcyn ær genemned,
> [þæt þe eft forhwearf eþle bedæled,
> Bene elohim, þæt is bearn godes.
> Anne hæfde dryhten deorestne geworht]
> Lucifer haten, leoht berende,
> On gear-dagum in godes rice.

Taking the text as it stands, *ær genemned* might mean "previously mentioned," that is, in this poem, as at ll. 20–21, or better "formerly," parallel to *on geardagum; genemned* and *haten* would also be parallel in syntax.   The awkwardness of this syntax favors some such explanation as that of Gollancz, though not necessarily such an elaborate one.   369 oferhyda] Cosijn, Beitr. XXI, 24, suggests *for oferhyde* or else *eawan* or *æfnan* in place of *agan*. Bright, MLN. XVIII, 130, defends the MS. reading and approves the translation in Bos.-Tol. II, 735, "he would give way to pride."   370 þa] All edd. read merely *Satanus* for l. 370*a*, except Clubb, who supplies *þa*, following Bright, MLN. XVIII, 130. Graz, Eng. Stud. XXI, 20, suggests *þær* before *Satanus*, or with Holthausen, Indog. Forsch. IV, 383, *seolf* after *Satanus*.   As alternatives Bright suggested *þæt* or *se* before *Satanus*.   geþohte] Thorpe, Bouterwek alter to *gesohte*. Ettmüller reads *Satanus swearta searwum geþohte*.   373 ordfruma] All edd. read *ordfruma*, though *ordfruman* might possibly, though very improbably, stand as

240 NOTES ON CHRIST AND SATAN

appositive to *him*, l. 373*b*. **375** in hynðo] The MS. reading *in to* is defective metrically and in meaning, though Grein and Wülker retain it. Ettmüller reads *in to henðo*. Graz, p. 58, suggests *heonon to geglidan*. Cosijn, Beitr. XXI, 24, reconstructs l. 375*b*–376*a* to read *him to gesiðum ‖ in þæt nearwe nið*. Kock, JJJ., p. 73, reads *in hatunge glidan*, "fall in the hate." Holthausen, Anglia Beibl. XXX, 4, proposes *in hete geglidan* or *glidan*. Clubb reads *in inðo* for the MS. *in to*, taking *inðo* as equivalent to *hinðo*, and this is the simplest reconstruction. **376** no seoððan] Dietrich supplies *wæs* between these words. **377** andwlitan seon] Thorpe, note, suggests *onwlitan*, a verb, for *andwlitan*, and Holthausen, Anglia Beibl. V, 233, Clubb supply *seon*. Graz, Eng. Stud. XXI, 21, reads *eagum wlitan* for l. 377*b*. Bright, MLN. XVIII, 130, transfers *mosten* from l. 377*a* to a place after *andwlitan*, taking *andwlitan* as an infinitive. **378** buton ende] Ettmüller, Grein, Cosijn, Beitr. XXI, 24, read *a buton ende*. **379** in] Graz, Eng. Stud. XXI, 21, omits. **382** ær nemdon] There is an obvious break in the sense here. Ettmüller supplied *fagum folce, forht geworden*. Grein reads *fagum folce ferhð geaclod*. **385** stronglic] Ettmüller supplied *strið* after *stronglic*. **387** fægere] Wülker retains *fæger*, though a comparative is needed and *fæger* leaves the line too short. Ettmüller, Grein read *fægerre*. Thorpe, Bouterwek, Clubb have *fægere*. **395** uppe] Grein, Graz, Eng. Stud. XXI, 21, read *up*. **397** yrreweorces] All edd. follow the MS. here, except Clubb, who reads *hereweorces*, with Graz, Eng. Stud. XXI, 21, for the sake of the alliteration. But if Clubb can read *inðo* in l. 375, he might read (*h*)*ēnðo* here and thus preserve *yrreweorces*. henðo] Ettmüller suggested *earfoðu* for *henðo*, and Holthausen, Anglia Beibl. V, 233, suggests *ermðo*.

401–500

406 ac] Thorpe, note, suggests *ac*, and so Bouterwek and Ettmüller, but the other edd. follow the MS. **419** onæled] Holthausen, Anglia Beibl. V, 233, reads *onælde*. **421** þan] Ettmüller, Grein read *þam*. **423** mægðe] Thorpe, Bouterwek assume a loss in the MS. after *mægðe*. Ettmüller supplies *feran* after *mægðe* and assumes a loss after *feran*. Graz, Eng. Stud. XXI, 21, would either read *fare* for *mægðe*, or assume a loss in the MS. But the text may stand, with the verb of motion omitted after *mæge and mote*. **428** Segdest] Ettmüller, note, suggests *sægde* and Grein reads *segde*. **433** fægen] Ettmüller, Holthausen, Anglia Beibl. V, 233, read *fægene*. freodrihten] Wülker retains the MS. reading *heora drihten* despite the lack of alliteration. Ettmüller reads *heora freadrihten*. Bouterwek has *freo drihten*, Holthausen, Anglia Beibl. V, 233, Graz, Eng. Stud. XXI, 21, Clubb have *freodrihten* as representing the MS. *heora drihten*. Grein alters *heora* to *feora*. **434** helle] Grein alters to *ham*. **437** minre] All edd. read *minre*, except Clubb, who retains *mire*, see l. 249, note. **440** and] All edd. omit *and* except Junius. **442** wuldre hæfde] Bouterwek, Erläut., p. 326, reads *hæftas* for *hæfde*, followed by *wites clommas feondum on fæstede*. For l. 442*a*, Grein reads *werud to wuldre*. Wülker indicates an omission before *wuldre*. But *wuldre* is adverbial, "gloriously" (Clubb, notes), and *clomma* the object of *hæfde...oðfæsted*.   clomma] Thorpe, note, suggested *clommas*, and so all edd. except Clubb, who reads *clomma* as an accusative plural. Grein, Germania X, 420, also returns to *clomma*. Sievers, Beitr. X, 514, Graz, Eng. Stud. XXI, 21, read *hæfde wites clom* for l. 442*b*, which requires an addition to l. 442*a*.   448 in] The sense would be improved, as Clubb, notes, remarks, by omitting *in*. The omission of *ah* would serve the same purpose.   449–451 ne hi...geworden] In the MS., p. 223, this passage is pointed as follows: ne hi ed cerres˅ æfre moton wenan ˀ Seoððan him wæs drihten god˅wrað geworden. This pointing has misled the edd., and the passage is simplified by placing a metrical point after *moton*. The only plausible change is the substitution of *weroda* for *god*, which would be placed before *drihten* for metrical regularity, but this is not necessary, see l. 259, note. Grein reads *ne hi edcerres æfre moton wenan*, ‖ *seoððan him wæs drihten god deofla cynne* ‖ *wrað geworden*. So also Wülker, except that he indicates a loss after *god* which he does not supply. Omitting *god*, Clubb reads *ne hi edcerres* | *æfre moton wenan*. ‖ *Seoððan him wæs Drihten wrað geworden,* | *sealde him wites clom*. Ettmüller supplied *dugeða aldor* after *god*. Holthausen, Anglia Beibl. V, 233, supplies *domes* or *dreames* before *wenan*. Dietrich first suggested taking *wenan seoððan* together.   451 clomm] Ettmüller reads *clommas*, to agree with *atole*, l. 452.   452 atole] Grein, Spr. I, 11, suggests *atolne*, to agree with the singular *clom*. Clubb reads *atol*, a noun, appositive to *clom*. Some such change might be made, though it is possible to take *atole* as adverbial.   453 dimne] Thorpe, note, suggested *dimne*, and so later edd.   454 hinsiðgryre] Thorpe, Bouterwek read *hinsið gryre*. Grein, Wülker have *hinsiðgryre*. Clubb reads *insiðgryre* for *hin-*. See l. 375, note. Ettmüller reads *hinsiðes gryre*.   455 Þæt, la, wæs] Grein reads *Þæt wæs la*.   458 him] Ettmüller, Holthausen, Anglia Beibl. V, 233, Graz, Eng. Stud. XXI, 22, omit *him*. Bouterwek, Erläut., p. 326, suggested supplying *on* before *handum*.   462 Þæt he swa wolde] The infinitive of action is omitted. Thorpe, Bouterwek suppose a loss in the MS. after *wolde*, and Ettmüller writes in a line. Bouterwek, Erläut., p. 326, suggests *swa* for *sawla*. Grein, Wülker, Clubb read *swa la*. Graz, Eng. Stud. XXI, 22, reads *wolde swa*.   466 ban] Thorpe, note, suggested *bendas* for *ban*. Grein reads *banan*. Translate, "their bones (i.e. bodies) failed (them) when," etc., and see Clubb, note, for this Biblical use of *ban*.   472–478 Þa...æghwær] Clubb places these lines within parentheses and regards them as an interruption in the direct discourse. The lines certainly seem less direct, but may be only unskilfully done.   474 on] Bouterwek supplies *geond*, but Ettmüller supplies *on*, and so later edd., except Wülker, who reads *middangearde* without a preposition. Thorpe, note, Ettmüller read *middangearde*, but Bouterwek, Grein, Klaeber, The Later Genesis, p. 34, Clubb read *middangeard*.   477 hie afyrde eft] Ettmüller assumed the loss of a half-line after *eft*, and in a note suggested *Þæt hie afyrrode eft se feorh-sceaða*. Bouterwek, Erläut., p. 326, reads *Þæt hie afirrde eft*. Dietrich reads *afyrde*, and *est* for *eft*. Grein reads *Þæt Þe* *afyrde freodrihtnes est,* but Grein, Germania X, 420, changes *þe* to *he.* Wülker indicates a loss after his reading *afyrde* but supplies nothing.   Klaeber, JEGPh. XII, 257, proposes *þæt he afyrde foldbuendum,* "that he, the enemy, removed it (= *eðel*) from men." Clubb omits *eft* and reads *he afyrde,* taking *þæt he...æghwær* as one line. Clubb takes *he* as equivalent to *hie,* plural object of *afyrde.* If anything is to be supplied, it may be added as well after *æghwær* as elsewhere.   481 æpla] Grein reads *æplas.*   482 beorhtan] Grein supplies *þa* before *beorhtan.*   484 ofergymdon] The MS. reading suits the sense but not the alliteration, but see l. 259, note.   Thorpe, note, Clubb read *oferhygdon.*   Bouterwek, Ettmüller, Grein read *oferhyrdon.* Wülker retains the MS. reading.   Grein-Köhler, p. 286, suggests supplying *hyge* before *ofergymdon.*   487 gereaw] For *gehreaw,* and so Dietrich and Grein read.   Ettmüller supplies *hearde* before *gereaw,* and Graz, Eng. Stud. XXI, 22, would supply *hearde* or *æt heortan.*   488 þæs] Grein and Wülker follow the MS., though this leaves l. 488*a* metrically incomplete. Ettmüller supplies *þæs* before *carcernes,* and so Clubb.   Ettmüller also changes *clom* to *clommas.*   Holthausen, Indog. Forsch. IV, 383, would supply *cwealm* before *ðrowade,* transferring *clom* to l. 488*a.*   Cosijn, Beitr. XXI, 24, suggests that *cealdan* or *cealdne* has dropped out before *clom,* and suggests *þises* as better than Ettmüller's *þæs.*   490 weorc] Grein alters to *word.*   495 tintregan fela and teonan micelne] So Thorpe and later edd. Sievers, Beitr. X, 514, rejects this on metrical grounds.   Holthausen, Anglia Beibl. V, 233, reads *tintregan micelne and teona fela.*   498 rædboran] All edd. read *rices boran,* with the MS., except Clubb, who has *rices rædboran,* following Sievers, Beitr. X, 454, Holthausen, Anglia Beibl. V, 233, and Graz, Eng. Stud. XXI, 23.   Dietrich had previously suggested *rice ræsboran.*   hrefnan] To normalize the alliteration, Ettmüller, Graz, Eng. Stud. XXI, 23, read *ræfnan.*   Dietrich has *refnan,* and Grein reads *arefnan.*   Holthausen, Anglia Beibl. V, 233, reads *refnan leten.*   500 þæt] Cosijn, Beitr. XXI, 24, supplies *ic* after *þæt.*

501–600

501 geara] Graz, Eng. Stud. XXI, 23, and Cosijn, Beitr. XXI, 24, would omit *geara.*   502 on þam minnan ham] Grein and Wülker, following Thorpe and Bouterwek, read *and þa minan ham lange* for this half-line, though Grein, note, suggests removing *ham.*   He translates, Dicht., p. 142, "wie die Meinigen verlange."   Thorpe, note, suggested *lædde* for *lange.* Ettmüller reads *munan* for *minan.*   Holthausen, Anglia Beibl. V, 233, reads *þæt mæl lange* for l. 502*b.*   Graz, Eng. Stud. XXI, 23, reads *in þam minnan ham,* omitting *lange.*   Clubb reads as in the text, and translates, notes, "I was mindful that this company in this wretched home were longing that I should lead them from their bonds [to their heavenly] home."   There is some question as to the authenticity of an adj. *minnan,* "vile," see Clubb, notes.   Perhaps one should emend here to *mircan.*   503 of hæftum] Holthausen, Anglia Beibl. V, 233, supplies *heo* before *of.*   Ettmüller supplied

hie before *ham.*   **504** agan sceolon] Ettmüller supplied *þær* after *agan,* Grein reads *agan moton,* Holthausen, Indog. Forsch. IV, 383, Graz, Eng. Stud. XXI, 23, read *agan sculon,* and Clubb reads *agan sceolon.*   **509** galgum] Clubb alters to *galgan.*   **510–511** and ic eft, etc.] There is no indication of loss in the MS.   Ettmüller supplied *to eðle minum* after *becom.* Holthausen, Anglia Beibl. V, 233, suggested *ece on dreamas.* In l. 511, Grein supplied *in heofonrice* after *drihtne.*   Clubb indicates a loss after *drihtne,* and takes *dreamas* as to be construed with some missing word.   But the sense of the passage is complete as it stands, "and I then attained eternal joys at the hands of (*to*) the holy Lord."   **513** ær on morgen] Holthausen, Eng. Stud. XXXVII, 205, and Clubb read *on morgen ær,* but see Gen. 574, note.   **515** stan] Grein and later edd. read *stan.*   **519** on] Dietrich, Grein, Wülker read *of.*   **520** andleofan, etc.] In this passage the MS. reads: 7 leofan gingran winum· 7 huru secgan het· simon petre· Grein reads *gingrum sinum* for *gingran winum* and Wülker reads *gingran sinum.* Dietrich would read *and eowan* or *æteowan gingran sinum* for l. 520*b.*   Holthausen, Anglia Beibl. V, 233, Graz, Eng. Stud. XXI, 23, Cosijn, Beitr. XXI, 25, Clubb omit *winum,* taking *andleofan* as meaning "eleven."   Clubb, notes, translates, "He bade the shining angels summon his eleven followers." Grein, Dicht., p. 143, translates, "hiess künden allglänzende Engel seinen elf Jüngern."   **526**] Thorpe, Bouterwek, Wülker, Clubb assume the loss of a half-line before *haligne.*   Grein supplies *ongeton* before *haligne.*   There is no certainty that the loss occurred before *haligne,* and it may have been after *sunu.*   But *bled,* l. 525, ends a line in the MS., and it may be that something dropped out in passing from one line to the next.   **528** þa on upp gestod] The earlier edd. follow the MS., except Grein, who omits *þa gingran.*   So also Holthausen, Indog. Forsch. IV, 383, and Graz, Eng. Stud. XXI, 23.   Holthausen would then supply *cwic,* reading *cwic on upp stod,* or *on upp gestod.*   Cosijn, Beitr. XXI, 25, suggests *þa upp astod* or *þær on upp astod.*   Clubb reads *þa on upp gestod.*   **537** on laðne bend] Bright, MLN. XVIII, 130, places *on* in l. 537*a* and alters l. 537*b* to *laðe* or *laðan benda.* **538** hæþene] So Grein and later edd.   **540** hie] Bouterwek, Grein, Wülker read *hit* for *hie.*   mode] So Thorpe, Bouterwek, Holthausen, Anglia Beibl. V, 233.   The other edd. read *mod,* except Grein, who changes *mod* to *soð.* Cosijn, Beitr. XXI, 25, would read *mode,* or assume that a final *-e* is unexpressed before a following word beginning with a vowel.   **544** feollon] Grein reads *feallan,* Wülker *feallon* as an infinitive after *forlet.* But *bæðe* is better taken as a nom. pl., subject of *feollon,* see Clubb, notes.   Grein, Wülker alter *bæðe* to *bæð,* as object of their infinitive *feallan.*   According to Clubb, the "baths" are the blood and water from Christ's wounds, or the reference may be "to Christ's passion itself as a *second baptism* of martyrdom."   **550** weorcum] Dietrich, Grein, Wülker read *wordum.*   **552** sceolon] Grein supplies *moton,* Holthausen, Indog. Forsch. IV, 383, Graz, Eng. Stud. XXI, 24, supply *sculon* after *agan.*   Clubb reads *sceolon.*   **553** drihtnes domas] Bouterwek and later edd. supply *and duguðe þrym* for the missing half-line.   **554–555**] Bouterwek, Grein, Wülker, Clubb take *and* *we...leoht* as one line.   Sievers, Beitr. XII, 477, assumes the loss of a half-line after *wynnum*.   Graz, Eng. Stud. XXI, 24, reconstructs l. 554 to read *wunian in wynnum* as a half-line.   If an alliterating word in *d*, e.g. *diere*, *deore*, is supplied in l. 554*a*, this half-line could complete l. 553*a* and the meter of the whole passage could be regularized.   **558** feowertig daga folgad folcum] So all edd., except Clubb, who reads *folgad folcum feowertig daga*, following a suggestion of Grein, note.   Graz, Eng. Stud. XXI, 25, reads as Clubb.   Cosijn, Beitr. XXI, 25, would omit *folgad* and read *feowertig daga folcum gecyðed* ‖ *meotod mancynnes*.   Kock, Anglia XLIV, 258, reads *feowertig daga folcum gecyðed* ‖ *mancynnes folgad, ær he*, etc., translating *mancynnes folgad* as "the help of men."   As the text stands, *folgad* is to be taken as a past participle from *folgian*, "followed," "served."   **559** mancynne] So Grein, Graz, Eng. Stud. XXI, 25, Clubb.   Wülker retains *mancynnes*, but grants, note, that *mancynne* is better.   **562** Astah up] Bright, MLN. XVIII, 130, reads *Up astah*.   **563** wolcna] Grein, note, suggests *wuldres* for *wolcna*.   **564** Mid wæs] Bright, MLN. XVIII, 130, reads *hond godes wæs mid*.   **570** tene] The edd. follow the MS. reading *ane*, except Clubb, who has *tene*, adopting Bright's suggestion, MLN. XVIII, 130, though Bright reads *þæt he ymb tyn niht þæs | twelf*, etc.   twelf] Holthausen, Anglia Beibl. V, 233, reads *andleofan*.   **578** innon] Grein, Wülker read *inn on*.   **585** encgel] Grein alters to *þengel*, and Wülker alters to *encgla*, genitive after *waldend*.   **587** swegl betolden] Dietrich reads *sweglbefalden*, and so Grein.   Thorpe, Bouterwek, Wülker read *sweglbehealden*. Clubb has *swegl betolden*, and he regards *swegl* as an uninflected instrumental. Perhaps one should read *swegle*.   **593** teala] The addition of *teala* with Dietrich, Grein and Clubb supplies the appropriate alliteration.   **595** þær] Grein reads *þæt*.   **598** ælmihtig god] All edd. assume a loss in the MS. after *god*, but there is no indication in the MS. of any loss, and the fact that *on*, the last word on p. 226, is repeated as the first word on p. 227, is an indication that the scribe was copying without break.   The sense of the passage is also complete as it stands.   Grein supplies *oðre siðe* for l. 598*b*.   The other edd. indicate a gap, but supply nothing.   **600** hluddre] Grein, Wülker read *hludre*.

601–700

602 geond foldan sceatas] Grein supplied *feower* before *foldan*, Holthausen, Indog. Forsch. IV, 383, Clubb read *þa feower*, to complete the line metrically.   **605** dinna] Thorpe, note, and later edd. read *dinna*, except Bouterwek, who has *dynna*.   **608** gesceadan] Thorpe, note, suggests *gesceadan* for the MS. *gesceawian*, and so Bouterwek, Graz, Eng. Stud. XXI, 25.   Grein, Clubb read *gescearian*.   But Grein, Germania X, 420, returns to the MS. reading.   **613** gongan in godes rice] Bouterwek supplied *gumena bearn* after *rice*.   Dietrich read *burhweallas* for *burh*, in l. 612, and placed *moton* in the next line. Grein supplied *glædmode*, and Grein, Germania X, 420, *gegnum*, before *gongan*.   The other edd. indicate an omission before *gongan* but supply

nothing.   **617** þær ge habbað] Clubb, following Graz, Eng. Stud. XXI, 26,
regularizes the alliteration by placing *habbað* before *ge*. Holthausen, Anglia
Beibl. V, 233, reads *habban sculon* for *habbað*, and Cosijn, Beitr. XXI, 25,
adds *nu* after *habbað*. But see Gen. 574, note.   **619** forworhtan] So all
edd. except Clubb, who reads *forhtan* with Graz, Eng. Stud. XXI, 26, for
the sake of alliteration. But it is doubtful if the metrical gain compensates
for the weakening of the sense. After *forworhtan*, Grein supplies *on þa
winstran hond*, as completing the line; *þa ðe firnedon* is the first half of the
following line, and he then adds *on foldan æfre* as a second half-line.   **624**
reordende] The corrected reading of the MS. would make *reordiende*, which
Junius reads as *reodiende*. All edd. read *reordiende*, except Clubb, who has
reordende, following Cosijn, Beitr. XXI, 25. Thorpe, note, Bouterwek,
Grein read *rodera waldend* for the missing second half-line, and Cosijn, ibid.,
reads *and reðe word*.   **630** leaðað] All edd. read *lædað*, except Clubb, who
reads *leaðað*. See l. 588.   **632** nið] The noun *nið*, "hate," "affliction,"
is usually masculine, but Grein, Spr. II, 292, supposes a neuter noun *nið*,
"abyssus," for this passage, and so also Clubb in his glossary.   Grein-Köhler, p. 504, suggests *niðer* for *nið*.   **634** earmlic] All edd. follow the MS.,
except Grein, Clubb, who read *þearlic* for alliteration. See l. 259, note.
637 on edwit] Bright, MLN. XVIII, 131, places a metrical stress on *on*, as
adverb, taking *edwit* as object of *asettað*, or he suggests changing to *hu hie
on him edwit* or *hu hie him edwit on*.   **638** stæleð feondas, etc.] The MS.
reads *stæleð fæhðe and in firne þær ðe hie drihten*. Thorpe and Bouterwek suppose a loss in the MS. after *firne*, and for *þær* Bouterwek reads *þæs*. Dietrich reads *in firnum, þæs ðe*, etc. Grein supplies *þonne Satanus* before *stæleð*,
omits *and*, changes *firne* to *firene* and *þær* to *þæs*. Wülker indicates a loss
before *stæleð*, omits *and*, but retains *firne* and *þær*. Clubb reads *stæleð
feondas ‖ fæhðe and firne*, taking *stæleð* as plural and *feondas* as subject.
Holthausen, Indog. Forsch. IV, 383, follows Grein, except that he reads only
Satan for Grein's *þonne Satanus*. Cosijn, Beitr. XXI, 25, reads *synna
stæleð ‖ fæhðe and firene, þæs*, etc. Kock, Anglia XXVII, 229, reads
Satanas stæleð ‖ fæhðe and firne, translating, "how Satan accuses them of
the enmity and crime in which they so oft forgot the Lord, the eternal
Monarch." In l. 639*b*, Grein, Clubb read *freodrihten*, but Wülker reads
drihten with the MS.   **641** þone þe hie] Thorpe, Bouterwek and Grein
read *þone hie*, but Wülker and Clubb read *þone þe hie*.   **646** selfe mid
swegle] Grein reads *mid swegle torht sunu*, translating, Dicht., p. 146, "mit
dem himmelsklaren Sohn." Wülker follows Grein. Grein, note, suggests
swegel-torhtne, which would accord with his translation, or *sunu* as a plural.
Holthausen, Eng. Stud. LI, 181, approves of Grein's reading except that he
omits *selfe*. Clubb takes *sunu* as a plural subject of *sittað*, omitting *torht*,
and this seems the simplest solution. Clubb calls attention to *eadige bearn*,
l. 143, as parallel to *eadige...sunu* here.   **652** þa ðe heonon ferað] Bouterwek completed by adding *heofonrice to*, Grein by adding *to heofonrice*.   **658**
up gelæddest] Grein, Clubb supply *up gelæddest*, to complete meter and sense.
668 of heofonum] Sievers, Beitr. X, 514, adds *heah* before *of*, and Graz,

Eng. Stud. XXI, 26, reads *of heofonrice* to regularize the line metrically.
669 þa costode] Grein, Wülker read *þæt he costode.*   674–676] Syntax and
meaning indicate a considerable loss in the MS. here which none of the edd.
have ventured to supply.   Clubb supposes a loss in the MS. also after
dreamas, l. 678.   **676** hafast] Grein changes to *hafað.*   **679**] Bouterwek,
Grein, Wülker take *on heofonrice...genom*, ll. 678–679*a*, as one line.   Graz,
Eng. Stud. XXI, 27, supplies *halig scyppend* for l. 679*b*, and Clubb reads
hæleða scyppend.   Grein, note, suggests *hine* for *he.*   See Gen. 703, note.
681 herm] Grein, Wülker, Clubb read *herm*, "malicious," "evil."   Grein,
note, suggests *bær* for *herm.*   Thorpe and Bouterwek made a compound,
hermbealowes.   Graz, Eng. Stud. XXI, 27, suggests *blac* for *herm.*   **684**
on þines seolfes dom] Junius, Thorpe retained the MS. *seoferdum*, but all
later edd. read *seolfes dom.*   Grein, Wülker, Clubb supply *on* before *þines.*
687 gif] Grein, Wülker read *þæt* for *gif.*   **692** gearo] Clubb retains *geara.*
698 hu wid and sid] Thorpe suggested that *sy* or *seo* had dropped out after
sid, see ll. 703, 706.   Dietrich supplies *sie* or *seo*, and Cosijn, Beitr. XXI,
25, adds *sio.*   Sievers in a note to Cosijn's note would place *sio* after *hu.*
Holthausen, Eng. Stud. LI, 181, proposes *hu wid sie*, taking *sie* as a disyllable.   Clubb supplies nothing, assuming that the form of the verb "to be"
is understood, and this is certainly a possible construction.   **699** helheoðo]
All edd. retain the MS. reading *helheoðo* except Clubb, who reads *hel heoro-
dreorig.*   This was suggested by Grein, note, and so Graz, Eng. Stud. XXI,
27, Holthausen, Eng. Stud. LI, 181.   Cosijn, Beitr. XXI, 25, suggested *hel
heaðodreorig.*   Trautmann, Bonner Beitr. II, 149, proposed *helheoðo deop
sig.*   Bouterwek, Erläut., p. 326, suggested that *heoðo* was for *heahðo*, but
the reading he prefers is *hel seo* for *helheoðo.*   Grein-Köhler, p. 325, *hel-heoðo*,
and in the lack of a satisfactory substitute, it seems best to retain the MS.
reading.   The fact that no other occurrences of the word are found is not
sufficient ground for rejecting it.

701–729

703 and hu sid seo] Thorpe, note, suggested that *and wid* should be added
after *sid*, and so Bouterwek, Williams, Short Extracts, p. 28.   Grein reads
swol-eðm for the MS. *eðm.*   Holthausen, Eng. Stud. LI, 181, omits *and* and
reads *hu sid seo | se swarta eðel.*   Cosijn, Beitr. XXI, 25, Clubb read *and hu
sid seo | se swarta eðm.*   **705** þonne hafast, etc.] Graz, Eng. Stud. XXI,
27, reads *þon handum | hafast ametene.*   **706** hu heh and deop] Sievers,
Beitr. X, 515, reads *hell inne seo* for the second half-line, and so Graz, Eng.
Stud. XXI, 27.   Cosijn, Beitr. XXI, 25, suggests *hu heh and deop seo || hell
inneweard*, transposing *seo* as in l. 703.   Sievers in a note to Cosijn's reading
would place *seo* after *hu.*   **707** grim] Sievers, Beitr. X, 515, reads *grimme*,
and so Graz, Eng. Stud. XXI, 27, Williams, Short Extracts, p. 28.   **708**
seondon] So all edd., except Wülker, who retains the MS. *seond*, presumably
as equivalent to *sind.*   Cosijn, Beitr. XXI, 25, reads *seon* as a disyllable.
709 merced hus] Cosijn, Beitr. XXI, 25, emends to *þæt merce* for *merced.*

710 werigan] So all edd. after Junius, except Clubb, who reads *werga*, dat. sg. masc. weak adjective, i.e. as equivalent to *wergan*.   wracu] All edd. after Junius read *wracu*, except Clubb, who reads *wrece* with the uncorrected MS. But Clubb interprets *wrece* as a nom. sg., equivalent to *wracu*.   **712** æglece] The earlier edd. read *æglæce*, Grein reads *earm æglæca* as a first half-line and supplies *in to helle* after this word as a second half-line. Wülker reads *æglæca*, but supplies nothing.   Grein also supplies *feond in fyrlocan* after his *in to helle* as the first half of the next line, his second half-line being *hwilum...mæt*. Holthausen, Anglia Beibl. V, 234, reads *earmum* for *folmum* to provide alliteration.   Clubb reads as in the text, taking *æglece* as an Anglian nominative.   **714** þes] Grein reads *þæs*.   **716** he] Thorpe and later edd. read *hie*, except Clubb, who retains *he* as a nom. pl., see l. 334. **717** Hæfdon gewunnon] Grein supplies *gryre* after *Hæfdon* and reads *gewunnen*.   Grein also supplies a full line after *andsacan*, reading *þonne him se atola andweard stod*. Wülker assumes a loss after *andsacan*, but supplies nothing. Williams, Short Extracts, p. 29, follows Wülker. Holthausen, Anglia Beibl. V, 234, supposes the loss to have occurred after *gewunnon* (for which he reads *gewunnen*). Clubb reads as in the text.   **722** sinne] All edd. read *synne* with the MS., except Clubb, who reads *sinne*, following Grein, Germania X, 420.   susle] Grein alters to *susl*.   **723** Ða he gemunde] Grein reads *þæt he gaste gemunde*. Holthausen, Indog. Forsch. IV, 383, proposes *gemde* for *gemunde* and *þæt* for the following *þa*, citing l. 719.   **726** deofla mænego] After *mænego*, Grein supplies *adreogan ne mihton*. In the following line he places *þonne up astag* and supplies *earmra gedræg* as a second half-line. Wülker indicates a loss after *mænego* and after *astag*, but supplies nothing. This is what Thorpe and Bouterwek had done. Clubb reads as in the text, translating, notes, "The perfidious and loathsome wight gazed through that wretched den until the dreadful multitude of devils arose." The word *gryre* in the phrase *egsan gryre*, omitted in Clubb's translation, may be taken as nominative, subject of *astag*, or as instrumental. It seems best to take it as nominative, with *mænego* as a dependent genitive. This satisfies the sense, though the line remains defective in alliteration, as in ll. 712, 717, 723. See l. 259, note.   **727** in witum] Grein reads *in witum*, and so Clubb. But Grein, Germania X, 420, Wülker read *inwitum*, as the earlier edd. had done. This would make *wordum inwitum* an adverbial phrase, "with wicked words."   þa] Thorpe and later edd. omit *on þa*, the MS. reading *þa on þa* being obviously redundant.   **728** reordian and cweðan] Grein supplies *wið heora rices boran* to complete the line.